Robert Michels, Socialism, and Modernity

OXFORD STUDIES IN MODERN
EUROPEAN HISTORY

General Editors

SIMON DIXON, MARK MAZOWER,
and
JAMES RETALLACK

Robert Michels, Socialism, and Modernity

ANDREW G. BONNELL

Great Clarendon Street, Oxford, OX2 6DP,
United Kingdom

Oxford University Press is a department of the University of Oxford.
It furthers the University's objective of excellence in research, scholarship,
and education by publishing worldwide. Oxford is a registered trade mark of
Oxford University Press in the UK and in certain other countries

© Andrew G. Bonnell 2023

The moral rights of the author have been asserted

First Edition published in 2023

Impression: 1

All rights reserved. No part of this publication may be reproduced, stored in
a retrieval system, or transmitted, in any form or by any means, without the
prior permission in writing of Oxford University Press, or as expressly permitted
by law, by licence or under terms agreed with the appropriate reprographics
rights organization. Enquiries concerning reproduction outside the scope of the
above should be sent to the Rights Department, Oxford University Press, at the
address above

You must not circulate this work in any other form
and you must impose this same condition on any acquirer

Published in the United States of America by Oxford University Press
198 Madison Avenue, New York, NY 10016, United States of America

British Library Cataloguing in Publication Data

Data available

Library of Congress Control Number: 2022940829

ISBN 978–0–19–287184–8

DOI: 10.1093/oso/9780192871848.001.0001

Printed and bound in the UK by
Clays Ltd, Elcograf S.p.A.

Links to third party websites are provided by Oxford in good faith and
for information only. Oxford disclaims any responsibility for the materials
contained in any third party website referenced in this work.

To my Sydney teachers and former colleagues.

Acknowledgements

This book has had a long gestation, and I regret that I may not be able to acknowledge all of the many debts I have accrued during the work on it.

Firstly, thanks are owed to all the archivists and librarians who assisted with the research for this book. I especially thank Stefania Martinotti Dorigo and Paola Giordana, custodians of the Archivio Roberto Michels in the Fondazione Luigi Einaudi, Turin, for their invaluable assistance with the Michels papers, especially the extensive correspondence files. Also in Italy, I would like to thank David Bidussa for kind assistance with the resources of the Fondazione Giangiacomo Feltrinelli, Milan, and the staff of the National Library of Italy in Florence.

It is always a great pleasure to work among the rich collections of the International Institute of Social History in Amsterdam—my thanks go to the staff there for their friendly and efficient assistance.

In Germany, I would like to thank the archivists and librarians at the Friedrich-Ebert-Stiftung, Bonn, the Hessisches Staatsarchiv in Marburg, the Landesarchiv Berlin, the Universitätsarchiv in Halle, the Landesbibliothek Schleswig-Holstein (especially Kornelia Küchmeister for assistance with the Tönnies papers), Dr. Ralf Breslau of the Handschriftenabteilung of the Staatsbibliothek Berlin, the Geheimes Staatsarchiv Preussischer Kulturbesitz, Berlin-Dahlem, and the Stiftung Archiv Parteien und Massenorganisationen der DDR at the Bundesarchiv Berlin-Lichterfelde. For assistance with access to rare newspapers, I would like to thank the librarians in the university libraries of Giessen and Marburg, the library of the Deutsches Historische Museum, Berlin, and the Leo Baeck Institute at the Jüdisches Museum, Berlin. Other libraries that assisted with the project were the Deutsche Nationalbibliothek in Leipzig, the Bibliothèque Nationale, Paris, the British Library, London, and the library of the University of Queensland (especially the Document Delivery staff).

Many colleagues assisted with the work on the book through discussions and offering feedback and suggestions. At an early stage of my work on this book, I benefited from discussions with Timm Genett, both in Turin and in Berlin. Other colleagues to whom I owe thanks include Frank Bongiorno, the late Dick Geary, Christian Gehrke, Christian Goeschel, Reiner Tosstorf, for generously supplying me with relevant press clippings, Heather Wolffram and her colleagues at the History research seminar at the University of Canterbury, New Zealand, the members of the Australasian Association for European History, for listening to multiple papers on Michels, and the colleagues at the 21st George Rudé seminar in French History and Civilisation at the Australian National University,

viii ACKNOWLEDGEMENTS

Canberra, in 2018. Special gratitude is owing to Jim Retallack, Toronto, for his interest in this project and for generously offering to read the manuscript, which his suggestions greatly improved. I would also like to thank the anonymous readers for Oxford University Press for helpful and supportive feedback.

This book could not have been written without regular periods of study leave from the University of Queensland, which is also gratefully acknowledged.

At Oxford University Press, I would like to thank Stephanie Ireland for her warm welcome to the press and assistance with the initial stages of publication, and her successor Hannah Doyle, and particular thanks to Emma Varley and her team for their editorial work. I would also like to thank the production team, in particular, Sindhuja Baskaran and Dolarine Fonceca.

Earlier versions of a section of Chapter 2 and Chapter 4 were published in the journals *German History* and *French History and Civilization* respectively, and I thank the editors and reviewers of those journals for their assistance.

As always, a large debt of thanks is owed to my wife Debbie, for putting up with my absences on research and absences at home at my desk, and for much else.

The book is dedicated to my former teachers and colleagues at the University of Sydney, especially Bob Dreher, who first introduced me to European intellectual history many years ago, and to the late Michael J. Birch, who for many years was the first reader of my work, and who always let me know if he thought it was boring.

Contents

Introduction	1

PART I: MICHELS AND SOCIALIST PARTIES

1. Robert Michels, a Career: From Young Radical to Elite Theorist	15
2. Michels and German Social Democracy: Activism and Ethical Superiority	25
From Marburg to Dresden	26
Agitation and Organization	45
Disillusionment after Bremen	51
From Participant to Outside Academic Critic of German Social Democracy	64
Analysing Oligarchy: Towards *Political Parties*	83
3. Socialism plus Temperament: Michels and Italian Socialists	89
4. Michels and French Socialists and Syndicalists	128

PART II: MICHELS, MODERN IDEAS, AND MOVEMENTS

5. Feminism and the Sexual Politics of a New Century	147
Feminism	147
The Sexual Question	163
6. Intellectuals, Masses, and Leaders	186
Intellectuals	186
Masses	194
Leaders	202
7. Internationalism, Patriotism, Nationalism	206
8. Ethnicity and Race	228
9. Michels and the Modern	254
10. Conclusions	265
Bibliography	269
Index	275

Introduction

Robert Michels has frequently been subjected to analysis as a theorist of social elites, and as a proponent of the 'iron law of oligarchy'. Michels is best known for his investigation of the tendency of political parties to generate self-serving, self-perpetuating bureaucracies which become ends in themselves, regardless of the party's ostensible ideological goals. First published in 1910/11, his work on *Political Parties* has long been a staple of Western political science, and is still invoked by critics of established parties of both left and right.

Michels' undisputed *magnum opus*, *Political Parties* was a *tour de force*—copious footnotes testified to Michels' knowledge of socialist literature in multiple languages, while the work clearly drew on his personal familiarity with the German Social Democratic Party, of which he had previously been an active member. Michels showed, in great detail, and with the German party as his prime case study, how the necessity for organizations to represent constituencies in labour struggles and modern politics inevitably led to the supersession of earlier forms of direct democracy. The 'masses' in a modern industrial society were not able to govern themselves directly—mass participation in increasingly complex and technical decision-making processes (as in the drafting of modern parliamentary legislation) was not feasible. Instead, the masses had to delegate their authority to functionaries and leaders, who gradually formed a separate social stratum, whose powers and privileges became more and more entrenched over time. Even socialist party activists who had once been manual workers became increasingly detached from the party base as they gained in education and knowledge, and adopted a more elite standard of living. A typical biography might be: skilled craft worker, party activist (and maybe publican in a pub frequented by party members), journalist, party official, then member of a state or national parliament. This itinerary provided a form of social mobility for some. Indeed, the more the bureaucratic structures of the party and labour movement expanded, the more they became a machine for social mobility for functionaries. Leaders also learned to cater to the masses' desire to be led. Intellectuals and full-time functionaries were necessary on a practical level in a mass party, but they also constituted an elite stratum that was increasingly distant from the proletarian rank and file (and even their own past lives), having much more to lose than chains, and they found themselves having more in common with the bourgeois leaders of other parties.[1]

---

[1] Robert Michels, *Zur Soziologie des Parteiwesens in der modernen Demokratie*, Leipzig, 1911.

Robert Michels, Socialism, and Modernity. Andrew G. Bonnell, Oxford University Press. © Andrew G. Bonnell 2023.
DOI: 10.1093/oso/9780192871848.003.0001

2   ROBERT MICHELS, SOCIALISM, AND MODERNITY

Michels' analysis seemed to explain much about the evolution of the German Social Democratic Party, which at the time he wrote was in the process of becoming the world's first million-member mass political party. The party seemed to be drifting from its radical, revolutionary early days, and becoming more cautious and bureaucratic. The fiery nineteenth-century people's tribunes—Wilhelm Liebknecht, August Bebel, and others—were passing the torch to men who seemed more like bureaucrats and administrators—men such as Friedrich Ebert, later the first President of the Weimar Republic, and Hermann Müller, later Chancellor in the Republic. But Michels' work resonated well beyond the circles of scholars interested in the trajectory of the German socialist party. The book made wider claims about the inherent limitations of democratic politics in a complex modern, industrial society. It was functionally inevitable that even a party with a radical, revolutionary, or at least reformist democratic platform would succumb to the dominance of a stratum of professional functionaries. Oligarchy was unavoidable, and democratic ideas did not provide any inoculation against this sociological 'iron law'.

Michels' work had a significant impact, not only in his native Germany, but also worldwide, being widely translated within just a few years into French, Italian, English, and even Japanese. The rapidity with which the book was translated illustrated the extent to which readers outside Germany saw Michels' pessimistic diagnosis regarding the possibilities for democracy to be relevant to contemporary political concerns. After the Second World War, especially after the republication of the English translation of *Political Parties* in 1949 (and again in 1962; with a new introduction by Seymour Martin Lipset), the book quickly became established as a classic in Western political science.[2] Michels' book chimed perfectly with many of the concerns in American sociology and political science during the Cold War: the rise of a technocratic 'power elite' (as diagnosed by C. Wright Mills), the 'end of ideology', and the rise of 'organization man' as large corporations and governments took on an increasingly similar bureaucratic complexion. Michels' functional analysis of power structures and the oligarchical tendencies of all large organizations was a good fit with the functionalist orientation of much American social science in this period (and an alternative to Marxist critiques of class structure—indeed, Michels' work reassuringly offered a case study of the futility of socialist transformative politics).

---

[2] Robert Michels, *Political Parties: A Sociological Study of the Oligarchical Tendencies of Modern Democracy*, with introduction by Seymour Martin Lipset, New York, 1968 [1962]. Lipset (p.38 of his 'Introduction') acknowledged a 'great intellectual debt' to Michels' book. On the postwar reception of Michels' book, see Frank R. Pfetsch, 'Einführung in Person, Werk und Wirkung', in Robert Michels, ed., *Zur Soziologie des Parteiwesens in der modernen Demokratie*, 4th edn., Stuttgart, 1989, pp.xxxiv–xxxviii; on the reception in the United States until the late 1950s, see Giorgio Volpe, *Italian Elitism and the Reshaping of Democracy in the United States*, London, 2021. Volpe even credits the elite theory of Mosca, Pareto, and Michels 'with having played a primary role in the renewal of political science' (p.178).

Over a century after its first publication, Michels' *Political Parties* is still in print in multiple languages. It is even possible that his ideas are experiencing a renewed popularity, given the often observed discontent with the extent to which contemporary Western democracies offer only a limited range of political choice, and given the tendency for political parties to become sophisticated and increasingly professionalized vote-getting machines, safeguarding their institutional interests, at the same time as the degree of ideological differentiation between 'catch-all' parties has diminished. The currency of the term 'Politikverdrossenheit' (roughly, the condition of being fed up with politics) in Germany from the 1990s on and the increasing de-alignment with the major parties since then; dissatisfaction with the blatantly manipulative cynicism of the professionalized politics of 'spin' in the United Kingdom under Tony Blair and his successors; the revolt against the so-called 'partitocrazia', or rule by a corrupt cartel of political parties in Italy in the 1990s; and the subsequent upsurge of populism in many European countries, which has taken on new and global dimensions following the 2008 global financial crisis, engulfing the United States in perhaps the most spectacular and erratic manifestation of the new populism—these all fit into this picture. It is not surprising, then, that the centenary of Michels' *Political Parties* saw something of a flurry of interest in his work.[3]

However, while Michels' *magnum opus* has continued to be influential among political scientists and pundits to this day, it is very much a product of the intellectual and political currents of the time in which it was written. This study does not seek to rehearse the existing analyses of Michels' work, rather it is concerned with the origins of Michels' work, and with the contemporary experiences and influences that made it the potent book that it became. These historical factors also led to the book's dated and idiosyncratic dimensions, which are sometimes overlooked in the desire to apply it to today's political phenomena. To understand all aspects of Michels' *Political Parties*, we need to be aware of his influences and own commitments in political life in different national contexts: in Germany, France, and Italy (Part I of this book reconstructs his involvement in these countries' socialist movements); his interest in feminism and the sexual question; and other major political and intellectual controversies of his day in which he became involved. This requires a careful historical reconstruction of Michels' itineraries in the decade leading up to the publication of his book at the end of 1910. Michels' career was perhaps unique in the degree to which he worked across national boundaries (especially in Germany, Italy, and France) and crossed political boundaries (between the socialist and the 'bourgeois') as well as working across multiple intellectual disciplines as he sought to carve out a reputation for himself in the nascent social sciences.

---

[3] See for example the German collection of essays published specifically to mark the centenary: Harald Bluhm and Skadi Krause, eds., *Robert Michels' Soziologie des Parteiwesens. Oligarchien und Eliten—die Kehrseiten moderner Demokratie*, Wiesbaden, 2012.

4   ROBERT MICHELS, SOCIALISM, AND MODERNITY

This present work makes no great claims for Michels' prescience or originality, the latter having already been the subject of some debate. Clearly, he borrowed much from James Bryce and Moise Ostrogorski, and was influenced in his thinking by the circle around the *Archiv für Sozialwissenschaft und Sozialpolitik*, Max Weber, Werner Sombart, and Edgar Jaffé, as well as by the Italian elite theorists such as Gaetano Mosca and Vilfredo Pareto. In a letter to Mosca in 1907, Michels gave Mosca credit (over the rival claims of Pareto) for discovering the dominance of the oligarchical principle in contemporary political life.[4] In his *Elementi di scienza politica* (1896) Gaetano Mosca had developed the theory of a 'political class' as a distinct social group and a political factor in its own right. And Pareto had followed this with his reflections on the theory of the 'circulation of elites' in his *Systèmes socialistes* (1902). Moise Ostrogorski's 1903 work, *La démocratie et l'organisation des partis politiques* had already outlined a 'discrepancy between the democratic ideals' to which parties claimed allegiance 'and the actual dominance of a party apparatus' within the organization; and Ostrogorski had supported this argument with a broad basis of empirical material drawn from British and American examples.[5] James Bryce's *The American Commonwealth* (1907) further developed this theme.

Michels' contribution lay less in theoretical originality than in presenting the most fully articulated, and richly documented, analysis to date of how the apparatus of a modern mass party came to assume the role of a functional oligarchy, whose self-perpetuation took precedence over the democratic and emancipatory, even revolutionary, principles of the party. As Arthur Mitzman wrote: 'The importance of Michels' thesis in the history of social theory lies not so much in its uniqueness (for others, before Michels, have elaborated the idea of the oligarchical substance of government) as in the living, concrete experience behind its formulation.'[6] Michels' study of the German Social Democratic Party has had a lasting influence on its historians, combining as it did his first-hand knowledge of the party and its leaders with a wealth of contemporary source material. To what extent his depiction of the party is a reliable guide to its workings will be examined in Chapter 2 of this book, along with the problematic aspects of Michels' relationship to the party as both an activist, for a time, and analyst, along with his own particular conception of his role as an intellectual in a working-class party.

---

[4] Michels to Gaetano Mosca, 10 May 1907, Archivio Roberto Michels (= ARM), in Fondazione Luigi Einaudi (= FLE). (Michels' correspondence is arranged by correspondent, chronologically within each correspondent's folder or folders). David Beetham has observed that given the notorious rivalry and acrimony between the two Italian elite theorists, 'it must be judged as something of an achievement that Michels kept on good terms with both of them'. David Beetham, 'Michels and His Critics', *Archives Européennes de Sociologie*, XXII, 1981, p.82. On the rival claims of Mosca and Pareto to primacy, see T. B. Bottomore, *Elites and Society*, London, 1964.

[5] As pointed out by Heinrich August Winkler, 'Robert Michels', in Hans-Ulrich Wehler, ed., *Deutsche Historiker*, Göttingen, 1973, pp.443–4.

[6] Arthur Mitzman, *Sociology and Estrangement: Three Sociologists in Imperial Germany*, New York, 1973, p.267.

INTRODUCTION   5

The classification (or even canonization) of Michels as an elite theorist, or critic of party politics, gives us only a very partial picture of Michels, however. Michels participated in, and was influenced by, a wide range of early twentieth-century debates which can be loosely characterized as reflecting concerns, even discontents, with aspects of 'modernity', or, in Michels' case, discontent with the obstacles to the realization of more 'modern' social conditions. Issues that exercised Michels' mind in the years leading up to the publication of his major work included the role of intellectuals in politics, the nature of mass society, the emancipation of women and the possibility of a new, secular approach to sexual morality, the possibility of a scientific understanding of society, including questions of ethnicity and race, as well as the more narrowly 'political' questions of democracy, socialism, and revolutionary politics (issues explored in Part II of this work).

For some writers, much of Michels' output on these disparate questions has been 'justly forgotten'.[7] From the point of view of contemporary social science, this judgement is understandable, but for intellectual historians (and, to some extent, historians of early twentieth-century political and social movements), Michels' more dated writings are no less interesting as products of their specific time than those that are still regarded as relevant by later political scientists. It will be argued in the present study that Michels' broader concerns with questions that helped to define 'modernity' in the early twentieth century should not be set aside from his political theory, as usually happens. Rather, Michels' political commitments, disillusionments and critical analyses are best understood within the context of these wider concerns.

Michels did not work in ivory-tower isolation. One of the characteristics that make Michels an intriguing subject for the intellectual historian is that before 1914 he maintained a probably unique network of correspondents across the world of politics and intellectual and academic circles, with contacts from the political left and right (to an extent unusual in the polarized ideological terrain of imperial Germany), and of an unusually transnational variety. Through his friendships with Werner Sombart and Max Weber, Michels was closely involved in the formation of sociology as an academic discipline in Germany, despite his own lack of a German university position. Michels' friendship with Max Weber, which lasted from 1906 to 1915, has been well-documented.[8] While Weber was both an intellectual mentor and academic patron for Michels (at least to the extent that was possible in the circumstances), Michels was able to act as an intellectual sparring partner for Weber who could give the latter insights into the ways

---

[7] Winkler, 'Robert Michels', p.447.

[8] See Wolfgang J. Mommsen, 'Max Weber and Robert Michels: An Asymmetrical Partnership', *Archives Européennes de Sociologie*, 22, 1981, pp.100–16; Wolfgang J. Mommsen, 'Robert Michels and Max Weber: Moral Conviction versus the Politics of Responsibility', in W.J. Mommsen and J. Osterhammel, eds, *Max Weber and His Contemporaries*, London, 1989; Lawrence A. Scaff, 'Max Weber and Robert Michels', *American Journal of Sociology*, 86, 1981, pp.1269–86.

6 ROBERT MICHELS, SOCIALISM, AND MODERNITY

of thinking of the politically committed activist.[9] With Weber's assistance and encouragement, Michels became a significant contributor to the flagship journal of German sociology, the *Archiv für Sozialwissenschaft und Sozialpolitik*, co-edited by Weber. By 1912, Michels was even thrusting himself forward as a member of the editorial committee of the journal, to the point that both Weber and Werner Sombart became alienated by his behaviour.[10] Not only did Michels publish some of his most substantial and important articles, on the social structure of German social democracy and on 'oligarchical tendencies in society', in this journal, he became a regular, indeed highly prolific, contributor of book reviews and review articles.

Weber's partner in the editing and running of the *Archiv*, Werner Sombart, also became a close friend and intellectual associate of Michels. Sombart had started his career as a radical middle-class advocate of social reform, although as his career progressed he would bow to political pressure to publicly endorse the imperialistic new *Weltpolitik* of the German Empire and the expansion of the imperial navy, and move progressively further right.[11] Michels' closeness to Sombart coincided with the former's increasingly strong disillusionment with radical socialist politics. When Sombart joined Hugo von Hofmannsthal, Richard Strauss, Georg Brandes, and Richard Muther in founding the ostensibly apolitical cultural review *Der Morgen*, Michels was among the journal's contributors.

Prior to his disillusionment with socialism, Michels was part of a rather different intellectual—and political—network. After Michels became personally acquainted with Karl Kautsky, the foremost Marxist theorist of the German Social Democratic Party, he joined the contributors of the party's theoretical journal *Die Neue Zeit*, which Kautsky edited. He also furnished the revisionist Social Democrat Eduard Bernstein's periodical *Documente des Sozialismus* with articles and reviews on the history of socialism in Italy and France, and contributed reports on the 1902 party congress of the Italian socialists to the German Social Democratic press. For a few years, Michels was an active member of the German Social Democratic Party and a contributor to a number of Social Democratic newspapers. At the same time, Michels became a regular correspondent with the French revolutionary syndicalist Hubert Lagardelle and a contributor to the syndicalist journal *Le Mouvement Socialiste*. He also became acquainted with other French syndicalists, Edouard Berth and Victor Griffuelhes, and with Georges Sorel, who was for some time also linked to *Le Mouvement Socialiste*. Michels also knew prominent Italian socialists such as Arturo Labriola and Anna Kuliscioff, and published in the Italian socialist press.

---

[9] As noted by Wolfgang Mommsen in the essays cited in the preceding note.
[10] See Edgar Jaffé to Robert Michels, 3 December 1912, ARM in FLE, Turin.
[11] On Sombart, see Friedrich Lenger, *Werner Sombart: 1863–1941*, Munich, 1994.

INTRODUCTION 7

Some of Michels' earliest articles for newspapers and periodicals dealt with feminism and women's issues. (Michels' wife Gisela Michels-Lindner was also a writer in her own right.) Michels' publications in feminist journals ranged from the Marxist feminist *Die Gleichheit*, edited by Clara Zetkin, to progressive liberal and even more conservative feminist journals. His correspondence includes letters from a veritable who's who of the German women's movement: Zetkin, and Ottilie Baader, another socialist feminist; Helene Stöcker, who represented the radical (sex reform) wing of the bourgeois feminist movement; Adele Schreiber, Anita Augsburg, Henriette Fürth, the progressive liberal Minna Cauer, and her associate Else Lüders; the pioneer social worker Alice Salomon, and Gertrud Bäumer, who occupied the conservative wing of the German women's movement. When Helene Stöcker and Adele Schreiber, along with Ruth Bré, formed the *Bund für Mutterschutz*, to improve the legal situation and welfare of unmarried mothers and their children, an organization that constituted the avant-garde of the German sex reform movement, Michels was one of the league's supporters, who also initially included Weber and Sombart. In 1911, within a year of the publication of his *magnum opus* on the oligarchical nature of organization in democratic parties, Michels published a book on the sexual question, *Die Grenzen der Geschlechtsmoral* (*Boundaries of Sexual Morality*), consisting mainly of essays he had published over the preceding decade.

Like Michels' political networks, his intellectual networks after he distanced himself from the socialist movement were transnational. Havelock Ellis took an interest in Michels' writings on sexual mores. In Italy, he became closely acquainted with the famous criminologist Cesare Lombroso, and with Lombroso's daughter Gina, a sociologist. His name is frequently linked with the Italian elite theorists, Gaetano Mosca (Michels' correspondence with him started in 1907, and continued until Michels' death in 1936) and Vilfredo Pareto (Michels corresponded with him from 1912 to Pareto's death in 1923). After the appearance of *Political Parties*, Michels initiated a correspondence with Gustave Le Bon, the influential proponent of 'crowd psychology', which led to the publication of the French edition of the book.

Robert Michels has been the subject of a wave of recent scholarly works: a major new study of Michels and the development of his political thought by Timm Genett and a companion volume of his selected writings in German; a substantial collection of essays on *Political Parties*; and a doctoral dissertation at the State University of New York; as well as an impressive number of articles and essays by the Turin researcher Federico Trocini.[12] Genett, to some extent follow-

---

[12] Timm Genett, *Der Fremde im Kriege. Zur politischen Theorie und Biographie von Robert Michels 1876–1936*, Berlin, 2008; Robert Michels, *Soziale Bewegungen zwischen Dynamik und Erstarrung. Essays zur Arbeiter-, Frauen- und nationalen Bewegung* (ed. Timm Genett), Berlin, 2008; Bluhm and Krause, *Robert Michels' Soziologie des Parteiwesens*; Peter A. LaVenia, 'Breaking the Iron Law: Robert Michels, The Rise of the Mass Party, and the Debate over Democracy and Oligarchy' (PhD diss.,

8   ROBERT MICHELS, SOCIALISM, AND MODERNITY

ing Pino Ferraris,[13] portrays Michels as a Social Democrat shaped by the positiv-ist Marxism of the period of the early 1900s, who then came under the influence of the crisis of positivism. In the process, an optimistic view of historical progress was replaced by a more pessimistic outlook, as manifested in *Political Parties* and its outlining of an 'iron law of oligarchy'. Against interpretations of Michels which emphasize an essential continuity from the young 'revolutionary syndicalist' Michels to the fascist, Genett stresses that Michels' later adherence to fascism was contingent and came relatively late in his life (1928). Genett's tome on Michels goes into lengthy exegeses of Michels' work and rests on an immersion in the Michels papers in Turin, but its contextualization of Michels' writings and career is uneven. The present study delves into archival sources overlooked by Genett to reconstruct his political activities in greater depth. Genett also tends to play down the place of ethnic and racial categories in Michels' work, which I view as signifi-cantly more consequential than does Genett.

The recent work on Michels builds on an older foundation of decades of research by political scientists and historians, much of which has been concerned with situating him within the body of theories of elites and oligarchies, while there has also been a focus on tracing Michels' notorious political trajectory from revolutionary left to fascist right. Michels identified increasingly with Italian nationalism and even imperialism following the 1911 Italian invasion of Libya, and ultimately became a fascist and ardent supporter of Benito Mussolini.

In a 1964 dissertation on Michels as a theoretician of elites, Frank Pfetsch viewed Michels through the prism of the Cold-War-vintage totalitarianism the-ory (one of the examiners of the dissertation was the totalitarianism theorist Carl J. Friedrich), seeing Michels as an example of the structural similarity of left- and right-wing extremism, and as a proponent of an idealized form of Rousseau-ean direct democracy which lent itself to the kind of 'totalitarian democracy' postulated by Jacob Talmon.[14] Arthur Mitzman's 1973 study of three sociologists in imperial Germany—Ferdinand Tönnies, Werner Sombart, and Robert Michels—took a broader view of Michels' thought and life in the pre-1914 period,

---

University of Albany, State University of New York, 2011); unfortunately the La Venia dissertation is more informative about the thinking of the US Greens Party about the 'mass party' problem than about Michels, partly because La Venia mainly relies on English-language material and opens up no new sources on Michels; among other publications, see Federico Trocini, *Tra internazionalismo e nazionalismo. Robert Michels e i dilemmi del socialismo di fronte alla guerra e all'imperialismo* (= Quaderni della Fondazione Luigi Salvatorelli Marsciano 7), Rome, 2007; Federico Trocini, 'Michels' Vergleich der deutschen Sozialdemokratie mit der italienischen sozialistischen Partei', in Bluhm and Krause, *Robert Michels' Soziologie des Parteiwesens*, pp.56–66. Another younger Italian scholar who has recently worked on Michels is Giorgio Volpe. See Giorgio Volpe, ed., *Il Carteggio fra Roberto Michels e i Sindacalisti Rivoluzionari*, Naples, 2018.

[13] Pino Ferraris, *Saggi su Roberto Michels*, Camerino, 1993.

[14] Frank Pfetsch, Die Entwicklung zum faschistischen Führerstaat in der politischen Philosophie von Robert Michels (diss., Heidelberg), 1964; see also Frank Pfetsch, 'Robert Michels als Elitetheoretiker', *Politische Vierteljahresschrift*, Jg.7, 1, June 1966, pp.208–27.

INTRODUCTION 9

drawing on a fairly wide selection of printed sources.[15] Mitzman views Michels as an example of the responses of German social thinkers to what Max Weber diagnosed as a process of disenchantment with the world, and to the increasing encroachment on social life of the 'iron cage' of 'bureaucratic and industrial modernity'.[16] In this perspective, Michels appears as a case study in the disillusionment of European intellectuals in the idea of progress. Mitzman argues that 'in the ten-year period from 1900 to 1910, Michels underwent a change from Condorcet-like optimism to a pessimistic rejection of progress and reason characteristic of the totalitarian epoch'.[17]

Wilfried Röhrich published a study of Michels' trajectory 'from the socialist-syndicalist to the fascist creed' in 1972, a *Habilitation* (the German second, post-doctoral thesis) at the University of Kiel.[18] Röhrich's 'ideologiekritisch' analysis depicted Michels as a revolutionary idealist, whose revolutionary romanticism began with his attraction to the 'proletarian aggressivity'[19] of the labour movement. There is a strong suggestion in Röhrich's writing that he was reacting against the perceived 'revolutionary romanticism' of the 1968 student movement. Thus, Michels allegedly came under the influence of Sorel and syndicalism, experienced the phenomenon of a growing bureaucratization of the labour movement, sapping its revolutionary idealism, and turned to Italian nationalism and a radicalized elite theory, and thence to fascism. Joachim Hetscher's 1993 study took a diametrically opposed approach from Röhrich's, from a Marxist perspective. Hetscher considered Michels to have exposed genuine contradictions within the socialist movement in terms of the structure of its organization becoming at odds with its democratic and revolutionary ideology, but he viewed Michels as regressing to a more conservative belief in the inevitability of social hierarchies from around 1908.[20] David Beetham criticized the interpretations of Mitzman and Röhrich and the emphasis on a supposed continuity in 'the psychopathology of political idealism' or Sorelian 'revolt against reason'; rather it was Michels' encounter with 'value-free' social science and his pursuit of social-scientific understanding of the Social Democratic Party that led to his disenchantment with socialism and democracy.[21]

---

[15] Mitzman, *Sociology and Estrangement*.
[16] Mitzman, *Sociology and Estrangement*, p.344; cf. Mitzman's study of Weber, *The Iron Cage: An Historical Interpretation of Max Weber*, New York, 1969.
[17] Mitzman, *Sociology and Estrangement*, p.270.
[18] Wilfried Röhrich, *Robert Michels. Vom sozialistisch-syndikalistischen zum faschistischen Credo*, Berlin, 1972.
[19] Röhrich, *Robert Michels*, pp.28, 168.
[20] Joachim Hetscher, *Robert Michels. Die Herausbildung der modernen Politischen Soziologie im Kontext von Herausforderung und Defizit der Arbeiterbewegung*, Bonn, 1993.
[21] David Beetham, 'From Socialism to Fascism: The Relation between Theory and Practice in the Work of Robert Michels', *Political Studies*, XXV, 1, 1977, pp.3–24 and 2, pp.161–81. See also the critical response of R.J. Bennett, 'The Elite Theory as Fascist Ideology—A Reply to Beetham's Critique of Robert Michels', *Political Studies*, XXVI, 4, pp.474–88, contesting both Beetham's emphasis on the

10 ROBERT MICHELS, SOCIALISM, AND MODERNITY

In Italy, Pino Ferraris gave research into Michels a new foundation, with in-depth studies of Michels' thought and activities in a number of areas: politics, relations with German Social Democracy, and engagement with feminism and the sexual question.[22] Basing his work on more substantial research in the surviving Michels papers in Turin than previous writers on Michels had done, Ferraris gave a more nuanced and rounded picture of Michels, questioning the assumption of some previous writers (e.g. Mitzman and Beetham) that Michels had come under the sway of revolutionary syndicalism (rather, it was one influence, among others), and even questioning whether Michels could be considered a syndicalist at all given his sceptical view of the trade union movement.[23]

Why, then, still read Michels today? Firstly, while his interpretation of his contemporary German Social Democratic Party may have been partial and tendentious, in failing to recognize the radical potential that still existed within the party's membership, he did put his finger on some real problems: the tendency to see the growth of organization as a good in itself, and the degree to which the party started to experience some bureaucratic inertia. The change from the party of August Bebel and Wilhelm Liebknecht to the party of Friedrich Ebert, Philipp Scheidemann, and Gustav Noske was due more than just to generational turnover. Secondly, Michels' interaction with the German Social Democrats on the one hand and French and Italian syndicalists on the other provides a vantage point for comparisons and contrasts between these different currents in the labour movement of the period. Thirdly, Michels was arguably unique in the extent of his political and intellectual networks in a highly fertile period for the evolution of both social movements and social science: Michels' engagement in socialist and feminist politics, while he also cultivated an extraordinary transnational network of European social scientists, makes him an intriguing prism through which to study some of the decisive political and intellectual currents of Europe before the First World War.

It is nearly half a century since Arthur Mitzman's study of Michels' intellectual trajectory as part of his work *Sociology and Estrangement*. There has been no full-length study of Michels in English since. A re-examination of Michels' intellectual and political development is overdue. The present work concentrates on the decade 1900–10, as the most fertile period of Michels' development, being characterized by his broadest and deepest engagement with the varied intellectual and political currents of the time, and it is also the period leading up to his most significant and influential work. After 1910, the originality and topical significance of Michels' writing diminishes, and it is as though he became an epigone of

---

continuity of Michels' thinking in *Political Parties* and his fascist period, and the linkage between elite theory and fascism. See also Beetham, 'Michels and His Critics'.

[22] Essays collected in Ferraris, *Saggi su Roberto Michels*.

[23] Ferraris, *Saggi su Roberto Michels*, pp.58–9, 172–5. Ferraris also takes issue with Röhrich's 'a dir poco, bizarra monografia', p.94.

himself. The focus on this formative period also allows a more thoroughly contextualized analysis of Michels' development than has been provided so far in the literature in any language, drawing on archival sources neglected by previous writers on Michels. I have also identified some 180 articles (mostly, but not exclusively, book reviews and brief articles) that have been omitted from the standard Michels bibliographies, and by previous Michels scholars, which allow a fuller consideration of his *oeuvre* as a full-time freelance writer prior to his academic career.

The first part of this study, after a brief biographical overview of Michels' career, examines his involvement with socialist parties and movements in Germany, Italy, and France, respectively. Michels' political involvement with the German Social Democratic Party, the Italian Socialist Party, and French socialism and revolutionary syndicalism were formative for his early development and attitudes on political organization and mass politics, and this deserves close comparative analysis, with due attention given to the specific national circumstances of the different parties and movements concerned. In the light of the importance of Michels' own experience of the German party in particular for his major work, the present book seeks to provide a more complete and accurate documentation of Michels' career as an active Social Democrat than available studies have hitherto provided.

The book's second part examines Michels' engagement with particular intellectual currents and movements outside the socialist labour movement. Michels' involvement with feminist movements (both socialist and 'bourgeois') deserves close examination, as does his participation in the emerging discourses about sexuality and 'sex reform' in the early 1900s. Drawing on his own experience as an intellectual (with academic career ambitions) in socialist parties, Michels' wider theoretical conclusions on the role of the intellectual will then also be analysed, along with the evolution of Michels' thoughts on 'the masses' and leaders. Michels produced a body of writing reflecting on internationalism, patriotism, and nationalism. His thought on these themes was inflected by his own political experiences and by the different national contexts within which he himself was operating, so again a closely contextualized reading will be useful. One of the main findings of this study is the importance of ideas of ethnicity and race, which run through Michels' *oeuvre*, and these themes will also be closely examined in the context of Michels' experiences and writings. Finally, Michels' writing is considered in the context of early 1900s discourses about modernism and modernity. In general, Michels expressed a positive view about 'modernity', and his impatience with political conditions in imperial Germany was partly influenced by what he saw as their anachronistic features. His view of modernity did not, however, attain the level of theoretical reflection developed by his friend and mentor Max Weber.

While Weber reflected on the costs of the historical process which he characterized as the 'disenchantment of the world', Michels was militant in his secular outlook. Whereas Weber reflected on the finite nature and limited possibilities of politics as a vocation, Michels sought satisfactions from politics that might transcend such limits and that would provide him with a sphere of activity and struggle that would enable him to demonstrate his own prowess and ethical superiority. Instead of picturing Michels as a fundamentally disillusioned democrat or syndicalist, it is important to appreciate Michels' essentially agonistic understanding of politics and his sense of political life as representing an arena that would allow exceptional individuals, like himself, to demonstrate their worth. The reconstruction of Michels' path from socialist activist to elite theorist is not intended to reduce his thought to the biographical dimension, but to allow the reader to better understand the complexity of the contemporary influences that shaped his still influential but flawed contribution to modern political thought.

PART I
MICHELS AND SOCIALIST PARTIES

1
Robert Michels, a Career
From Young Radical to Elite Theorist

Robert Michels was born on 9 January 1876 in Cologne. He was the son of a part-French, patrician, upper-middle-class Catholic family. That this background remained significant to him in later life is demonstrated by the lengthy biographical essay he devoted to his grandfather Peter Michels in 1930.[1] According to an obituarist, Michels was fond of describing himself as 'renano di nascita, di sangue francese, ma italiano di cuore'.[2] Michels was born in the years of Bismarck's *Kulturkampf* against the Catholic church, and it appears there was no love lost in the Michels household for the militaristic and illiberal Prussian rule over the Rhineland (with the exception of Michels' father, who seems to have espoused the conventional middle-class patriotism of the *Kaiserreich*). The young Michels was sent at the age of 9 to study at the prestigious French Gymnasium in Berlin, then to Eisenach, where he attended the Carl-Friedrich-Gymnasium. In 1895, he entered military service, joining a Saxon regiment in Weimar. In 1896, he was an officer cadet with the infantry in Hannover, something he later dismissed as a 'young man's folly, which I soon made good by taking up university study'.[3] He also later stated that during his time as an officer cadet in Hannover, he encountered the Reichstag speeches of August Bebel, reprinted in the Reichstag proceedings reports in the conservative newspapers then available to him, and that what he read of Bebel's speeches awakened an interest in socialism.[4] After a sojourn in England, he heard lectures at the Sorbonne in Paris, then at Munich University. In 1897, he enrolled at Leipzig for a year, where he studied history, including German cultural history up to the mid-eighteenth century with Karl Lamprecht. He also heard lectures on the 'materialist view of history'. Lamprecht was then a pioneer of an approach to history that embraced cultural history and engaged with broader concerns than the great actions of state that preoccupied so many

---

[1] Robert Michels, 'Peter Michels und seine Tätigkeit in der rheinischen Industrie, in der rheinischen Politik und im rheinischen Gesellschaftsleben', *Jahrbuch des Kölnischen Geschichtsvereins e.V.*, 12, 1930, pp.1–98.

[2] 'Rhinelander by birth, French by blood, but Italian in his heart'. *Neue Zürcher Zeitung*, 7 July 1936, quoted in Winkler, 'Robert Michels', p.442.

[3] Robert Michels, 'L'Allemagne et la guerre contre la France', *L'Européen. Courrier International Hebdomadaire*, 6, no.216, 20 January 1906, p.33n1.

[4] *Protokoll über die Verhandlungen des Parteitages der Sozialdemokratischen Partei Deutschlands. Abgehalten zu Dresden vom 13. bis 20. September 1903*, Berlin, 1903, p.229.

Robert Michels, Socialism, and Modernity. Andrew G. Bonnell, Oxford University Press. © Andrew G. Bonnell 2023.
DOI: 10.1093/oso/9780192871848.003.0002

16   ROBERT MICHELS, SOCIALISM, AND MODERNITY

late-nineteenth-century German historians. Michels then transferred to Halle, where after a few more semesters of lectures and seminars (from the winter semester of 1898/9 to the summer semester of 1900) he took a doctorate in history with Gustav Droysen. The latter was the son of the renowned Prussian-German historian Johann Gustav Droysen. According to a Halle colleague, the younger Droysen was talented but something of a frustrated artist, whose creative inclinations had perforce given way to the family pressure to pursue a scholarly career, and the younger Droysen formed no historical school of his own.[5] Michels' studies in Halle included economics with the prominent representative of the *Staatswissenschaften*, Johannes Conrad, compiler of a multi-volume standard reference handbook of the *Staatswissenschaften*, and Gustav Schmoller's successor in the Halle professorial chair in that field. Conrad's seminars continued the Halle tradition of preparing students for the service of the state. Conrad's own politics were National Liberal, and he had been an adviser on economic policy to Chancellor Caprivi and had also been involved in the second commission on the drafting of Germany's new Civil Code.[6] Michels' other *Nebenfach* (secondary field of study, after history) was philosophy—he attended introductory lectures by Edmund Husserl, then still a *Privatdozent* (untenured, and unsalaried, lecturer), and other philosophy lectures by Alois Riehl. Interestingly, Michels' studies in Halle also included a course on Darwinism by the geographer Alfred Kirchhoff, a keen supporter of German colonial expansion,[7] who also introduced Michels to the subject of 'Anthropogeographie', introducing a biological strand of thought into Halle's curriculum of political and social sciences, and Michels also heard lectures on criminal psychology.

Most of Michels' historical studies in Halle were undertaken with Theodor Lindner, whose daughter Gisela he married.[8] Lindner was a student of Leopold von Ranke, and had lamented in the 1890s the extent to which the trend to specialization among historians was driving 'spirit and life' out of historical writing, complaining that within the historical profession, 'instead of great leaders, only subalterns [had come] forward'.[9] Michels' doctoral dissertation, on Louis XIV's

---

[5] Johannes Conrad, *Lebenserinnerungen. Aus seinem Nachlass*, ed. Else Kesten-Conrad and Herbert Conrad, n.p., n.d. [printed as manuscript, 1917], pp.151–2.

[6] On Conrad, see his memoirs: Conrad, *Lebenserinnerungen*. Conrad's son wrote: 'In his words and in his writings, he was a life-long opponent of Social Democracy as a party and of socialism as a theory'. Herbert Conrad, 'Zum Gedächtnis meines Vaters', in Conrad, *Lebenserinnerungen*, p.243.

[7] For a brief biographical sketch of Kirchhoff, see Willi Ule, *Alfred Kirchhoff. Ein Lebensbild*, Halle a.S., 1907. Timm Genett points to the retention of a notebook filled with notes from Kirchhoff's lectures, the only Halle lecture notes preserved in Michels' papers, as evidence of the impact that Kirchhoff's Darwinistic thought had on the young . Michels Timm Genett, *Der Fremde im Kriege. Zur politischen Theorie und Biographie von Robert Michels 1876–1936*, Berlin, 2008, p.148.

[8] See 'Curriculum Vitae' in Robert Michels, *Zur Vorgeschichte von Ludwigs XIV. Einfall in Holland* (diss.), Halle a.S., 1900, pp.42–3; Decanat Haym. Promotionen vom 1. Juli 1900 bis Januar 1901, no.8: Robert Michels (unfoliated), Universitätsarchiv, Halle, including certified transcripts of Michels' leaving certificate (*Reifezeugnis*) from Eisenach and his academic records from Leipzig and Halle.

[9] Quoted in Roger Chickering, *Karl Lamprecht. A German Academic Life (1856–1915)*, New Jersey, 1993, p.37.

invasion of Holland in 1672, was a conventional enough exercise on great acts of state, notable for its display of linguistic expertise (citing sources in several languages) and as an indication of Michels' interest in French history (the work necessitated archival research in Paris, among other places). The dissertation's occasional references to Cologne's history may also reflect a certain Rhenish local patriotism on the author's part.[10]

Michels cannot be said to have gained his doctorate with flying colours. The printed version of the dissertation was accepted as an introductory part of a larger whole (never published). Gustav Droysen praised the diligent and detailed research that was apparent in the work so far—the dissertation was judged 'diligenter scripta'—even if the text was in need of some editing. The oral examination—the *rigorosum*—was less than convincing. Johannes Conrad found some notable gaps in Michels' command of economics, concluding that his knowledge of the subject was 'adequate for a *Nebenfach*'. The Dean of the Philosophical Faculty (roughly, the Arts Faculty), the venerable Rudolf Haym, arrived at a similar conclusion after questioning Michels in philosophy. Gustav Droysen found Michels on the whole well-informed on matters connected with Louis XIV, the subject of his dissertation, but lacunae soon appeared in other areas on which he was questioned. Droysen credited Michels with a 'lively interest' in history, but more hard work was needed for him 'to penetrate into the depths' of the subject. Michels was awarded the grade of 'probabliliter' for the oral examination, a not uncommon result at this time, judging by the other Halle dissertations from the second half of 1900, but less impressive than the other possible results: pass outright, *cum laude*, or *magna cum laude*. However, two weeks after the oral examination, on 7 November, Michels mounted his defence in the formal disputation and was awarded the doctorate.[11]

Michels was an industrious researcher in his chosen furrow and a fluent writer, with an obvious flair for languages, and he was clearly well-connected for a newly minted PhD. Not only that, but his affluent family background could provide him with the material means for an academic career, an essential prerequisite at this time. If Michels' performance in his doctoral examination had not been particularly distinguished, the dissertation was accepted as a promise of more substantial work to come. In the normal run of things, Michels might have expected to go on to complete his professorial dissertation, or *Habilitation*, and to pursue a career as a history professor at a German university. His involvement in socialist politics was to frustrate his academic ambitions, however.

Michels spent close to a year from May 1900 to May 1901 (interrupted by his doctoral exams) in and near Turin, following his marriage to Gisela Lindner. He

---

[10] Michels, *Zur Vorgeschichte.*
[11] Michels, *Promotion* file, Universitätsarchiv, Halle (as in note 5), with Droysen's report on the dissertation, and proceedings of the oral examination on 22 October 1900, with comments by Conrad, Droysen, and Haym.

18   ROBERT MICHELS, SOCIALISM, AND MODERNITY

spent some of his time in Turin doing archival research for a projected *Habilitation* on relations between Prussia and Piedmont in the seventeenth century.[12] He also involved himself in helping to found a short-lived cultural periodical, *La Commedia*.[13]

From the Hessian university town of Marburg, where Michels hoped to be able to pursue his *Habilitation*, Michels commented in early 1902 on the current debate on objectivity in the historical profession, noting that the spectrum of opinion allowed under the rubric of 'objectivity' seemed to encompass mainly opinion of a 'conservative or National Liberal shade', to which recently 'a sufficiently nationalistically tinged Catholic *Weltanschauung*' had been added.[14] However, Michels went on to argue that another approach to history was effectively banished from German universities, the socialist idea of history, despite the fact that it was '*at least as* scientific and *surely much more idealistic* than another', being free of the religious or national prejudice that usually militated against objectivity.[15] For Michels, not only explicit partisans of the Borussian-national school, like Treitschke and Sybel, fell short of the ideal of 'objectivity'; even Ranke, for all the sobriety of his narrative voice and his apparent aristocratic detachment above the fray, could not attain that ideal, as his sources were largely confined to the courts of Europe: 'a historiography, that excludes the "people" and their sufferings [...] simply *cannot* be objective'.[16] And yet in the recent controversy over academic freedom in Prussia, the 'Arons case', 'no Mommsen broke a lance for objectivity' (alluding, presumably, to the way in which Theodor Mommsen had intervened in the dispute over Treitschke's anti-semitism in the late 1870s).[17] If apologists for the status quo took refuge in pointing to the need for universities to act like the state bodies they were, they should give up invoking phrases such as 'the academic freedom of instruction' or the 'republic of scholars'.[18]

---

[12] Timm Genett has suggested (drawing on research by Francesco Tuccari) that the village of Cossila San Grato was a discreet place of exile for the newlyweds, avoiding possible social disapproval in Germany after the Michels' first child, a daughter called Italia (who only lived a few months) was born in August 1900, just three months after the wedding in Halle on 16 May 1900. Timm Genett, 'Einleitung: Robert Michels—Pionier der sozialen Bewegungsforschung', in Robert Michels, *Soziale Bewegungen zwischen Dynamik und Erstarrung. Essays zur Arbeiter-, Frauen- und nationalen Bewegung*, ed. Timm Genett, Berlin, 2008, p.14. For the wedding date, see Stadtarchiv Halle (Saale), Eheregister und Namensverzeichnisse; Bestand A 2.1; Signatur: A 2.1 3_H_1900_1, also accessible through www.ancestry.de. The engagement appears to have been in February 1898, see Karl Lamprecht to Robert Michels, 10 February 1898, ARM/FLE.

[13] Robert Michels,'Der ethische Faktor in der Parteipolitik Italiens', in *Zeitschrift für Politik*, Bd.3, no.1, 1910, p.66n1.

[14] Robert Michels, 'Zur Voraussetzungslosigkeit der Geschichtswissenschaft auf den deutschen Hochschulen', *Das freie Wort*, Jg.1, no.22, 20 February 1902, p.673. Michels characterized the journal *Das freie Wort* as a non-party forum for 'the liberal-minded of all shades and social democrats, ethicists and scholars', standing on a 'politically purely democratic and economically social-reformist point of view'. Robert Michels, review of *Das freie Wort. Eine Auswahl...*, in *Ethische Kultur*, vol. XI, no.19, 9. May 1903, p.151.

[15] Michels, 'Zur Voraussetzungslosigkeit der Geschichtswissenschaft', p.674. Emphases in original.

[16] Michels, 'Zur Voraussetzungslosigkeit der Geschichtswissenschaft', p.675. Emphasis in original.

[17] Michels, 'Zur Voraussetzungslosigkeit der Geschichtswissenschaft'.

[18] Michels, 'Zur Voraussetzungslosigkeit der Geschichtswissenschaft', p.676.

In December 1901, Michels wrote to Karl Kautsky, editor of the leading Marxist theoretical journal *Die Neue Zeit*, offering him articles on Italian socialism. Introducing himself as a socialist with a close knowledge of Italy, and announcing his intention to complete a *Habilitation* in Marburg and work there as *Privatdozent*, Michels wrote optimistically that 'I don't believe I will do too much damage to my advancement if I occupy myself with non-German socialism, even publicly'.[19] This proved to be a major miscalculation on Michels' part, with fundamental consequences for his subsequent biography. In February 1902, Michels wrote to Josef Bloch, editor of the revisionist Social Democratic periodical *Sozialistische Monatshefte*, to offer him a couple of essays for publication in that journal. Michels again introduced himself by explaining that 'I am a socialist, however I intend to gain my *Habilitation* as a *Dozent* in economic history at the university here [in Marburg] shortly'.[20] By October the same year, prospects in Marburg (or anywhere in Prussia) were evidently looking dim, as Michels wrote to the Bavarian socialist Georg von Vollmar asking him, 'as someone very well-informed about conditions in Munich', and as a 'comrade', for Vollmar's judgement on whether Michels as a known Social Democrat might have a chance of employment as a *Privatdozent* in modern history or economic history.[21] Michels' sanguine view of his academic career prospects, and his (initial) expectation that they were achievable at a Prussian university, are remarkable in view of the much publicized Arons case at the University of Berlin a couple of years earlier, which Michels himself alluded to at almost the same time as his letter to Bloch, in the article in *Das freie Wort* referred to above. In early 1900, the physicist Dr Leo Arons was dismissed from his position as *Privatdozent* (unsalaried and untenured lecturer) at the University of Berlin as a result of his activities as a member of the Social Democratic Party (despite Arons' adherence to the moderate, revisionist tendency of the party). The dismissal was forced through by the Prussian state government on the basis of a law passed in 1898 to increase the state's powers to discipline *Privatdozenten*, the so-called *lex Arons*.[22]

Michels seems to have felt acutely frustrated in his academic ambitions, judging by the angry article he contributed to the journal *Ethische Kultur* on 'capitalism in science'. Michels took aim at what he considered to be a number of evils present in the German university system: the propensity of some professors to act as selfish monopolists, protecting their own special field against outsiders, rather than seeking to spread or advance knowledge for the sake of knowledge; the

---

[19] Michels to Karl Kautsky, 6 December 1901, International Institute of Social History (= IISH), Amsterdam, Archief Kautsky, K D XVII, no.534.

[20] Michels to J. Bloch, 7 February 1902, ARM/FLE (photocopy: original in Bundesarchiv Koblenz, now in IISH, Sozialistische Monatshefte Archives, 129).

[21] Michels to G. v. Vollmar, 4.10.1902, IISH Vollmar Nachlass, 1438.

[22] For a recent account of the Arons case, see Stefan L. Wolff, 'Leo Arons—Physiker und Sozialist', *Centaurus*, Vol.41, 1999, pp.192–9. See also the documentation by E[dward] S[hils], 'Academic Freedom Then and Now: The Dismissal of Leo Arons from the University of Berlin', *Minerva*, Vol.18, 3, 1980, pp.499–520.

20   ROBERT MICHELS, SOCIALISM, AND MODERNITY

feudal dominance of a few academic 'authorities', and the servility inculcated in their students, especially their epigonal doctoral candidates. Michels painted a picture of an academic world governed by power and corruption, rather than values based on the advancement of science.[23] The article had originally been offered to Karl Kautsky for publication in *Die Neue Zeit*, but Kautsky thought it theoretically flawed: what Michels called 'capitalism' in academia was closer to a guild, traceable to the 'still half-medieval guild-like privileges of scholars', characterized by monopolistic use of one's own labour power rather than the use of capital to exploit others' labour power.[24] Rather than re-work the article in accordance with Marxist economic theory, as Kautsky suggested, Michels found an outlet for his discontent in the life-reform movement journal *Ethische Kultur*.

Despite identifying himself with the left of the Social Democratic Party, Michels wrote regularly for 'bourgeois' periodicals. During 1903, Michels contributed to the *Ethische Kultur* (*Wochenschrift für sozial-ethische Reformen*) on an almost weekly basis, even if many of these contributions were only short notices or book reviews. In some respects, this journal of radical liberal social reformers, whose regular contributors included the pacifist Friedrich Wilhelm Foerster, seemed a natural home for Michels' political views at this time, with his emphasis on the ethical dimension of socialism, and his anti-militarism. As a regular contributor to *Ethische Kultur*, Michels straddled the bourgeois reform milieu and the democratic wing of left liberal opinion, while simultaneously aligning himself with the militant left of Social Democracy (which was philosophically committed to intransigent class struggle and non-cooperation with the middle class).

At this time, Michels was starting to engage in serious study of the history of the socialist movements of France and Italy, research that was reflected in a number of reviews he published in Eduard Bernstein's periodical *Documente des Socialismus*. From 1904 on, Michels became a regular contributor to Hubert Lagardelle's *Le Mouvement Socialiste*, a theoretical journal of a small group of French radical syndicalist intellectuals (albeit largely without any substantial working-class base). Michels also evinced vicarious sympathy for Italian radical syndicalists such Arturo Labriola, although he also maintained cordial relations with Italian reformist socialist intellectuals, such as the economist Achille Loria and Cesare Lombroso, both of whom became his colleagues when he took up a lectureship at the University of Turin.

In 1907, Michels was finally successful at securing a position at a university, but in Turin, Italy, not in Germany. Timm Genett's recent major study of Michels has rightly drawn attention to the extent to which Michels' ambition for a chair at a German university never really left him (a fact that arises clearly from Max

---

[23] Dr Robert Michels, 'Der Kapitalismus in der Wissenschaft', *Ethische Kultur*, Jg.XI, Nr.24, 13 June 1903, pp.186–8.
[24] Karl Kautsky to Robert Michels, 9 October 1902, ARM/FLE.

Weber's letters to Michels, albeit this being the only side of that correspondence to survive).[25] Michels developed much warmer and more patriotic sentiments towards his adopted homeland of Italy than he showed towards the Empire of Kaiser Wilhelm II, where he was allergic to manifestations of officially promoted nationalism. His views on the question of nationalism and patriotism would come to diverge depending on the national context he was writing in. The preface to Michels' study of the political sociology of the Italian socialist movement, published in Italian in book form in 1908, was dated 'Turin, Via Andrea Provana, 1 February 1907'. Here Michels professed his love for his adopted country and for all things Italian (describing himself as 'straniero benchè italiano di adozione').[26] In December 1913, Michels formally applied to renounce his German citizenship, and the request was granted the following month.[27]

By the time he moved to Turin, Michels was increasingly disillusioned with the bureaucratic character of the German Social Democratic Party and its emphasis on parliamentarism, complaining of the 'intellectually and morally corrupting, anti-proletarian tendencies of parliamentarism'.[28] In his inaugural lecture at Turin (on the topic 'Homo Oeconomicus and Cooperation'), Michels displayed his expertise on the theory of socialism, but he was now displaying some academic distance from the movement. He dismissed individualism as the solution to the social problems produced by capitalist industrialization, noting the increasing tendency of employers as well as workers to organize themselves. But he left open the question of whether his highly esteemed senior colleague at Turin, Gaetano Mosca, was correct in disputing the feasibility of socialism, merely indicating that 'a growing number of scholars' concurred with Mosca, and pointing to his own writing on the inherently oligarchical tendency of organizations.[29] Elsewhere, Michels cited Mosca's and Pareto's views on elites and oligarchy, testing the notion that conflicts between democracy and autocracy were a screen for the mere replacement of the domination of one minority by another. Michels took the example of the parliamentary leadership of the German Social Democratic Party as a test case. The party also demonstrated the propensity of bureaucracies to expand and acquire more power. Michels acknowledged the tension between the

---

[25] Genett, *Der Fremde im Kriege*.

[26] 'A foreigner although Italian by adoption'. Roberto [Robert] Michels, *Il proletariato e la borghesia nel movimento socialista italiano*, Turin, 1908 (reprint New York, 1975), pp.8–9.

[27] Hessisches Staatsarchiv Marburg, Bestand 165 Kassel—Preussisches Regierungs-Präsidium, N2.6420, Bd.89. See also the documents gathered for Michels' Italian citizenship application in September 1920 in ARM/FLE, Documenti personali.

[28] Robert Michels, 'Proletariat und Bourgeoisie in der sozialistischen Bewegung Italiens', *Archiv für Sozialwissenschaft und Sozialpolitik*, Vol.22, 1906, p.717. Michels added comments in the Italian book version of this article series to the effect that German backwardness was evident in that Germans still saw democracy as something desirable, whereas French and Italian thinkers were already tiring of parliamentarism. Michels, *Il proletariato e la borghesia*, p.383.

[29] Robert Michels, 'Der Homo Oeconomicus und die Kooperation', *Archiv für Sozialwissenschaft und Sozialpolitik*, Bd.29, 1909, pp.50–83, here p.65; cf. Italian original in *La Riforma Sociale*.

22   ROBERT MICHELS, SOCIALISM, AND MODERNITY

views of Mosca and Pareto on the one hand, and the Marxist view of history on the other, but he deferred the attempt to resolve the conflict.[30]

It was during his time at Turin, at the end of 1910, that Michels published his major statement on oligarchy in party organization, *Zur Soziologie des Parteiwesens in der modernen Demokratie*, known in English more succinctly as *Political Parties*.[31] Following the success of Michels' *Political Parties*, he was able to look forward to a career as an established academic. Not, however, in Germany, where the universities remained closed to someone with his radical past, even though he was crab-walking away from the organized left. In mid-1913, Michels was called to take up a chair in economics at the University of Basel. He was only accepted after Max Weber repeatedly and emphatically assured him that he had absolutely no prospects of a professorship in Germany.[32] At the end of 1913, prior to his move to Basel, Michels renounced his German citizenship, intending to apply for Italian citizenship.[33] Because of the outbreak of war and Michels' move to Switzerland, his Italian citizenship formalities were not completed until after the First World War.[34]

Despite the fact that Michels' citizenship was in limbo while he was in Switzerland, he increasingly identified with the Italian cause in the First World War, and he declared his support for Italian participation in the war. Michels cooperated actively with the Italian diplomatic representatives in Switzerland, and with the Italian cultural organization, the Dante Alighieri Society.[35] Michels' pro-Italian sympathies led, as Michels himself foresaw, to a break with his German colleagues. Michels initially suggested to Weber that his name be removed from the title-page of the *Archiv für Sozialwissenschaft und Sozialpolitik*.[36] Subsequently, Weber broke off relations with Michels over the latter's public statements in the Swiss press about the war.[37] Michels was also denounced (perhaps by a German

---

[30] Roberto [Robert] Michels, 'L'oligarchia organica constituzionale. Nuovi studi sulla Classe Politica', *La Riforma Sociale*, Vol.XVIII, series 2, anno XIV, December 1907, pp.961–83. (Reprinted in Roberto [Robert] Michels, *Potere ad oligarchia. Organizzazione del partito ed ideologia socialista (1900–1910)*, ed. Ettore A. Albertoni, Milan, 1989, pp.431–57.)

[31] Leipzig, 1911 (date on title page, but date on paper cover is 1910, which is also when the first copies became available).

[32] Weber to Gisela Michels-Lindner, 30 June and 10 July 1913, Max Weber, *Briefe 1913–1914* (= *Gesamtausgabe* II, 8), ed. M.R. Lepsius and W.J. Mommsen, Tübingen, 2003, pp.257–8, 268. See also detailed note on Michels' appointment in Basel on p.256. Timm Genett has rightly stressed Michels' persistent, but doomed, ambition to gain a chair in Germany. Genett, *Der Fremde im Kriege*, pp.614–26.

[33] Hessisches Staatsarchiv Marburg, Bestand 165, Nr.6420, Bd.89.

[34] Folder: Cittadinanza Italiana, Arichivio Roberto Michels / Fondazione Luigi Einaudi, Turin.

[35] Federico Trocini, 'Robert Michels a Basilea tra 1914 e 1920. Gli rapporti con la R. Legazione d'Italia e con la Società Nazionale "Dante Alighieri"', *Annali della Fondazione Luigi Einaudi*, XLIII, 2009, pp.137–68; and Trocini's detailed documentation: *Robert Michels e la Prima Guerra Mondiale. Lettere e documenti (1913–1921)*, Florence, 2019.

[36] Max Weber to Robert Michels, 27 May 1915, in Weber, *Briefe 1915–1917* (= *Gesamtausgabe* II/9) (ed. Gerd Krumeich and M. Rainer Lepsius), Tübingen, 2008, p.54.

[37] Max Weber to Robert Michels, 20 June, 9 September, and 21 October 1915; and Weber to Gustav Schmoller, 10 January 1916, *Briefe 1915–1917*, pp.65–7, 132–5, 145–6, 246–51. See also the dossier on

colleague) to German military and police authorities for his ostentatiously pro-Italian sympathies and he was suspected of working as an anti-German agent in Switzerland. (Michels was also accused of writing the anti-*Kaiserreich* tract *I Accuse, By A German*, which was actually written by the pacifist Richard Grelling.)[38]

Timm Genett has justifiably questioned earlier interpretations of Michels as rebounding from an extreme left, or fundamentalist-democratic position, to an extreme right, fascist position. Between his definitive disillusionment with socialists' failure to uphold the International in 1914 to his return to Italy and his eventual adhesion to fascism, Michels took up centrist, even liberal-conservative, political positions, quite in keeping with the habitus of a Swiss economics professor, in fact.[39]

While a professor in Basel, Michels continued to follow developments in Italy with great interest, and developed an admiration for Benito Mussolini, writing to the *Duce* from January 1923, when he sent Mussolini copies of articles he wrote on fascism for the Swiss press. From then on, Michels served as an intellectual promoter of Italian fascism.[40] While travelling in Italy in 1924, Michels witnessed a couple of public appearances by Mussolini and later expressed his admiration for the way that this man who was 'born from the masses' was capable of mastering the masses with his charisma.[41] Michels also had a personal interview with Mussolini in the grand hall in the Palazzo Chigi, where Mussolini received his official visitors and granted them an audience, and gave Michels the benefit of his thoughts on the genuine leader of the masses, who needed above all to be decisive (in contrast to a reflective and hesitant intellectual) and who also needed to keep personal contact with the masses.[42]

Michels had another formal meeting with Mussolini in March 1927, in which, he wrote to his wife Gisela: 'Mussolini, handsome, cultivated & kind as always, asked me: what can I do for you? I answered: preserve your friendship for me, and I left the Palazzo Chigi with my head high'. It seems Michels declined Mussolini's offer of a professorship in Italy, reluctant to appear as a political appointment imposed on a faculty: 'they must want me of their own free will'. But while Michels described his apparent renunciation as a 'sacrifice', he was still clearly confident of

---

Michels in Geheimes Staatsarchiv Preussischer Kulturbesitz, Berlin-Dahlem VI. HA, Nl. Schmoller, Nr.158. Fall Michels.

[38] Landesarchiv Berlin, No.16386: Akten der Abteilung VII-4 des Königlichen Polizei-Präsidiums zu Berlin, A. Pr. Br. Rep. 030, betreffend den Schriftsteller, Professor Dr Robert Michels 1903–1917, Bl.23. The denunciation came from a Lieutenant Braun, possibly Gustav Braun, a German professor of geography at Basel who volunteered to serve in the German army at the outbreak of war.

[39] Genett, *Der Fremde im Kriege*, pp.661–70, 722–38.

[40] Loreto Di Nucci, 'Roberto Michels "ambasciatore" fascista', *Storia Contemporanea*, Vol.XXIII, 1, February 1992, p.91.

[41] Robert Michels, *Italien von heute*, Zurich and Leipzig, 1930, pp.268–70, quotation p.268.

[42] Michels, *Italien von heute*, pp.269–70.

24 ROBERT MICHELS, SOCIALISM, AND MODERNITY

gaining a professorial chair in Italy, perhaps in Perugia.[43] (It is doubtful that Mussolini was taken in by Michels' show of false modesty.) Michels had, in fact, been lobbying Italian government officials for a professorship in Italy since 1926. After Michels turned down a position in Messina (a hardship posting remote from Michels' preferred haunts in the North such as Turin, or perhaps Rome), an appointment to a chair in Perugia followed in November 1927.[44] Perugia's Faculty of Political Science had just been founded that year, and was intended to serve as an elite academy for fascist leadership cadres. Shortly after arriving in Perugia, Michels joined the National Fascist Party, on 6 June 1928.[45] In the years between taking up his position in Perugia and his death in 1936, Michels put his abilities as a lecturer and writer, and his international academic networks, in the service of promoting the Italian fascist regime in Italy and abroad.[46]

It will have been apparent in the brief account of Michels' career so far that the intellectual, political, and personal paths that led to the ideas expressed in this book were not simple or straightforward. This is reflected in the large bodies of secondary literature that grapple with either Michels' contributions to political theory or his personal political trajectory, or both. In the chapters to follow, I seek to reconstruct the spectrum of different political and intellectual influences that shaped Michels' major, and only enduring work.

---

[43] Robert Michels to Gisela Michels-Lindner, 25 March 1927, ARM/FLE.

[44] Di Nucci, 'Roberto Michels "ambasciatore" fascista', pp.92–6.

[45] Di Nucci, 'Roberto Michels "ambasciatore" fascista', p.91.

[46] Di Nucci, 'Roberto Michels "ambasciatore" fascista', pp.97–101. A. James Gregor calls Michels 'a distinguished and committed Fascist intellectual', and, rather generously, continues: 'one of the principal ideologues of Fascism. Much of the intellectual substance of Fascism was a product of his multifaceted intelligence, research acumen, and scholarly diligence'. A. James Gregor, *Phoenix: Fascism in our Time*, New Brunswick, NJ, and London, 2004, pp.54, 55. See also A. James Gregor, ed., *Roberto Michels e l'ideologia del fascismo*, Rome, 1979. Like some of Michels' other, more critical, conservative and liberal readers, Gregor tends to overstate the continuities between the 'revolutionary syndicalist' Michels and the Fascist ideologue Michels.

2

Michels and German Social Democracy

Activism and Ethical Superiority

Michels' 1910 work on the oligarchical organizational structure and sociology of political parties was to impress both his contemporaries and later scholars not only by the mass of footnotes and empirical material on his principal case study, the German Social Democratic Party, but by the fact that he wrote with the authority of someone who, as Seymour Martin Lipset wrote in his introduction to the 1962 American re-publication of *Political Parties*, had been 'long active personally in the German socialist movement.'[1] As already noted, Arthur Mitzman considered that the 'importance of Michels' thesis in the history of social theory' lay less in its conceptual originality than 'in the living, concrete experience behind its formulation.'[2] Robert Michels was an active member of the German Social Democratic Party over a number of years, something which prevented him from realizing his long-cherished ambition of an academic career in the Kaiser's Germany. He was a frequent contributor to German Social Democratic newspapers and periodicals in the period 1903–5. He attended the party congresses of 1903, 1904, and 1905 as a delegate of the electoral districts of Marburg-Kirchhain-Frankenberg and Alsfeld-Lauterbach-Schotten. He was acquainted, and corresponded, with a number of prominent members of the party. However, in important respects, Michels' experience of the German Social Democratic Party was atypical. In particular, Michels' experience of Social Democratic Party organization in the small Hessian university town of Marburg was hardly representative of life in the wider Social Democratic labour movement, and Michels was also highly conscious of his identity as a bourgeois intellectual in what was still strongly identified as a working-class party. In Michels' view, this voluntary identification with the cause of the working class was a mark of ethical distinction, an attitude on his part which would strongly colour his relations with the party.

[1] Seymour Martin Lipset, 'Introduction', to Robert Michels, *Political Parties*, trans. Eden and Cedar Paul, New York and London, 1968 (reprint of 1962 edn), p.15.

[2] Arthur Mitzman, *Sociology and Estrangement: Three Sociologists of Imperial Germany*, New York, 1973, p.267. For an empirically grounded critique of Michels' portrayal of the German labour movement, see Christiane Eisenberg, 'Basisdemokratie und Funktionärherrschaft. Zur Kritik von Robert Michels' Organisationsanalyse der deutschen Arbeiterbewegung', in *Mitteilungsblatt des Instituts zur Erforschung der europäischen Arbeiterbewegung*, 9, 1989, pp.8–30.

Robert Michels, Socialism, and Modernity. Andrew G. Bonnell, Oxford University Press. © Andrew G. Bonnell 2023.
DOI: 10.1093/oso/9780192871848.003.0003

26   ROBERT MICHELS, SOCIALISM, AND MODERNITY

From Marburg to Dresden

In December 1901, the 25-year-old recent PhD in history wrote to Karl Kautsky, editor of the leading Marxist theoretical journal in Germany, and for that matter in Europe, *Die Neue Zeit*, offering his services as an author of articles on conditions in Italy, concluding: 'In the hope, that you will not turn away a "doctor" from contributing his small portion to the great liberation'.[3] Kautsky was initially reserved, assuring Michels that he was 'by no means opposed to "doctors"', but the weekly journal suffered from such a shortage of space that he had had to decline 'articles from proven party comrades on conditions in Italy'.[4] However, once Kautsky had made Michels' personal acquaintance, Michels joined the contributors of *Die Neue Zeit*. It is worth noting, however, that Michels—prolific writer that he was—contributed relatively little to the weighty Marxist journal during his involvement with German Social Democracy. While Michels developed a broad knowledge of European labour movement history and an enthusiasm for revolutionary politics, his interest in questions of Marxian theory seems to have been limited.

In February 1902, there is the first recorded instance of Michels attending a political meeting in Marburg, but this was a gathering of the National Social Party, at which the liberal aristocrat Hellmuth von Gerlach spoke, and not a Social Democratic meeting. Michels did, however, state at the meeting that he was not an adherent of the National Social Party, apparently without declaring himself a Social Democrat.[5] A marginal note on the police report of the meeting recorded that the authorities were already aware that Michels was planning to write his *Habilitation*—his second, professorial dissertation—in Marburg.[6] The small Hessian university town (out of a population of about 17,500 around this time, some 1,150 were students) was well away from centres of industry and labour movement organization.[7] Marburg was a 'town of the university, public servants and rentiers', with virtually no industry and close to its rural hinterland.[8] It was an attractive home for the widows of schoolteachers and clergymen, who sought to make a modest living out of renting out rooms to students and professors.[9] Much of the town's population worked in the tertiary, service sector, increasingly

---

[3] Michels to Karl Kautsky, 6 December 1901, International Institute for Social History, Amsterdam (IISH), Archief Kautsky, K D XVII, no.534.

[4] Michels to Kautsky 6 December 1901 (original IISH); Kautsky to Michels, 21 December 1901, ARM/FLE.

[5] Report of Fuss-Gendarm Volkenand, incorrectly dated 18 October [*recte*: February] 1902, Hessisches Staatsarchiv Marburg [HStAM], 180/752.

[6] Report of Fuss-Gendarm Volkenand, 18 October [*recte*: February] 1902.

[7] Bernhard vom Brocke, 'Marburg im Kaiserreich 1866–1918', in Erhart Dettmering and Rudolf Grenz, eds., *Marburger Geschichte. Rückblick auf die Stadtgeschichte in Einzelbeiträgen*, Marburg, 1982, p.377.

[8] Vom Brocke, 'Marburg im Kaiserreich 1866–1918', p.369.

[9] Vom Brocke, 'Marburg im Kaiserreich 1866–1918', p.428.

MICHELS AND GERMAN SOCIAL DEMOCRACY 27

oriented around the needs of the university, its staff and students.[10] Michels took up residence at 30 Barfüssertor, an address suited to the status of a young academic—on the edge of the picturesque *Altstadt* and close to the university. The social gap between the Michels' family's circumstances in Marburg and those of the workers is encapsulated in a letter from Gisela Michels-Lindner to Robert in which she describes how their son Mario was shocked at the sight of a workman's dirty boots.[11]

Michels offered articles to Social Democratic journals during 1902, and wrote reports on the Italian Socialist Party Congress at Imola in September 1902 for three German party papers. He wrote to Joseph Bloch, who edited and ran the revisionist journal *Sozialistische Monatshefte* in February 1902, offering him an essay on the Italian writer Edmondo de Amicis, and introducing himself as 'a socialist, but I plan to do my *Habilitation* at the university here as a *Dozent* (lecturer) in economic history'.[12] Michels appears to have believed that he would not 'do too much damage to my advancement if I occupy myself with non-German socialism, even publicly', as he told Karl Kautsky.[13] As suggested above, this miscalculation on Michels' part would have decisive consequences for his intended academic career in the Kaiser's Empire.[14] In February 1903, Michels attended his first (on record, at least) local party meeting in Marburg.[15] From then on, at the latest, his party membership was known to the Marburg police and civil service, and the Prussian Political Police in Berlin would subsequently start a file on him as well.[16] The following month, on 14 March, Michels spoke at the 'März-Feier' (March Celebration) of the Marburg Social Democrats, speaking on the subject of 'Karl Marx'. (The March Festival was a regular fixture in the Social Democratic calendar, commemorating the 1848 revolution.)[17]

Presumably this talk followed the lines of Michels' leading article in the *Mitteldeutsche Sonntags-Zeitung* dated the following day, on 'What Does Karl

---

[10] Vom Brocke, 'Marburg im Kaiserreich 1866–1918', p.429.

[11] Gisela Michels-Lindner to Robert Michels, 17 September 1904, ARM/FLE.

[12] Michels to Joseph Bloch, 7 February 1902, ARM/FLE (photocopy, original in Bundesarchiv, Koblenz; now in International Institute of Social History (IISH), Amsterdam, Sozialistische Monatshefte Archives, 129).

[13] Michels to Karl Kautsky, 6 December 1901, IISH, Archief Kautsky, K D XVII, no.534.

[14] In light of Michels' letter to Kautsky suggesting that occupying himself with Italian socialism would not harm his prospects of a *Habilitation*, Jürgen Kaube's assertion that Michels knew his involvement with socialism would cost him his academic career needs to be qualified. Jürgen Kaube, *Max Weber. Ein Leben zwischen den Epochen*, Berlin, 2014, p.316.

[15] The Report of Wachtmeister Kuhlmann on Social Democratic Party meeting in Jesberg's pub on 7 February (dated 10 February) 1903, Hess. StaM, 180/752, notes the attendance of Michels and Gisela Michels-Lindner, but Michels is not recorded as speaking at this meeting, nor was he among those elected to the election committee at this meeting.

[16] Landesarchiv Berlin (LAB), A. Pr. Br. Rep. 030 Tit.95, No.16386: Akten der Abteilung VII-4 des Königlichen Polizei-Präsidiums zu Berlin, betreffend den Schriftsteller, Professor Dr Robert Michels 1903–1917.

[17] Advertised in 'Aus dem Kreise Marburg-Kirchhain', *Mitteldeutsche Sonntags-Zeitung*, no.10, 8 March 1903.

28 ROBERT MICHELS, SOCIALISM, AND MODERNITY

Marx Mean to Us?'.[18] The article raises the question of Michels' theoretical understanding of Marxism, given that Marxist theory tended not to feature conspicuously in his writings of this period, even in his articles for the Social Democratic press. Michels' essay, on the occasion of the twentieth anniversary of Marx's death, began by emphasizing that there was no room for a cult of personality in the *Weltanschauung* of social democracy, but that this did not mean that one should not commemorate the achievements of socialism's pioneers. Marx, Michels wrote, was not infallible, his theory was not at all identical with socialism *per se*, and it was conceivable that his doctrines might one day be superseded. Before dealing with the doctrines themselves, Michels paused to consider Marx as an individual personality:

> I will not speak here of how the highly educated young Doctor of Philosophy, son of a well-off family, had to give up his cherished plan of a professorial career at a German university for the sake of social democracy; nor will I recall here how the thorough researcher and scholar, who left all the penny-a-dozen academics on German professorial chairs so far, far behind, had to do without the recognition of the world to which he originally belonged by his origins and by his education; nor do I wish finally to repeat at length how the active popular speaker and writer was chased by bourgeois governments from one country to another, until he finally found asylum for himself and his own in hospitable England. These are all things that every social democrat who is more prominent than usual similarly experiences.[19]

Of course, in Marc-Antony-like fashion, Michels was drawing attention to these elements in Marx's biography by the rhetorical device of denying that he was going to do so. It is hardly reading too much into these lines to detect a degree of identification with Marx on Michels' part, or an element of concealed autobiography: Michels saw himself (a young Doctor of Philosophy from a rich family) as someone whose brilliant academic career was being sacrificed for the sake of his political engagement with Social Democracy, an engagement that was entering its most active phase. 'Martyrdom and socialism are, it seems, closely connected with each other, albeit very much involuntarily', Michels reflected.[20]

As far as Marx's thought was concerned, Michels presented him as a grand synthesizer, who had brought all the 'socialist, communist, and collectivist social theories that had arisen before him' into a single intellectual whole, at the same time rejecting everything in them that was 'unhealthy' or impracticable, and who had brought this structure into harmony with reality and with science. There is an

---

[18] Michels, 'Was bedeutet uns Karl Marx?', *Mitteldeutsche Sonntags-Zeitung*, no.11, 15 March 1903 (leading article).
[19] Michels, 'Was bedeutet uns Karl Marx?'.   [20] Michels, 'Was bedeutet uns Karl Marx?'.

echo here of Engels' expression 'from utopia to science', but Michels' formulation makes Marx sound more eclectic and synthetic in his approach. Michels singles out for mention the *Communist Manifesto*, and the discovery of the materialistic conception of history that 'the history of all peoples and times is ultimately nothing but a long series of persisting struggles of the different classes among one another'. Michels mentioned the concepts of the intensification of the class struggle, the relations of production, and the notion of 'the whole juridical, social, moral and intellectual culture, or un-culture, of the individual ages *only as a kind of superstructure*'. Michels noted that Marx's emphasis on the primacy of the given relations of production meant that voluntaristic *putsch* attempts would be futile unless the development of the economic foundation of society had reached a certain level of development. Michels also referred to *Das Kapital*, and the theory of surplus value. Finally, he praised Marx as the first Social Democrat who had successfully united theory and practice.[21] Michels' brief discussion of Marxian theory was a little general and imprecise, although one needs to bear in mind that it was a commemorative article for a regional newspaper, and not a treatise for the more scholarly theoretical organ *Die Neue Zeit*. In February 1904, in an obituary for the Italian historical materialist philosopher Antonio Labriola, Michels credited Labriola (rather vaguely) with having been one of Marx's successors who had 'completed Marx's theories in some respects, developed them further in others, and in yet others modified them'. Michels' Labriola was 'a convinced Marxist, without in any way being a blind stickler for fixed principles'; he mocked dogmatism, but was a determined opponent of any attempts to water down the scientific foundations or tactical principles of socialism, and was therefore a merciless critic of Eduard Bernstein, even to the point of becoming unfairly condescending towards him (although, while often scathing in his comments about revisionism and reformism, Michels always remained respectful and cordial in his dealings with Bernstein personally). Once again, in this article Michels shows himself sympathetic to radicalism, but vague when it comes to the specifics of Marxist theory, which he suggests is still plastic and open-ended, without stating precisely in what respects.[22] In 1905, writing for the Italian syndicalist newspaper *Avanguardia Socialista*, Michels gave the impression that he found Marx difficult to read: he stated that Marx was difficult to follow unless one had completed university courses in Hegelian philosophy, while Kautsky's style, by contrast, was as 'limpid and clear as an Alpine stream'.[23]

Later in 1903, in the bourgeois reform-movement journal *Ethische Kultur*, Michels defined socialism as not a party with a party doctrine but a

---

[21] Michels, 'Was bedeutet uns Karl Marx?'; emphasis in original.

[22] Dr Robert Michels, 'Antonio Labriola', *Mitteldeutsche Sonntags-Zeitung*, no.7, 14 February 1904.

[23] Roberto [Robert] Michels, 'Idee e uomini. Karl Kautsky', *Avanguardia Socialista*, vol.III (2nd series), no.111, 28 January 1905, p.1.

'Weltanschauung', more precisely a 'social-ethical *Weltanschauung*'. Those who profess it, according to Michels, had only joined together to form a party out of necessity (*notgedrungen*) for the practical life of politics. Furthermore, mere material deprivation could never make a socialist out of anyone, in Michels' view—the desire of socialists to improve society represented 'an idealistic form of dissatisfaction'.[24]

Michels began to contribute to a wide range of German Social Democratic publications (alongside many others as well). In the course of 1902, Michels became a regular contributor to Eduard Bernstein's periodical *Documente des Socialismus*. As the name suggests, Bernstein's journal was a forum for the publication of archival sources on the history of the socialist movement, as well as including a running bibliography on socialist literature, with critical reviews by the journal's contributors of works on socialist history and theory. Michels contributed documentations on the history of French socialism and regular reviews of Italian socialist publications. As well as being international in its scope, Bernstein's *Documente* were relatively ecumenical in the political spectrum of contributors, in keeping with the journal's scholarly make-up. Michels' regular collaboration with the *Documente* was not necessarily a sign of ideological affinity with Bernstein's revisionism. However, a reading of his early contributions to the journal would hardly dispel any assumption that Michels was close to the revisionist camp. Michels' reviews for *Documente des Socialismus* often confined themselves to summarizing the content of Italian publications for the benefit of German readers, and he seems to have made an effort to give a balanced evaluation of the writings under review. However, he expressed some critical distance from the works of such Italian radical socialists as Ottavio Dinale and Enrico Ferri, in which the latter polemicized against reformism.[25] Michels gave (qualified) praise for Benedetto Croce's critique of orthodox Marxism. Croce's strictures against the 'disciples of Marx' were formulated in terms not unlike those of German revisionism.[26] Michels took issue with Eugenio Ciacchi's complaint against the non-proletarian composition of Italy's socialist parliamentary caucus. Michels' praise for the idealism and selflessness of the bourgeois supporters of socialism in Italy mirrored Bernstein's emphasis on idealism over class motives in the latter's commentary on non-proletarian elements' support for social democracy.[27]

---

[24] Robert Michels, 'Sprechsaal', *Ethische Kultur*, Jg. XI, Nr.35, 29. August 1903, pp.278–9.

[25] Robert Michels, review of Ottavio Dinale, *Diversità di Tendenze o Equivoco?*, in *Documente des Socialismus*, Vol.1, 1902, p.337; Robert Michels, review of Enrico Ferri, *Il Metodo Rivoluzionario*, in *Documente des Socialismus*, Vol.1, 1902, pp.530–2.

[26] Robert Michels, review of Benedetto Croce, *Materialismo Storico ed Economia Marxistica, Saggi Critici*, *Documente des Socialismus*, Bd.1, 1902, p.530.

[27] Robert Michels, review of Eugenio Ciacchi, *Cos'è la Camera del Lavoro?*, *Documente des Socialismus*, Bd.1, 1902, p.381.

MICHELS AND GERMAN SOCIAL DEMOCRACY   31

In his series of essays published as *Die Voraussetzungen des Sozialismus* in 1899, seen as the founding text of revisionist Marxism, Bernstein had invoked 'Kant against Cant', in order to argue that Marxism was in need of being augmented by the conception of ethics found in Kantian philosophy, although there is no evidence of a systematic study of Kant on Bernstein's part.[28] Michels' sojourn in Marburg would have brought him into the intellectual environment of neo-Kantianism. Thanks to the Marburg philosopher Hermann Cohen, Marburg was the centre of neo-Kantianism in Germany in the 1890s and early 1900s.[29] Michels came into contact with neo-Kantianism through some of his academically educated Marburg associates there, such as the German-Russian student of Cohen, Otto Buek, as indicated in his 1932 autobiographical essay on his Marburg experiences.[30] However, Michels did not identify himself as a neo-Kantian in this period, and, as with Bernstein, there is little evidence of systematic engagement with Kant's thought on his part. (Perhaps unsurprisingly, only a few German Social Democrats, such as Kurt Eisner, did engage closely with Kant's ideas, despite the efforts of the Cohen student Karl Vorländer to promote a synthesis of Kant and Marx.)[31] Moreover, on the level of political strategy and tactics, Michels took up positions diametrically opposed to those of the revisionists. What seems most likely is that the neo-Kantians' emphasis on ethics harmonized in a congenial manner with Michels' own conception of his socialist affiliation being determined by his own ethical qualities, without his seeking to integrate these ideas into a coherent philosophical system. The neo-Kantian emphasis on the ethical dimension of socialism would have reaffirmed his own convictions on this point, derived from his reading of his own biographical experiences. By 1908, Michels was praising Vorländer for his 'fruitful synthesis of Kant and Marx', and for Vorländer's affirmation of the decisive importance of the moral factor vis-à-vis economic and material factors.[32]

---

[28] Eduard Bernstein, *Die Voraussetzungen des Sozialismus*, ed. Günther Hillmann, Reinbek bei Hamburg, 1969 [1899], pp.199–218.

[29] On Marburg neo-Kantianism, see Tim Keck, 'Practical Reason in Wilhelmian Germany: Marburg Neo-Kantian Thought in Popular Culture', in Seymour Drescher et al., eds., *Political Symbolism in Modern Europe: Essays in Honor of George L. Mosse*, New Brunswick, NJ, and London, 1982, pp.63–80.

[30] Robert Michels, 'Eine syndikalistisch gerichtete Unterströmung im deutschen Sozialismus (1903-1907)', in Robert Michels, *Masse, Führer, Intellektuelle. Politisch-soziologische Aufsätze 1906–1933*, ed. Joachim Milles, Frankfurt and New York, 1987, p.65 (first published in *Festschrift für Carl Grünberg zum 70. Geburtstag*, Leipzig, 1932, pp.343–64).

[31] According to Keck, 'Kurt Eisner was the only consistent advocate of the Marburg position', having worked as a journalist on the Marburg newspaper *Hessische Landeszeitung* in the mid-1890s. Keck, 'Practical Reason in Wilhelmian Germany', p.68. On Vorländer, see pp.66–8.

[32] Robert Michels, 'Le côté éthique du socialisme positiviste', *La Société Nouvelle*, Vol.14 (2nd series), no.3, September 1908, pp.305–12, reference to Vorländer on p.305n. As a regular contributor to the *Archiv für Sozialwissenschaft und Sozialpolitik*, Michels would by then have been familiar with Vorländer's article, 'Die Stellung des modernen Sozialismus zur philosophischen Ethik', *Archiv für Sozialwissenschaft und Sozialpolitik*, 22, 1906, pp.727–64. Vorländer acknowledged that the 'leading theoretical capacities [of the Social Democratic Party] were...subject to the demands of the political

32 ROBERT MICHELS, SOCIALISM, AND MODERNITY

In April 1902, Michels contributed the first of what would later become several articles to Clara Zetkin's *Die Gleichheit*, dealing with the socialist women's movement in Italy. The language of Michels' article indicates an author who identified himself fully with the cause of the socialist party.[33] This article was followed by a series by Michels on the socialist women's movement in Italy, starting in August 1902. Michels noted that in some respects, for example, in its improvements in women's access to higher education, the Italian state was more advanced than Germany. Writing on educational reforms for women in Italy since the 1870s (admission to university study, improvement of training and status for women high school teachers), Michels praised these as 'just and modern' actions of the Italian state.[34]

Michels seems to have enlisted the help of Clara Zetkin and the brilliant militant left-wing socialist Rosa Luxemburg in placing his articles in the party press, specifically his reports from the Italian socialist congress at Imola in September 1902, which appeared in the party's flagship newspaper *Vorwärts* as well as the south-west German *Schwäbische Tagwacht*. Luxemburg undertook to write to Gustav Jaeckh, the editor of the radical left paper in Leipzig, the *Leipziger Volkszeitung*, to encourage him to carry Michels' reports from the congress.[35] In this context it is worth noting that while keen to publish widely (in both the socialist and non-socialist press), Michels does not seem to have sought a full-time paid position as an editor in the Social Democratic Party press, although such a position might well have been open to him. Full-time work in the party press was modestly remunerated and carried the constant occupational hazard even after the expiry of the anti-Socialist law in 1890 of arrest for political offences such as *lèse-majesté*.[36] Michels would come to see paid party work as a means of social advancement for men from working-class backgrounds, but such employment was less attractive to a young man from a wealthy background with hopes of an academic career.

During 1903, Michels was highly active in party work and wrote frequently for the Hessian socialist newspaper, the *Mitteldeutsche Sonntags-Zeitung* (based in Giessen). Reports in this paper and the Marburg police files show Michels to have been closely involved in the political activities of the Social Democratic Party in

struggle to a great extent'—as Bernstein and Kautsky had both stressed in explanation of their limited engagement with abstract philosophical questions, although he also considered the influence of Marx and Engels partially responsible for the abstention from philosophical 'speculation' (p.737).

[33] Dr Robert Michels, 'Der Kampf um das Arbeiterinnenachutzgesetz in Italien', *Die Gleichheit*, Jg.12, no.9, 23 April 1902, pp.68–9.

[34] Dr Robert Michels, 'Die Frauenbewegung in Italien', *Die Gleichheit*, Jg.12, no.19, 10 September 1902, p.150.

[35] Luxemburg to Clara Zetkin, 18 August 1902, in Rosa Luxemburg, *Gesammelte Briefe*, Bd.1 (ed. Institut für Marxismus-Leninismus beim ZK der SED), Berlin, 1984, p.643.

[36] See Waltraud Sperlich, *Journalist mit Mandat. Sozialdemokratische Reichstagsabgeordnete und ihre Arbeit in der Parteipresse 1867 bis 1918*, Düsseldorf, 1983; Alex Hall, *Scandal, Sensation and Social Democracy: The SPD Press and Wilhelmine Germany 1890–1914*, Cambridge, 1977.

the lead-up to the June 1903 Reichstag elections. Thereafter, Michels continued to be active in the Marburg party organization between the elections and the 1903 Dresden party congress of the Social Democratic Party. Michels and his wife Gisela were also active in the foundation of a consumers' cooperative association in Marburg.[37]

Michels showed himself to be an active and effective agitator in the Marburg election campaign. He stood as a so-called *Zählkandidat* (a candidate running in a constituency the Social Democrats had no hope of winning in order to register the level of support for the party nationwide) in the electorate of Hessen III: Lauterbach-Alsfeld, adjacent to Marburg-Frankenberg-Kirchhain, as well as campaigning for the party in Marburg itself. Speaking to a gathering of (approximately forty) stonemasons on the subject of the value of trade union organization in April 1903, Michels addressed the concerns of stonemasons whose recently legally mandated nine-hour day had resulted in wage reductions, stressing that only effective trade union organization offered an answer. According to the report in the regional Social Democratic press, his speech met with undivided agreement, and about half of those present signed themselves up for the proposed union branch and elected an organizer.[38] At a Social Democratic election rally in May, the principal speaker was the Social Democratic Party candidate for the Reichstag district, the writer Paul Bader. His National Social Party opponent Hellmuth von Gerlach responded and Michels followed with an hour-long response to Gerlach, attacking militarism and the contradictions in the National Social Party programme.[39] In addition to his occasional leading articles for the *Mitteldeutsche Sonntags-Zeitung*, Michels also contributed occasional short reports on election campaign meetings, and polemical rejoinders to political opponents such as von Gerlach.[40]

One of Michels' leading articles for the *Mitteldeutsche Sonntags-Zeitung* refuted the charges of the Social Democrats' opponents in the campaign, including the National Socials, that the party sought to destroy the *Mittelstand*, arguing that the Social Democratic Party, with its principled opposition to tariffs, which increased

---

[37] 'Aus dem Kreise Marburg-Kirchhain', *Mitteldeutsche Sonntags-Zeitung*, no.14, 5 April 1903; 'Aus dem Kreise Marburg-Kirchhain', *Mitteldeutsche Sonntags-Zeitung*, no.20, 17 May 1903. Gisela Michels-Lindner was also instrumental in starting a *Konsumverein* (consumers' cooperative) in the nearby town of Alsfeld in 1905, Hessisches Staatsarchiv Darmstadt (HStAD), G15 Alsfeld Q11 (unfoliated), Gendarmerie report dated Alsfeld, 27 November 1905.

[38] 'Aus dem Kreise Marburg-Kirchhain', *Mitteldeutsche Sonntags-Zeitung*, no.15, 12 April 1903.

[39] 'Aus dem Kreise Marburg-Kirchhain', *Mitteldeutsche Sonntags-Zeitung*, no.21, 24 May 1903. Von Gerlach's *Hessische Landeszeitung* subsequently took issue with Michels' 'comments that were unseemly and offensive to religion' in this meeting. 'Aus der Wahlbewegung', *Hessische Landeszeitung*, no.115, 17 May 1906; Michels' rejoinder in 'Aus der Wahlbewegung. Erklärung', *Hessische Landeszeitung*, no.117, 20 May 1903.

[40] 'Aus dem Kreise Marburg-Kirchhain': R.M., report on meeting of the Evangelische Bund, *Mitteldeutsche Sonntags-Zeitung*, no.12, 22 March 1903; 'Aus dem Kreise Marburg-Kirchhain', R.M., response to *Hessische Landeszeitung*, *Mitteldeutsche Sonntags-Zeitung*, no.16, 19 April 1903.

34   ROBERT MICHELS, SOCIALISM, AND MODERNITY

the cost of living, as well to indirect taxes to support militarism and naval expansion, which had the same effect, was the true friend of all small artisans and independent craftsmen—a demographic that was not insignificant in Marburg, which lacked large-scale industry.[41]

In addition to speaking to supporters of the Social Democratic Party in their own meetings, Michels also relished the confrontation with political opponents at meetings convened by the latter. The strategy of attending other parties' election rallies to challenge their speakers not only offered the benefit of taking the battle into the opponents' camp, it was also a practical response to the scarcity of venues available to Social Democrats, as a result of measures such as the military boycott of pubs that made their rooms available for Social Democratic assemblies. Thus Michels took on von Gerlach in his own meetings, for example, claiming a link between the government's conservative protectionist tariff policy, which von Gerlach opposed, and its militarism, which the National Socials tended to endorse.[42] Michels also joined the local Social Democratic Party Reichstag candidate, the writer Paul Bader, in tackling the conservative candidate von Pappenheim in the latter's own election meeting a fortnight before the election. Von Pappenheim seems to have been close to being outnumbered at his own rally (which von Gerlach and his National Social supporters also attended), and Michels spoke up to reject 'in an appropriately sharp manner' the conservative's pejorative characterization of the Social Democrats.[43]

The election outcome nationally was a triumph for the Social Democratic Party, which received over three million votes (31.7 per cent of votes cast) and a total of eighty-one Reichstag seats after the run-off elections. In Lauterbach-Alsfeld, Michels won 1,084 votes, or 8.5 per cent of votes cast, while the National Liberals went on to win the run-off election against the rightist pro-agrarian *Deutsche Soziale Partei*.[44] In Marburg, the result was a run-off election between von Gerlach and the anti-semitic candidate, with Bader running third. The Marburg Social Democrats voted to observe neutrality in the run-off election. In his memoirs, von Gerlach later claimed that Michels explained to him why he favoured abstention on the part of the Social Democrats, rather than supporting the more progressive candidate against the conservatives, arguing that: 'If you are

---

[41] Dr Robert Michels, 'Die Mittelstandspolitik der Sozialdemokratie', *Mitteldeutsche Sonntags-Zeitung*, no.23, 7 June 1903.

[42] 'Aus der Wahlbewegung', *Hessische Landeszeitung*, no.106, 7 May 1903.

[43] G.M. [Gisela Michels-Lindner?], 'Aus dem Kreise Marburg-Kirchhain', *Mitteldeutsche Sonntags-Zeitung*, no.24, 14 June 1903.

[44] Carl-Wilhelm Reibel (ed.), *Handbuch der Reichstagswahlen 1890–1918. Bündnisse, Ergebnisse, Kandidaten* (2 vols, Düsseldorf, 2007), pp.1327–31. Michels does not seem to have had a measurable personal impact on the Social Democratic vote in Lauterbach-Alsfeld. In 1898, the Social Democrat candidate Schmidt polled 809 votes, amounting to 10.6 per cent, while in 1907, in keeping with the nationwide results of the so-called 'Hottentot elections', the Social Democrats held their vote in absolute terms, polling 1,194 for their candidate Orbig, while the percentage fell slightly to 7.9 per cent (p.1329).

elected, the Social Democrats have no prospect of later taking the seat. If the reactionary wins, on the other hand, our chances will be good'.[45] However, to Michels' particular annoyance, the central party newspaper, *Vorwärts*, called on Social Democratic voters to support the National Social candidate as the lesser evil. The key consideration in this decision was the issue of 'bread profiteering' (*Brotwucher*): the agrarian landowners' support for higher tariffs on grain which would result in bread becoming more expensive, whereas Gerlach opposed the conservatives' tariff bill.[46] Michels was incensed at this intervention, claiming that it was less a matter of whether the local party meeting had been correct in their decision to abstain from endorsing Gerlach, than of the way in which the local party was being overridden and contradicted by the central newspaper, with a resultant loss of face for the local organization that had already publicized its earlier resolution. Michels was the main speaker at the meeting at which, after lively debate and some voices against Michels' position, a resolution was passed protesting against *Vorwärts'* intervention and was conveyed to the paper for publication.[47] Michels' irritation with *Vorwärts'* intervention was exacerbated by the fact that the revisionist Social Democratic Reichstag member, Wolfgang Heine, reportedly gave von Gerlach, with whom he was personally acquainted, advance notice by telegram of the *Vorwärts* announcement about the decision, with the result that von Gerlach found out about the notice before the Marburg Social Democrats themselves.[48] Heine brusquely rejected the complaint of the Marburg party members, claiming that he had only telegraphed von Gerlach after seeing the *Vorwärts* announcement in print, when it was already therefore in the public domain.[49]

Michels was clearly unwilling to let the matter rest with the publication of the Marburg resolution in *Vorwärts*. The Marburg party organization sent a second missive to *Vorwärts*, over the name of the former Reichstag candidate Paul Bader, but the party's central paper continued to shrug off the protest with the assertion that it had acted in the party's interests and consistently with the policy of opposing higher duties on foodstuffs.[50] Even after this second rebuff, a third letter from Marburg was sent to *Vorwärts*, this time signed by Michels, his friend Thesing, and the new local party chairman Härtling, again failing to elicit any apology or

---

[45] Hellmut von Gerlach, *Von rechts nach links*, Frankfurt/Main, 1987; 1st edn, 1937, p.160.
[46] For the wording of the announcement and call on members in Marburg to vote for von Gerlach, see 'Im Wahlkreise Marburg' (under the rubric 'Streifzüge durch das Wahlfeld') in *Vorwärts*, no.144, 24 June 1903.
[47] 'Aus dem Kreise Marburg-Kirchhain', *Mitteldeutsche Sonntags-Zeitung*, no.27, 5 July 1903 (report on party meeting of 29 June); Vorwärts, no.164, 17 July 1903: 'Partei-Nachrichten'. 'Aus Marburg', with a short dismissive commentary by the *Vorwärts* editors. See also Dr Ernst Thesing, 'Zur Marburger Stichwahlangelegenheit', and editor's comment, *Mitteldeutsche Sonntags-Zeitung*, no.32, 9 August 1903.
[48] See *Vorwärts*, no.184, 9 August 1903, 1. Beilage, 'Partei-Nachrichten', 'Zur Marburger Stichwahl-Angelegenheit'.
[49] *Vorwärts*, no.187. 13 August 1903, 'Partei-Nachrichten. Zur Marburger Stichwahl-Angelegenheit'.
[50] 'Partei-Nachrichten. Die Marburger Stichwahl', *Vorwärts*, no.169, 23 July 1903.

36   ROBERT MICHELS, SOCIALISM, AND MODERNITY

self-criticism from the editors.[51] Michels also discussed the incident in an article he contributed to the Italian left-syndicalist newspaper *Avanguardia Socialista*, in which he subjected the Social Democrats' electoral tactics to a critical analysis. He stylized the *Vorwärts* dispute as one between the 'reformists in Berlin', and the local 'intransigent' Marburg party organization. Michels claimed that *Vorwärts* distorted the 1902 party congress resolution on electoral tactics in run-off elections, but he was unable to make a wholly convincing case that the Marburg decision to vote for a 'reactionary of the purest water' against von Gerlach, a more progressive candidate in most respects, but still a representative of 'militarists' and 'ultra-imperialists', was a completely principled one.[52]

Perhaps too much has been made of Michels' 1932 autobiographical article on a 'forgotten current of syndicalism in Germany'.[53] Michels' account of the 'Marburg group' of syndicalists was written a quarter of a century after the events it describes, and while parts of the essay are well documented, it would be misleading to take it as evidence of a significant organized syndicalist group in Germany. For all of Michels' retrospective stylization of his leadership of the small Marburg *Wahlverein* (or the 'Marburger Gruppe') into a syndicalist tendency in German socialism, at the time, writing again to *Avanguardia Socialista* in 1905, to real (Italian) syndicalists, he was more candid: 'A last word on German syndicalism: it doesn't exist'.[54]

Somewhat ironically, in view of the Marburg Social Democrats' insistence on the legally binding character of their resolutions, they did not actually possess a formally constituted *Wahlverein*, or electoral association—effectively, a local party branch did not yet formally exist in Marburg, a situation that the Marburg comrades moved to remedy in the following weeks, in order to maintain the organizational gains made during the election campaign.[55] The initial membership list included twenty-six names (reaching about forty-five by the end of August), with Michels as chairman of the provisional executive committee, followed by Georg Härtling, a typesetter, and the local *Vertrauensmann*, or Social

---

[51] 'Zur Marburger Stichwahl' (under 'Partei-Nachrichten'), *Vorwärts*, no.174, 29 July 1903.

[52] Dott. Roberto [Robert] Michels, 'La tattica dei socialisti tedeschi alle Elezioni Generali Politiche', *Avanguardia Socialista*, Anno II, no.28, 5 July 1903. An editorial note of the *Avanguardia Socialista* erroneously identified Michels as the Social Democratic candidate for Marburg.

[53] Michels, 'Eine syndikalistisch gerichtete Unterströmung', pp.63–79.

[54] Roberto [Robert] Michels, 'Sciopero generale, sindacalismo, Jena e Labriola', *Avanguardia Socialista*, Anno III (2. serie), no.149, 21 October 1905. This was not strictly true—there was a minority working-class syndicalist current among organized workers in Berlin (the 'localists' among Berlin trade unionists) and in the Ruhr, but Michels had little contact with German working-class syndicalism. Michels did acknowledge in this article the efforts of Raphael Friedeberg to create an anarchist-syndicalist movement in Germany—but not a Marxist one, Michels noted—but he did not think Friedeberg would be successful in achieving this.

[55] See 'Aus dem Kreise Marburg-Kirchhain', *Mitteldeutsche Sonntags-Zeitung*, no.29, 19 July 1903. Judging from this report, the initiative for the foundation seems to have come from Eduard Krumm, from Giessen, rather than from Michels, although Michels was still active in the Marburg party, addressing a trade union celebration on 19 July.

Democratic organizer, as his deputy.[56] Significantly, the local authorities quickly established the names of the employers of the working-class executive committee members, thereby opening up the possibility for discrimination, even black-listing, against socialists at their workplaces.[57] Michels was not as immediately susceptible to such economic pressure, but any hopes he may have once had of becoming a professor, or at least of gaining the essential professorial qualification of the *Habilitation* in Marburg, were clearly increasingly unlikely to be realized.

Michels did not take on a formal organizational role in the *Wahlverein*, officially constituted at the beginning of September 1903, but he continued to take the lead in what he regarded as its agitational work. Michels planned to hold a series of oral presentations (*Referate*) for the purpose of training members as agitators. He would give the first such talk, followed by his academic comrade Dr Ernst Thesing, four weeks later. The resemblance to a university seminar is striking. Much has been written about the supposed 'proletarian anti-intellectualism' in the German Social Democratic Party.[58] There is little evidence of it in the Marburg branch, where members in the printing, book-binding, and similar trades were perhaps accustomed to being economically dependent on, and hence deferential to, university academics. Michels and his university-educated colleague Dr Ernst Thesing were placed at the top of the list of party members submitted to the authorities and continued to be in demand as speakers at meetings.[59] Comrade Herr Doktor Michels and Comrade Herr Dr Thesing seem to have been accorded a certain amount of deference by rank-and-file party members in Marburg. But then, Marburg was not the most typical Social Democratic Party branch. At its foundation, it numbered just forty-four members, about thirty-five of whom were counted as 'organized workers'. The membership included fourteen book printers, seven wood-workers, five shoemakers, three stencil cutters, two tailors, one wallpaper printer, one brewery worker, one stoker, one cooper, one sculptor, one (male) domestic servant, one fitter, one gardener, one publican, one doctor of medicine, and—one doctor of philosophy.[60]

Michels reflected on the social composition of the Social Democratic Party in an article he contributed to the Italian review *La Riforma Sociale*, again commenting on the June Reichstag elections. The Social Democrats' programme he considered the same as that of the Italian socialists. The party displayed impressive organization, and 'marvellous tenacity in never losing sight of its high

---

[56] HStAM, Königliches Landratsamt Marburg 180/752, report of 13 July 1903; cf. also HStAM 180/752, 30 July 1903; HStAM 180/2318, reports of 31 August and 4 September 1903.

[57] HStAM 180/2318, reports of 30 July 1903.

[58] A central contention of Stanley Pierson, *Marxist Intellectuals and the Working-Class Mentality in Germany, 1887–1912*, Cambridge, MA, 1993.

[59] HStAM 180/2318, report of 31 August 1903.

[60] 'Aus dem Kreise Marburg-Kirchhain', *Mitteldeutsche Sonntags-Zeitung*, no.36, 6 September 1903. Michels' party membership card is in ARM/FLE, Documenti personali, showing stamps for paid membership dues (20 Pfennig a month) from September 1903 to December 1905 inclusive.

38 ROBERT MICHELS, SOCIALISM, AND MODERNITY

idealistic final goals even while pursuing essentially practical politics'.[61] One difference between the German and Italian parties was in the social composition of the parliamentary parties: of thirty-three socialist deputies in Italy, Michels reckoned only two or three (Rigola, Chiesa, and Bertesi) to be of proletarian origins, while in Germany there were, in the Reichstag of 1898–1903, fourteen Social Democrat deputies of bourgeois origins, twelve of 'petit bourgeois' background, and thirty 'of authentic proletarian origin'.[62] After the second round of the 1903 Reichstag elections, Michels counted fifty-three out of eighty-one Social Democratic deputies as having come from genuine working-class occupational backgrounds. However, he qualified this by commenting:

> Obviously, these 'authentic' proletarians as deputies have not been able to remain workers. It is not possible to lay bricks for a house at 2 o'clock and at 3 o'clock give a speech on social questions in the Chamber. Consequently the proletarian deputies are now almost all either newspaper editors or trade union employees, or (5 or 6) publicans, or have at least become independent artisans.[63]

In pointing this out, Michels insisted he did not want to detract from the fact that most German Social Democrat parliamentarians knew the life of the workers at first hand and that it was a testament to the intelligence of the German workers that workers like August Bebel and Ignaz Auer had raised themselves up to the position of being among the most noted men in the national parliament.[64]

As the 1903 Dresden party congress approached, three months after the impressive gains in the Reichstag elections, Michels prepared himself for an active role in the party debates. In particular, he still wished to pursue his dispute with *Vorwärts*, and with Wolfgang Heine, and the Marburg party organization submitted a formal motion to the congress calling on guidelines to be established for the conduct of the party paper towards local party bodies.[65] Michels and a group of twenty-four Marburg comrades subsequently followed this motion up with a late motion demanding that the party congress censure Wolfgang Heine for his conduct in notifying von Gerlach of the *Vorwärts* intervention and for Heine's

---

[61] Dott. Roberto [Robert] Michels, 'Psicologia e statistica delle elezioni generali politiche in Germania (Giugno 1903)', *La Riforma Sociale*, Fasc.7, Anno X, vol.XIII, seconda serie, 15 July 1903, pp.541–67, p.14 in offprint.

[62] Michels, 'Psicologia e statistica', pp.14–15.

[63] Roberto [Robert] Michels, 'L'analisi del Reichstag germanico', *La Riforma Sociale*, Fasc.3, Anno XI, vol.XIV (Seconda serie), pp.208–20, here pp.11, 12 of offprint.

[64] Michels, 'L'analisi del Reichstag germanico', p.12. Michels also noted, however, the absence of any farmers or peasants in the Social Democrat caucus as evidence of the failure of the party to make much headway in the countryside.

[65] *Protokoll über die Verhandlungen des Parteitages der Sozialdemokratischen Partei Deutschlands. Abgehalten zu Dresden vom 13. bis 20. September 1903*, Berlin, 1903, p.121 (motion 43).

MICHELS AND GERMAN SOCIAL DEMOCRACY   39

subsequent criticism of the Marburg party organization.[66] Michels also turned to the party leader August Bebel, with whom he and Gisela Michels-Lindner had become acquainted a year earlier when they visited him at his family home in Küsnacht near Zurich. Michels complained to Bebel about Heine's conduct and his brusque dismissal of the Marburgers' concerns in his response of 13 August in *Vorwärts*. Bebel sympathized with the Marburgers' position. Even if their endorsement of the more reactionary candidate had been mistaken, they were justified in thinking that they were acting in the spirit of a 1902 party congress resolution that warned against deals with liberal and progressive candidates; Heine's response to the Marburg complaint had been arrogant, his communication with von Gerlach a breach of protocol, to say the least, and *Vorwärts* had been at fault in its unilateral dismissal of the Marburgers' concerns. Bebel indicated that he would be happy to deal with this matter at the Dresden party congress, adding that he 'wish[ed] that the Marburg comrades would send someone to Dresden with hair on his teeth, then I will state my opinion in all clarity'.[67] It was Michels himself who took on this role as delegate for Marburg at the party congress.

In August, Michels also addressed the controversial question of whether the party should strive to take the mainly ceremonial position of one of the vice-presidents of the Reichstag (comparable to deputy speaker), to which the Social Democratic parliamentary party was now entitled on the grounds of its numbers, even if it meant having to seek an audience with the Emperor to formalize the appointment. The revisionists in the party, such as Eduard Bernstein and Wolfgang Heine, and more atheoretical reformists like Georg von Vollmar, supported the vice-presidency, even if it meant bowing to the Emperor who personified the most anti-democratic features of the state's constitution. For Michels, writing in the *Mitteldeutsche Sonntags-Zeitung*, the question of principle had to take precedence over pragmatic considerations, whereby the question of principle was reinforced by the personality of Kaiser Wilhelm II and his extreme anti-socialist utterances before the election (the King of Italy or the Grand Duke of Hesse might not be so bad, Michels suggested). For Michels, a shift from a principled position to one of weighing costs and benefits would 'open the door to the worst kind of opportunism'. For Michels, 'a party like ours, which in all questions of humanity takes the lead as the proud standard-bearer of reason and morality' had to be especially careful not to do anything that detracted from its dignity—with Michels' essentially ethical conception of the socialist idea is apparent here. He feared that the desire to seek 'practical gains' at any price was becoming a

---

[66] *Protokoll Dresden 1903*, p.134f (motion 139). Copies of the motion also in the folder on Wolfgang Heine in Michels' correspondence, ARM/FLE.

[67] Bebel to Michels, 15 August 1903, in August Bebel, *Ausgewählte Reden und Schriften*, Bd. 9 (ed. Anneliese Beske and Eckhard Müller), Munich, 1997, pp.57–9, quotation on p.58.

40   ROBERT MICHELS, SOCIALISM, AND MODERNITY

danger for the Social Democratic Party. 'Praktikertum' was spreading in the party, regardless of the still fundamentally hostile attitude of the state to the party.[68] Consequently, Michels instigated another motion for the Dresden party congress the following month, calling on the Reichstag caucus of the party to uphold the 'republican-democratic principles of our party'.[69] Michels regarded a defence of the party's republican principles as indispensable, a point of view that he articulated even more frankly in the Italian socialist press, where the risk of a charge of *lèse-majesté* (ever-present in the German Reich and an occupational hazard for Social Democratic newspaper editors) was less severe.

For example, in January 1903, Michels had commented in the Neapolitan socialist paper *La Strada* on the mildness of the reaction of the German Social Democrats to the Kaiser's anti-socialist diatribes on the occasion of the Krupp scandal: 'The German socialists, strong in energy and spirit, were enraged in the Krupp scandal...in all quietness, but openly they did not dare to make any mischief.' Michels acknowledged the real legal constraints imposed by the law of *lèse-majesté* on the Social Democrats, who risked gaol if they made comments that could be construed as derogatory to the throne.[70] From this, Michels drew the conclusion that 'international socialism has two adversaries: *the capitalism of capital and the capitalism of the aristocracy [di stemma], i.e. feudalism'.* If feudalism, with the monarchy at its head, were to disappear, that would be one enemy less.[71]

Shortly before the Dresden party congress in September, the Hessian Social Democrats had their own state congress in the village of Steinbach im Taunus, attended by 120 delegates from 101 local branches, as well as the Hessian state committee members, the *Vertrauensleute*, or organizers, of the nine Reichstag electoral districts in Hesse, plus representatives from the party press.[72] Michels used the occasion to continue to pursue his conflict with *Vorwärts*, presenting a motion to the congress that: 'The state conference is of the view that the

[68] Dr Robert Michels, 'Der Kaisergang und die Sozialdemokratie', *Mitteldeutsche Sonntags-Zeitung*, no.33, 16. August 1903; an almost identical text appeared in the *Rheinische Zeitung* (Cologne), Jg.12, no.184, 13 August 1903, albeit with an editorial disclaimer distancing the paper from Michels' views. Some of this material re-appears in Dr Robert Michels, 'Le congrès de Dresden et sa psychologie', *L'Humanité Nouvelle*, vol.VII, 53, November 1903, pp.740–54. On the role of atheoretical pragmatists, so-called 'Praktiker', in the Social Democratic Party, typified by Ignaz Auer, see Hans-Josef Steinberg, *Sozialismus und deutsche Sozialdemokratie* (5th edn.), Berlin and Bonn, 1979.
[69] *Protokoll Dresden 1903*, p.124 (motion 69).
[70] Roberto [Robert] Michels, 'L'affare Krupp e l'idea repubblicana', *La Strada*, Vol.2, no.2, 16 January 1902, pp.37–8. On the *lèse-majesté* law and the striking frequency with which it was used against Social Democratic newspaper editors, see Alex Hall, 'The Kaiser, the Wilhelmine State and Lèse-Majesté', *German Life and Letters*, 27, 1973–74, pp.101–15.
[71] Michels, 'L'affare Krupp e l'idea repubblicana', p.38, emphasis in original. On the Social Democratic Party's attitude towards republicanism, see Andrew G. Bonnell, *Red Banners, Books and Beer Mugs: The Mental World of German Social Democrats, 1863–1914*, Leiden, 2021, chapter 8.
[72] 'Landeskonferenz der hessischen Sozialdemokraten', *Mitteldeutsche Sonntags-Zeitung*, no.37, 13 September 1903.

unauthorized intervention of comrades into the electoral affairs of a district should definitely cease henceforth'. An amendment was moved to the effect that tactical differences between comrades concerning run-off elections were to be resolved by the state committee, watering down Michels' assertion of local autonomy somewhat. Michels also joined in the debate on the question of the vice-presidency of the Reichstag.[73]

It is worth noting that while Michels was an impassioned supporter of the Party Left against the revisionists at the 1903 party congress in Dresden, he did not actually share the left's insistence that comrades should not write for the bourgeois press, which was still a significant source of income for him. However, this was one of the most hotly contested points between radicals and revisionists at the congress, at which the Party Left, vigorously supported in print by the Social Democratic historian and journalist Franz Mehring, advocated a hard line against collaboration with bourgeois periodicals and newspapers.[74] (This issue had been precipitated by the revisionist Georg Bernhard, who had voiced criticisms of the party leadership in the weekly journal *Die Zukunft*, edited by Maximilian Harden.) Here Michels was on his own in the Party Left with which he was otherwise keen to identify himself. Michels, declining to take an editorship or other salaried position within the party, chose to continue to rely on earning his living by his pen, and he did not confine himself to the party press in his pursuit of honoraria and royalties for his writings.[75] Michels, attending the congress as representative of both the Marburg and the Alsfeld constituencies, spoke on the resolution prepared by the party executive. While agreeing with the executive, especially in relation to newspapers published by the party's adversaries, Michels warned of grey areas when it came to proposed exemptions for scholarly periodicals. He also insisted that there were worthy bourgeois periodicals which opposed specific negative manifestations of bourgeois society from an 'ethical point of view', and that (no doubt with his own regular work for the bourgeois reform journal *Ethische Kultur* in mind) it must be permissible to write for such journals. Michels also suggested that publishing in non-party outlets offered opportunities for proselytizing for the socialist idea, taking it into new circles. Here he cited his own previous experience as a young bourgeois officer cadet who encountered Bebel's speeches excerpted in the Reichstag reports printed in right-wing conservative newspapers. Along the way, Michels took a swipe at Wolfgang Heine with a barely veiled reference to the experience of the Marburg party of being disadvantaged by party colleagues acting out of friendship with their political opponents. Coming at the end of the second day of the party congress pro-

---

[73] Landeskonferenz der hessischen Sozialdemokraten', *Mitteldeutsche Sonntags-Zeitung*, no.37, 13 September 1903.
[74] HStAM 180/752, report of meeting 17 August 1903.
[75] See Michels to Luigi Einaudi, 14 December 1905, cited in Pino Ferraris, *Saggi su Roberto Michels*, Camerino, 1993, p.59n149.

42   ROBERT MICHELS, SOCIALISM, AND MODERNITY

ceedings, and immediately following a fulminating oration by Bebel in which he had castigated those revisionists who were accused of undermining the party through collaboration with its enemies in the press, and that closed amidst 'long-lasting, stormy applause', Michels' contribution would have been more than a little anti-climactic.[76] Equally anti-climactic was Michels' motion on the need for the Social Democratic Reichstag deputies to uphold 'republican-democratic principles' in the question of the Reichstag vice-presidency. Michels withdrew the motion as the separate formal debate on the question rendered it redundant, and he assured the party congress that no criticism of the conduct of the party's Reichstag caucus to date was implied.[77] Finally, Michels withdrew his motion of censure against Heine after the latter expressed some regret for the sharp form in which he had responded to the Marburgers' complaint. Michels explained that he did not want to detain the party congress with disputes about individuals when there had already been so much personal comment at the congress.[78] Michels had already had the vindication of Bebel publicly criticizing *Vorwärts* and Wolfgang Heine for their treatment of the Marburg branch in his speech to the congress on the matter, which in itself amounted to a public censure of Heine and the paper.[79] While Michels experienced some vindication thanks to Bebel's support, his position on the question of writing for the bourgeois press was at least partially at cross-purposes with the position of the party radicals, and his concerns were somewhat overshadowed by the wider clash between the Party Left and the revisionists at the congress.

In September, just after the Dresden party congress, the journal *Ethische Kultur* printed an article by the revisionist Social Democrat Max Cohen (Frankfurt/M.) criticizing the resolution banning writing for the bourgeois press, and taking issue with Franz Mehring's views on the matter.[80] This same issue was taken up in a couple of columns by the journal's regular contributor: Robert Michels. Clearly, both Cohen and Michels interpreted the Dresden resolution limiting collaboration with the bourgeois press broadly enough to exclude *Ethische Kultur* from the ban. However, that journal did not refrain from criticizing the Social Democratic Party for the developments seen at the Dresden congress. On 3 October, *Ethische Kultur* carried a leading article by F. (Friedrich Wilhelm Förster), that declared that the Dresden party congress was 'the greatest moral defeat' that the Social Democratic Party had suffered, and expressed fears that the party was losing sight of its ethical mission for the sake of abstract ideological quarrels.[81]

---

[76] *Protokoll Dresden 1903*, p.229.   [77] *Protokoll Dresden 1903*, p.284.
[78] *Protokoll Dresden 1903*, p.421.   [79] *Protokoll Dresden 1903*, p.268.
[80] Max Cohen, 'Dürfen Sozialdemokraten an bürgerlichen Blättern mitarbeiten?', *Ethische Kultur*, XI. Jg., 38, 19 September 1903, pp.299–300.
[81] F., 'Der sozialdemokratische Parteitag', *Ethische Kultur*, Jg.XI, 40, 3 October 1903, pp.313–14.

Michels subsequently published a lengthy, two-part article in *Ethische Kultur*, canvassing questions of Social Democratic strategy in the columns of a journal run by bourgeois, non-socialist advocates of social reform. He began by glossing over the controversy over whether the 'movement' or the 'goal' should take priority (picking up the two terms which had been used to denote polar positions within the party during the revisionism controversy), ironically presenting the two as complementary, and managing to cite both Rosa Luxemburg and the Hessian revisionist Eduard David approvingly.[82] Michels devoted most of the article to an ethical justification of socialism, defending the socialist idea against Rudolf Penzig's criticisms. Penzig, the editor of *Ethische Kultur*, had criticized the concept of class struggle, and presented socialism as a potentially coercive doctrine. Michels defended socialism on ethical grounds. He pointed to the fact that while socialism could not hope to win over entire social classes whose interests were opposed to it by persuasion alone, it had succeeded in winning over individuals from these classes:

> Socialist doctrine has indeed managed to win over many a 'son of the bourgeoisie' and to take possession of them so firmly that they abandoned father and mother, friends and relatives, social position and the respect of 'society', only to devote their lives to the high goal of the liberation of humanity; but these are exceptions to the rule, which can only be explained by the fact that these [class] suicides are either absolutely logical reasoners, who draw the conclusions for their position in social conflict from their scientific convictions, or—as is mostly the case—are outstanding individuals of finer feelings relative to the average of their class, whose heart drives them to make their small contribution to the struggle for a morally more elevated human race, cost it what it might.[83]

Michels, it would seem, counted himself among the majority of bourgeois converts to socialism who had made the decision on the basis of an emotional identification with the struggle for the improvement of humanity, rather than on the basis of a rigorously logical conviction of the objective correctness of Marxian theory. Despite his glossing over of the differences between revisionists and radicals in the first part of his article, Michels concluded by arguing that revisionists were more likely to be ready to settle for quickly achievable, tangible reforms than were more revolutionary thinkers like Kautsky or Enrico Ferri, and thus they ran the risk of frittering away the 'innermost core of the socialist idea'. Michels

---

[82] Dr Robert Michels, '"Endziel", Intransigenz, Ethik', *Ethische Kultur*, Jg.XI, no.50, 12 December 1903, pp.393–5; no.51, 19 December 1903, pp.403–4.
[83] Michels, '"Endziel", Intransigenz, Ethik', pp.394–5.

44   ROBERT MICHELS, SOCIALISM, AND MODERNITY

concluded: '*Only through an intransigent class struggle, closely tied to the undistorted idea of the final goal, will the socialism of the ethicist be able to be realized.*'[84]

Michels published another commentary on the Dresden party congress in the French journal *L'Humanité Nouvelle* in November 1903. In this article, he referred to the Social Democratic Party as the 'party in which the socialist idea has found its political crystallization' (although Michels' formulation implied that the idea might be capable of existing outside or without the party). The socialist idea, for its part, was taking 'giant strides', as shown by the German elections of 1903.[85] Given the resounding success of winning three million votes in June, Michels reflected that it might seem surprising that the tone of the Dresden party congress in September was not more celebratory, but rather was characterized by division and rancour.[86] The reason, according to Michels' account, had been Bernstein's article in the *Sozialistische Monatshefte* broaching the question of whether the Social Democrats should claim the position of vice-president of the Reichstag to which the party's number of seats entitled it.[87] Michels characterized this suggestion as a break with the party's 'old anti-Hohenzollern tactics', which would 'overturn at one blow an important part of the most evident and sublime principles of socialism'.[88] Michels explained to non-German readers that the intransigent policy of the German Social Democrats regarding pragmatic alliances with bourgeois parties had good reasons which lay in the history of the German liberals.[89] Social Democracy was isolated in Germany, where 1848 revolutionaries had turned into monarchists, and bourgeois republicanism was virtually non-existent.[90] There was a good reason why German socialists had taken on the name Social Democrats: because in Germany the socialist movement was the 'only possible refuge for any genuine democrat'.[91] Michels insisted on the fundamental importance of republicanism for the Social Democrats: 'It is the product of [the party's] scientific positivism which cannot admit a hereditary rule of an *Aristos Kai Kalistos* [i.e. the excellent and good]'.[92] 'Socialism is the mortal enemy of the Hohenzollern monarchy and vice versa.'[93] The question of the Reichstag

---

[84] Michels, '"Endziel", Intransigenz, Ethik', p.404. Emphasis in original. Cf. the rejoinder of Rudolf Penzig, 'Die Unvernunft des Klassenkampfes', *Ethische Kultur*, Jg.XI, No.52, 26 December 1903, pp.409–11. Penzig reproached Michels for his 'temperament' (p.409), which led him into impatience in the pursuit of his struggle against injustice. Michels' response to Penzig, reaffirming both the historical necessity and the ethical imperative of the class struggle: 'Zur Ethik des Klassenkampfes', *Ethische Kultur*, Jg.XII, no.3, 1 February 1904, pp.21–2.

[85] Michels, 'Le congrès de Dresden et sa psychologie', p.740.

[86] Michels, 'Le congrès de Dresden', p.741.

[87] Eduard Bernstein, 'Was folgt aus dem Ergebnis der Reichstagswahlen?', *Sozialistische Monatshefte*, 1903.

[88] Michels, 'Le congrès de Dresden', p.742.   [89] Michels, 'Le congrès de Dresden', p.744.

[90] Michels, 'Le congrès de Dresden', p.746.   [91] Michels, 'Le congrès de Dresden', p.747.

[92] Michels, 'Le congrès de Dresden', pp.747–8.

[93] Michels, 'Le congrès de Dresden', p.748. Michels added that this situation was compounded by the 'particularly medieval character of Wilhelm II'.

MICHELS AND GERMAN SOCIAL DEMOCRACY   45

vice-presidency, for Michels, had to be considered first and foremost from the perspective of the '*dignity of the idea*'.[94]

In Michels' idealistic conception of socialism, the dignity of the idea was non-negotiable. For him, socialism was in the vanguard of modernity: The socialist party could pride itself on 'representing a completely new conception of the dynamic of the universe... In all serious questions of modern life, it marches at the head of progress like a proud standard-bearer of reason and morality.'[95] The idea could not therefore be sullied by short-term considerations of political utility. An article that Michels wrote around this time, for the mass-circulation workers' almanac and calendar the *Hessischer Landbote*, also reflects this idealistic definition of socialism. Here, Michels equated social democracy with religion, albeit without metaphysics. Michels emphasized that neither economic need nor the insight into the scientific justification of socialism was sufficient to make someone a 'genuine social democrat'. This required altruism and high ethical goals: 'Socialism is science, socialism is economic and social movement towards a predetermined goal, socialism is also, however, a religion, and namely a religion of love of humanity and peace between peoples, which puts the capitalistic-Christian churches in the shade as far as ethical content is concerned.'[96] With his appearance as a delegate at the Dresden congress, Michels had attained national prominence in the party, which also meant that he was henceforth of interest to the Prussian Political Police in Berlin, as well as the local authorities in Marburg.[97]

Agitation and Organization

After the Dresden party congress, Michels travelled to Paris, where he planned to give talks to German, French, and Italian socialist groups.[98] In France, he had the opportunity to observe the participation of French socialists in the French bourgeois coalition government. On balance, Michels' evaluation, as conveyed in the *Magdeburg Volksstimme*, was negative: the contributions of Millerand and Jaurès to the defence of the (bourgeois) democratic republican state form were seen as positive, but limited. On the other hand, and here Michels used the French example for an implied critique of the German revisionists, the fixation on day-to-day work in parliament led to the 'final goal' of socialism becoming lost to view, and the French socialists found themselves having to share responsibility for

---

[94] Michels, 'Le congrès de Dresden', p.750. Emphasis in original.

[95] Michels, 'Le congrès de Dresden', p.750.

[96] Dr Robert Michels, 'Die Religion ist Privatsache und die Sozialdemokratie eine Religion', *Hesssicher Landbote. Ein Kalender für das werthätige Volk*, Offenbach, [1904], pp.11–13, quotation p.13.

[97] LAB 16386.

[98] 'Aus dem Kreise Marburg-Kirchhain', *Mitteldeutsche Sonntags-Zeitung*, no.45, 8 November 1903.

46   ROBERT MICHELS, SOCIALISM, AND MODERNITY

outright reactionary and oppressive decisions of the coalition government, with the result that the left wing of the party was breaking away.[99] The following month, Michels was hailing the expulsion of Millerand from Jaurès's French socialist party as a major setback for revisionism and opportunism everywhere, singling out Wolfgang Heine for special mention as an example of that tendency.[100]

During 1904, Michels continued to be active in the Marburg Social Democratic Party and for the Hessian regional party press, although less intensively than in the previous year. In January 1904, he contributed an article to the *Mitteldeutsche Sonntags-Zeitung* in which he poured scorn over the work of a *Privatdozent* (unsalaried lecturer) in philosophy in Halle, one Dr Hermann Schwarz, who chastised socialist workers for their confusion, class hatred, and ingratitude towards their employers. Michels accused Schwarz of treating the ethical questions as if in a vacuum, ignoring the economic facts of the case, and concluded by suggesting that if Schwarz were to fail to gain a professorship, the bosses of Crimmitschau, where textile workers were engaged in a bitter industrial struggle, might have a use for him. It may not be reading too much into Michels' attack on Schwarz to see in it some bitterness that ignorance of social questions was no barrier for the university career from which the more talented and better-informed Dr Michels was excluded.[101] No doubt Michels saw in Schwarz one of the *Schmarotzer* (parasites) monopolizing seats of learning whom he had already attacked in *Ethische Kultur*.[102]

Michels displayed his own credentials as an emergent social scientist in an article for *Die Neue Zeit* published in July 1904 on comparative electoral statistics for socialist parties in a series of different countries, adding to his growing reputation as an authority on the international socialist movement. Michels compiled a range of statistical data on election results in several countries in the latter part of the nineteenth century (up to the German Reichstag elections of 1903, by far the most impressive result to date in any of the countries listed), with some general comments on their interpretation. The actual findings of the article were somewhat tentative at best, with Michels digressing for a whole page on the voting figures for French socialists in 1848 (with data from an old research topic of Michels being pressed into service for the occasion). Michels' remark that the lack of a strong socialist vote in Britain demonstrated 'the remarkable incapacity of the

---

[99] Robert Michels, 'Die Teilnahme an der Macht', *Volksstimme* (Magdeburg), no.304, 31 December 1903.
[100] Robert Michels, 'Das Ende vom Liede Millerand', *Volksstimme* (Magdeburg), Jg. 15, Nr.8, 10 January 1904, pp.1–2.
[101] Dr Robert Michels, 'Begriffsverwirrung und Klassenhass', *Mitteldeutsche Sonntags-Zeitung*, no.5, 31 January 1904.
[102] Dr Robert Michels, 'Der Kapitalismus in der Wissenschaft', *Ethische Kultur*, Jg.XI, Nr.24, 13 June 1903, pp.186–8.

English workman for political thinking' was indicative of his occasional tendency to resort to essentializing ethnic stereotyping.[103]

While awaiting the publication of the article on comparative election statistics, Michels wrote to Kautsky on 20 June 1904, offering him another essay for the *Neue Zeit* on the state of 'confusion' in the international socialist movement.[104] Michels' essay offered a survey of several issues in which the actions or public statements of socialists in different European countries: Germany, Austria, France, Italy, and Denmark appeared to contradict both each other and common socialist principles. Using often anecdotal evidence, Michels gave examples of what he regarded as inconsistencies in the areas of religion (German socialists opposed exceptional legislation against the Jesuits, while some Italian socialists sought to uphold such laws), the question of duelling (this referring more to the actions of individual socialist leaders than any theoretical principles), trade policy, the question of nationalities policy, and the attitude to monarchy. Michels urged Kautsky to publish the article as a matter of urgency, so that it could appear before the Amsterdam international socialist congress. Michels apparently hoped that the appearance of the article before the Amsterdam congress would help inspire the congress to pull all deviants from correct socialist principle into line.[105] Kautsky responded immediately with a long and patient critique of the article, declining to publish the article in the *Neue Zeit*, and advising Michels to refrain from publishing it elsewhere as it would do more than harm than good. While calling Michels' article interesting, and allowing for the fact that Michels had put his finger on some regrettable inconsistencies between European socialist parties, Kautsky felt that Michels was leaping a step too far in equating a lack of uniformity with confusion. Kautsky agreed that it was necessary to work towards consistency in socialist theory, especially in key points such as class struggle and the need to conquer political power, but to achieve harmonious international collaboration with the socialist parties of other countries, there had to be respect and understanding for the distinctive characteristics of different national situations— 'your article does not provide this', Kautsky judged. He would have been prepared to print Michels' article if it were more constructively framed, distinguishing between different national contexts on the one hand and common socialist goals on the other, and providing more of a 'well-meaning survey' of such differences 'than a pejorative critique of "confusion"' but Kautsky strongly suspected that Michels would not agree to this. Alternatively, Michels could provide a more indepth analysis of the national differences in their own social and political contexts when it came to a single issue (such as religion or duelling) rather than

---

[103] Dr Robert Michels, 'Zu einer internationalen Wahlstatistik der sozialistischen Parteien', NZ, Jg.22, 2, 1904, pp.496–503, quotation p.502.
[104] Robert Michels to Karl Kautsky, Eisenach, 20.6.1904. IISH. Nachlaß Kautsky, D XVII, 540.
[105] See Robert Michels, 'Le incoerenze internazionali del socialismo contemporaneo', *La Riforma Sociale*, fasc. 8, Anno X, vol.XIII (seconda serie), 15 August 1904, pp.644–52.

48 ROBERT MICHELS, SOCIALISM, AND MODERNITY

superficially touching on a series of different issues in list form. Here, too, Kautsky saw potential for more harm than good: 'a cursory list of differences seems to me to be hardly suited to bring about improvement. It will just create irritation and misunderstandings.'[106] However, Michels could seldom be dissuaded from publishing any of his essays at least once, and he promptly submitted it to *La Riforma Sociale* in Turin, where it appeared in August.[107] Michels was starting to turn to 'bourgeois' periodicals to air criticisms of the socialist labour movement, and in September 1904 he turned to the *Archiv für soziale Gesetzgebung und Statistik*, soon to be renamed the *Archiv für Sozialwissenschaft und Sozialpolitik*, to offer the journal an article on conditions in Italy.[108]

By the summer of 1904, Michels appears to have been increasingly bored with the practical day-to-day organizational work suggested by party functionaries like the Hessian Social Democrat Eduard David. While David, in his correspondence with Michels, stressed the need for persistent, patient work to build up the party organization in the area around Marburg and Alsfeld, Michels argued that good speakers should be brought into the *Wahlkreis* (electoral district), from outside Hessen if necessary, to conduct agitation among the workers there. Even if the industrially undeveloped region was unpromising territory for socialist agitation, there were, Michels insisted, already comrades there ready and willing to demonstrate self-sacrifice for the party.[109] Michels displayed little interest in the mundane side of party (or trade union) organization. Rather, demonstrating the sort of 'spontaneism' sometimes unfairly attributed to Rosa Luxemburg, he seemed to believe that sufficiently charismatic speakers might be able to revolutionize even relatively unpromising terrain. Michels' work in seeking to radicalize the masses through agitation in person was not entirely confined to Hesse, however. In March 1905, he spent a week giving speeches to party meetings in the Lower Rhine-Ruhr region, from Elberfeld to Duisburg, with Gisela Michels-Lindner also speaking at other meetings. Michels' topics included: 'Workers, Socialism, and Science.'[110]

---

[106] Karl Kautsky to Robert Michels, 21 June 1904, in ARM/FLE.

[107] Michels, 'Le incoerenze internazionali del socialismo contemporaneo'.

[108] Edgar Jaffé to Robert Michels, 17 September 1904, in ARM/FLE.

[109] See Eduard David to Robert Michels, 1 August 1906, in folder Eduard David, ARM/FLE; see the account of the debate between Michels and David at the congress of Hessian Social Democrats in 1904 in 'Unsere Landeskonferenz', *Mitteldeutsche Sonntags-Zeitung*, no.32, 7 August 1904, clipping in folder *Mitteldeutsche Sonntags-Zeitung*, ARM/FLE.

[110] Announcement of Agitations-Komitee Niederrhein, 27 January 190[5?], in the Michels correspondence, ARM/FLE. *Freie Presse* (Elberfeld), 18 March 1905 (Gisela on 'Social Democracy's Position on Religion', 20 March 1905, 21 March 1905 (announcing Gisela speaking on 'Woman and the Family', with a report on 24 March 1905), 23 March 1905 (reporting on Michels' successful lecture in Elberfeld)). I thank Reiner Tosstorf for generously supplying me with copies of the relevant newspaper excerpts. Gisela Michels-Lindner's agitational talks were also reported on in *Die Gleichheit*, Jg.15, no.3, 3 May 1905, p.52 (rubric 'Aus der Bewegung', report by g.m. = Gisela Michels-Lindner).

Some of Michels' impatience with German conditions and with the persisting influence of revisionism in the Social Democratic Party found vent at this time in an article for the Milan syndicalist paper *Avanguardia Socialista*. In this article, Michels attacked revisionism as based on an overoptimistic and illusory view of society, which denied the reality of class conflict.[111] Michels wrote scathingly of Jean Jaurès' ill-founded optimism regarding the prospect of peaceful collaboration across class divisions, and cited an article by Eduard Bernstein in the *Sozialistische Monatshefte* following the Crimmitschau textile workers' strike as another example of an overly sanguine view of social conflict by a revisionist theorist.[112] In particular, Michels may have been irritated by Bernstein's diagnosis that the end of the direct labour dispute and the shift to trying to influence the legislative sphere instead was a sign of progress.[113] This overoptimistic vision of 'class collaboration' Michels saw as common to reformists like Millerand and the Italian party leader Filippo Turati. Michels went on to cite conditions in Germany as an example of the clearest form of class conflict, where the most diverse groups within the bourgeoisie would unite politically to exclude socialists and the proletariat from power. He even claimed that in the 1903 Reichstag elections the anti-semites supported a bourgeois candidate 'Jewish by race and religion' against a (non-Jewish) Social Democratic candidate in a run-off election. (Unfortunately, Michels did not name the constituency.) Further, and rather curiously, he claimed that 'at the same time we have seen the rabbis in Kassel preach from the height of their pulpit that it was the duty of all Jewish believers to give their vote to the enemies of their confession rather than to give it to the enemies of capital', i.e. Jews had supposedly been enjoined to vote for anti-semites rather than Social Democrats. Across confessional boundaries, and from

> the Count of Kanitz—ultra-conservative—to the deputy Eugen Richter—radical—all politicians of the bourgeoisie loyally reach out their hands to help each other in that supreme task of their life, in the name of the Holy Trinity of 'God', 'Fatherland' and 'Capital—to crush the idea of socialism.[114]

For Michels, Germany was the case study par excellence of the reality of class struggle, where the bourgeoisie consciously submerged their internal differences to resist the growth of socialism.

Michels thus approached the September 1904 congress of the German Social Democratic Party in Bremen in a frame of mind of increasing impatience with

---

[111] Roberto [Robert] Michels, 'A proposito di socialismo illusorio', *Avanguardia Socialista*, Anno II, no.88, 6 August 1904.

[112] Eduard Bernstein, 'Capitalmacht und Gewerkschaftsmacht. Ein Beitrag zur Dynamik des Gewerkschaftskampfes', *Sozialistische Monatshefte*, VIII (new series), 2, 1904, pp.129–37.

[113] Bernstein, 'Capitalmacht und Gewerkschaftsmacht', p.136.

[114] Michels, 'A proposito di socialismo illusorio'.

50   ROBERT MICHELS, SOCIALISM, AND MODERNITY

deviations from what he believed was the correct interpretation of the 'socialist idea', and especially with revisionism, and wishing for a more direct approach to militant agitation instead of the emphasis on organization of the party's practitioners of reformism.

Michels attended the annual party congress as the delegate for Alsfeld-Lauterbach-Schotten. He spoke in the debate on colonialism and the war in south-west Africa, in which the revisionist advocate for colonialism Max Schippel was held up to censure. Michels condemned the German colonial war in south-west Africa, and argued that even Bebel's position on national self-defence needed to be qualified—it should not extend to actions that might militate against the rights of self-determination of national minorities within the borders of the Reich (such as the Poles in Germany's eastern provinces).[115] Michels also spoke in support of his own motion (supported by nineteen comrades) congratulating the Italian socialists on their recent successful struggle, won through a 'political mass strike'. The motion congratulating the Italian comrades was carried after Michels withdrew the words 'political mass strike' in order to avoid precipitating a wider debate on the merits of a political general strike.[116]

Michels also took part in the women's conference at the party congress—by this time, Michels was an occasional contributor to the party's women's paper *Die Gleichheit* (Equality), edited by Clara Zetkin, as well as writing more widely on feminism and women's issues, including in non-socialist feminist journals.[117] At the women's conference, Michels took a counter-intuitive position for an intransigent opponent of revisionism, questioning why the Social Democratic women's organization had declined to participate in the bourgeois women's congress for women's suffrage in Berlin in the previous June. While acknowledging the principal differences between the socialist and the bourgeois women's movements, and explicitly distancing himself from revisionism, Michels argued that the socialist women could have had a positive impact on the bourgeois women's suffrage convention, and that it would have been a good propaganda opportunity.[118] Michels' speech was energetically rebutted by Luise Zietz, who stressed the gulf between bourgeois feminist suffrage efforts and those of the socialist women. Zietz argued that bourgeois suffrage advocates, such as Käthe Schirmacher, wanted 'votes for ladies', not for all women, as they did not oppose other forms of discriminatory franchise for voters. Zietz also pointed to the bourgeois feminists' formal visit to both the Kaiser and Chancellor Bülow, who of course refused to grant the vote to women, as evidence of the compromised nature of the bourgeois women's organizations. In Zietz's view, the bourgeois congress would have been an unjustifiable

---

[115] *Protokoll über die Verhandlungen des Parteitages der Sozialdemokratischen Partei Deutschlands. Abgehalten zu Bremen vom 18. bis 24. September 1904*, Berlin, 1904, p.206.
[116] *Protokoll Bremen 1904*, p.321, wording of the motion (no.145) on p.139.
[117] See Chapter 5 below.   [118] *Protokoll Bremen 1904*, pp.342–4.

distraction from the vital organizational work of the Social Democratic women.[119] Somewhat paradoxically, Michels managed to sound less radical as a participant in the women's conference than he had in the wider party congress. Michels maintained cordial relations with the editors of bourgeois feminist journals to which he contributed in a way he would perhaps not have done with male politicians from rival parties, while Zietz did not make a distinction between liberal feminists and male liberal politicians.

Disillusionment after Bremen

If one can pin-point a moment at which Michels' disillusionment with the German Social Democracy started to set in, it would appear to be the Bremen congress. Michels' disappointment was muted in his first comments on the congress, written for German and Italian party papers, but increasingly showed through and was vented at length in the Italian *Avanguardia Socialista* in mid-October and in an article also written in October but published at the beginning of December 1904 in *Le Mouvement Socialiste*, which began Michels' association with the small group of French revolutionary syndicalists.

Michels wrote a critical resumé of the Bremen congress for the Roman socialist newspaper *Avanti!*, which published it as its first-page leading article. On the one hand, the Bremen congress had achieved little, in Michels' view, and had been timid in its handling of the controversy over Max Schippel and in its reception of Karl Liebknecht's proposals for agitation among working-class youth, among other issues. However, Michels' article finished on a positive note, concluding that, faced with increasingly determined opposition from the German state, churches, the nobles, and the bourgeoisie, the order of the day at Bremen had been to consolidate the unity of the party, and this had been achieved: 'It was the congress of fraternity, of solidarity in the face of the enemy, of internal peace, or at least a truce.'[120] A reader might have been skeptical as to whether this premium on harmony within the party fully accorded with Michels' own preferences, given his recently expressed desire to stamp out deviations from correct socialist principles.

Michels pulled fewer punches in a commentary for the *Mitteldeutsche Sonntags-Zeitung*, where he again criticized the relative timidity of the congress on a number of key issues: the question of a separate youth organization, the reluctance to engage in specifically anti-militarist agitation among army recruits (which would have brought the party into direct conflict with the law), and the reluctance to have a full discussion of the question of the general strike. Michels

[119] *Protokoll Bremen 1904*, pp.344–5.
[120] Roberto [Robert] Michels, 'A Brema', *Avanti!*, Anno 8, no.2811, 1 October 1904.

singled out as symptomatic the criticism which Kautsky's telegram of congratulations (seconded by Michels) had received for the Italian socialists on the success of their recent mass strike encountered at Bremen. As in the *Avanti!* article, Michels ended by recognizing the gains in party unity at Bremen, but the overall tenor of the article was critical, and the article appeared with an editorial note distancing the editor of the paper from some of Michels' views.[121]

Michels gave even less restrained vent to his frustrations over the Bremen congress in the Italian radical syndicalist *Avanguardia Socialista*, in an article entitled 'A Funereal Congress', lamenting the 'absolute lack of practical and theoretical results' of the 'diplomatic', 'timorous', and 'inconclusive' congress, contrasting the state of the German party with the revolutionary energy demonstrated by the organized Italian proletariat in their recent general strike. Unlike the Italians, the Germans rejected the notion of an economic general strike, and deferred the debate over the political general strike 'to the Greek calends'. Michels complained that with a few honourable exceptions the majority of the congress showed itself indifferent or even hostile to 'this, the only weapon that we have in our battles against reaction'. In this syndicalist paper, Michels identified himself more strongly with a revolutionary syndicalist position than in his other articles. In an article published in Italy, Michels could also be more outspoken about linking the question of anti-militarist youth organization to the need to combat Wilhelmine Germany's arch-militarist culture: 'in no other country in Europe is the military so pathologically faithful to its king' as in Germany, where a condition of 'military hypnotism coupled with passive obedience' affected 'the masses', even those who voted socialist. Michels openly expressed dismay, even disgust, at the poor reception the congress gave to the radical minority such as Karl Liebknecht on this issue, while showing 'ecstasies of approbation' for 'the note of the basest parliamentary opportunism' articulated by Vollmar. On Vollmar's argument that one needed to be able to petition the war minister in good faith that the sons of socialists be given equal treatment in the army, Michels exploded: 'It seems improbable, incredible, blasphemous, but yet it is true'. Vollmar was putting the collegial good relations between himself as a member of the Reichstag and the imperial war minister before the chance to undertake useful direct socialist propaganda. Michels retorted that one might as well give up socialism altogether if it disturbed one's good relations with the government. For Michels, the outcome of the Bremen congress showed that Jean Jaurès's criticism of the German Social Democratic Party was correct: the party had energy, tenacity, discipline, but completely lacked the factor essential for victory: *élan* (i.e. revolutionary sentiment, aggressive courage). While Michels acknowledged the positive aspects of the congress in terms of greater party unity, he feared the cost of this was too high, and

---

[121] Dr Rob. [Robert] Michels, 'Bremer Erbschaften', *Mitteldeutsche Sonntags-Zeitung*, Jg.11, no.43, 23 October 1904.

MICHELS AND GERMAN SOCIAL DEMOCRACY   53

that the congress had revealed 'an indolent mass in the breast of the German socialist party', a mass among whom conservative and petit bourgeois ideas prevailed, which rested too easily on its past days of glory and which would be increasingly hard to shift as times changed.[122]

Michels' dissatisfaction with the state of German Social Democracy as reflected at the Bremen congress seems to have festered and intensified as the weeks after the congress passed, although this was also a reflection of the political complexion of the journals he was contributing to. In December 1904, he published a severe critique of the German Social Democratic Party in the French radical syndicalist journal *Le Mouvement Socialiste*. Despite three million votes, the German party was as far as ever from attempting the 'conquest of power':

> But if a party which disposes of such electoral strength is completely incapable of bringing about the least change; if such a party remains in the condition of a microcosm, if not invisible, at least negligible and impotent even to influence the state in a liberal direction, it thereby demonstrates a manifest sterility, and a lack of strength barely credible for anyone ignorant of the history of the German socialist party and the milieu in which it has been evolving.[123]

Michels characterized the German Reich as the most backward state in Europe, with the exceptions of Russia and Turkey.[124] However, despite the party's voting strength, its resources and organization, Michels predicted that in the case of an outbreak of war, or of the government abolishing the universal (manhood) suffrage, the German Social Democratic Party would do nothing, other than pass a protest resolution (worded as a 'very revolutionary manifesto'). Its record suggested it would tamely submit to 'legality'.[125] A number of factors, in Michels' view, accounted for the degree to which the German Social Democrats were prone to passivity: unlike the French socialists, they faced a united bourgeois bloc, given the high degree of political polarization in Germany along class lines. There were also factors of history—Germany's lack of a strong revolutionary tradition—and 'race': the passive, slow, ponderous German national character.[126] Ultimately, what the German proletariat lacked was '*the courageous will to action*,

---

[122] Roberto [Robert] Michels, 'Un congresso funebre', *Avanguardia Socialista*, Anno II, no.97, 14 October 1904.

[123] Robert Michels, 'Les dangers du Parti socialiste allemand', *Le Mouvement Socialiste*, no.144, 1 December 1904, p.193. (The article was subsequently re-published in Italian as 'Gli errori del partito socialista tedesco', in *Il Pensiero*, Vol.III, 4, 1 February 1905, pp.56–8; 5, 1 March 1905, pp.69–71. The 'dangers' for the party had now become its 'errors'. Also published in *The Socialist: Official Organ of the Socialist Labour Party*, Vol.III, no.29, January 1905, pp.2–3, 'Dangers of the German Socialist Party'.)

[124] Michels, 'Les dangers du Parti socialiste allemand'.

[125] Michels, 'Les dangers du Parti socialiste allemand', pp.196–7.

[126] Michels, 'Les dangers du Parti socialiste allemand', p.199.

54   ROBERT MICHELS, SOCIALISM, AND MODERNITY

the *revolutionary ferment*.[127] For this, the party was largely responsible: its propaganda concerned itself too little with questions of principle and theory, and its meetings and regular agitation were filled with routine organizational matters and mundane day-to-day concerns. The party did not sufficiently raise the workers' consciousness about programmatic issues such as republicanism, the equality of the sexes, or the rights of nations to self-determination, and instruction in Marxist theory was lacking.[128] The result was that 'extraordinary confusion' prevailed on questions of socialist doctrine, not only among the rank-and-file members, but among many of the second-tier leaders.[129] There was a deeper malaise: the German party professed a 'pretended radicalism', but had ceased to do the work of creating 'socialist personalities, socialist consciousness' among the workers (a problem not confined to Germany, in Michels' view: he saw the same trend in Italy and France). Parliamentarism was killing '*socialism conceived of in its most profound aspects, substituting for them a one-sided political socialism*'. The 'idealist side of our system of ideas' was being neglected.[130] Socialism as a 'faith', which spoke to the 'whole man' was being replaced by a 'misunderstood historical materialism' that was narrowly economistic. Michels' quoted Guglielmo Ferrero's admiration expressed in 1897 for '*lo spirito religioso*' of German socialism, a spirit which Michels saw as having been displaced by a concern for electoral success.[131] Michels concurred with the German syndicalist Raphael Friedeberg that German Social Democracy was losing some of its moral impetus: its preoccupation with economic matters resulted in losing sight of, in Michels' words, the 'eternal truth that will and energy, too, can exert a strong force on our actions, sometimes even in contradiction of the material exigencies of life'.[132] But he did not believe that Friedeberg's prescription of revolutionary syndicalism would work in the German labour movement. 'Unfortunately', in Michels' view, the German trade unions were completely 'trade-unionist' ('trades-unionisés') in the English sense, and revisionism and opportunism were rampant in them.[133] For all its glorious past achievements, Michels concluded, the German party 'is marching into a dead-end'. It needed to remember its mission of inspiring the masses with the goals of socialism.[134] Michels criticized the party's refusal to engage in anti-religious agitation: the programmatic statement that religion was a private matter was electorally expedient, but it meant abstaining from campaigning against religious superstition in the masses, and allowed people with the most backward views into

---

[127]   Michels, 'Les dangers du Parti socialiste allemande', p.200.
[128]   Michels, 'Les dangers du Parti socialiste allemande', pp.200–1.
[129]   Michels, 'Les dangers du Parti socialiste allemande', p.199.
[130]   Michels, 'Les dangers du Parti socialiste allemande', p.201.
[131]   Michels, 'Les dangers du Parti socialiste allemande', p.202.
[132]   Michels, 'Les dangers du Parti socialiste allemande'.
[133]   Michels, 'Les dangers du Parti socialiste allemande', pp.207–8.
[134]   Michels, 'Les dangers du Parti socialiste allemande', p.212.

the party.[135] Michels' conception of socialism as, in effect, a substitute for religion, and a scientifically superior replacement for religion, is evident in this passage and his quotation from Ferrero.

In January 1905, Michels used the columns of the Italian socialist journal *Il Divenire Sociale* to attack the 'illness' of legalism, taking issue with Eduard David's article in the *Sozialistische Monatshefte* on the need for a purely legal and parliamentary conquest of power (even though Michels was careful to add parenthetically that David was a man of real spirit).[136] Michels was starting to strain himself in seeking to balance his personal esteem and continuing collegial relations with German socialist leaders with his increasingly acerbic criticism of the party for failing to live up to the socialist ideal. He penned a laudatory portrait of Kautsky for *Avanguardia Socialista* as not only the 'most authentic disciple' of Marx, but also an independent thinker whose writing surpassed Marx's writings at least in its clarity. Kautsky was 'perhaps the greatest political economist in modern Germany'. He was also of 'immense importance' as a man of political action, in his resolute opposition to reformist tendencies within the German and, more widely, European socialist movement.[137] However, his article in *Le Mouvement Socialiste* was still critical of Kautsky for failing to dispel the prevalent 'parliamentary opportunism' within German Social Democracy, and even Bebel, despite possessing, deep down, a 'revolutionary temperament', was at fault in this respect.[138]

In February 1905, Michels published a piece in the *Leipziger Volkszeitung* that now came close to articulating a syndicalist position within Germany, while still managing to invoke Kautsky in support of his views. Michels argued that the hazards of parliamentarism meant that a revolutionary trade union movement was essential as a counterweight to the political party. Michels cited a recent article by Kautsky in *Die Neue Zeit* which had warned against the danger that parliamentarism, as a means of bourgeois rule, carried with it the latent risk that parliamentarians, even those with proletarian backgrounds, could become the masters of the people rather than their servants, effectively becoming the servants of the bourgeoisie. Michels argued that the trade union movement, unlike parliament, was fundamentally anti-bourgeois as a collective organization of workers. A revolutionary trade union movement was thus an indispensable counterweight to 'the sinking into the parliamentary swamp [*parlamentarische Versumpfung*], that unpleasant by-product of every political party'. A revolutionary trade union movement 'is a constant fountain of youth for the party', but that presupposed

---

[135] Michels, 'Les dangers du Parti socialiste allemande', p.203.

[136] Roberto [Robert] Michels, 'Violenza e egalitarismo come fattori della tattica socialista', *Il Divenire Sociale*, I, no.2, 16 January 1905, pp.25–7, here p.26. Michels cites Eduard David, 'Die Eroberung der Macht', *Sozialistische Monatshefte*, vol.VIII (new series), 1, pp.9–18.

[137] Michels, 'Idee e uomini, p.1.

[138] Michels, 'Les dangers du Parti socialiste allemande', pp.203–4.

56   ROBERT MICHELS, SOCIALISM, AND MODERNITY

that the trade unions grasped the connections between politics and economics. Michels lamented that the German trade unions did not seem to have gained this level of insight. He noted that the German trade unions had shown themselves to be anything but revolutionary, for example in their attitudes to the May Day demonstrations and the question of the general strike; and he poured scorn on unionists' arguments that such revolutionary manifestations should be avoided as they were not provided for in collective agreements: 'collective agreements have never made a bourgeois society abdicate power'.[139] For Michels, the biggest stumbling block for syndicalism as a solution for the problems confronting the socialist idea in Germany was the reality of the German trade union movement, which was even more reformist and bureaucratic than the party, which at least had a vigorous left wing. In *Le Mouvement Socialiste*, in February 1905, Michels pointed to the gap between revolutionary rhetoric and quietist political conduct on display at the congress of the Prussian Social Democrats, alluding sarcastically to 'revolutionary Buddhists', and drawing hope only from the existence of the revolutionary left faction around Karl Liebknecht.[140]

During 1905, Michels continued to contribute regularly to *Le Mouvement Socialiste* and articulated increasingly critical views vis-à-vis the German labour movement, which tended to converge with militant syndicalist positions even if he did not fully embrace syndicalism in theory. His criticisms focused on what he saw as the overcautious and bureaucratic nature of the leadership of Germany's labour movement, as shown by its response to industrial disputes, and its failure to adopt sufficiently strong anti-militarist and anti-imperialist positions in the face of the German Empire's increasingly assertive *Weltpolitik*. Thus, during the Morocco crisis of 1905, Michels warned against the risk of war between Germany and France over Morocco, and called for immediate talks between French and German Social Democrats to help to avert a war.[141]

In January 1905, a large-scale strike of Ruhr miners broke out. Over 200,000 workers (at the height of the strike, over 85 per cent of the workforce) went on strike over three weeks, with the union leadership being forced to respond to the demands from the rank and file for strike action over a number of grievances: longer shifts, threatened job losses at some mines, health and safety issues, fluctuations in real wages, and other concerns. The outcome of the strike proved inconclusive, with union leaders breaking it off after receiving vague promises from the Prussian government for improved regulation of working conditions,

[139] Robert Michels, 'Zum Kapitel Gewerkschaftsbewegung', *Leipziger Volkszeitung*, no.41, 18 February 1905, 4. Beilage.
[140] Robert Michels, 'Le congrès des socialistes de Prusse à Berlin', *Le Mouvement Socialiste*, no.149, 15 February 1905, pp.239–51 (here pp.246–7) (written in Marburg, January 1905).
[141] Robert Michels, 'Die deutsche Sozialdemokratie und Marokko', *Arbeiter-Zeitung. Sozialdemokratisches Organ für das Rheinisch-Westfälische Industrie-Gebiet*, no.148, 28 June 1905.

MICHELS AND GERMAN SOCIAL DEMOCRACY 57

and following an erosion of unity among the striking workers.[142] In the pages of *Le Mouvement Socialiste*, Michels was scathing about the '*worker bureaucratism*' of the miners' union leadership after the workers had called on them to declare a strike: 'Depressing proof of what a long period of *worker bureaucratism* can do to make the masses forget how to decree their own actions.'[143] The strike was not at all revolutionary in its aims, but was enough to start alarming the German bourgeoisie.[144] Not only was Michels unimpressed by the performance of the miners' union leader Otto Hué, he was incensed at the fact that a chain of party meetings in Berlin called on the Ruhr mines to be nationalized, that is, put under control of the existing semi-feudal undemocratic Reich of Wilhelm II. For Michels, this *étatisme* displayed, as clear as day, 'the total lack of Marxist spirit in the daily political life of German Social Democracy.'[145] Michels wrote that in all of Germany there was no boss more tyrannical than the German state.[146] He condemned the union leaders who, having been reluctant to call on the strike, decided to end it—an 'oligarchical order' over the heads of the mine-workers.[147] He concluded that, after the strike: 'The masses are convinced that the parliamentary, neutralist and legalitarian tactics of their chiefs are bankrupt, and at their cost.'[148]

After the *Correspondenzblatt* of the Free Trade Unions published a polemical response to Michels' critique, depicting it as a crude caricature of the course of events,[149] Michels reiterated his criticisms of the union 'bosses', whose conduct was 'dictated by the worst kind of bureaucratic and oligarchical spirit.'[150] He renewed his criticisms of the German trade union leaders when he wrote a commentary on the 1905 congress of the Free Trade Unions in Cologne, in which he contrasted the German unions unfavourably with the revolutionary syndicalism on display in France and Italy. The German unions were following English-style

---

[142] Helga Grebing, *Arbeiterbewegung. Sozialer Protest und kollektive Interessenvertretung bis 1914*, Munich, 1985, p.34; cf. Dieter Fricke, *Der Ruhrbergarbeiterstreik von 1905*, Berlin, 1955 (an East German orthodox Marxist-Leninist account stressing 'betrayal' on the part of right-wing union leaders, but based on detailed research).

[143] Robert Michels, 'La grève générale des mineurs de la Ruhr', *Le Mouvement Socialiste*, 152, 1 April 1905, pp.481–9, here p.481. Emphasis in original.

[144] Michels, 'La grève générale des mineurs de la Ruhr', p.483.

[145] Michels, 'La grève générale des mineurs de la Ruhr', p.484.

[146] Michels, 'La grève générale des mineurs de la Ruhr', p.485.

[147] Michels, 'La grève générale des mineurs de la Ruhr', pp.486–7.

[148] Michels, 'La grève générale des mineurs de la Ruhr', p.489.

[149] E.B., 'Ein Aprilscherz?!', *Correspondenzblatt der Generalkommission der Gewerkschaften Deutschlands*, 15. Jg., no.18, 6 May 1905, pp.278–9. Cf. the same journal's analysis of the lessons of the strike's failure (citing lack of a unified miners' organization in the face of better organized, cartelized employers, the low-fee competition of the Catholic miners' trade union, and the conservatism of some miners) in 'Die Lehren des Kampfes im Ruhrkohlenrevier', in *Correspondenzblatt der Generalkommission der Gewerkschaften Deutschlands*, 15. Jg., no.12, 25 March 1905, pp.177–80 and no.13, 1 April 1905, pp.193–6.

[150] Robert Michels, 'A propos de la grève de la Ruhr', *Le Mouvement Socialiste*, No.149, 1 July 1905, pp.341–4, here p.341.

58   ROBERT MICHELS, SOCIALISM, AND MODERNITY

trade unionism, based on the pursuit of limited improvements in pay and conditions, rather than the syndicalist prosecution of class struggle through direct action.[151]

Michels criticized the notion of the party-political neutrality of the German trade unions which was becoming prevalent among the union leadership. Michels also took issue with intemperate comments aimed at party intellectuals at the congress. Michels felt that the delegates should have shown more appreciation for the role of party intellectuals in helping to explain the 'ill-defined and obscure needs and tendencies of the proletariat', and in challenging the complacency of party officials.[152]

While recognizing the organizational growth of the German Free Trade Unions, with over a million members and substantial cash reserves, Michels at the same time mocked this 'outward strength', suggesting that the union leaders were so preoccupied with getting peace and quiet to tend to their cash reserves that they had forgotten their *raison d'être* of the class struggle.[153] Michels lamented that the Social Democratic Party, 'being itself on a scarcely revolutionary path', had failed to react against the drift to opportunism of the trade unions.[154] Michels also cited the debates at the Cologne Trade Union Congress on May Day and the mass strike question as evidence of this growing opportunism.[155] Stepping up the rhetorical register, Michels attacked the German trade union 'bosses' for their 'detestable fear of any movement, of any risk, of any slightly hazardous enterprise', as they had becoming fixated on protecting their material gains and finding an accommodation with the existing state. 'The bureaucratism of the minority of the "bosses" is crushing any free movement of the majority of the organized.'[156] He expressed the fear that if the party and unions were in agreement on essential issues, as party newspapers seemed to indicate, this would mean 'the rapid death of socialism in Germany'.[157]

Michels' insistence on viewing strikes in essentially ethical terms was illustrated by a curious contribution he wrote for the Dutch socialist journal *De Nieuwe Tijd*, and the debate that ensued with the Dutch Social Democrat Joseph Loopuit. Michels composed an essay seeking to demonstrate the ethical justification of strikes. He argued that the strike was a morally justified instrument of workers seeking to realize their rights (citing both Kant and Marx, *Kapital*, vol.I), and that, furthermore, *every* strike was morally justified in a larger cause: '*every* strike involves a forward step, consciously or unconsciously, for the working class

---

[151] Robert Michels, 'Le congrès syndical de Cologne', *Le Mouvement Socialiste*, No.149, 1 July 1905, pp.313–21.

[152] Michels, 'Le congrès syndical de Cologne', pp.318–19.

[153] Michels, 'Le congrès syndical de Cologne', pp.314–15.

[154] Michels, 'Le congrès syndical de Cologne', p.315.

[155] Michels, 'Le congrès syndical de Cologne', pp.315–18.

[156] Michels, 'Le congrès syndical de Cologne', p.319.

[157] Michels, 'Le congrès syndical de Cologne', p.321.

on the path towards its ideal goal, the new just society'.[158] Joseph Loopuit responded to the essay. He was clearly somewhat baffled by the first step in Michels' argument, objecting that no Social Democrat had ever queried that strikes were morally justified, making Michels' slightly laboured and abstract ethical justification of strike action redundant, at least within the pages of a socialist journal. As for the second step in the argument—that *every* strike was ethically justified, Loopuit argued that the strike was a weapon, the use of which was dependent on tactical considerations, and on the presence of factors such as organization and discipline. An unsuccessful strike could indeed bring disadvantages to the workers involved in it. He wrote: 'as social democrats...we are empiricists and not in the first instance ethicists'. Decisions such as whether to embark on a strike had to made on the basis of objective material necessity, not on a subjective sense of being in the right.[159] In a rejoinder to Loopuit, Michels conceded that the concept of 'ethical socialism' had been brought into some discredit by revisionists, but he cited the importance of moral factors in history, giving the persistence (or otherwise) of national identities as an example.[160] If moral factors would not decide the victory of the working class over the bourgeoisie, they had at least led to the defection of some 'sons of bourgeois papas' to the ethically superior doctrine of socialism.[161] Michels expressed support for Henriette Roland Holst's views on the general strike question, thereby intervening in the Dutch debate on the topic.[162] At the same time, Michels sought to contest the view among Dutch trade unionists that the German unions were an example to follow.

Michels also carried his critical opinion of the evolution of the German labour movement to Britain, which he visited briefly in the summer of 1905. In an interview with *The Socialist. Official Organ of the Socialist Labour Party*, he stated:

> The need for a revolutionary spirit in the German Party is great. I and others are striving to create that spirit; the parliamentarism of the party and its tactics in the past have so tied its hands that one feels its energy is being to a great extent run to earth and wasted.

---

[158] Robert Michels, 'Over de "rechtvaardigheid" der werkstaking', *De Nieuwe Tijd*, Vol.10, nos.7–8, 1905, pp.480–4, here pp.483–4. A version of this article was re-published by Michels in German in 1907: see Robert Michels, 'Über die Gerechtigkeit des Streiks', *Polis. Sozialpsychologische Rundschau* (Zurich), four-page offprint in FLE, dated 1907.

[159] Jos. Loopuit, 'De praktijk der werkstaking. (Antwoord aan Robert Michels.)', *De Nieuwe Tijd*, Vol.10, 9, September 1905, pp.593–7, quotation here on p.596 (ellipsis added).

[160] Robert Michels, 'Iets over de betrekking tusschen ethiek en klassenstrijd', *De Nieuwe Tijd*, Vol.10, 9, September 1905, pp.598–607.

[161] Michels, 'Iets over de betrekking tusschen ethiek en klassenstrijd', p.604.

[162] Michels, 'Iets over de betrekking tusschen ethiek en klassenstrijd', p.601. For a brief account of this debate in its Dutch context, in which the Dutch Social Democratic paper *Het Volk* also participated, see Henny Buiting, *De Nieuwe Tijd. Sociaaldemokratisch Maandschrift 1896–1921. Spiegel van socialisme en vroeg communisme in Nederland*, Amsterdam, 2003, pp.272–3.

60 ROBERT MICHELS, SOCIALISM, AND MODERNITY

Michels went on to state that the sole purpose of socialist representatives in parliament should be to act as propagandists. 'The Government should be voted against, never supported.... The line for Socialism is, no connection. Always front the opposing force in a fighting attitude.'[163]

As the 1905 Social Democratic Party congress in Jena approached, Michels continued to step up his criticism of parliamentarism and reformist-bureaucratic trade unionism in the struggle for socialism. However, even while he was wont to characterize the Prussian-German state as absolutist and 'half-Russian' by comparison with republican France,[164] he stopped short of seeing the revolutionary movement then under way in Tsarist Russia as suitable for Germany. In the Dortmund *Arbeiter-Zeitung*, Michels wrote on the absolute necessity of the proletariat (and those 'allied to their ideas'—'und die ihm ideell Verbundenen') seizing power from the existing bourgeois state. While socialism valued human life, respect for human life being one of its highest principles, Michels believed that it was illusory to expect peaceful evolution towards socialism while the ruling elite remained stubborn. The ruling classes would not be converted to social justice by 'begging and asking' alone, or by 'convincing them that they are ethically in the wrong'. 'Never yet in human history has a class given up its existing, i.e. historically and legally developed, privileges out of the goodness of its heart. It will not yield to reason, but to force.' It was thus 'utopian' to seek to achieve socialism through parliamentarism, or through trade unionism or consumer cooperatives. If ever the Social Democratic Reichstag caucus were in a position to seriously threaten the interests of the ruling class, it would swiftly be removed. 'To rely on parliamentary tactics as the exclusive and sole means of salvation would be just as foolish as to try to travel from Germany to America by bicycle.' Michels qualified his endorsement of revolutionary means in the second half of his article. Where autocracy insisted on its absolute power, revolutionary means were entirely justified, as in Russia (alluding to the events of the 1905 Russian revolution). In general, however, revolution and evolution were not mutually contradictory—revolution was a phase of the wider evolution of society, and the extent to which revolutionary means were necessary was directly dependent on the degree of intransigence of the ruling class. Michels wrote 'we are essentially ethical people, and only the impossibility of achieving our goal by legal means forces us to look around for other means'.[165]

---

[163] G.S. Grose, 'The Right Road for Socialism: Special Interview with Dr Robert Michels', *The Socialist: Official Organ of the Socialist Labour Party*, Vol.III, no.35, July 1905, p.5.

[164] E.g. in Michels, 'Die deutsche Sozialdemokratie und Marokko'.

[165] Robert Michels, 'Die Eroberung der Macht', *Arbeiter-Zeitung. Sozialdemokratisches Organ für das Rheinisch-Westfälische Industrie-Gebiet*, no.182, 6 August 1905. Cf. r.m., 'Russische Sklaverei und deutsche "Freiheit"', *Rheinische Zeitung*, no.277, 23 November 1905. In this article, Michels disowned any intention of 'making a revolution' on Russian lines in Germany, even though conditions in Germany were not that different from Russia. Absolutism in Germany was just thinly veiled behind a

MICHELS AND GERMAN SOCIAL DEMOCRACY 61

Michels' enthusiasm for the radical syndicalist wings of the French and Italian labour movement, and his mounting criticism of the German party and unions, started to concern his allies on the Marxist left of the German Social Democratic Party. Almost on the eve of the Jena party congress, Heinrich Ströbel took Michels to task over one of his articles in the Frankfurt *Volksstimme*. Ströbel considered that Michels was falling into the error of confusing '*temperamental* radicalism with a radicalism of *conception*,—of *logically developed conceptions of the party*'. Ströbel also charged that Michels was '*overestimating* the revolutionary nature, or rather the explosive *temperament* of the Latin nations, just as you underestimate the latent revolutionary strength of Marxist socialism in Germany'. Ströbel suggested that outbreaks of radical enthusiasm in the Latin nations might prove ephemeral, while the pent-up energy of the German proletarian had the potential to awaken to much greater effect, provided Social Democracy did not end up being enervated by revisionism and reformism.[166]

Michels again took part in a Social Democratic Party congress, in Jena in September 1905, once again representing the Alsfeld constituency while Georg Härtling represented Marburg-Kirchhain, and he arrived prepared to do battle with revisionism and excessive parliamentarism in the party. For Michels, the fact that Germany only had sham parliamentarism did not lessen the dangers of excessive parliamentarism in the party: 'Wherever there is a parliament', Michels told the congress, 'there is parliamentarism, and if Eisner told Friedeberg, that we had no parliament, and therefore no parliamentarism, he was wrong', taking the side of the anarcho-syndicalist Raphael Friedeberg against the revisionist Kurt Eisner.[167] Michels also spoke on the question of anti-war resolutions, criticizing the fact that the party had been too 'lukewarm' in its opposition to the government's foreign policy during the Morocco crisis, and calling for anti-war resolutions to be worded as unambiguously as possible.[168] Michels also added his voice to the debate on the question of the political mass strike.[169] August Bebel had put up a resolution commending the political mass strike as a defensive weapon of the labour movement in the event of an attack on workers' right to vote or their right to organize in unions. At the same time, Bebel stipulated that the essential precondition for any successful mass strike would be the greatest possible extension of the development of the 'political and trade union organisation of the

---

pretence of parliamentary government, but 'we are of the most steadfast resolve, not to desecrate our ideal with bloodstains.'

[166] Heinrich Ströbel to Robert Michels, 14 September 1905, ARM/FLE. The article referred to by Ströbel is not identified, as existing microfilm runs of the Frankfurt *Volksstimme* (both in the Friedrich Ebert Stiftung and commercially available) are incomplete.

[167] *Protokoll über die Verhandlungen des Parteitages der Sozialdemokratischen Partei Deutschlands. Abgehalten zu Jena vom 17. bis 23. September 1905*, Berlin, 1905, p.182.

[168] *Protokoll Jena 1905*, pp.216–17.

[169] For background and key texts on the 'mass strike debate', see Antonia Grunenberg, ed., *Die Massenstreikdebatte*, Frankfurt/M., 1970.

62   ROBERT MICHELS, SOCIALISM, AND MODERNITY

working class and the incessant education and enlightenment of the masses by the labour movement press and agitation both by word of mouth and by writing'.[170] Bebel's speech criticized the revisionists and some trade unionists on the one hand, for whom the thought of a mass strike for political ends, as opposed to more delimited strikes for specific economic goals, was anathema; on the other hand, he criticized Raphael Friedeberg for the belief that a mass strike on its own could revolutionize the working class, with less need for a preoccupation with organization. Robert Michels was among the speakers responding to Bebel's main speech on the political mass strike. He gave a partial defence of Raphael Friedeberg's position, while stipulating that he did not agree with Friedeberg on everything (specifically, Michels distanced himself from Friedeberg's criticisms of Marx, his underestimation of parliamentarism, and his 'Psychismus', which might be rendered as 'psychologism'). Michels argued that the anarcho-syndicalists around Friedeberg were a product of the Social Democratic Party's own errors and equivocations. However, he argued that Friedeberg had a point in so far as the party's successes in terms of votes counted in its favour had not been accompanied by a corresponding increase in 'socialistic spirit' among the rank and file. Michels argued that the passivity of German workers was evident in the problem of the abuse of recruits in the army, a topic that was the subject of regular Social Democratic campaigns—he suggested that French and Italian workers in uniform simply would not tolerate what German workers put up with in the army. Michels also complained that pro-monarchist views among German workers were too persistent, and that the Russian revolution was viewed merely as a distant and exotic spectacle by many Germans.[171] Unlike the party congress in Dresden in 1903, at which Bebel had made a point of indicating support for Michels and the Marburg party members, this time Bebel did not bother to respond to Michels' comments in his speech in reply. At one point, responding to Robert Schmidt, a revisionist who had once been among the radical members of the party, Bebel said: 'If I wanted to get personal, I could point to a few people, who have given ultra-radical speeches today, and of whom I could say that I don't know how long they will stay that way'.[172] There is no evidence that Bebel was singling out Michels with this barb, but as things turned out, it would have been apt if he had been.

Once again, Michels gave vent to his dissatisfaction with the course of a party congress in the pages of *Le Mouvement Socialiste*. For him, the Jena congress had demonstrated that the party was at a crossroads between parliamentarism and the general strike: the resolution of this conflict in favour of the latter against the former was the paramount duty. With its approximately 400,000 members, the party was losing its homogeneity, and becoming a heavy and cumbersome machine. As

---

[170] *Protokoll Jena 1905*, pp.142–3 (motion 151), 285–313 (Bebel's speech), 335–41 (Bebel's address in response to critics).
[171] *Protokoll Jena 1905*, p.325.   [172] *Protokoll Jena 1905*, p.336.

MICHELS AND GERMAN SOCIAL DEMOCRACY 63

this process gathered momentum, the spiritual unity of the party faded: there was now an absence of a preparedness for self-sacrifice in German Social Democracy, as it was 'too parliamentary and too optimistic'.[173] Michels saw this growth of the party as a threat rather than a strength: 'A sect can remain homogeneous; a large party loses its homogeneity in the same measure as it grows in number'.[174] The ideal factor, so central to Michels' conception of socialism, was being crowded out by bureaucracy and parliamentarism. He was critical both of the role of the trade unionists in the mass strike debate and of Bebel's speeches.

In an article written for a French readership, Michels put particular emphasis on his criticism of the Social Democratic Party for its weak position vis-à-vis German imperialism and the threat of war. He criticized Bebel's 'socialist patriotism' (the affirmation of the right of national self-defence) as indistinguishable from 'bourgeois patriotism', and complained that his own anti-war speech had been truncated in the official protocol of the congress.[175] He also criticized the weakness of the party's response to the Morocco crisis earlier that year: 'War could have broken out without finding the least impediment in the three million socialist voters. In the hours of danger, this splendid collection of votes, this model bureaucratic organization which is German socialism, did not count for anything: it was asleep'.[176]

In a contribution to the Italian syndicalist paper *Il Divenire Sociale*, Michels professed to feel isolated within the party. He wrote: 'we, the Marxists, the revolutionaries, the syndicalists, and those committed to the class struggle—have remained separate, each man for himself... This has been the most fundamental cause of what is, when all is said and done, our manifest political weakness: the dissolution, the isolation'.[177] Significantly, Michels added a footnote qualifying his identification with syndicalism: 'I consider as syndicalism the general tendency of shifting socialist tactics away from the bourgeois-political field of parliamentarism onto the economic-proletarian field, with a frankly held socialist confidence in the direct action and the exertion of pressure by the class'.[178] In another essay for *Le Mouvement Socialiste*, Michels gave a syndicalist interpretation—in his

---

[173] Robert Michels, 'Le socialisme allemande et le Congrès d'Iéna', *Le Mouvement Socialiste*, no.166–7, November 1905, pp.281–307, quotation p.296. For another critical summary of Jena aimed at a syndicalist readership, see Michels, 'Sciopero generale, sindacalismo, Jena e Labriola'.

[174] Michels, 'Le socialisme allemande et le Congrès d'Iéna', p.281.

[175] Michels, 'Le socialisme allemande et le Congrès d'Iéna', pp.290–1.

[176] Michels, 'Le socialisme allemande et le Congrès d'Iéna', p.291. See also Robert Michels, 'L'Allemagne et la guerre contre la France', *L'Européen. Courrier International Hebdomadaire*, 6, no.216, 20 January 1906, p.34, in which Michels again criticized what he regarded as a feeble response by German Social Democrats to the conduct of the German government in the recent Morocco crisis: 'Certainly, this silence and abstention at such a moment are inexcusable, and I said so at the Congress of Jena'.

[177] Roberto [Robert] Michels: 'Kautsky e i rivoluzionari italiani', part of the feature: 'Attorno alla mozione di Brescia—Verso le nuove assisi del Partito', *Il Divenire Sociale. Rivista di Socialismo Scientifico*, Anno I, no.21, 1 November 1905, pp.326–9, quotation p.329.

[178] Michels: 'Kautsky e i rivoluzionari italiani'.

64   ROBERT MICHELS, SOCIALISM, AND MODERNITY

sense of the term—of the failure of the strike (and lock-out) by Berlin metal-workers in late 1905, blaming the overreliance on centralized organization and a lack of courage and readiness for struggle on the part of the Free Trade Unions.[179] Michels wrote mockingly of the belief of the trade union functionaries of the importance of the number of workers' pennies (*Groschen*) in their treasuries, when these were pitted against the millions of the bosses.[180]

From Participant to Outside Academic Critic of German Social Democracy

After Jena, despite his increasingly vocal criticisms of the party, Michels continued to be active in agitation for German Social Democracy. In November 1905, he took part in the campaign for the Marburg local council elections, even running unsuccessfully as a candidate for town councillor.[181] At the same time, Michels was increasingly engaged with non-socialist social scientists and their journals, especially the *Archiv für Sozialwissenschaft und Sozialpolitik* edited by Max Weber and Werner Sombart with the assistance of Edgar Jaffé. Michels contributed a long series of articles on Italian socialism to the *Archiv* in 1905.[182] In December of that year, Jaffé sought to persuade Michels to give the German party the same treatment for the journal. He did his utmost to persuade Michels to write an extended, objective analysis of German Social Democracy, promising him a generous allocation of space in the *Archiv* (which came with an honorarium per printer's sheet), and holding out the strong possibility of a book publication by the *Archiv*'s publisher, Paul Siebeck. Jaffé argued that Michels was uniquely qualified to write such a work—on the one hand, he was sufficiently close to the party to have inside knowledge of its workings; on the other hand, he said that Michels was 'completely able to view the developments objectively and in a scholarly manner [*wissenschaftlich*]'. Jaffé continued:

> It would of course involve more than an analysis of the composition of the Social Democratic voter base, and a discussion of the different tendencies within the party, but above all to describe the organisation of Social Democracy as a political party, that which the Americans call the <u>party machine</u>, both in <u>personal</u> and in <u>objective</u> terms. Social Democracy is indeed the only party in Germany which possesses such a party machine, and which has developed it to a highly

---

[179] Robert Michels, 'La grève des métallurgistes de Berlin', *Le Mouvement Socialiste*, no.170, 15 January 1906, pp.96–100 (dated Marburg, December 1905).

[180] Michels, 'La grève des métallurgistes de Berlin', p.100.

[181] *Volksstimme* (Frankfurt/M.), Jg.16, no.266, 13 November 1905, Beilage; no.271, 18 November 1905.

[182] Robert Michels, 'Proletariat und Bourgeoisie in der sozialistischen Bewegung Italiens', *Archiv für Sozialwissenschaft und Sozialpolitik*, 21, 1905, pp.347–416; 22, 1906, pp.80–125, 424–86, 664–720.

advanced level, as is otherwise only to be seen in America. (You will of course be acquainted with the relevant discussions by Bryce in his two-volume book on America).[183]

It is not too far-fetched to see in this letter the germ of Michels' *Political Parties*. Not only did Jaffé seek to commission an analysis of German Social Democracy from Michels, Werner Sombart had already also raised this possibility, asking Michels in November whether he might like to give German Social Democracy a similar treatment in the fourth part of his series on Italian socialism, 'outlining its politics, revisionism, revolutionary romanticism, party boss-rule [*Parteibonzentum*], danger of parliamentary ossification, syndicalism, etc. etc.'[184] Sombart thus offered Michels a number of keywords for a critical analysis of the German party. Not long after his exchanges of letters with Sombart and Jaffé, Michels began what would become an extensive correspondence with Max Weber. Michels seems to have broached the idea of an article on German Social Democracy with Weber, who indicated that a proposed contribution by Michels 'is particularly interesting for me, just as your previous articles for the *Archiv* have been'. Weber also looked forward to meeting Michels in person in Heidelberg at the next opportunity, warning only of the possibility that Michels might arrive on one of Weber's 'black days', when he was 'completely useless for human society', which happened roughly one day out of five or six.[185] By late March 1906, Weber was giving Michels advice on how to proceed with his articles on German Social Democracy. Weber encouraged Michels to analyse the formal, organizational side of the party, while acknowledging that German Social Democracy differed from the American party machines described by James Bryce in so far as the German party represented an explicit *Weltanschauung*. He even offered to help Michels to get hold of a copy of Bryce and some other relevant literature (e.g. Sidney Low on the governance of England) through the university inter-library loan system. Weber recommended that Michels consider the relationship between organization and *Weltanschauung*.[186] The first meeting in person between Michels and Max and Marianne Weber took place on 13 April 1906 in Heidelberg, with Marianne finding Michels a 'very attractive Social Democrat'.[187] At this first encounter, Michels clearly sounded out Weber about the chances of achieving his *Habilitation* at a

---

[183] Edgar Jaffé to Robert Michels, 8 December 1905, ARM/FLE (underlining in original).

[184] Werner Sombart to Robert Michels, 28 November 1905, ARM/FLE. Michels had been corresponding with Sombart since April 1905 about contributions to the *Archiv*.

[185] Max Weber to Robert Michels, 1 January 1906, ARM/FLE, published in Max Weber, *Briefe 1906–1908* (ed. M. Rainer Lepsius and Wolfgang Mommsen = Max Weber *Gesamtausgabe*, Abteilung II: Briefe, Bd. 5), Tübingen, 1990, p.19. Only Weber's side of the correspondence has survived. Anyone working on these letters is in the debt of the editors and co-workers of the Weber *Gesamtausgabe* for their work in transcription of Weber's letters, which are frequently challenging to read in the original.

[186] Max Weber to Robert Michels, 26 March 1906, ARM/FLE, also in Weber, *Briefe 1906–1908*, pp.56–8, and 2 July 1906, ARM/FLE, Weber, *Briefe 1906–1908*, pp.99–100.

[187] Weber, *Briefe 1906–1908*, p.19n3.

66   ROBERT MICHELS, SOCIALISM, AND MODERNITY

German university. Weber suggested sounding out Professor Julius Pierstorff at Jena, but the response from Jena a few weeks later was that there was no chance of Michels, an 'organized Social Democrat', being successful there.[188] Michels' manuscript for the article on German Social Democracy reached Weber in May. Weber advised Michels that publication in the July issue of the *Archiv* was impossible, but it could well make the September issue, 'so that, one can hope, it appears before the party congress', referring to the Mannheim congress of the Social Democratic Party.[189] This suggests that Weber expected Michels' work might well have a political impact.

Even though Michels chose Marx's eleventh thesis on Feuerbach as an epigraph for the *Archiv* article on German Social Democracy ('The philosophers have hitherto only interpreted the world differently, the point is to change it'), it marked a step towards Michels treating the party as an object of social-scientific analysis, rather than expressing the view of an activist within the party.[190] Rudolf Blank had already written on the social composition of Social Democratic voters in the *Archiv*,[191] so Michels focused more on the social composition of the party's membership. He drew on numerous extant local statistical studies on labour movement membership by their trade, and even added his own data from Marburg (which he tersely described as follows: 'Small university town. Economically, a dead spot.'[192]) Before proceeding to analyse the available data on party members, he made a characteristic reference to the ethical dimension of socialism: 'If we were to try to estimate [the number of Social Democrats] in accordance with the equation: socialism equals applied ethics + economic-historical understanding, the result of our reckoning, assuming it were feasible, would produce a terrifyingly low number'. In light of the impossibility of measuring how many people, within or outside the party, qualified as socialists in terms of their ideals and mental grasp of socialist ideas, Michels was obliged to count the holders of party membership cards.[193] He drew the conclusion from his data that, '*in its social composition*, the party *has remained an overwhelmingly **proletarian** one*'.[194] The Social Democrats were still a party 'of the industrial proletariat'—rural workers and workers in the state sector were still underrepresented, partly as a result of repressive measures against their right to organize.[195] Michels also pointed out

---

[188] Max Weber to Robert Michels, 18 April 1906, ARM/FLE; Weber, *Briefe 1906–1908*, pp.84–5 and p.84n2.

[189] Max Weber to Robert Michels, 21 May 1906, ARM/FLE; Weber, *Briefe 1906–1908*, p.94.

[190] Robert Michels, 'Die deutsche Sozialdemokratie', *Archiv für Sozialwissenschaft und Sozialpolitik*, 23, 1906, pp.471–556.

[191] Rudolf Blank, 'Die soziale Zusammensetzung der sozialdemokratischen Wählerschaft Deutschlands', *Archiv für Sozialwissenschaft und Sozialpolitik*, 20, 1905, pp.507–53.

[192] Michels, 'Die deutsche Sozialdemokratie', p.508.

[193] Michels, 'Die deutsche Sozialdemokratie', p.476.

[194] Michels, 'Die deutsche Sozialdemokratie', p.510.

[195] Michels, 'Die deutsche Sozialdemokratie', p.511.

MICHELS AND GERMAN SOCIAL DEMOCRACY   67

that members of the so-called 'labour aristocracy', skilled workers with a trade, were more likely to join the party than unskilled labourers.[196]

Michels devoted some pages of his analysis to considering the role of bourgeois intellectuals in the party (including a discrete discussion on Jewish intellectuals). He contrasted the German situation with Italy as far as the relative rarity of '*Akademiker*' (university graduates) in the German party was concerned.[197] Turning to the question of the social origins of *Akademiker* in the German party, Michels took issue with the stereotype of the '*déclassé*' intellectual, protesting against their social decline. On the contrary, Michels argued that *déclassé* intellectuals, in the sense of 'gypsy-like' existences were relatively rare in Social Democracy: such individuals 'are much more likely to find rewards in bourgeois journalism than in the poorly paid, work-intensive and in many respects dangerous labour movement press'. Indeed, Michels claimed to know of 'very many cases, in which bourgeois intellectuals, driven on by their conscience as researchers, carried out the transition to Social Democracy precisely in the moment in which the prospects for their bourgeois career were at their very zenith!'[198]

Arthur Mitzman perceptively noted that: 'The dichotomy of egoistic versus unselfish or self-sacrificing behaviour runs throughout Michels' work.'[199] For example, in the 1908 Italian book publication of some of Michels' essays on Italian socialism, he would stress the social and career sacrifices that a bourgeois had to make in Germany if he threw his lot in with the socialist labour movement, writing that it required 'heroic fortitude'.[200] There is an element of self-stylization at work here—as we have seen, Michels' break with his bourgeois career seems to have been at least partly involuntary, stemming from his mistaken belief that writing about Italian socialism would not hinder his chances of a *Habilitation* in Marburg, and he never really broke with his bourgeois freelance writing career to take up full-time work in the 'poorly paid, work-intensive and in many respects dangerous labour movement press'. Despite their willingness to sacrifice themselves, however, *Akademiker* in Michels' account did not succeed in overcoming the barriers between themselves and the 'mass of comrades with a shared outlook'. Despite 'all common feeling and the love of the cause', an *Akademiker* had different 'kinds of economic needs, and in any case a different educational background and different communicative practices than the mass of workers, whose company he had joined, and on the whole he will be felt to be a foreign body by

---

[196] Michels, 'Die deutsche Sozialdemokratie', p.517.
[197] Michels, 'Die deutsche Sozialdemokratie', p.518.
[198] Michels, 'Die deutsche Sozialdemokratie', p.523.
[199] Mitzman, *Sociology and Estrangement*, p.278.
[200] Roberto [Robert] Michels, *Il proletariato e la borghesia nel Movimento socialista italiano*, Turin, 1908, pp.312–13.

68 ROBERT MICHELS, SOCIALISM, AND MODERNITY

the proletariat wherever he goes'. 'Class conflicts' within the party that are denoted by the term '*Akademiker*-question' are common knowledge.[201]

Michels than turned to an analysis of the social composition of the party leadership and to a consideration of the relations between party leaders and the mass of ordinary party members—which would become the major theme of *Political Parties* a few years later. Michels noted that of the Social Democratic Reichstag deputies elected in 1903, 65 per cent came from skilled working-class backgrounds, and another 18.5 per cent could be classified as 'proletarianized petits bourgeois', adding up to 75–80 per cent who could be considered of proletarian background.[202] However, such parliamentary representatives of the workers, whose speeches testified to a knowledge of workers' lives, 'cannot remain workers. One cannot do one's job as a stonemason on a building site at 3.00 in the afternoon and at 4.00pm deliver a speech in the Reichstag on legislation to regulate the stock exchange'.[203] Michels went on to state that 'the originally proletarian Reichstag caucus has now become thoroughly petit bourgeois'.[204]

With its growing complex of organizations and workers' associations, and its increasing number of paid positions, the Social Democratic Party was starting to function as a 'class elevation machine' for a stratum of its functionaries. In this respect, Michels compared the party machine to the Catholic church, which had traditionally provided a mechanism for social advancement for the intelligent sons of the peasantry and the petite bourgeoisie. With the great demand for able people to fill the large number of party offices, Social Democracy served the advancement of intelligent members of the working class.[205] More provocatively for anti-militarist socialists, Michels compared the social mobility the party machine offered workers to that afforded by the Prussian army, which offered men from modest backgrounds a degree of economic security if they became non-commissioned officers.[206] In this process, however, workers by hand became brain-workers, and functionaries became estranged from the proletariat out of which they came, becoming more petit bourgeois in income and habits.[207] Michels concluded: 'As paradoxical as it may sound, the imposing political struggle between the classes representing capital and labour ends in a very similar fashion to the economic to-ing and fro-ing of supply and demand in economic

---

[201] Michels, 'Die deutsche Sozialdemokratie', p.536.
[202] Michels, 'Die deutsche Sozialdemokratie', p.527.
[203] Michels, 'Die deutsche Sozialdemokratie', p.529.
[204] Michels, 'Die deutsche Sozialdemokratie', p.552.
[205] Michels, 'Die deutsche Sozialdemokratie', p.541.
[206] Michels, 'Die deutsche Sozialdemokratie', pp.544–5. Michels re-used some of this part of the article in a piece for a Belgian anarchist journal: Dr Robert Michels, 'Over den tegenwoordigen Toestand van het Socialisme in Duitschland', Antwerp, 1907 [offprint from *Ontwaking*, VII, February 1907, pp.49–62].
[207] Michels, 'Die deutsche Sozialdemokratie', pp.542, 543.

competition: in a social exchange within the classes themselves.'[208] The end result was that 'there is a social difference between the leadership and the party masses, even if it is moderated by the origin of this leadership and by strong ideal factors'. Michels considered that this gulf had significant consequences for party organization and tactics, which he promised to explore in a future article.[209]

Michels followed up this lengthy article for the *Archiv für Sozialwissenschaft und Sozialpolitik* with another lengthy contribution, a review article on recent literature on socialism. Michels took aim at a couple of 'bourgeois' experts on socialism, Karl Diehl and the Leipzig *Privatdozent*, W. Eduard Biermann. He rhetorically suggested that every self-respecting university academic seemed to feel the need to write a popular refutation of socialist and anarchist thinkers, based only on superficial knowledge. Michels' self-image as an outsider in the profession was partly on display here, along with his 'insider' knowledge of international socialism.[210] Stressing the idealistic basis of socialism, as ever, Michels took issue with Karl Diehl: 'Diehl wants to kill social democracy with its materialist view of history by summoning up idealism…, as if idealism were not, as experience has shown, always the best nourishment for socialism itself'.[211] At the same time, however, Michels had fulsome praise for the works of Sombart, whom he lauded as an international expert on socialism, whose works were distinguished by a 'wealth of ideas and intellectual eminence'.[212] Michels did point to what he felt was a potential contradiction in Sombart's critique of Social Democracy: on the one hand, Sombart recommended that the party confine itself to 'realistic' objectives and methods (i.e. legal and parliamentary), and on the other hand, he complained that the party had lost its idealism and *élan* in the 'dusty air of day-to-day (Social Democratic) politics'. At this point, Michels directed his sarcasm towards the Social Democratic Party, not its bourgeois analyst, as he had in the cases of Biermann and Diehl. He diagnosed the cause of the loss of 'idealism, the feeling for high and wide goals, for the capacity for self-sacrifice' in Social Democracy in

---

[208] Michels, 'Die deutsche Sozialdemokratie', p.544.

[209] Michels, 'Die deutsche Sozialdemokratie', p.556. Some of the material in this article was also used in R. [Robert] Michels, *L'Allemagne, le socialisme et les syndicats*, Paris, 1906 (a separate printing of an article for the *Revue Internationale de Sociologie*). Here, too, Michels gave priority to socialism as a 'movement of ideas' (p.1), before moving to consider socialism as the movement of a specific class, the proletariat, pursuing the selfish goal of its own emancipation. The movement of ideas needed intellectuals to promote it (p.3). Michels also writes here about the psychology of the German workers (a tendency to passivity, respect for authority, and discipline (p.7), which reinforced the backward nature of the German state). Michels did hold out a prospect that the conflict of interests between classes in Germany would continue to manifest itself, leading German workers to push for a new 'era of peace and progress' (p.12).

[210] Robert Michels, 'Literatur. Zur Geschichte des Sozialismus', *Archiv für Sozialwissenschaft und Sozialpolitik*, 23, 1906, pp.786–843, here p.798.

[211] Michels, 'Literatur. Zur Geschichte des Sozialismus', p.797.

[212] Michels, 'Literatur. Zur Geschichte des Sozialismus', p.799.

70   ROBERT MICHELS, SOCIALISM, AND MODERNITY

precisely that barren and idiotic only-parliamentarism, that contented willingness to give up putting one's own person at stake (which doesn't yet have to
mean 'revolution'!), that patiently bureaucratic ballot-paper-counting and formulation of modest legislative motions which feed the waste-paper baskets of
the Reich and state parliaments, which is the sum total of the majority of the
contemporary socialist parties' work.[213]

Michels largely endorsed Sombart's analysis of Social Democracy, with some
reservations as far as Sombart's critique of Marx was concerned, and disagreeing
with Sombart's perception of a 'tendency towards uniformity' among the socialist
parties of different countries. Michels praised Sombart for seeing socialism as a
class movement, not as 'the expression of the confused or criminal thoughts of a
handful of *déclassé* individuals and the immanent stupidity of gullibility of an
eternally envious multitude.'[214]

Michels' incipient collaboration with Sombart and Weber was also reflected in
increasingly cordial references to Sombart in non-German socialist publications.
In a warm review of Sombart's work on the German economy in the nineteenth
century for *Il Divenire Sociale*, Michels recommended Sombart to Italian socialists as a 'more or less marxistoid' writer.[215] A few months later, Michels praised
the latest edition of Sombart's book on 'socialism and the social movement', in
which he seconded Sombart's criticisms of the German Social Democratic
Party—namely, its lack of *élan*, and its contradictory utterances on patriotism.[216]
Michels' attempt to build bridges between the radical left and Sombart is a little
ironic in view of Sombart's steady shift to the political right since his earlier sympathies for reformist Social Democracy, conditioned at least in part by career
considerations.[217] On 7 November 1905, Sombart had in fact expressed to
Michels his impatience with what he called 'Marx-scholasticism', adding that
while he was not getting closer to (the conservative sociologist) Gustav Schmoller,
he was moving further away from Marx.[218]

While Michels was increasingly closely collaborating with 'bourgeois' scholars
on an analysis of the German Social Democratic Party, he continued to criticize it
from the left, especially when he saw the party as falling short of internationalist

---

[213] Michels, 'Literatur. Zur Geschichte des Sozialismus', p.800.

[214] Michels, 'Literatur. Zur Geschichte des Sozialismus', p.805.

[215] Roberto [Robert] Michels, Review of Werner Sombart, *Die Deutsche Volkswirtschaft im XIXten
Jahrhundert*, in *Il Divenire Sociale. Rivista di Socialismo Scientifico*, Anno I, no.23, 1 December
1905, p.372.

[216] Robert Michels, Review of Werner Sombart, *Sozialismus und Soziale Bewegung*, in *Le
Mouvement Socialiste*, tome XIX, no.174/175, May/June 1906, pp.178–80.

[217] See Friedrich Lenger, *Werner Sombart. 1863–1941*, Munich, 1994. On the relationship between
Michels and Sombart, see Federico Trocini, 'Sombart e Michels. Due itinerari paralleli?', *Annali della
Fondazione Luigi Einaudi*, 48, 2014, pp.269–91 (followed by an edition of their correspondence edited
by Trocini, pp.291–364).

[218] Werner Sombart to Robert Michels, 7 November 1905, ARM/FLE.

and anti-militarist ideals. For example, in early 1906, Michels renewed his criticism of the weakness of the Social Democratic Party's response to the German imperial government's conduct in the Morocco crisis, specifically on the occasion of French trade union leader Victor Griffuelhes' (secretary of the Confédération Générale du Travail; CGT) visit to Germany in January 1906, in an attempt to enlist the support of the German trade unions for a concerted French-German anti-war demonstration, only to be effectively rebuffed by his German counterparts.[219] Endorsing Griffuelhes' complaints against the German unions' (and the Social Democratic Party's) repeated failure to support internationalist and anti-war initiatives, Michels saw the German unions as adhering pusillanimously to rules and statutes in the face of an international emergency. He accused the German labour movement, with a few exceptions (e.g. the *Leipziger Volks-Zeitung*, and his own contributions to the *Frankfurter Volksstimme*) of bureaucratic formalism and timidity.[220] Michels diagnosed 'an absence of energy', linked with a 'lack of self- confidence and revolutionary spirit' and 'pusillanimity' among German Social Democrats and unionists.[221] In Michels' view, the large party and union organizations and treasuries were part of the reason for the German labour movement's weakness, and not sources of strength:

> The fear of losing its voters and its savings is the *supreme law* of Social Democracy. It is this fear that explains its indolent strategy and its passivity. It is this fear which, making the German socialist party the weakest of the socialist parties—despite its prodigious resources of men and money, gives us the key to its attitude towards war and militarism.[222]

Michels' article on Morocco and Griffuelhes' unsuccessful visit elicited a lengthy rebuttal by Eduard Bernstein in the revisionist *Sozialistische Monatshefte*. Bernstein conceded that socialists outside Germany had wondered at the passivity of the German party during the Moroccan crisis, but found some of Michels' arguments tendentious.[223] Bernstein's explanation for the phenomenon of the party's relative inaction during the Moroccan crisis was simple: 'German Social Democracy, for all its internationalist sentiments, simply has no foreign policy'. This was because no German political party really had a foreign policy, because parties were unable to make foreign policy in Germany, where only governments determined foreign policy—governments that were not made by parties.[224]

---

[219] Robert Michels, 'Les socialistes allemands et la guerre', *Le Mouvement Socialiste*, no.171, 15 February 1906, pp.129–39 (signed Marburg, 10 February 1906).
[220] Michels, 'Les socialistes allemands et la guerre', pp.132–5.
[221] Michels, 'Les socialistes allemands et la guerre', p.136.
[222] Michels, 'Les socialistes allemands et la guerre', pp.138–9, quotation p.39.
[223] Eduard Bernstein, 'Das vergrabene Pfund und die Taktik der Sozialdemokratie', *Sozialistische Monatshefte*, X, 4, April 1906, pp.287–95.
[224] Bernstein, 'Das vergrabene Pfund und die Taktik der Sozialdemokratie', p.292.

72   ROBERT MICHELS, SOCIALISM, AND MODERNITY

Bernstein disagreed with Michels' 'quite superficial' argument that the labour movement was too concerned about protecting its cash reserves. Rather, Bernstein argued that the German people lacked revolutionary feeling, as far as a permanent willingness to challenge the authorities was concerned. He went on to diagnose a gap between the language of German Social Democracy and its actual behaviour: 'We are not a revolutionary party, we are a party of legal-parliamentary action. From year to year, we are ever more thus.'[225] The increasing involvement of the party in practical parliamentary work at a local government level and above was not, as Michels suggested, because of the preference of party officials, 'but rather because it corresponds to the whole nature of German development and German conditions'.[226] Bernstein maintained that 'the *pusillanimous* German trade union movement, piling up its funds' (as Michels had characterized it), had achieved more for its members than the French CGT or 'the new theory of violence of [Georges] Sorel, now the theoretician of *revolutionary syndicalism*' (and a member of the circle around *Le Mouvement Socialiste*). Bernstein characterized 'this *revolutionary* playing at trade-unionism [*Gewerkschaftlerei*]' as a symptom of a prolonged infantile stage.[227] Bernstein disagreed with Michels' accusation that the Social Democratic Party was impotent, and he concluded by reiterating the revisionist position that the party could be more effective if it dispensed with revolutionary phraseology and recognized the parliamentary nature of its struggle.[228] Michels responded to Bernstein's article in another article in *Le Mouvement Socialiste*, in which he began by arguing that Bernstein had essentially agreed with his analysis of the state of Social Democracy—diagnosing passivity in the face of crises—but that he had drawn opposite conclusions from Michels' own.[229] Michels lamented that Bernstein, 'so subtle, so sharp-minded in the diagnosis of the maladies of socialism—and we have all learned much from him—could be so superficial, so illogical, in the prescription of remedies'. Bernstein's recommendations would not counter the passivity of the Social Democratic labour movement but would instead make it more docile by de-radicalizing it, Michels argued.[230]

Shortly after he had written his article for *Le Mouvement Socialiste* on the German Social Democrats and Morocco, Michels was in Paris, where, among other engagements, he gave a lecture to French workers in the Palais du Travail, in Belleville, on 21 February 1906. This lecture was then published as a series of articles in the journal of the German 'localist' trade unions, *Die Einigkeit*.[231] Michels

---

[225]   Bernstein, 'Das vergrabene Pfund und die Taktik der Sozialdemokratie', p.293.

[226]   Bernstein, 'Das vergrabene Pfund und die Taktik der Sozialdemokratie', p.294.

[227]   Bernstein, 'Das vergrabene Pfund und die Taktik der Sozialdemokratie'.

[228]   Bernstein, 'Das vergrabene Pfund und die Taktik der Sozialdemokratie', pp.294–5.

[229]   Robert Michels, 'Polémiques sur le socialisme allemande', *Le Mouvement Socialiste*, no.176, 15 July 1906, pp.228–37, here pp.228–9 (dated Marburg, May 1906).

[230]   Michels, 'Polémiques sur le socialisme allemande', p.229.

[231]   Dr [Robert] Michels, 'Die Kriegsgefahr und die deutsche Arbeiterbewegung', *Die Einigkeit. Organ der Freien Vereinigung deutscher Gewerkschaften*, no.21, 26 May; no.22, 2 June; no.23, 9 June; no.24, 16 June; no.25, Beilage, 23 June 1906.

was evincing more and more signs of sympathizing with the German 'localist' unions, which represented a more militant syndicalist, grass-roots orientation than the centrally organized Free Trade Unions, but he had no illusions about the size or influence of the localists in Germany, whose numbers he cited as just over 1 per cent of the membership of the Free Trade Unions.[232] Michels' rationale for publishing the lecture in German was to counter what he claimed had been misrepresentations of his speech in *Vorwärts* and in the *Korrespondenzblatt* of the General Commission of Free Trade Unions, among other German labour movement papers.[233] Michels once again professed his alarm at the inactivity of the leadership of the German labour movement, especially of the Free Trade Unions, in the face of the threat of war over Morocco. His lecture, Michels explained, was designed to try to explain this inactivity to French workers, and to dispel any misunderstanding that the German union leaders were driven purely by old-fashioned 'patriotism'.[234] Michels argued that the German Social Democratic Party had succeeded in attracting the votes of all Germans who favoured democratic reform, not just socialist workers, but had become a captive of its electoral success, and of these 'masses of voters'. Social Democracy now

> lives in constant fear of losing the three million voters, or the concern to add further millions to these millions. That is no brilliant basis for energetic actions, much less considering the fact that Social Democracy has taken over much from the state that it opposes, to some extent has had to take over much. One can indeed say that Social Democracy has become strong through the use of means quite similar to those of the Prussian Junker state. The numerical values which have made it strong were organisation, a convinced and conscientious corps of officials and a voluntary, but nonetheless iron, discipline. Thus it represents to the present an admirable whole, considered from the standpoint of

---

[232] See Roberto [Robert] Michels, *I sindacati tedeschi e la lotta contro la disoccupazione*. Relazione svolta al I Congresso internazionale per la lotta contro la disoccupazione (n.d. [1906]), copy in FLE, p.8, in Michels cited membership figures from 1904: Free Trade Unions 1,116,000 members and 'localists' 13,000. He noted, however, the principled adherence of the 'localists' to the concept of class struggle and their rejection of party-political 'neutrality'; Michels, 'Die deutsche Sozialdemokratie', pp.497–8.

[233] Robert Michels, 'Kriegsgefahr', *Die Einigkeit*, no.21, 26 May 1906. See Robert Michels, 'Aus den deutschen Gewerkschaften', *Correspondenzblatt der Generalkommission der Gewerkschaften Deutschlands*, Jg.16, no.10, 10 March 1906, p.155, where the mining union's paper *Die Bergarbeiterzeitung* is quoted angrily rejecting Michels' alleged slur that union bosses had opposed a continuation of the Ruhr strike because they feared for their salaries as functionaries. The union paper threatened to expose 'the elevated standard of living of certain ultra-radicals' if such divisive rhetoric did not cease. Michels responded in 'Eine Entgegnung', *Correspondenzblatt der Generalkommission der Gewerkschaften Deutschlands*, no.13, 31 March 1906, pp.201–2, stating, among other things, that his income did not exceed that of some union leaders, while arguing that his criticism went beyond claims of personal greed to broader questions of clinging to organizational structures at the expense of their ostensible purposes, which prompted another rebuttal from the *Correspondenzblatt der Generalkommission der Gewerkschaften Deutschlands*, p.202; see further, 'Dr Michels gegen die deutschen Gewerkschaften in Frankreich', *Correspondenzblatt der Generalkommission der Gewerkschaften Deutschlands*, no.15, 14 April 1906, pp.232–3.

[234] Michels, 'Kriegsgefahr'.

74   ROBERT MICHELS, SOCIALISM, AND MODERNITY

administration, a giant administrative body, with its officials, statutes, its complicated organisms, its well-filled treasuries, and its newspapers, edited with great care, but it shares the weaknesses of all widely ramified and well-founded mechanisms: it can only be set into motion with difficulty and its immanent concern for itself hinders the rise of movements of great boldness and clear energy.[235]

With this analysis, Michels might be said to have anticipated the later concept of 'negative integration', which the Weber scholar Guenther Roth applied to the German Social Democratic Party in a highly influential work in 1963, half a century after Michels' own *Political Parties*.[236]

Michels' lecture continued, asserting that despite its successes, Social Democracy still represented a movement of the persecuted:

> The intellectuals from the bourgeoisie who have joined it are virtually boycotted by the class from which they stem. In Prussia a special ministerial decree forbids them from lecturing positions at universities.... Nor do workers fare better, who participate in the Social Democratic movement....[237]

Here it is striking that Michels mentions his own situation as a bourgeois intellectual banned from university positions before mentioning the plight of the more numerous rank-and-file party members from the working class. Michels then turned to consider the Free Trade Unions, which he heavily criticized for their lack of socialist ideology and party-political neutrality, contrasting them with the French CGT, which maintained a commitment to class struggle.[238]

Michels did not attend the Social Democratic Party congress at Mannheim in September 1906, a congress that was notable for sealing the political 'neutrality' and equal standing of the Free Trade Unions with the party, reinforcing the opposition of the trade union leaders to the notion of a political general strike.[239] Max Weber was an observer at the congress during the mass strike debate, and, in

---

[235] Michels, 'Kriegsgefahr', III, *Die Einigkeit*, no.23, 9 June 1906.

[236] Guenther Roth, *The Social Democrats in Imperial Germany*, Totowa, NJ, 1963. Roth considers 'negative integration' to have ultimately contributed to the stabilization of imperial Germany's political system prior to the outbreak of the First World War. The term 'negative integration' was further developed by Dieter Groh, *Negative Integration und revolutionärer Attentismus. Die deutsche Sozialdemokratie am Vorabend des Ersten Weltkrieges*, Frankfurt/M., Berlin, Vienna, 1973.

[237] Michels, 'Kriegsgefahr', III, *Die Einigkeit*, no.23, 9 June 1906.

[238] Michels, 'Kriegsgefahr', IV, *Die Einigkeit*, no.24, 16 June 1906.

[239] On the Mannheim congress, see John A. Moses, *Trade Unionism in Germany from Bismarck to Hitler, 1869–1933*, Vol.1, Totowa, NJ, 1982, pp.159–62; Michael Schneider, *Kleine Geschichte der Gewerkschaften. Ihre Entwicklung in Deutschland von den Anfängen bis heute*, Bonn, 1989, pp.97–8; Karl Christian Führer, *Carl Legien 1861–1920. Ein Gewerkschafter im Kampf um ein 'möglichst gutes Leben' für alle Arbeiter*, Essen, 2009, p.133. Führer points out that as the party had 384,000 members while the Free Trade Unions numbered 1.7 million, the unions' claim for parity was hard to resist.

MICHELS AND GERMAN SOCIAL DEMOCRACY   75

a reversal of roles, sent an account of the congress to Michels, who was in Italy. Weber's account mixed aesthetic disdain for the 'utterly petit-bourgeois habitus, the many stolid publicans' physiognomies, the lack of any *élan*' with a critique of the party's political strategy, or rather lack of one: 'without the resolution to draw the logical conclusions of a swing to the "right" if the way to the "left" is blocked, or is assumed to be'. Weber summed up his impression of Mannheim: 'These gentlemen don't frighten anyone anymore'. Weber also reported to Michels that he was mentioned in absentia by the union leader Carl Legien as close to the 'localists'.[240] Legien cited a reference to the 'localists' by Michels in his *Archiv* article as opening their organization to anarchists in support of his (Legien's) argument that the 'localists' did not belong in the Social Democratic Party. Legien cited Michels as a reliable source on the 'localists', on the basis that he had published an article series in their newspaper (*Die Einigkeit*).[241]

Following Mannheim, Michels stepped up his criticism of the Social Democratic Party in radical left papers outside Germany. *In Le Mouvement Socialiste*, he wrote that the Mannheim congress had been a worse defeat for the Social Democratic Party than the one Napoleon inflicted on Prussia a century earlier (a centenary that had been the subject of much discussion in Germany during the year): 'even before the battle was joined, it capitulated, handing its sword—its principles, its *raison d'être*—over to the adversary: the General Commission of the reformist-centralist trade unions'.[242] In the Belgian anarchist journal *Ontwaking*, Michels lamented that the congress had been far from a 'page of glory' in the party's history.[243] Michels contrasted the localist trade unions, as revolutionary socialists, with the neutral Free Trade Unions. Unfortunately, the localists were failing to grow in numbers and were neglected, or worse, by the Social Democratic Party.[244] While excommunicating anarchists, the party was too indulgent towards its right wing.[245] Not only did Michels bemoan the growing influence of the reformist right-wing union leaders, and of revisionists like the Hessian Eduard David (now described as a 'eunuch of a Hessian deputy'), but Bebel himself had turned into a 'pure-blooded revisionist'.[246] Not only did Bebel agree with the trade union leaders that building up union organization was the essential precondition of any mass strike action, he even warned against attempting a general strike at the outbreak of war, when millions of men would be

[240] Max Weber to Robert Michels, 8 October 1906, ARM/FLE, also in Weber, *Briefe 1906–1908*, pp.172–3.

[241] *Protokoll über die Verhandlungen des Parteitages der sozialdemokratischen Partei Deutschlands. Abgehalten zu Mannheim vom 23. bis 29. September 1906*, Berlin, 1906, pp.242–3.

[242] Robert Michels, 'Le socialisme allemand après Mannheim', *Le Mouvement Socialiste*, IX, no.182, 1907, pp.5–22, quotation p.5.

[243] Michels, 'Over den tegenwoordigen Toestand van het Socialisme in Duitschland', p.3.

[244] Michels, 'Le socialisme allemand après Mannheim', pp.8–9.

[245] Michels, 'Le socialisme allemand après Mannheim', p.7.

[246] Michels, 'Le socialisme allemand après Mannheim', pp.11, 12.

76   ROBERT MICHELS, SOCIALISM, AND MODERNITY

immediately placed under arms and under martial law—for Michels this statement of Bebel's was a shocking indictment of the failure of socialist education within the party's ranks.[247] The radical left in the party was losing ground, as indicated by the resounding failure of Kautsky's motion on the mass strike question.[248] Once again, Michels concluded by diagnosing bureaucracy and the fetishization of organization for organization's sake as the root of the party's malaise. Bureaucratization was turning proletarians into *petits bourgeois*, sapping their revolutionary sentiments, even though Michels concluded that the party still contained some surviving militants who saw socialism as a real and urgent goal.[249]

In the elections of January 1907, known as the 'Hottentot elections' after Chancellor Bülow called a snap 'khaki election' after opposition from the Social Democrats and the Catholic Centre Party to increased spending on Germany's war in south-west Africa, Michels campaigned for the Social Democratic Party one more time.[250] Michels took part in a public disputation with nationalistic students in Marburg,[251] but he left most of the election campaigning in Marburg to Robert Dissmann, an official of the metal-workers' union and Social Democratic Party activist. By this time, Michels had already decided to move to Turin, abandoning for the time being his goal of achieving a *Habilitation* at a German university, to take up a position with the economics professor and moderate socialist Achille Loria.[252] Even as he prepared to leave Germany to take up an academic career in Italy, Michels responded to the Social Democratic Party's dramatic loss of Reichstag seats in the 1907 elections with a renewed round of criticism of the party.

Michels analysed the 'Hottentot elections' for the Italian journal *La Riforma Sociale*. While he stressed that the defeat of the German Social Democratic Party was only relative—they gained nearly 250,000 votes compared with 1903, but the higher turnout for other parties resulted in a loss of seats from eighty-one to forty-three—he also criticized the party for its failure effectively to oppose the government's exploitation of nationalism: they had not dared to try to rally support behind a higher idea of humanity, or behind the principles of historical

---

[247] Michels, 'Le socialisme allemand après Mannheim', pp.16–18.

[248] Michels, 'Le socialisme allemand après Mannheim', pp.13–14.

[249] Michels, 'Le socialisme allemand après Mannheim', pp.20–2.

[250] On the 'Hottentot elections', see George Dunlap Crothers, *The German Elections of 1907*, New York, 1941 (reprint edn. 1968); Jonathan Sperber, *The Kaiser's Voters: Electors and Elections in Imperial Germany*, Cambridge, 1997, pp.240–54.

[251] 'Wahlkreis Marburg-Kirchhain', *Volksstimme* (Frankfurt/M.), Jg.18, Nr.20, 24 January 1907, 2. Beilage.

[252] See Max Weber to Robert Michels, 27 November 1906, ARM/FLE, also in Weber, *Briefe 1906–1908*, p.185; Weber to Loria, 1 January 1907, Weber's letter of recommendation for Michels, in Weber, *Briefe 1906–1908*, p.207.

MICHELS AND GERMAN SOCIAL DEMOCRACY 77

materialism, focusing instead on complaints about the costs of colonies.[253] The election defeat left the Social Democrats without any possibility of using parliamentary means (by voting with the Centre Party and the minorities) of imposing any restraint on the foreign policy of the Reich.[254] Michels adopted a sharper tone while reiterating some of the same analysis in an article in *La Guerre Sociale*, the mouthpiece of the French radical socialist and anti-militarist Gustave Hervé. For *La Guerre Sociale*'s readers, Michels began by emphasizing that he did not see a smaller number of parliamentarians as necessarily a misfortune in itself—the fewer the members of parliament, the less the risk of succumbing to the temptation of compromise with one's enemies. However, the electoral defeat was of concern in so far as it showed the weakness of support for socialism among parts of the German working class. In trying to paint themselves as the better patriots, German Social Democrats had failed to proclaim the truth of Marx's dictum that the proletariat has no fatherland. The ideological timidity of the German party was in part to blame for its electoral setback. Marx's lesson that patriotism and militarism were outgrowths of capitalism had not penetrated into the German workers, 'who are lacking in temperament and in revolutionary traditions', a state of affairs that Social Democrats were neglecting to remedy.[255] Michels addressed the problem of what he regarded as confused ideas about patriotism within German Social Democracy in an article entitled 'Proletarian Patriotism' in Essen's *Arbeiter-Zeitung*. However, the editor of the paper, while endorsing Michels' internationalist standpoint, felt compelled to preface Michels' article with the qualification that Michels' criticisms of the party's failure to articulate a sufficiently clear rejection of bourgeois patriotism were somewhat 'one-sided', and editorial glosses distanced the paper from some of Michels' more critical remarks on the party and its leadership. The paper noted that 'comrade Dr Robert Michels' was departing from Germany, and would in future be active in Italy.[256]

Michels contributed *to La Guerre Sociale* again in May 1907, with a short article devoted to the question of whether there were revolutionaries in Germany. He concluded that there were revolutionaries in Germany, but that taken as a whole the German Social Democratic Party was far from revolutionary. Social Democracy was 'in effect, almost completely lacking in revolutionary spirit.' Michels went on: 'There is little wanting for it to be solely a Millerandist party.

---

[253] Roberto [Robert] Michels, 'La vittoria dei conservatori nelle elezioni germaniche del 1907. Appunti storici e statistici', *La Riforma Sociale*, Anno XIV, vol. XVII, 2nd series, 15 February 1907, pp.133–51, here cited from the offprint, pp.16–17.

[254] Michels, 'La vittoria dei conservatori nelle elezioni germaniche del 1907', p.21.

[255] Robert Michels, 'Un antipatriote allemande aux antipatriotes français', *La Guerre Sociale*, 1, no.13, 13–19 March 1907; this also appeared in Italian in the anarchist paper *Il Pensiero*: Roberto [Robert] Michels, 'Il partito socialista tedesco dopo le elezioni', *Il Pensiero*, V, no.7, 1 April 1907.

[256] Genosse Michels, 'Proletarischer Patriotismus', *Arbeiter-Zeitung* (Essen), no.77, 5 April 1907, p.1 (leading article). A translation of this article appeared in the Antwerp anarchist periodical, *Ontwaking*. 'Duitsche Toestanden', in *Ontwaking. Maandschrift*, Nieuwe Reeks, a. VII, no.5, pp.195–9.

78   ROBERT MICHELS, SOCIALISM, AND MODERNITY

There is already more than one Millerand in its ranks…'. There *were* party radicals, but they could not yet see how serious the decay of the party was becoming through the advance of the reformists. Michels concluded that the decomposition of the party had some way to go before the remaining revolutionaries would become alert to the internal threat to the party. Then it might split, but for Michels the possible loss of party unity was of lesser importance than the possibility of a renaissance of revolutionary spirit.[257]

In *Le Mouvement Socialiste*, in a rejoinder to an article by Edouard Berth, Michels reiterated his concern that the German Social Democrats lacked '*élan* and self-sacrificing idealism', stating that 'class egoism' was not enough for a revolutionary movement.[258] Michels insisted on the need for need for 'ethical sentiment' to augment workers' material economic interests for a socialist movement to achieve its goals: Krupp workers' economic interests might be quite consistent with militarism and an arms race, for example, without any ethical motives. Michels emphasized: '*The economic factor is impotent without the coefficient of moral paedagogy. Without it, the "mission of the proletariat" will never be accomplished.*'[259] Here, Michels saw a role for a revolutionary syndicalist ferment within the wider socialist movement, as it 'guaranteed the preservation of a remnant of a revolutionary base', even though there were only a mere 13,000 localist trade unionists (in French: 'syndicalistes "syndicalistes"') in Germany, compared with 1.3 million 'reformist trade unionists'.[260] Michels elaborated on these reflections when he spoke to a gathering in Paris of European revolutionary syndicalists from different European countries on 3 April 1907. He painted a bleak picture of conditions in Germany, where 'there are few symptoms of rebirth', unlike in France, where revolutionary syndicalists sought to keep the revolutionary socialist idea alive. Being born in Germany was no longer any cause for pride. The days of the great German thinkers, Goethe, Schiller, Kant, were over, and the life of the mind in Germany was now 'venal and servile', with no idea what it meant to be independent and free.[261] The lack of political freedom and democracy in Germany had favoured the rise to primacy of the political party, even while the party remained weak on its own parliamentary terrain, exhibiting timidity when it comes to consideration of weapons such as the general strike. The party's bureaucratic, hierarchical structure was in large part responsible for this weakness and timidity.[262] There were a few syndicalists and youthful radical elements in German Social Democracy, but on the whole: 'The current tactic of Social

---

[257] Robert Michels, 'L'Allemagne est-elle révolutionnaire', *La Guerre Sociale*, 1ère année, no.21, 8–14 May 1907.

[258] Robert Michels, 'Controverse socialiste', *Le Mouvement Socialiste*, no.184, March 1907, pp.278–88, here pp.279–80.

[259] Michels, 'Controverse socialiste', p.280.   [260] Michels, 'Controverse socialiste', p.288.

[261] Robert Michels, 'Le syndicalisme et le socialisme en Allemagne', *Le Mouvement Socialiste*, no.188, July 1907, pp.58–63, here p.59.

[262] Michels, 'Le syndicalisme et le socialisme en Allemagne', pp.60–1.

MICHELS AND GERMAN SOCIAL DEMOCRACY   79

Democracy, prudent, indecisive, legalitarian and parliamentarian, can only prolong the ruling system and prevent the successful emergence of vigorous youthful elements.' The grip of the party's leaders, including Bebel, had become harmful, and only syndicalism offered the chance of a rebirth for socialism.[263]

In the lead-up to the Socialist International Congress held in Stuttgart in August 1907, Michels continued his criticisms of the German party for its parliamentarianism and bureaucratic nature, and for its reluctance to support more radical anti-militarist agitation, as advocated by Karl Liebknecht. He went so far as to suggest that it would now be the duty of the Socialist International to expel the German party if the International could not oblige it to be more conscious of its duties as a socialist party, rather than as a patriotic party.[264] Michels took his criticisms of the German party leadership's position on 'defensive war' outside of the Social Democratic and labour movement press, publishing an article in *Der Morgen*, a 'weekly periodical for German culture', edited by his friend Werner Sombart, in conjunction with Richard Strauss, the Danish literary critic Georg Brandes, and Hugo von Hofmannsthal.[265] Sombart pointedly distanced himself from Michels' 'revolutionary syndicalist' views in a preface to the article. Michels took issue with the stated position of August Bebel and Gustav Noske that the German Social Democratic Party would support a defensive war. He made two telling points: how would the party be able to determine which belligerent was in the wrong when the government might have a monopoly of information on the diplomatic moves that led to war, and would have a self-evident interest in obfuscating the issue, which might then continue to be debated by historians for decades? (This is in fact largely what happened in July 1914, when Chancellor Bethmann Hollweg fed the revisionist Social Democrat Alfred Südekum misleading intelligence presenting Russia as the aggressor and the German government as doing its utmost to avoid war. On this point, Michels was prescient.) Secondly, from a socialist point of view, if wars were the product of competing capitalist interests, the moral question of the distinction between a war of aggression and a defensive war did not even arise. Michels also pointed to the logical inconsistency of a position in which on the one hand Social Democrats voted against the army budget but on the other hand were willing to countenance the possibility of sharing a common (external) enemy with the ruling classes.[266] While Michels argued from the basis of assuming class antagonisms within the nation, a position that Sombart clearly did not share, the criticism of the party in a bourgeois periodical

---

[263] Michels, 'Le syndicalisme et le socialisme en Allemagne', pp.62, 63.

[264] Robert Michels, 'Le prochain Congrès socialiste international', *Le Mouvement Socialiste*, no.188, July 1907, pp.38–46, especially p.46; Robert Michels, Review of *Militarismus und Antimilitarismus* by Karl Liebknecht, in *Le Mouvement Socialiste*, tome XXII, July–December 1907, pp.253–4.

[265] Robert Michels, 'Die deutschen Sozialdemokraten und der internationale Krieg', *Der Morgen*, no.10, 16 August 1907, pp.299–304.

[266] Michels, 'Die deutschen Sozialdemokraten und der internationale Krieg', p.304.

80   ROBERT MICHELS, SOCIALISM, AND MODERNITY

marked an increasing distance between Michels, now a *Privatdozent* in Turin, and the German party, and was a significant breach in Social Democratic Party etiquette, at the very least.

Michels observed the Socialist International Congress in Stuttgart as a delegate of the Italian Socialist Party.[267] Michels also enjoyed the company of his friend Werner Sombart at the congress, with whom he seems to have shared days of pleasure jaunts around Stuttgart. Michels also introduced Sombart to a number of syndicalists 'und ihnen nahestenden Revoluzzern' ('and sundry red revolutionaries of a similar bent'), as Michels put it, with a touch of irony.[268] While making these exotic acquaintanceships, Sombart came to a very similar view to Michels with respect to the theoretically revolutionary German Social Democrats: they had become a 'legal-parliamentary party', and the distinction between revisionists and radicals had lost its significance.[269] As Friedrich Lenger points out, Sombart's own interests at this time were moving away from party politics and towards conservative cultural criticism, as reflected in his involvement with the journal *Der Morgen*.[270]

Following the Stuttgart congress, and the subsequent German party congress in Essen, at which Bebel had reaffirmed the principle of the right of a nation to self-defence, Michels continued to criticize the weakness of German Social Democrats' position on anti-militarism, for example in an interview with Hervé's *La Guerre Sociale* (in which he was still described as a member of German Social Democracy).[271] For Michels, the patriotism of the German socialists had become a threat to the rest of the movement in Europe, paralysing its progress: 'It is clear, for example, that that part of the French socialists who oppose Hervé's propaganda or the anti-militarism of the CGT draw particular inspiration from German practice and use it as a brake to prevent any forward progress.'[272] German socialists had a particular duty to be critical of their fatherland given its backward and ultra-militarist nature—a duty they were neglecting.[273] The willingness of German Social Democrats to defend the fatherland overlooked the extent to which it was 'a fatherland composed for the one part of provinces stolen from the Poles, the Danes and the French, and for the other part of capital stolen from the workers by the barons of industry and finance.'[274] With its weak position against

---

[267] Timm Genett, *Der Fremde im Kriege. Zur politischen Theorie und Biographie von Robert Michels 1876–1936*, Berlin, 2008, p.377.

[268] Lenger, *Werner Sombart. 1863–1941*, pp.153, 174, 435n92.

[269] Lenger, *Werner Sombart. 1863–1941*, p.153.

[270] Lenger, *Werner Sombart. 1863–1941*, pp.154, 160.

[271] 'Nos Interviews. Stuttgart. Opinion de Robert Michels, membre de la Social-Démocratie', *La Guerre Sociale*, 1ère Année, no.40, 18–24 September 1907.

[272] Robert Michels, 'Le patriotisme des socialistes allemands et le congrès d'Essen', *Le Mouvement Socialiste*, année X, no.194, 15 January 1908, pp.5–13, here p.12.

[273] Michels, 'Le patriotisme des socialistes allemands et le congrès d'Essen', pp.10–11.

[274] Michels, 'Le patriotisme des socialistes allemands et le congrès d'Essen', pp.11–12.

militarism, the German party was now losing its claim to leadership in the international socialist movement.[275] Elsewhere, he complained of the 'decadence of the socialism of the old, so-called revolutionary, Marxist style in Germany', as displayed in the Stuttgart congress.[276] Somewhat curiously, at the same time as he supported the party's radical left in ultra-left French and Italian journals, Michels submitted an article to the revisionist *Sozialistische Monatshefte*, on the socialist Italian (and Torinese) painter Luigi Onetti, returning to his earlier mode of interpreting Italian culture to German readers.[277]

Michels expanded on his theme of German Social Democracy's loss of standing in the international socialist movement in another lengthy essay for the *Archiv für Sozialwissenschaft und Sozialpolitik*, which again blended moralistic criticism of the party and analysis couched in social-scientific terms.[278] Michels began by reflecting (with an ironic undertone) on the leading role that the German party had hitherto claimed to exercise in the international socialist movement: after the war of 1870–1, the German military, state structure, legal institutions, and universities had been regarded abroad as successful models to be emulated, and the same had applied to German Social Democracy.[279] Michels acknowledged some reasons for the hegemony of German Social Democracy in the International: the identification of the German party with Marxism, which had succeeded in marginalizing other forms of socialist theory, the evidence of electoral success, and the example of the Germans' organization and discipline, as well as the benefits from Germany's growing influence in world affairs.[280] But Michels regarded that hegemony as having been sterile in terms of its influence on other socialist parties, endorsing French syndicalist Hubert Lagardelle's criticism that the German party's influence 'has not made us receptive to new ideas'.[281] Michels lined up a whole series of critics of German Social Democracy, from radical left syndicalists to the Fabian George Bernard Shaw, and cited their negative comments on the party. Enrico Ferri had complained that German resolutions were always composed of ifs and buts and equipped with back doors.[282] Arturo Labriola argued that the Germans made a great deal of noise about beating bourgeois society on

---

[275] Michels, 'Le patriotisme des socialistes allemands et le congrès d'Essen', p.12.

[276] Robert Michels, Review of *Internationaler Sozialisten-Kongreß zu Stuttgart 18. bis 24. August 1907* (Protokoll), in *Archiv für Sozialwissenschaft und Sozialpolitik*, 27 (neue Folge), 1908, pp.841–4.

[277] Robert Michels, 'Luigi Onetti, ein Maler-Sozialist', *Sozialistische Monatshefte*, Jg.12, 9, September 1907, pp.767–70. See also a subsequent article on Edmondo de Amicis, Robert Michels, 'Edmondo de Amicis', *Sozialistische Monatshefte*, Jg.13, 6, June 1909, pp.361–8.

[278] Robert Michels, 'Die deutsche Sozialdemokratie im internationalen Verbande. Eine kritische Untersuchung', *Archiv für Sozialwissenschaft und Sozialpolitik*, 25, 1907, pp.148–231.

[279] Michels, 'Die deutsche Sozialdemokratie im internationalen Verbande, p.152.

[280] Michels, 'Die deutsche Sozialdemokratie im internationalen Verbande, pp.156–61.

[281] Michels, 'Die deutsche Sozialdemokratie im internationalen Verbande, p.162, citing Lagardelle, 'Mannheim, Rome, Amiens', *Le Mouvement Socialiste*, October 1906, p.6.

[282] Michels, 'Die deutsche Sozialdemokratie im internationalen Verbande', p.163.

82 ROBERT MICHELS, SOCIALISM, AND MODERNITY

the head during elections, only to leave things the same after the elections.[283] Shaw wrote that: 'political experience has made the German party so far opportunist and constitutional...they have...studied the art of giving an extreme and catastrophic air to very ordinary and harmless proposals'.[284]

Michels linked the increasing decline of the hegemony of German Social Democracy in international socialism partly to growing awareness of the real impotence of the party within the German state, and partly to the deficiencies in the party's own commitment to internationalism and especially anti-militarism. Michels used gendered language to characterize the impotence of the German party:

> What the boy socialism never suspected, the youth socialism suddenly saw with stark clarity. The door which led to the bridal chamber of his ardently desired one, the goddess of power, which he had sallied forth to conquer, remained hermetically sealed despite all his furious efforts. The law of the state did not keep pace with the revolutionizing of people's heads. Parliamentarianism showed itself to be impotent when it came to creating new rights for the people, or indeed even when it came to energetically resisting the worsening of their existing rights.[285]

One possible remedy for this impotence would be the resort to a general strike, but Germany compared poorly to other countries in the party's willingness to resort to such a tactic.[286] Similarly, German socialists showed less resolution in espousing anti-militarism than socialists in other countries, with Michels stating that 'Germany has remained the only country, in which there is still not a trace of an anti-militarist movement in the socialist party'.[287] The Morocco crisis had exposed both the 'impotence of German Social Democracy' and the 'slight international feeling within this party'.[288] Unfortunately, German Social Democracy had never paid sufficient attention to criticism by socialists in other countries. This was partly due to linguistic limitations, according to Michels, who noted that the journalists of the German Social Democratic press are recruited mainly from 'proletarian and petit bourgeois elements', thus lacking in knowledge of foreign languages.[289] However, on a more fundamental level, the most profound cause of the weakness of the German party 'lies in the party-political quintessence of Social Democracy itself as a party exclusively of newspaper readers and voters

---

[283] Michels, 'Die deutsche Sozialdemokratie im internationalen Verbande', p.170.
[284] Michels, 'Die deutsche Sozialdemokratie im internationalen Verbande', p.170n42.
[285] Michels, 'Die deutsche Sozialdemokratie im internationalen Verbande', p.176.
[286] Michels, 'Die deutsche Sozialdemokratie im internationalen Verbande', pp.176–9.
[287] Michels, 'Die deutsche Sozialdemokratie im internationalen Verbande', p.189.
[288] Michels, 'Die deutsche Sozialdemokratie im internationalen Verbande', p.190.
[289] Michels, 'Die deutsche Sozialdemokratie im internationalen Verbande', p.221.

with a large bureaucratic apparatus'. In conflict with a centralized state, it had centralized itself. The party had come to rely exclusively on electoral politics, and had become preoccupied with maintaining the organization in being—the party was therefore becoming 'mentally lazy and indolent'. The party disciplined its followers, but only trained them thereby into cowardice. German Social Democrats became imbued with 'the great plus—or is it minus?—of the character of the German people, the herd-like quality of capacity for obedience, suited for organization, and the subordination in administrative affairs'. In consequence, they displayed a lack of *élan* (*Schwung*) and idealism (in contrast with Italian socialism).[290] International observers diagnosed in the German party a lack of 'ethical forcefulness and revolutionary feeling, of the will and capacity for action'.[291] Michels consequently predicted that as long as prevailing political conditions in Germany continued, the German party would continue to decline and lose authority within the international socialist movement.[292]

By early 1908, Michels, now an academic residing in Turin, had largely placed himself outside the German Social Democratic Party. Karl Kautsky pronounced Michels' virtual excommunication in April 1908. Acknowledging receipt of an article sent him by Michels, Kautsky wrote:

> I have to remark that while I do reciprocate your personal sympathies, I am very uncomfortable with the fact that you publish your outpourings against the party in a bourgeois paper. Amongst us, that counts as indecent. It at any rate demonstrates a lack of party sentiment. Furthermore, I consider your politics to be ruinous and disorganizing. We don't want to transplant Italian chaos into Germany. We therefore have no reason to treat you gently.[293]

Analysing Oligarchy: Towards *Political Parties*

As Michels moved away from involvement in socialist politics and settled into the life of an academic in Turin, his essays on German Social Democracy shifted to a greater focus on sociological questions. In December 1907, he wrote an essay on the oligarchical tendencies of the political class, which appeared first in the Italian journal *La Riforma Sociale*, and then in an expanded form in the German *Archiv*

---

[290] Michels, 'Die deutsche Sozialdemokratie im internationalen Verbande', p.230.
[291] Michels, 'Die deutsche Sozialdemokratie im internationalen Verbande', p.227.
[292] Michels, 'Die deutsche Sozialdemokratie im internationalen Verbande', p.231. Michels revisited this argument in his last contribution to the French syndicalist journal *Le Mouvement Socialiste* in 1910: Robert Michels, 'L'ancienne hégémonie du socialisme allemand', *Le Mouvement Socialiste*, no.225, November 1910, pp.241–51.
[293] Karl Kautsky to Robert Michels, 3 April 1908, ARM/FLE. Kautsky closed with his customary greeting to Michels 'from my house to yours'.

84   ROBERT MICHELS, SOCIALISM, AND MODERNITY

für Sozialwissenschaft und Sozialpolitik.[294] Michels described the tendency of bureaucracy to expand, as an instrument of the domination of the political class and the state. Michels reiterated his observations made in his earlier *Archiv* article on the extent to which the Social Democratic Party served as a mechanism for upward social mobility of a few intelligent members of the working class, who then became 'deproletarianized'. Michels incorporated a discussion of the elite theory of his senior colleague at Turin University, Gaetano Mosca, and Vilfredo Pareto. He made use of Pareto's notion of the 'circulation of elites', while stipulating that this should be seen as a process of amalgamation rather than replacement of social groups.[295] He concluded by acknowledging a conflict between Mosca's and Pareto's notions of the inevitability of oligarchy with the Marxist view of history and promised to analyse that conflict further in an forthcoming article.[296] In his expanded, German version of the article, Michels classified the complex of tendencies hindering the realization of democracy into three levels: in human nature, in the nature of the 'political class' (here referencing the Italian elite theorists) and in the nature of organization.[297] Drawing on mass psychology, Michels diagnosed an unlimited degree of need for leadership on the part of the masses, which was also manifest among organized workers, along with 'Misoneismus', a fear of novelty, or an aversion to new things or ideas, a term which Michels seems to have acquired from Cesare Lombroso.[298]

Michels also diagnosed among the masses—and that also included the rank and file of the socialist labour movement, a definite desire for distinguishing themselves from others of lesser status (*Abhebungsbedürfnis*). This was evident among the so-called labour aristocracy. With a striking indication of the degree to which Michels was now distancing himself from socialist and syndicalist views, he also saw this characteristic at work in organized workers' attitudes towards strike-breakers. Tellingly, Michels used the term applied to strike-breakers by employers: 'Arbeitswillige', workers willing to work, rather than 'strike-breakers', let alone the more pejorative terms used by actual workers on strike. Gratuitously, Michels also borrowed a term from the Italian physiologist Angelo Mosso to

---

[294] Roberto [Robert] Michels, 'L'oligarchia organica constituzionale. Nuovi studi sulla Classe Politica', *La Riforma Sociale*, Vol.XVIII, series 2, Anno XIV, December 1907, pp.961–83, reprinted in Roberto [Robert] Michels, *Potere ad oligarchia. Organizzazione del partito ed ideologia socialista (1900–1910)*, ed. Ettore A. Albertoni, Milan, 1989, pp.431–57; Robert Michels, 'Die oligarchischen Tendenzen der Gesellschaft. Ein Beitrag zum Problem der Demokratie', *Archiv für Sozialwissenschaft und Sozialpolitik*, Vol.27 (new series), 1908, pp.73–135. See also Robert Michels, 'Der konservative Grundzug der Partei-Organisation', *Monatsschrift für Soziologie*, Jg.1, April 1909, pp.228–36; May 1909, pp.301–16.

[295] Michels, 'L'oligarchia organica constituzionale', p.451 in the Albertoni volume; Michels, 'Die oligarchischen Tendenzen der Gesellschaft', pp.75,77, 129.

[296] Michels, 'L'oligarchia organica constituzionale', pp.452–3.

[297] Michels, 'Die oligarchischen Tendenzen der Gesellschaft', p.79.

[298] Michels, 'Die oligarchischen Tendenzen der Gesellschaft', pp.83–4. See Cesare Lombroso, *Gli anarchici*, Turin, 1895.

describe this conflict: *Ergomachie*, the fight for the trough.[299] Within a relatively short time, Michels had moved from being an ardent sympathizer with revolutionary syndicalism, regarding a general strike as the best cure for the ills of parliamentary politics, to denigrating the motives of striking workers.

Michels continued to be critical of the parliamentary representative system of government, but he now drew arguments from conservatives as well as radicals like Lagardelle and anarchists. Michels cited both Rousseau ('in the moment in which a people gives itself representatives, it is no longer free') and Mosca (the 'falsity of the parliamentary legend').[300] A reader of Michels' essay might almost conclude that the last adherents of parliamentarianism were German Marxists—it was practically 'the only weapon' they had.[301]

In addition to citing Mosca, Michels also named Pareto and the latter's concept of the 'circulation of elites' as confirmation of his own view of the inherently oligarchical nature of all party organization.[302] He also cited a statement of Cesare Lombroso (writing in the Italian socialist newspaper *Avanti!*) on the potentially corrupting effects of organization and bureaucracy: 'the more the proletariat approaches the takeover of power and the wealth of the bourgeoisie, the more it takes on the vices of its opponents and becomes itself an instrument of corruption'.[303] Michels drew eminently conservative conclusions from his reflections on the oligarchical nature of organizations, conclusions which bore the stamp of Mosca's concept of the 'political class':

> History seems to teach us, that no popular movement, however strong and energetic it is, can summon forth lasting and organic changes in the social structure of civilised humankind, because the most outstanding elements of this popular movement themselves, the men who once led it on and inspired it, will separate themselves more and more from the masses, to be absorbed into the 'political class', to which they bring perhaps not so much 'new ideas', but all the more youthful creativity and practical intelligence. This they help to preserve the political class in a constantly renewed process of rejuvenation.[304]

At best, as a fall-back position, Michels conceded that the pressure from an oppositional party might help partly to mitigate the excesses of oligarchical rule, and that the labour movement was at least capable of producing its own internal critics, who, albeit against the wishes of its leadership, were critical of authority

---

[299] Michels, 'Die oligarchischen Tendenzen der Gesellschaft', pp.89–90, with a reference to A. Mosso, *Vita moderna degli Italiani*, Milan, 1906.

[300] Michels, 'Die oligarchischen Tendenzen der Gesellschaft', p.92.

[301] Michels, 'Die oligarchischen Tendenzen der Gesellschaft', p.94.

[302] Michels, 'Die oligarchischen Tendenzen der Gesellschaft', p.129.

[303] Michels, 'Die oligarchischen Tendenzen der Gesellschaft', p.128, citing Cesare Lombroso, 'I frutti di un voto', *Avanti!*, no.2987, 27 April 1905.

[304] Michels, 'Die oligarchischen Tendenzen der Gesellschaft', p.130.

86   ROBERT MICHELS, SOCIALISM, AND MODERNITY

and were willing to keep raising the question of the movement's ultimate *raison d'être*.[305]

Despite Michels' willingness to align his own arguments with those of socialism's more conservative critics, he still referred to 'our movement' (although perhaps no longer 'our party', 'movement' being a broader concept) in an essay he sent to the *Sozialistische Monatshefte* in response to Eduard Bernstein's criticism of his pessimistic formulations about the possibility of democratic change.[306] Michels' criticisms of the shortcomings of internal democracy within the party, despite its annual congresses representing every local branch of the party and its annual elections of the party executive, were also rebutted by the party paper *Vorwärts*.[307] Both Bernstein and *Vorwärts* focused on one of Michels' examples of bureaucratic control: the fact that ballot papers for the election of the executive at the annual party congresses showed a pre-printed list of candidates. *Vorwärts* corrected Michels by pointing out that the printed lists of candidates were not prepared by the executive but by the bureau of the party congress, and that the lists were composed of nominations put forward by the delegates. 'Every delegate has the right, up to a specified deadline, to make suggestions for the list.' Naturally, in practice, informal caucuses representing different tendencies of the party conferred at the congress about nominations, 'in order to avoid excessive splintering of votes'. Michels' analogy, comparing the situation to the German government printing lists of Reichstag candidates it wanted people to vote for, was misleading. In fact, the practice was comparable to a democratic election under proportional representation, in which ballot papers carried the names of candidates nominated by all parties. *Vorwärts* stated that although Michels had attended a few party congresses, he had either failed to understand the conduct of business of these 'parliaments of the party' or had managed to 'sweat away' any memory his knowledge of the party since moving to Italy.[308] Michels was not deterred by such empirical details from reasserting his principal thesis, arguing in general: 'wherever you say organization, you say tendency towards the formation of oligarchies'.[309] More specifically, other socialist parties, for example the Italian party, had made more efforts than the German party to resist the tendency towards oligarchy. The German party 'had been driven onto that course in the period of

---

[305] Michels, 'Die oligarchischen Tendenzen der Gesellschaft', pp.134, 135.

[306] Robert Michels, 'Einige Bemerkungen zum Problem der Demokratie. Eine Erwiderung', *Sozialistische Monatshefte*, Jg.12 (New series), no.25, 17 December, 1908, p.1615. See Eduard Bernstein, 'Die Demokratie in der Demokratie', *Sozialistische Monatshefte*, Jg. 12 (New series), no.18/19, 1908, pp.1106–14. The columns of the *Sozialistsche Monatshefte* had always been open to non-socialists, the magazine being run its editor Josef Bloch's own business, and it was not owned by the party.

[307] *Vorwärts*, no.296, 18 December 1908, 'Blühenden Unsinn' (under rubric 'Politische Übersicht').

[308] 'Blühenden Unsinn'. On internal democracy within the German Social Democratic Party, and for a response to Michels' arguments by a later scholar of the party's history, see Gerhard A. Ritter, *Die Arbeiterbewegung im wilhelminischen Reich*, Berlin, 1963 [1959], pp.48–51.

[309] Michels, 'Einige Bemerkungen zum Problem der Demokratie', p.1621.

MICHELS AND GERMAN SOCIAL DEMOCRACY   87

persecution during the anti-Socialist law and through the rigid, militaristically predisposed and organized milieu' of imperial Germany since then.[310]

If Michels used the words 'our movement' in debating Bernstein in the *Sozialistische Monatshefte*, he was increasingly referring to socialists in the third person in his contributions to bourgeois social science and economics journals, as in his 1909 critique of the Marxist concept of the 'immiseration' of the workers for an Italian economics journal.[311] In 1908, he sought to get a retainer from a Social Democratic Party newspaper for regular articles on Italy, but he explained to Max Weber that this was an attempt to top up his limited income as a *Privatdozent* in Turin.[312] His observations on German Social Democracy in 1909–10, during the completion of his major book on *Political Parties*, were overwhelmingly negative, and often accompanied by polemical or sarcastic turns of phrase. The German Social Democratic Party had displayed a decline in its level of idealism as it became more bureaucratic and more of an engine of economic improvement and social mobility for 'intelligent workers'.[313] German Social Democracy had always been the most nationalist and militarist of all socialist parties, something for which Bebel bore considerable personal responsibility.[314] Michels dismissed Catholic fears of the electoral successes of the Social Democratic Party: an accumulation of ballot papers could only ever become 'dangerous' if ballot papers had the power to transform society, and if the men casting them were conscious of the innate idea of socialism and willing to sacrifice themselves for it—which was evidently not the case.[315] Even in a largely positive review of a work by Kurt Eisner, which he praised for its wit and its engagement with German idealist philosophy, Michels included a back-handed pejorative description of the decadent state of German Social Democracy:

> They [Eisner's sketches] are an eloquent proof for the fact that, however much the organisational character of the party has denuded the revolutionary proletarian movement of its ethical-religious costume, there is still some room in this practical and *realpolitisch* accumulation of newspapers, ballot papers and professional officials for old-fashioned German idealism, and we find it on the very

---

[310] Michels, 'Einige Bemerkungen zum Problem der Demokratie', pp.1618–19, quotation p.1618.

[311] Roberto [Robert] Michels, 'Delucidazioni sulla teoria dell'immiserimento', *Giornale degli Economisti e Rivista di Statistica*, vol.39, series 2, no.5–6, November–December 1909, pp.417–53.

[312] Max Weber to Edgar Jaffé, 21 May 1908, in Weber, *Briefe 1906–1908*, p.574. The newspaper is only identified here as *Die Volksstimme*, possibly the Frankfurt paper of that name, which Michels had frequently contributed to in the past.

[313] Robert Michels, 'La solidarité sociale en Allemagne', *Annales de l'Institut International de Sociologie*, Vol.XII, 1910, p.23 of offprint.

[314] Review of Hellmut von Gerlach, *August Bebel, ein historischer Essay*, in *Archiv für Sozialwissenschaft und Sozialpolitik*, 28 (neue Folge), 1909, pp.827–8.

[315] Robert Michels, Review of Theodor Wacker, *Entwicklung der Sozialdemokratie in den zehn ersten Reichstagswahlen (1871–1898)*, in *Archiv für Sozialwissenschaft und Sozialpolitik*, 29, 1909, pp.257–8.

88 ROBERT MICHELS, SOCIALISM, AND MODERNITY

watershed between crude, prosaic epigonal Marxism and busy and business-like opportunism.[316]

Most significantly, for Michels, 'whoever says organization, says tendency towards oligarchy', and there was a 'profoundly aristocratic character' innate to organization. As for the German Social Democrats, they were 'fanatical partisans of the idea of organization'.[317] He concluded an article on the fundamentally conservative tendency of all organization with the following summary of the state of the party:

> The men of the party have expended their efforts and their sweat for half a century to create an exemplary organisation. Now three million workers are organized, and a bureaucracy has been called into being which rivals that of the state itself for its sense of duty, its punctiliousness and its obedience to a hierarchical order, the treasuries are full, a complex of financial and psychological interests has been constituted across the whole country. An energetic and bold tactical approach would risk everything: the work of many decades, the existence of many thousands of major and minor leaders, in short of the whole 'party'. This thought gradually becomes almost impossible to conceive of.... Thus the organisation becomes an end in itself instead of a means to an end.[318]

On one level, Michels offered a structural analysis of the sociology of large organizations. But his critique of Social Democracy also functioned on another level, that of ethics. Ultimately, in Michels' view, the masses of organized workers were incapable of demonstrating the same level of willingness to sacrifice themselves and to profess an idealistic commitment to high ethical principles that an exceptional individual like himself, whose economic interests were not those of the working class, was able to exemplify.

---

[316] Robert Michels, Review of Kurt Eisner, *Feste der Festlosen*, in *Archiv für Sozialwissenschaft und Sozialpolitik*, 28 (neue Folge), 1909, pp.805–6, quotation p.806.
[317] Michels, 'Der konservative Grundzug der Partei-Organisation', pp.232, 231.
[318] Michels, 'Der konservative Grundzug der Partei-Organisation', p.313.

3

Socialism plus Temperament

Michels and Italian Socialists

There is a long history of German visitors becoming entranced with Italy. Goethe's *Italian Journey* is just the best known of many examples of this.[1] Robert Michels, conscious of his own 'Latin' origins as a part-French Rhinelander, was happy to identify with Italy and Italians, and he became especially Italophile during his honeymoon sojourn in northern Italy with his wife Gisela, between the completion of his doctorate and marriage, and his move to Marburg in his quest for a professorship. Michels even joined the Italian Socialist Party before he joined the German party, signing up to the Turin section in November 1902. At the same time he also enrolled in the Turin Camera del Lavoro (a workers' secretariat combining representational, educational and welfare functions for organized workers).[2] Prior to this, in August, Michels had already procured introductions, such as one from Filippo Turati to a group of Milan socialists, to assist him with studies of the Italian labour movement.[3] Thus began an association with Italian socialism which supplied Michels, although always slightly on the periphery of the Italian party, with a notably wide range of contacts, from moderate (and professorial) socialists such as Achille Loria and Cesare Lombroso in Turin, to revolutionary syndicalists such as Arturo Labriola in Milan.[4] Initially, Michels played the role of interpreter of Italian conditions for a German audience (especially in the labour movement press and periodicals). He then also became an occasional contributor to the Italian socialist press, especially its radical syndicalist

---

[1] For a valuable survey of recent literature on the German-Italian relationship, see Christian Goeschel, 'A Parallel Relationship? Rethinking the Relationship between Italy and Germany, ca. 1860–1945', *Journal of Modern History*, Vol.88, 2016, pp.610–32.

[2] Membership cards for both organizations in ARM/FLE, Documenti personali. On the *camere di lavoro*, see Robert Michels, Review of Eugenio Ciacchi, *Cos'è la Camera del Lavoro?*, *Documente des Socialismus*, Bd.1, 9, 1902, p.381.

[3] Letter from Turati to Gruppo Scaramuccia, Milan, in ARM/FLE (Turati folders), 9 August 1902. Turati introduced the 'comrade and economist Dr. Robert Michels' as a 'friend of Clara Zetkin, the strongest socialist women's agitator in Germany'. The letter stated that Michels wanted to get to know the Camera del Lavoro in Milan.

[4] On the professorial socialists of Turin, see Paolo Spriano, *Storia di Torino operaia e socialista*, Turin, 1972, pp.37–60. Spriano writes (p.45): 'The Turinese socialist intellectuals do not in fact identify with the working class: they want to assist it, but do not consider it the protagonist of its own emancipation'. On Italian revolutionary syndicalism, see Gian Biagio Furiozzi, *Il sindacalismo rivoluzionario italiano*, Milan, 1977; Giovanna Cavallari, *Classe dirigente e minoranze rivoluzionarie*, Camerino, 1983, and Giorgio Volpe, *La disillusione socialista. Storia del sindacalismo rivoluzionario in Italia*, Rome, 2015.

Robert Michels, Socialism, and Modernity. Andrew G. Bonnell, Oxford University Press. © Andrew G. Bonnell 2023.
DOI: 10.1093/oso/9780192871848.003.0004

90 ROBERT MICHELS, SOCIALISM, AND MODERNITY

publications. From 1907, Michels lived and worked in Italy, after which his academic and scholarly persona began to replace his activist persona in relation to the Italian socialist movement. Michels admired the temperament of Italian socialists, which he saw as being in contrast with their German counterparts. He found the political climate in liberal Italy more congenial than that of the Kaiser's empire, and also appreciated the more liberal climate in Italian intellectual life which permitted university professors to be socialists, and vice versa.

Michels seems to have been struck by three characteristics of the Italian socialist movement that all offered marked contrasts to the situation within German Social Democracy: the prominence of Italian bourgeois intellectuals, including many university academics, in the socialist party; the greater opportunities for productive collaboration between socialists and middle-class radical parties; and a less intransigent and hostile attitude on the part of state authority towards the socialist labour movement. All three elements are strongly apparent in his reports to German social democratic newspapers on the September 1902 Italian Socialist Party congress at Imola, which Michels attended as a representative of the German Social Democratic Party.[5]

In his report to *Vorwärts* on the Imola congress, Michels remarked that a German observer was struck first of all by the fact that the Italian state railways provided concession tickets (with a discount of up to 60 per cent) to congress delegates. Such a cooperative attitude on the part of the state was quite unheard of for a German socialist—indeed, not that long before, German Social Democrats had had to hold their congresses clandestinely, outside their country.[6]

Michels did not mention that the relatively benign and mild treatment of the socialist movement by the Italian state was an even more recent development. Michels arrived in Italy shortly after Francesco Crispi's policy of harsh repression of the labour movement had been replaced by Giolitti's policy of cautious liberalization, after repression had failed to stop the growth of the labour movement.[7]

No less impressive for Michels than the hospitality of the state railways was the fact that Imola was one of the thirty-five municipalities in Italy (by Michels' count) to be governed by a socialist mayor, and the socialist delegates who arrived by train were greeted at the station not only by workers, peasants, and artisans, but also by lawyers, university professors, and doctors—'in short, all estates

---

[5] The attendance of Robert and Gisela Michels as representatives of *Vorwärts* and other German socialist newspapers is noted in the official protocol of the conference. Partito Socialista Italiano, *Rendiconto del VII Congresso Nazionale (Imola 6-7-8-9 Settembre 1902)*, Rome, 1903, p.6.

[6] Robert Michels, 'Der Kongreß der italienischen socialistischen Partei', *Vorwärts*, no.210, 9 September 1902; Dr Robert Michels, 'Ein Blick in den "Zukunftsstaat"' [I], *Mitteldeutsche Sonntags-Zeitung*, no.10, 8 March 1903.

[7] See Antonio Landolfi, *Storia del PSI. Cento Anni di Socialismo in Italia da Filippo Turati a Bettino Craxi*, Milan, 1990, pp.25, 28–31; Emilio Gentile, *Le origini dell'Italia contemporanea. L'età giolittiana*, Bari, 2003.

SOCIALISM PLUS TEMPERAMENT 91

except the clergy and the military'.[8] Even the church bells were mobilized along with all other bells in the town to salute the party congress on its first morning, to Michels' undiminished wonderment.[9] Members of the bourgeois parties did not show the same intransigent hostility to the socialists as was the norm in Germany: Michels noted that 'radicals, republicans, and even monarchists of all shades of the spectrum' showed hospitality to the delegates. Michels summed it up in an article for the *Schwäbische Tagwacht*: 'Here in Italy one lives in a freer country'.[10] Michels' report for the *Schwäbische Tagwacht* emphasized the part played by intellectuals in the Italian party:

The first thing that strikes one is what a huge percentage of the participants consists of intellectuals. As is well-known, lawyers and university academics are no rarity in the socialist party of Italy, which, as we know, is not only the party of the class of manual workers, that is, the so-called proletariat, but is also at the same time the party of the most highly educated. Indeed, among the 30 members of parliament no fewer than 28 are non-proletarians and thus only two men come from the working class. That often gave rise to a peculiar impression in so far as every time a 'genuine' proletarian spoke, a long murmur ran through the hall: 'That man was once a worker'. It is superfluous to say that this murmur did not at all call forth mockery, as in a bourgeois assembly, but honest admiration.[11]

On the second day of the congress, the congress delegates and local workers staged a demonstration march through the town of Imola, with some 5,000 participants marching to the town's old town hall. At the town hall, socialist leaders like Andrea Costa, Turati, Bissolati, and others spoke, and 'the German comrade Dr. Robert Michels also spoke at Costa's request, to celebrate the idea of the internationalism of the socialist proletariat'.[12] The deep impression these days made on Michels is shown by the series of articles he wrote on Imola for the *Mitteldeutsche Sonntags-Zeitung*, which appeared six months later and were dedicated less to analysis of the course of the congress (which was no longer recent news when these articles appeared) than to a reportage on the welcome extended by the town of Imola and the feelings of comradeship engendered there. The title of the series

---

[8] Michels, 'Ein Blick in den "Zukunftsstaat"' [I].

[9] Michels, 'Ein Blick in den "Zukunftsstaat"' [II], *Mitteldeutsche Sonntags-Zeitung*, no.11, 15 March 1903.

[10] R.M. [Robert Michels], 'Eindrücke vom Kongress der italienischen sozialistischen Partei in Imola', *Schwäbische Tagwacht*, no.226, 29 September 1902.

[11] [Michels], 'Eindrücke vom Kongress der italienischen sozialistischen Partei in Imola'. According to Michels, in 1902 the polisher Pietro Chiesa and the carpenter Rinaldo Rigola were the only Italian socialist members of parliament out of thirty who were of proletarian birth. Robert Michels, Review of Angelo Celli, Angiolo Cabrini, Pietra Chiesa, and Luigi Majno, *La difesa della vita. Documente des socialismus*, Bd.1, 11, 1902, p.482.

[12] 'Kongreß der italienischen socialistischen Partei', *Vorwärts*, 10 September 1902.

92   ROBERT MICHELS, SOCIALISM, AND MODERNITY

for the *Mitteldeutsche Sonntags-Zeitung*, 'A Look into the "Future State"' suggested that socialist-administered Imola had already realized a bit of socialism in the present, while Michels' enthusiastic descriptions of Italian warmth and hospitality may have owed as much to his Italophilia as to his socialist views.[13]

Michels' report for *Vorwärts* also focused on the two ideological tendencies in the Italian party, the reformists (represented by Filippo Turati, Leonida Bissolati, Claudio Treves, Anna Kuliscioff, and others) and the revolutionary wing of the party (represented by Enrico Ferri, Arturo Labriola, and others).[14] In another report, for the *Schwäbische Tagwacht*, Michels characterized the reformists as 'the quantitatively intellectual' tendency in the party, because of the large number of intellectuals among the 'transigent' leadership, and the radicals under Ferri as 'the qualitatively intellectual', in recognition of the distinction of Ferri and his confederates. The radicals were outvoted, with Ferri's 'intransigent' resolution on the party line defeated, and a compromise resolution from Ivanoe Bonomi succeeding. Michels confided to *Schwäbische Tagwacht* readers that he would have been happy to see the resolution on the party's tactics lean more strongly to the side of Ferri and his supporters, but with an eye to party unity Michels felt that it might not have been beneficial if Ferri had entirely got his way on the resolution.[15] At the end of the congress, Michels' report to *Vorwärts* stressed the importance of the fact that the party had avoided a split and had strengthened its unity at Imola. In addition to the outcome that allowed the differences between the two wings of the party to appear relatively minor, Michels also approved of the fact that the party executive had retained oversight of the individual sections of the party: 'The Roman character seems to resist centralisation, nonetheless we consider centralisation the precondition not only of the power to act, but also of the ideal unity' of the party. 'That even within a centralised party the individual sections can conduct themselves freely, and that even under tight centralisation intellectual freedom does not need to suffer, is shown best by German Social Democracy' (a view which Michels would depart from in subsequent years, of course). He closed by hoping that the Latin centrifugal tendencies would not prevail over a functioning party organization that allowed the party to offer a united front and retain a capacity to act.[16]

Subsequently, Michels contributed an article to the Italian party newspaper *Avanti!*, in which he compared the Imola congress with the German party's

---

[13] Michels, 'Ein Blick in den "Zukunftsstaat"' [I], and subsequent issues.

[14] Robert Michels, 'Der Kongreß der italienischen socialistischen Partei', *Vorwärts*, no.211, 10 September 1902. On the conflict between Arturo Labriola and Turati, see Richard Drake, *Apostles and Agitators: Italy's Marxist Revolutionary Tradition*, Cambridge, MA, and London, 2003, pp.93–9.

[15] R.M. [Robert Michels], '7. Kongreß der italienischen sozialistischen Partei zu Imola', *Schwäbische Tagwacht*, no.214, 15 September 1902.

[16] Robert Michels, 'Der italienische Kongreß', *Vorwärts*, no.214, 13 September 1902. In the *Schwäbische Tagwacht*, Michels also stressed that it was a great success for the conference to have banished the danger of a schism. [Michels], '7. Kongreß der italienischen sozialistischen Partei'.

Munich congress. He began by drawing a contrast between the Munich congress, which had dealt with numerous concrete questions of high foreign and domestic politics (tariffs, the right of association and assembly, militarism, etc.), and the Imola congress, at which the Italian Socialist Party was largely preoccupied with its own internal matters. He also contrasted the prominent role of women at the Munich congress with Imola, at which 'not a single woman spoke'. Michels also pointed to the greater divisions over theoretical questions in Germany, suggesting that the Germans disagreed over 'how to see things', while the Italians disagreed over 'how to act'. One major difference between the two parties was that while Imola approved alliances with bourgeois radicals, August Bebel's resolution passed by the Munich congress imposed such strict conditions on alliances with bourgeois parties as to make them virtually unachievable. Michels explained to readers of *Avanti!* that the difference between the two parties on this point was more apparent than real, as the German party had no credible allies, given that even the left of the German bourgeois party spectrum were outright imperialists and militarists. Michels concluded by stressing the importance of party unity, which both congresses had succeeded in reaffirming. France was a dire example of how disunity could weaken the movement of the proletariat. There was also the sad example of England, with its four 'socialist parties', which could barely muster half a dozen members of parliament between them.[17]

Even before the Imola congress, and before taking up his membership of the Italian Socialist Party, Michels had written an appreciative account of the Italian party for the Frankfurt bourgeois reformist journal *Das freie Wort* in November 1901. Socialism, Michels wrote, had had its origins in northern Europe and was a relatively recent transplant in southern Europe. In Spain and Italy, anarchism and radical republicanism had preceded it. Only in the early 1880s did Italian translations of the works of Lassalle, Marx, and Louis Blanc begin to have an influence, the emergence of socialism in Italy being marked by the entry of the economist (and former follower of Bakunin) Andrea Costa into the Italian parliament in 1882. By 1900, the number of socialist parliamentary deputies had reached thirty-three. For the benefit of German readers, Michels compared and contrasted the Italian Socialist Party with its German counterpart, adopting the standpoint of a sympathetic German observer. Michels found that the idea of the 'state of the future' played less of a role in Italian socialism compared with German Social Democracy, but the campaign for the eight-hour day, as shown by the Italian industrial disputes of spring 1901, was in full swing, thanks to the 'keen propaganda of the leaders and the selfless mutual support of the workers'.[18] The

---

[17] Roberto [Robert] Michels, 'Fra due congressi. Imola e Monaco', *Avanti!*, Anno VI, no.2097, 8 October 1902.

[18] Robert Michels, 'Der Sozialismus in Italien', *Das freie Wort*, Jg.1, no.16, 20 November 1901, pp.492–8, quotation p.495.

organization of women workers was more advanced in Italy than in Germany (although this was not yet manifest at party congresses, as Michels discovered at Imola). Despite the many similarities between the two parties, Michels noted that the Italian socialists differed from the Germans in that while the German Social Democrats remained strictly isolated from other parties, the Italian socialists were more ready to collaborate with bourgeois reformist parties, the radicals and republicans, and with bourgeois intellectuals, a collaboration that Michels found had positive advantages, in that the bourgeois reformists did not spend as much time attacking their rivals on the left as did their counterparts in Germany. Italian socialism also enjoyed a more heterogeneous social base than did the mainly working-class German party. While the 'great majority of the propertied and educated' remained hostile to the 'new ideas' of Social Democracy in Germany, these new ideas had reached 'almost all strata of the population' in Italy. This trend was helped by the fact that the Italian party spectrum as a whole leant more to the left than in Germany, thanks to the more 'democratic tendency of the whole people' in Italy, and their 'innate tolerance for differences in opinion'. Michels again pointed to the significant number of Italian intellectuals who sympathized with socialist ideas, while the Italian Socialist Party itself counted significant intellectuals such as Enrico Ferri in its ranks.[19]

In another article for *Das freie Wort*, in 1902, Michels described the growth of socialist organization in rural Italy, particularly in the north of the country.[20] Whereas Italian socialism, like its German counterpart, had originally been strongest in the industrial cities, growing inequality in more capitalistically organized agriculture, especially in the Po valley, was leading to the growth of socialism among Italian rural labourers. Michels stressed the moral benefits of socialist organization to the lives of Italian workers, including educational efforts to combat illiteracy (important for electoral purposes in a country where literacy qualifications were needed for voting), and a reduction in alcohol abuse and even the crime rate.[21] Michels also described the successes of the strike movement of rural labourers (including the severely exploited women rice-growers), which he described as distinguished by its 'chivalry', and which also benefited from an unusually neutral attitude on the part of the state authorities.[22] He concluded by citing Filippo Turati on 'the modern class struggle': 'Only through this can a noble spirit still be seized by a sacred fire, only through this can collapsing religions be replaced, only through this can life be endowed anew with worth and with an

---

[19] Michels, 'Der Sozialismus in Italien', pp.496–7.

[20] Robert Michels, 'Der italienische Sozialismus auf dem Lande', *Das freie Wort*, Jg.2, no.2, 1902 (offprint in FLE). In part, Michels drew here on Ivanoe Bonomi and Carlo Vezzani's work on the proletarian movement around Mantua, which he reviewed for *Documente des Sozialismus*, Vol.1, 6, 1902, pp.247–8.

[21] Michels, 'Der italienische Sozialismus auf dem Lande', pp.8–10 of offprint.

[22] Michels, 'Der italienische Sozialismus auf dem Lande', pp.10–11.

ideal.'[23] While Michels was partly framing his account of the Italian class struggle for the non-socialist bourgeois reformist journal, this emphasis on the ideal values embodied in the socialist movement is typical of his early writings. For example, Michels returned to the theme in March 1903 in the journal of the Gesellschaft für Ethische Kultur (Society for Ethical Culture), drawing on some of the same sources (Bonomi and Vezzani) as well as on work by Enrico Ferri and others to document the work of moral improvement accomplished by Italian socialism, with violence and drunkenness declining where socialist organization was successfully established.[24]

As noted in Chapter 2, Michels wrote to Kautsky in December 1901 offering to contribute articles on Italy to *Die Neue Zeit*.[25] In the following months, Michels set about making himself the German Social Democratic press's expert on Italian conditions, contributing work to a range of newspapers and journals. In April 1902, he contributed the first of a series of articles on the Italian women's movement to Clara Zetkin's *Die Gleichheit*. He stressed the recent rapid growth of the Italian Socialist Party, which was swiftly gaining the allegiance in both the urban and the rural proletariat in northern and central Italy, as well as gaining support among '*the best elements*' of other strata of society, 'especially among the educated'.[26] Over most of 1903, Michels then contributed a series of articles to *Die Gleichheit* on the history of the proletarian women's movement in Italy, paying tribute to the work of pioneering socialist feminists like Anna Maria Mozzoni and Anna Kuliscioff.[27]

Michels wrote numerous reviews of works on Italian socialism for Eduard Bernstein's *Documente des Socialismus*, a journal dedicated to the history and literature of socialism. Given the documentary character of the publication, and its ecumenical approach to the different currents of socialism, Michels avoided striking a polemical note in his accounts of Italian socialist writing. He frequently commented on the extent to which Italian university professors were engaged in the socialist cause (clearly a point close to his heart), noting the existence of a 'very numerous group of university lecturers, who put their body and soul into the struggle for socialism'.[28] Elsewhere, in a piece for *Ethische Kultur*, Michels

---

[23] Filippo Turati, *La moderna lotta di classe*, Milan, 1897, p.10, cited at p.14.

[24] Dr Robert Michels, 'Einfluß des Sozialismus in Italien auf die Sittlichkeit der Bevölkerung', *Ethische Kultur*, Jg. XI, Nr.10, 7. März 1903, pp.76–7.

[25] Michels to Karl Kautsky, 6 December 1901, IISG, Archief Kautsky, K D XVII, no.534.

[26] Dr Robert Michels, 'Der Kampf um das Arbeiterinnenachutzgesetz in Italien', *Die Gleichheit*, Jg.12, no.9, 23 April 1902, p.68; emphasis in original.

[27] Dr Robert Michels, 'Rückblick auf die Geschichte der proletaischen Frauenbewegung in Italien', *Die Gleichheit*, Jg.13, 1, 1 January 1903, pp.2–3; no.2, 14 January 1903, pp.11–13; no.5, 25 February 1903, pp.36–8; no.8, 8 April 1903, pp.58–60; no.11, 20 May 1903, pp.83–5; no.17, 12 August 1903, pp.131–4.

[28] Dr Robert Michels, Review of Giovanni Lombardi, *Lo Stato. Saggio di Sociologia*, in *Documente des Socialismus*, Vol.1, 8, 1902, p.338. See also Dr Robert Michels, Review of Arnaldo Lucci, *Giustizia Nuova*, in *Documente des Socialismus*, Vol.1, 8, 1902, p.338; Dr Robert Michels, Review of Ettore

96 ROBERT MICHELS, SOCIALISM, AND MODERNITY

refuted an anti-socialist polemic by a Neapolitan academic by enumerating the university professors and lecturers who belonged to the socialist party or supported Marxian ideas (Enrico Leone, Arturo Labriola, Ernesto Cesare Longobardi, Benedetto Croce), describing them as 'men who not only have an excellent academic reputation, but who have entered the socialist movement out of the purest idealism, despite the fact that they must have known that they would not be able to satisfy their supposed ambition by this path.'[29] Michels gently took issue with a booklet by Eugenio Ciacchi on the *camere di lavoro*, in which Ciacchi criticized the degree to which non-proletarian elements were starting to get involved in these workers' bodies and extended the same criticism about the parliamentary caucus of the socialist party. While Michels sympathized with Ciacchi on the first point, he argued that the involvement of bourgeois intellectuals in parliament for the socialist party had been beneficial: 'In no other country, in my view, does the proletariat owe as much gratitude to the intelligentsia from bourgeois circles for the most selfless action in service of their rights as in the homeland of the author.'[30]

Michels did express sympathy for the radical left wing of Italian socialism, giving a friendly account of the Milan revolutionary syndicalist Arturo Labriola's pamphlet on *Ministries and Socialism*, a polemical tract against Filippo Turati's support for parliamentarianism. Michels cited Labriola's (characteristically polemical) broadside against reformism, equated with 'comfortable, cretinous legalitarianism' (*cretino e comodo legalitarismo*) and noted that Labriola regretted that that the intransigent wing of the German Social Democrats were no longer seen as providing a model to the Italian party. The idea of a 'step-by-step evolution' had come to be too influential in the Italian party, according to Labriola. However, Michels expressed regret over Labriola's call for the expulsion of Turati from the party.[31] If Turati appeared to be a cautious moderate to Michels in 1902, it is worth recalling that a few years earlier, as part of a state crackdown on the

---

Ciccotti, *La Guerra e la Pace nel Mondo antico*, *Documente des Socialismus*, Vol.1, 8, 1902, pp.381–2; Dr Robert Michels, Review of Giovanni Montemartini, *Le leghe di Miglioramento fra i Contadini nell'Oltrepò Pavese*, *Documente des Socialismus*, Vol.1, 8, 1902, p.383.

[29] Dr Robert Michels, Review of R. Fornelli, '*Dove si va?*', *Appunti di Psichologia Politica*, in *Ethische Kultur*, Jg. XI, Nr.30, 25. Juli 1903, p.239. See also Michels' obituary for Antonio Labriola, in which Michels stressed the fact that Italian socialists could become university professors, a sign of greater academic freedom in practice than that which prevailed in Germany, where universities were forced into 'the straitjacket of state-upholding purity'. 'Antonio Labriola', *Mitteldeutsche Sonntags-Zeitung*, Jg.XI, Nr.7, 14 February 1904, p.6.

[30] Michels, Review of Ciacchi, *Cos'è la Camera del Lavoro?*.

[31] Robert Michels, Review of Arturo Labriola, *Ministero e Socialismo. Risposta a Filippo Turati*, *Documente des Socialismus*, Bd.1, 9, 1902, p.382. On Arturo Labriola (not to be confused with the older Italian philosopher and Marx scholar, Antonio Labriola), see Dora Marucco, *Arturo Labriola e il sindacalismo rivoluzionario in Italia*, Turin, 1970; D. Marucco, 'Arturo Labriola', in Franco Andreucci and Tommaso Detti, eds., *Il movimento operaio italiano. Dizionario biografico 1853–1943*, Vol. III, Rome, 1977, pp.39–51. On Turati, see I. Barbadoro, 'Filippo Turati', in Andreucci and Detti, eds., *Il movimento operaio italiano*, Vol.V, Rome, 1978, pp.131–44.

Italian labour movement, Turati had been imprisoned for fourteen months by a military tribunal (his wife Anna Kuliscioff was also detained), out of a sentence of twelve years' imprisonment, for telling demonstrators that the hour of action had not *yet* struck.[32]

Michels also introduced the writing of the criminologist Enrico Ferri, from the revolutionary faction of the Italian Socialist Party, to the readers of Bernstein's journal, giving a detailed review of Ferri's *Il metodo rivoluzionario* ('the revolutionary method'). Ferri identified himself in his book as a member of the 'revolutionary-intransigent tendency' within the party, in opposition to Turati's 'ministerial ultra-reformism' and the 'moderate reformism' of Bissolati and the majority of the party. In Michels' summary of Ferri, these tactical differences had their roots in the psychological characteristics of their leading representatives ('e.g. combative nature (*Kampfeslust*), tendency to indolence, insufficient contact with the actual proletariat'). Ferri sought to advance the cause of socialism by promoting the 'formation of socialist consciences', a term Michels equated with 'class consciousness'.[33] Later, in 1908, Michels would publish a German translation of Ferri's *Metodo rivoluzionario*, as he engaged more closely with Ferri's militant and ethically grounded variety of socialist thought (and with the 'social anthropological' premises of Lombroso's disciples).[34]

Michels sought to give fair treatment to Filippo Turati and the reformist wing of Italian socialism within the pages of *Documente des Socialismus*, although he gave a pamphlet by Turati a third of the space he devoted to a pamphlet by Turati's critic Arturo Labriola in the same issue of the journal. Michels credited Turati with being a brilliant stylist (as even his opponents acknowledged). In addition to being a distinguished writer and advocate, Turati was also, in Michels' view, a 'thoroughly scientifically educated Marxist'.[35] Michels also gave an even-handed review of Achille Loria's critique of Marx, which he presented as analogous to Bernstein's revisionism in Germany, although he noted that Loria might have done more to address 'the well-known Neapolitan university professor' Benedetto Croce's criticisms of Loria's own work.[36] Loria's contribution to Italian socialist thought has recently been characterized as 'derived less from Marx and Engels than from a medley of positivism and determinism'. This is manifest in Loria's

---

[32] Barbadoro, 'Filippo Turati', p.135.

[33] Robert Michels, Review of Enrico Ferri, *Il metodo rivoluzionario*, *Documente des Socialismus*, Bd.1, 12, 1902, pp.530–2, quotations p.531.

[34] Enrico Ferri, *Die revolutionäre Methode* (trans. Robert Michels), Leipzig, 1908. On Ferri, see F. Andreucci, 'Enrico Ferri', in Andreucci and Detti, eds., *Il movimento operaio italiano*, Vol.III, pp.342–8.

[35] Robert Michels, Review of Filippo Turati, *Le riforme urgenti del processo penale*, *Documente des Socialismus*, Bd.1, 9, 1902, p.383.

[36] Robert Michels, Review of Achille Loria, *Marx e la sua dottrina*, *Documente des Socialismus*, Bd.1, 10, 1902, p.435. On Loria, see S. Panciroli Camporesi, 'Achille Loria', in Andreucci and Detti, eds., *Il movimento operaio italiano*, Vol.III, pp.157–64. At this time, Loria was a professor of economics at the University of Padua. He moved to a professorship at Turin in 1903.

essay on Charles Darwin and Marx, which posited a law of progressive meliorative development and a single principle of evolutionary development underlying both the natural and social worlds.[37] In this respect, Loria's thinking was fairly typical of Italian socialism at this time.[38] Michels was full of praise for Benedetto Croce's own critical essays on Marxism, which he described as 'rich in content and deeply thoughtful', although he did not engage explicitly with Croce's theoretical philosophical position. Instead, Michels noted the vigour with which Croce criticized both Marx's German epigones and the critics of Marxism.[39]

While evincing particular sympathy for representatives of the 'intransigent' tendency within Italian socialism, Michels preferred to take the position in his reviews for Bernstein's journal that the differences within the party did not amount to a 'crisis of Marxism' in Italy, and generally took an irenic approach to these factional conflicts in the Italian party.[40] Thus Michels gave a positive review of Giovanni Lerda's brochure on *Socialism and its Tactics*, which argued against electoral alliances between socialists and other parties of the 'left', on the grounds that such a coalition would lead to an inner weakening of the socialist party. At the same time, he noted Bernstein's disagreement with Lerda's position.[41] Lerda still allowed for the conception of Italian socialism as a broad church, which included not only Marxists. Furthermore, Michels cited Lerda as arguing that: 'The few real Marxists in the Italian party have become unsteady in many of their views, for example, in their belief in the materialist view of history, for they had seen what role is played in the education of the masses by precisely the *moral* factor'.[42] In this, Lerda's views seem to have been congenial to Michels, who was drawn to Italian socialism not by the purity of its Marxist doctrines, but by its *élan* and the ethical qualities of its struggles for social and political progress.

In addition to introducing German readers to the range of opinion in the Italian labour movement, Michels also reviewed a wide variety of works on Italy for the pages of *Documente des Socialismus*, covering Italian social thought, legal issues, the condition of the peasantry and rural workers, women's issues, literature, and other topics. Michels also contributed historical essays to Bernstein's journal, dealing for example with the founding of the Partito Operaio as an exclusively proletarian movement in Milan in 1882–3. Michels described the belief of

[37] Panciroli Camporesi, 'Achille Loria', p.160.

[38] Ilaria Porciani and Mauro Moretti, 'The Polycentric Structure of Italian Historical Writing', in Stuart Macintyre et al., eds., *The Oxford History of Historical Writing, Volume 4: 1800–1945*, Oxford and New York, 2011, p.235.

[39] Robert Michels, Review of Benedetto Croce, *Materialismo storico ed economia Marxistica, saggi critici, Documente des Socialismus*, Bd.1, 12, 1902, p.530.

[40] Robert Michels, Review of Giovanni Lerda, *Il socialismo e la sua tatttica* (2nd edn), *Documente des Socialismus*, Bd.1, 10, 1902, p.434.

[41] Michels, Review of Giovanni Lerda, *Il socialismo e la sua tatttica* (2nd edn), pp.434–5.

[42] Michels, Review of Giovanni Lerda, *Il socialismo e la sua tatttica* (2nd edn), p.434. On the ideological divide within Italian socialism, see also Michels' Review of Ottavio Dinale, *Diversità di tendenze o equivoco?*, in *Documente des Socialismus*, Vol.1, 8, 1902, p.337.

the founders of the Italian workers' party that people of bourgeois origins had to be excluded from the party as an expression of the Italian labour movement's immaturity.[43] He characterized the founding of the Partito Operaio as an important step leading to the later unification of the 'manual workers of the *Partito Operaio* with the intellectual workers of the *Socialisti* to form a comprehensive socialist party' in 1891.[44] In 1905, Michels contributed an essay on Giuseppe Garibaldi's links with socialism. Michels counted Garibaldi as a socialist, in part because of his sympathy for the Workers' International Association, but largely for his great idealism and his republican convictions.[45] Michels acknowledged that Garibaldi had only a vague understanding of class struggle and adhered to conservative views on property rights and inheritance, but quoted Garibaldi as saying that socialism was the 'sun of the future': 'Il Socialismo è il sole dell'Avvenire!'.[46] Michels also noted that while Garibaldi considered himself a citizen of the world, he retained a strong patriotic feeling of attachment to Italian irredentism.[47]

In articles for the non-socialist, bourgeois reformist journal *Ethische Kultur*, Michels repeatedly stressed the ethical qualities of Italian socialism. He made use of an advertisement in the Roman party paper *Avanti!* to mock the anti-socialist cliché that socialist agitators lived the high life at the expense of workers who gave up their hard-earned pennies to the party. He pointed out that the socialist newspaper editor needed good qualifications, including some literary ability and economic knowledge, had to conduct agitational lectures and organizational work in addition to editorial duties, and had to cope with hostile conditions in a small, priest-ridden town, all for a salary that only amounted to the average wage for a worker. In this depiction of the life of a dedicated socialist party functionary (who had to 'either be a bourgeois idealist with private means or be living in genuinely patriarchal simplicity'), there is no hint of the gap between party officials and rank and file that would later be at the core of Michels' critique of socialist parties.[48]

In a June 1903 article for the same journal, Michels also stressed the ethically uplifting qualities of the Italian socialist movement, citing at length a piece from the Turin socialist newspaper *Il Grido del Popolo* on the negative effects of a militarist education. Michels commended *Il Grido del Popolo* for its efforts in educating the proletariat, 'for the more quickly and more refined the emotional life of the working class develops, the sooner the latter will be in a position to break the

---

[43] Dr Robert Michels, 'Eine exclusiv proletarische Bewegung in Italien im Jahre 1883', *Documente des Socialismus*, Vol.4, 2, 1904, pp.64–9, here p.64.

[44] Michels, 'Eine exclusiv proletarische Bewegung in Italien im Jahre 1883', p.69.

[45] Dr Robert Michels, 'Die Beziehungen Giuseppe Garibaldis zum Sozialismus', *Dokumente des Sozialismus*, Vol.V, 4, 1905; pp.183–6; Heft 6, pp.275–9.

[46] Michels, 'Die Beziehungen Giuseppe Garibaldis zum Sozialismus', pp.185, 277–9.

[47] Michels, 'Die Beziehungen Giuseppe Garibaldis zum Sozialismus', p.184.

[48] Dr Robert Michels, 'Wie die sozialdemokratischen Hetzer vom Arbeitergroschen leben', in *Ethische Kultur*, Jg. XI, Nr.9, 28 February 1903, p.71.

100   ROBERT MICHELS, SOCIALISM, AND MODERNITY

hold of the social and economic privileges of the possessing and ruling class.' Michels seemed to consider moral education a precondition of success in the class struggle, rather than as a possible outcome of such a struggle.[49] In a subsequent article for *Ethische Kultur*, Michels praised the high moral sense of *Avanti!* for the way it reported a murder out of jealousy. The socialist paper refused to speak of a 'crime of love', defining love as the opposite of vanity, desire for revenge, and jealousy shown by the murderer. Michels contrasted this ethically serious outlook on the part of the *Avanti!* with the sensationalism typical of much of the bourgeois press.[50]

In further examples of Michels' emphasis on the services of the Italian socialist movement to the moral improvement of its country, he approvingly cited the Venetian socialist writer Carlo Monticelli's condemnation of the resort to violent means of settling disputes. In the face of what Michels called the 'tradition of the dagger among a section of republicans' in Italy, and the tendency 'of supporters of anarchism to all manner of violent acts... especially in the minds of the passionate inhabitants of the Romagna', Michels considered it noteworthy that the civilizing effects of socialist ideas were making headway against such 'atavism of particular strata of the proletariat'.[51] He also cited the Mantua socialist newspaper *La Nuova Terra* on the relief of Italian landowners at the fact that stealing was being reduced as local labourers became organized. Michels did not omit to add, however, that while the landowners were right to note the effects of ethical improvement and the discipline of socialist organization, they would do well not be too complacent at the growth of a powerful workers' organization.[52] In September 1903, describing conditions in southern Italy in an article for the bourgeois feminist journal *Die Frau* (on the role of women in strikes in Italy), Michels wrote that in this part of Italy, 'the labour movement has not yet sufficiently civilized the masses'.[53] It is clear from his writings for middle-class reformist journals that Michels saw the 'civilizing of the masses' as part of the work of the Italian socialist movement, even if he was also framing the discussion of the Italian movement in ways that would meet with the approval of his readers.

In addition to reporting on the Italian socialist movement for a German readership, Michels also began to intervene in debates within the Italian party. While Michels' articles on Italy for German readers tended to stress the ethically admirable nature of the Italian movement and used the (then) more liberal political

---

[49] Robert Michels, 'Geflügelverkäuferin und Geschichtsunterricht, eine Parabel', in *Ethische Kultur*, Jg. XI, Nr.24, 13. Juni 1903, p.189.

[50] R. [Robert] Michels, 'Was heißt "Liebe"?', *Ethische Kultur*, Jg. XI, Nr.28, 11 July 1903, p.222.

[51] R.M. [Robert Michels], 'Die Erziehung des Proletariats zur Selbstbeherrschung', in *Ethische Kultur*, Jg.XI, Nr.29, 18. Juli 1903, pp.229–30.

[52] RM [Robert Michels], [under the rubric 'Streiflichter'] 'Gott sei dank, nun stehlen sie nicht mehr!', in *Ethische Kultur*, Jg. XI, Nr.31, 1 August 1903, S.246.

[53] Dr Robert Michels, 'Die Frau als Streikende im Lohnkampf', *Die Frau*, Jg.10, Nr.12, September 1903, p.757.

climate in Italy as a foil to critique political conditions in Germany, from 1903 Michels used his commentaries in Italian newspapers and journals on developments in Germany as a springboard for interventions in Italian socialist politics, in which Michels sided with the left around Arturo Labriola and criticized the reformist tendencies of Filippo Turati.

In January 1903, Michels used the occasion of the Krupp scandal in Germany to subject Turati's lukewarm position on republicanism to a gentle critique in the Neapolitan socialist journal *La Strada*, while stressing at the outset that he admired not only Turati's 'intellect but also the clarity of *some* of his views'.[54] Michels showed how in Germany the Kaiser, far from being above the party-political fray, was able to conduct the most intemperate propaganda campaign against the largest political party in the country with complete impunity because the *lèse-majesté* laws gagged the opposition from responding directly against the Kaiser, except in the mildest possible terms. For Michels, '*all socialists must be unambiguously republicans, not only in semi-feudal Germany but, it seems to me, also in no less semi-feudal Italy*'.[55]

In July 1903, Michels contributed a critical analysis of the electoral tactics of the German Social Democrats to the Milan syndicalist paper *Avanguardia Socialista*, where it appeared alongside a leading article by Arturo Labriola which rejected any suggestion that the Italian socialists should try to participate in parliamentary government in the current state of the Italian parliamentary system. A note by the editor introduced Michels to the readership as a candidate in the recent German Reichstag elections, and promised more articles in future from 'l'ottimo compagno Michels', a description that clearly aligned Michels' with Labriola's left-syndicalist tendency.[56] Labriola had warmly welcomed Michels' offer of an article on this topic, even though he had to tell Michels that 'we have no money to pay anyone'.[57] For Michels to waive his usual honorarium (especially given that he depended on honoraria and royalties for an income) suggests a significant degree of political affinity with Labriola at this time.

Michels also contributed an article on the elections to the Rome-based socialist newspaper *Avanti!*, which also stressed the discomfiture of the divided bourgeois

---

[54] Roberto [Robert] Michels, 'L'affare Krupp e l'idea repubblicana', *La Strada*, Vol.2, no.2, 16 January 1903, pp.37–8; emphasis added. On the suicide of the arms manufacturer and friend of the Kaiser Fritz Krupp after the Social Democratic press had aired reports of Krupp's homosexuality during his visits to Capri, see Alex Hall, *Scandal, Sensation and Social Democracy: The SPD Press and Wilhelmine Germany, 1890-1914*, Cambridge, 1977, pp.176–81. A wave of raids on the Social Democratic press and Reichstag deputies followed the revelations in *Vorwärts*, reflecting the ties between the Krupp family and the state. The complicity of Neapolitan politicians and press in the Krupp scandal made the story of particular interest to the socialist papers of Naples.
[55] Michels, 'L'affare Krupp e l'idea repubblicana', p.38; emphasis in original.
[56] Dott. Roberto [Robert] Michels, 'La tattica dei socialisti tedeschi alle Elezioni Generali Politiche', and a. l., 'Parentesi. Participazione al potere', *Avanguardia Socialista*, Anno II, no.28, 5 July 1903.
[57] Labriola to Michels, 23 June 1903, ARM/FLE; also in Giorgio Volpe, ed., *Il carteggio fra Roberto Michels e i sindacalisti rivoluzionari*, Naples, 2018, pp.119–20.

102 ROBERT MICHELS, SOCIALISM, AND MODERNITY

democratic or left-liberal parties at the hands of the Social Democrats, as well as attacking the bourgeois left-liberals for their inconsistent behaviour in supporting reactionary candidates in many of the second-round elections. Michels took issue with Bernstein, who regretted the weakening of the bourgeois democratic groups. Michels welcomed the clearer division in the landscape between clearly bourgeois parties and the socialist democrats.[58] Michels published a lengthier treatment of the German elections in the non-socialist periodical *La Riforma Sociale*. In this article he again emphasized the non-existence of a bourgeois radical left in Germany, unlike Italy: '*A* [bourgeois] *extreme left, anti-monarchical and clearly anti-militarist, does not exist in Germany.*'[59]

After the Dresden congress of the German Social Democrats, which was generally viewed as a victory over the revisionist wing of the party left, Michels provided a commentary for the *Avanguardia Socialista*, suggesting a common cause in his fight against revisionism in the German party and Arturo Labriola's opposition to Turati's reformism. Michels portrayed the congress as a 'complete victory for the revolutionary tactic' against the revisionist tendency, with the overwhelming majority of delegates rejecting 'sterile and impotent reformism'. However, Michels cautioned that reformism still disposed of its newspapers, periodicals, and circles within the party, and would seek to continue to reinterpret the party line. The wording of the resolution itself, Michels, noted, by reaffirming that the party was revolutionary 'in the best sense of the word', left a back door open for possible interpretation and qualification of the word 'revolutionary'.[60]

After the Dresden congress in Germany, Michels' commentaries on Italian socialism for the German party press became more openly partisan in their criticisms of Turati and the Italian reformists. In January 1904, writing about the expulsion of the French 'ministerialist' socialist Millerand from the French party, Michels drew a comparison with other socialist parties where practical revisionism was at work, including in Italy: 'Comrade Turati and his friends, who do not even see anything wrong with a socialist accepting a minister's position in a monarchy, will hit on a clear warning signal on their path to His Majesty's ministry. Now the air will probably be going out of them too.'[61] At the same time, Michels offered Kautsky a critique of Italian revisionism for the *Neue Zeit*, which would complement the writings of Rosa Luxemburg and Kautsky himself on the

---

[58] Dott. Roberto [Robert] Michels, 'Democrazia e socialismo in Germania (Dopo le elezioni)', *Avanti!*, Anno VII, n.2375, 18 July 1903 (leading article).

[59] Dott. Roberto [Robert] Michels, 'Psicologia e statistica delle elezioni generali politiche in Germania (Giugno 1903)', *La Riforma Sociale*, Fasc.7, Anno X, Vol.XIII, seconda serie, 15 July 1903, pp.541–67, quotation p.13 of offprint; emphasis in original.

[60] Roberto [Robert] Michels, 'Dalla Germania. I resultati del congresso di Dresda', *Avanguardia Socialista*, Anno II, no.41, 4 October 1903.

[61] Robert Michels, 'Das Ende vom Liede Millerand', *Volksstimme* (Magdeburg), Jg. 15, Nr.8, 10 January 1904, pp.1–2.

SOCIALISM PLUS TEMPERAMENT   103

situation in France, albeit warning that it could provoke a feud with Turati, Claudio Treves, and others linked to the German *Sozialistische Monatshefte*.[62]

In March 1904, Michels intervened directly in the Italian party's Bologna congress, in support of Arturo Labriola's motion condemning Millerand-style ministerialism, a resolution clearly aimed at the Turati wing of the party. Not only did Michels himself intervene, he also contrived to get Kautsky to weigh in on the Labriola resolution. Michels sent Kautsky a copy of Labriola's proposed resolution, which Kautsky subjected to careful criticism, stressing the need to avoid formulations which could be considered to lend support to anarchist positions. 'Some sentences', Kautsky warned, 'could be given a more extreme interpretation than is presumably intended'. Kautsky drew a distinction between 'ministerialism' and actively engaging in the implementation of social reform legislation in the interest of the workers.[63] Michels translated Kautsky's letter and sent it to the *Avanguardia Socialista*, which published it under the title: 'Are We Anarchists? A Letter from Karl Kautsky'. Walter Mocchi in the *Avanguardia Socialista* (co-editor of the paper with Arturo Labriola) proudly proclaimed the adhesion to the *Avanguardia*'s line of Kautsky, 'the most authentic and recognized interpreter of Marxist thought, which tradition he continues, the leading editor of the *Neue Zeit*', while playing down Kautsky's more critical comments. The *Avanguardia* also published an accompanying letter from Michels, addressed to Labriola:

> Dear Labriola,
> Here, *in a most conscientious translation*, is the response of comrade Karl Kautsky to your question. *I believe you will be content, especially as Kautsky has left no doubt of where his sympathies lie in the internal (intestina) struggle in the Italian party.*
>> As far as I am concerned, you know that—for the main part—I am with you.
>> It is especially [the issue of] monarchism that separates me from Turati.
>> We shall see each other at Bologna.
>> Cordially yours,
>>> Roberto Michels.[64]

---

[62] Michels to Karl Kautsky, 10 January 1904, IISG Archief Kautsky K D XVII, 536.

[63] Kautsky to Robert and Gisela Michels, 11 March 1904, ARM/FLE.

[64] Karl Kautsky, 'Siamo noi anarchici? Una lettura di Carlo Kautsky', *Avanguardia Socialista*, II, 65, 20 March, 1903, with comments by Walter Mocchi and an accompanying letter by Roberto [Robert] Michels. Emphases in original. A couple of years later, Michels contributed a laudatory profile of Kautsky to the *Avanguardia Socialista*, stressing Kautsky's opposition to reformist opportunism, and citing his 'almost unconditional support for the *Avanguardia* wing for the congress of Bologna' as a key example. Roberto [Robert] Michels, 'Idee e uomini. Karl Kautsky', *Avanguardia Socialista*, Vol.III

104   ROBERT MICHELS, SOCIALISM, AND MODERNITY

In its reporting of the Bologna congress, the *Avanguardia Socialista* gave a prominent place to Michels' address, in which Michels' role was ostensibly to bring greetings from German comrades (he was attending as a correspondent for the left-radical *Leipziger Volkszeitung*).[65] Michels stated that the eyes of all Germans socialists were turned on Italy, with love and the solicitude of a big brother towards a younger brother struggling with a serious illness (the *Avanguardia* noted vigorous applause here). Michels recalled the recent triumphs of the German party and stressed the lessons of the Dresden party congress in reaffirming the 'republican essence of the socialist party' (greeted with more applause).[66]

Michels in turn reported on the proceedings of the Bologna congress for the German Social Democratic press. In the *Sächsische Arbeiter-Zeitung*, Michels described the Italian party as being at a 'crossroads':

> The congress...will decide whether the party will persist in the more or less shame-faced position it has adopted of being a party of government, indeed, whether it will extend this position even further by taking a royal ministry, or whether it wants to escape from the *cul de sac* in which it has managed to lose itself und once again march forward on the broad highway [*Heerstrasse*], which may not lead to a comfortable ministerial palace, but which sets a straighter path against the enemy.[67]

Michels warned of the risk that the Italian party, in the event that the reformist wing under Turati prevailed, would succumb to 'French Millerandism', made worse by the compromise with the monarchy that participation in an Italian government would entail. Turati's position, motivated by a number of factors, including the desire to see concrete improvements as soon as possible, and an overestimation of the potential of parliamentary activity, risked breaking with fundamental principles of Marxism. In his search for allies in the 'moderate bourgeoisie', Turati's wing of the party was declaring war on its revolutionary elements. Michels suggested that 'long years of work in bureaucratic mind-numbing details'

(2nd seriers), no.111, 28 January 1905, p.1. On this exchange, see Volpe, *La disillusione socialista*, pp.65–6.

[65] Michels' credentials for the Bologna Congress in ARM/FLE: Documenti personali, dated April 1904.

[66] Robert Michels, 'VIII Congresso Nazionale', *Avanguardia Socialista*, Anno II, no.69, 1 April 1904. (Michels' name is singled out in large bold type, in the style of a sub-heading); transcript also in Partito Socialista Italiano, *Rendiconto dell'VIII Congresso Nazionale, Bologna 8-9-10-11 Aprile 1904*, Rome, 1904, pp.7–8. Michels of course was taking a liberty in construing the Dresden debate to be about republicanism.

[67] Robert Michels, 'Vor der Entscheidung', *Sächsische Arbeiter-Zeitung*, Jg.15, no.76, 2 April 1904. Cf. Robert Michels, 'Die neue Parteitaktik in Italien', *Leipziger Volkszeitung*, Jg.11, no.81, 9 April 1904, 5. Beilage, where Michels speaks of a premature 'crisis of puberty' in the development of the Italian party, and develops an even sharper criticism of Turati as a potential Jaurès or even Millerand, whose dominance of the party might lead to the exclusion of the revolutionary wing under Labriola.

had made the reformists blind to the major social and political issues of the struggle for a socialist society. However, Michels discerned a growing resistance within the Italian party to the drift towards 'ministerialism', and the 'most courageous voice in the fray' was 'Comrade Professor [Arturo] Labriola', along with the *Avanguardia Socialista* (despite some rhetorical excesses in the latter, such as the call to purge the party of members of bourgeois origins, which would of course excise Michels himself). Michels concluded that the decision was imminent: 'The Party congress will decide, whether socialism in Italy will henceforth remain proletarian or...become royal, that is, whether to be or not to be'.[68] 'The taking of a seat in the ministry of a monarchically ruled state', in Michels' view, 'is tantamount to voluntary imprisonment or a betrayal of all party principles'.[69] In light of Michels' polemics against ministerialism, it is worth noting that while Turati recommended parliamentary cooperation with Giolitti's government to bring about or improve social reform legislation, he had declined Giolitt's offer of a place in his ministry in October 1903.

Michels furnished the German party press with a dramatic account of the showdown between the opposing wings of Italian socialism at the Bologna congress. He described an atmosphere of great tension at the start of the congress, with rumours of a party split in the air and no fewer than four main tendencies becoming apparent. Michels related that the hotel where Enrico Ferri, spokesman of the left, was staying was constantly surrounded by cheering crowds. The 'extreme right' of the party, or the 'ultra-revisionist tendency', led by Filippo Turati, Claudio Treves, and Ivanoe Bonomi, moved a resolution which advocated making use of 'the existing [i.e. monarchical, Michels inserted] institutions' so far as was possible, and opposing these institutions only in so far as they proved to be an 'immediate obstacle' to the efforts of the proletariat. Between this revisionist group and the far left, which had put up its own resolution, that of Arturo Labriola, which had received (carefully qualified) endorsement from Karl Kautsky, were a centre-right and centre-left group. The latter, represented by Enrico Leone and Francesco Ciccotti, were critical of the right's concessions to monarchism.[70] The main focus of the congress was the 'question of tactics', and the confrontation between the revisionists and the revolutionaries. For Michels,

---

[68] Michels, 'Vor der Entscheidung'. Cf. also the very similar article in the *Hamburger Echo*, where Michels wrote that the 'disease of ministerialism' had already entered the Italian party, complaining that Turati had not been punished for speaking in parliament of collaboration between classes. R.M. [Robert Michels], 'Revisionismus und Partei in Italien', *Hamburger Echo*, Jg.18, no.79, 3 April 1904, 1. Beilage; also, under the pseudonym 'Mario', 'Die beiden Tendenzen in der sozialistischen Partei Italiens', *Volksstimme* (Magdeburg), Jg.15, no.80, 6 April 1904.

[69] R.M. [Robert Michels], 'Revisionismus und Partei in Italien'.

[70] Robert Michels, 'Der Kongreß der italienischen Sozialisten', *Sächsische Arbeiter-Zeitung*, Jg.15, no.82, 11 April 1904. Michels recorded 'storms of applause' from the left delegates for the foreign comrades who had brought greetings to the congress, including of course himself. In his greetings to the congress, Michels invoked the example of the German party and stressed the need for strong party discipline. Michels also placed reports from the congress in the *Hamburger Echo*, the *Frankfurter*

106 ROBERT MICHELS, SOCIALISM, AND MODERNITY

the highlight of the congress was the rhetorical duel between Turati and Labriola, in which Michels considered Labriola the clear winner.[71] In the second round of voting, an anti-ministerialist, centre-left resolution moved by Ferri, which also reaffirmed the need for party unity, was passed (after competing resolutions by Turati and Labriola both fell short of an absolute majority), giving rise to fears of a party split, with some revisionists favouring the founding of a separate organization. Michels felt that the narrow majority for a compromise resolution had failed to bring about the necessary 'clarification', and saw 'storm clouds' in the near future of the Italian party, given the large number of reformists who were openly dissatisfied with the outcome, even if Turati's push towards 'ministerialism' had been halted for the time being.[72] Michels' article for the *Hamburger Echo* after the congress's conclusion was strongly critical of revisionism, in Italy, France, and Germany, for its emphasis on individualism to the point of denying socialist principles and destroying 'the most effective weapon of democracy, the united organization, conscious of its goal and guided by the will of the whole'.[73] At this stage, Michels still seems to have regarded a strong central party organization as an asset—as long as it was controlled by the party's Left.

Michels continued his campaign against revisionism and its associated manifestations such as reformism and ministerialism with a leading article for the *Avanguardia Socialista* in August 1904, in which he attacked revisionism as being based on an overoptimistic and illusory view of society, which denied the reality of class conflict.[74] Michels wrote scathingly of Jean Jaurès' ill-founded optimism regarding the prospect of peaceful collaboration across class divisions, and cited a recent article by Eduard Bernstein in the *Sozialistische Monatshefte* following the Crimmitschau textile workers' strike as another example of an overly sanguine view of social conflict by a revisionist theorist.[75] This overoptimistic vision of 'class collaboration' Michels saw as common to reformists like Millerand and Turati. Michels went on to cite conditions in Germany as an example of the clearest form of class conflict, where the most diverse groups within the bourgeoisie would unite politically to exclude socialists and the proletariat from power.

Volksstimme, the *Magdeburger Volksstimme* (under the pseudonym 'Mario'), and the *Schwäbische Tagwacht*.

[71] Robert Michels, 'Der Kongreß der italienischen Sozialisten', *Sächsische Arbeiter-Zeitung*, Jg.15, no.87, 16 April 1904.

[72] Robert Michels, 'Der achte Kongreß der sozialistischen Partei Italiens', *Schwäbische Tagwacht*, Jg.24, no.86, 14 April 1904; Michels, 'Der Kongreß der italienischen Sozialisten', SAZ, 16 April 1904. See also Gisela Michels' resumé of the congress which concluded her husband's series of reports: gm [Gisela Michels], 'Das Resultat', *Sächsische Arbeiter-Zeitung*, Jg.15, no.88, 18 April 1904.

[73] Robert Michels, 'Einheit der Partei', *Hamburger Echo*, Jg.18, no.88, 15 April 1904.

[74] Roberto [Robert] Michels, 'A proposito di socialismo illusorio', *Avanguardia Socialista*, Anno II, no.88, 6 August 1904.

[75] This was Eduard Bernstein, 'Capitalmacht und Gewerkschaftsmacht. Ein Beitrag zur Dynamik des Gewerkschaftskampfes', *Sozialistische Monatshefte*, VIII, Bd. 1, February 1904, pp.129–37.

If Michels had previously pointed to the German party as offering positive lessons for its Italian counterpart, he also vented his frustration and incipient disillusion with the German party in the radical socialist press in Italy, after the Bremen party congress of September 1904. Michels submitted an article to the *Avanguardia Socialista*, entitled 'A Funereal Congress', contrasting the German party with the 'revolutionary energy' demonstrated by the organized Italian proletariat in their general strike. (The general strike in Italy, from 16 to 20 September, commenced just before the Bremen congress, 18–24 September, but had already ended in failure by the end of the congress.) Michels complained that with a few honourable exceptions the majority of the congress showed itself indifferent or even hostile to 'this, the only weapon that we have in our battles against reaction'. In this syndicalist paper, Michels identified himself more strongly with a revolutionary syndicalist position than in his previous articles. Surveying the state of the German party, which Michels portrayed as increasingly torpid and prey to petit bourgeois ideas, he summoned his Italian syndicalist readers to be a constant example and a warning to their German comrades.[76] It is, however, worth remembering Pino Ferraris' strictures on Michels as a supposed syndicalist. While he evinced sympathy for the action of a general strike, in structural terms he continued to prioritize the political party over the trade union movement. Michels' sympathy for revolutionary syndicalism sprang more from his ethical-idealist and agonistic conception of politics than from Marxian theory.

In January 1905, a new periodical of the Italian revolutionary syndicalist factions appeared, *Il Divenire Sociale* ('the social future') headed by Enrico Leone, who also garnered support from Walter Mocchi, Arturo Labriola, and a number of other prominent syndicalists.[77] Michels contributed an article to the second issue, dealing with the topic of 'Violence and legalism as factors in socialist tactics'.[78] Michels began by pointing to the debate within the international socialist movement over socialists' stance towards the existing legal and social order, drawing a somewhat simplified dichotomy between the adherents of 'legalitarismo' on the one hand and the advocates of violence on the other, a dichotomy he went on to critique on the way to expounding his own views. These included a statement of the 'ethical necessity' of aversion to violence as brute force and bloodshed. Michels stressed the ethical principles of socialism, including its opposition to war between peoples, and individual acts of violence such as assassination and duelling. For Michels, the brutalization of society that a recourse to violence would bring with it would run counter to the ultimate goals of a socialist society.

---

[76] Roberto [Robert] Michels, 'Un congresso funebre', *Avanguardia Socialista*, Anno II, no.97, 14 October 1904.

[77] See Willy Gianinazzi, 'Il divenire sociale et pagine libere', *Cahiers Georges Sorel*, 5, 1987, pp.119–30; Cavallari, *Classe dirigente e minoranze rivolzionarie*, pp.69–79.

[78] Roberto [Robert] Michels, 'Violenza e egalitarismo come fattori della tattica socialista', *Il Divenire Sociale*, I, no.2, 16 January 1905, pp.25–7.

'Our revolution proceeds by means of the brain, influenced by the external development of social life.'[79] However, if violence was an illness, so too was 'legalism', in Michels' view, and an even more dangerous one, an epidemic of which was currently breaking out in international socialism. Legalism, Michels wrote, was 'the dry fruit of the tree of parliamentarism' in a situation in which parliaments were still the playthings of the ruling class.[80] For Michels, it was 'absolutely utopian' to suppose that the existing constitutional order, with its undemocratic features such as upper houses of parliament and monarchs, could of its own volition give birth to a new socialist order of things. The abolition of undemocratic upper houses and monarchies was a precondition of achieving socialist objectives, and these would not simply dissolve themselves under the current laws of the land.[81] Michels resolved this apparent impasse by citing 'his friend' Arturo Labriola's definition of violence, that violence was the 'immediate modification of the state of things'. Michels distinguished between violence as physical force (which could still become necessary if forced on socialists by their reactionary opponents) and the purely legal violence of people defying the existing laws. Against the existing constitution and laws, Michels counterposed the alternative democratic legitimacy of the principle of popular sovereignty, as expressed in the Declaration of Rights of Man and the Citizen of 1789.[82] Michels' article drew a response from Enrico Leone, who queried Michels' emphasis on republicanism, countering that it was just another form of rule by the bourgeoisie.[83] Michels continued to view compromise with monarchy as an essential point of difference between the revolutionary socialist left and reformists such as Turati.[84]

Michels continued to vent his criticisms of the German party in the Italian socialist press, placing an Italian version of his December 1904 article from *Le Mouvement Socialiste* on the 'dangers of the German socialist party' in the periodical *Il Pensiero*. While this was in keeping with Michels' usual practice of re-using his own material, often in multiple languages, the republication of this critique of the German party in an Italian journal also served as a warning to Italian socialists to beware similar dangers of parliamentarism (or 'parliamentary

---

[79] Michels, 'Violenza e egalitarismo come fattori della tattica socialista', p.25.

[80] Michels, 'Violenza e egalitarismo come fattori della tattica socialista'.

[81] Michels, 'Violenza e egalitarismo come fattori della tattica socialista', p.26.

[82] Michels, 'Violenza e egalitarismo come fattori della tattica socialista', p.27.

[83] Enrico Leone, 'Postilla', *Il Divenire Sociale*, I, no.2, 16 January 1905, pp.27–8. On Leone, see Willy Ganinazzi, *L'itinerario de Enrico Leone. Liberismo e sindacalismo nel movimento operaio italiano*, Milan, 1989; and particularly on his 'pure' syndicalist period the very detailed study by Daniele D'Alterio, *La capitale dell'azione diretta. Enrico Leone, il sindacalismo 'puro' e il movimento operaio italiano nella prima crisi del sistema giolittiano (1904–1907)*, Trento, 2011.

[84] A point Michels reaffirmed in Robert Michels, 'Eine Psychologie der sozialistischen Bewegung', *Leipziger Volkszeitung*, no.8, 4 January 1905 (a critical review of Ettore Ciccotti, *Psicologia del movimento socialista*).

opportunism') and the domination of cautious party leaders.[85] Michels contrasted Italian syndicalism favourably with the compromises of the German party in his contributions to the French syndicalist journal *Le Mouvement Socialiste*. In his description of the German trade union congress in Cologne, Michels contrasted this revolutionary syndicalism, based on class struggle, as found in both France and Italy, with English-style trade unionism, based on the pursuit of limited improvements in pay and conditions, and argued that the German trade unions were following the latter tendency.[86] Michels praised this revolutionary syndicalism in the following terms: 'It is the organizer of the social war, against all peace, all compromise, all diplomacy, thus constituting the eminently necessary counterweight to the parliamentarism of the party. It only knows struggle and only lives in struggle.'[87] In another article in *Le Mouvement Socialiste*, Michels chided the journal of the German trade unions, the *Korrespondenzblatt*, for misrepresenting the support for the strategy of a general strike among the Italian unions at their congress at Genoa. According to Michels, no-one at the congress had raised a voice against the general strike, which would be called in any situation in which the ruling classes resorted to armed force against the workers.[88]

In August 1905, Michels returned to the columns of *Il Divenire Sociale* to write about 'the justice of the strike and socialism'. Michels wrote a number of articles on the ethical justification of strikes, making surprisingly heavy weather out of a point that might have been self-evident to a left-wing socialist and sympathizer with syndicalism, but this again underlined Michels' essentially ethical and idealist conception of socialism.[89] Michels also took the opportunity to aim criticism at the reformist right wing of socialist parties for whom the 'justice' of a strike depended on its prospects of success. These people, Michels argued, confused the essentially ethical category of justice with the tactical category of opportunity: 'Philosophy rightly teaches us that justice is not, and cannot be, dependent on success.'[90] Ultimately, Michels argued, the strike was innately just, as it offered a means to the end of an abolition of the capitalist and the emancipation of the

---

[85] Roberto [Robert] Michels, 'Gli errori del partito socialista tedesco', in *Il Pensiero*, Vol.III, 4, 1 February 1905, pp.56–8; 5, 1 March 1905, pp.69–71.

[86] Robert Michels, 'Le congrès syndical de Cologne', *Le Mouvement Socialiste*, No.149, 1 July 1905, pp.313–21.

[87] Michels, 'Le congrès syndical de Cologne', p.313.

[88] Robert Michels, 'A propos de la grève de la Ruhr', *Le Mouvement Socialiste*, No.149, 1 July 1905, pp.341–4, here pp.343–4.

[89] Roberto [Robert] Michels, 'La "giustizia" dello sciopero e il socialismo', *Il Divenire Sociale. Rivista di Socialismo Scientifico*, I, no.15, 1 August 1905, pp.235–6 (an extended Italian version of Dr Robert Michels, 'Begriffsverwirrung und Klassenhass', *Mitteldeutsche Sonntags-Zeitung*, no.5, 31 January 1904, a polemic against the bourgeois polemic against bourgeois economist Hermann Schwarz (University of Halle), for failing to recognize the ethical justification for workers to go on strike. While such a justification might seem redundant in the pages of *Il Divenire Sociale*, it reflects Michels' habit of recycling his work).

[90] Michels, 'La "giustizia" dello sciopero e il socialismo', pp.235–6.

proletariat. Strikes had the potential to lead towards a new social order in a way that peaceful pacts with the privileged classes would not.[91]

Controversy over the general strike, and its possible political uses, loomed large in the German Social Democratic Party, as the party left, against the background of strikes and revolutionary movements in the Russian Empire, pushed for a stronger line on the use of a mass strike at the 1905 Jena party congress. Again drawing connections between the debates in Germany and Italy, Michels published a leading article in *Avanguardia Socialista* on the general strike issue, the German Social Democrats' Jena congress, and Labriola.[92] Arturo Labriola had published a critical commentary on the Jena congress and its equivocal outcome on the mass strike question, and posed the question of whether Jena would come to mark the start of the decline of the moral hegemony of German socialism in the international socialist movement.[93] Michels partially endorsed Labriola's critique of the Jena congress, stating that a distant observer like Labriola could sometimes see things more clearly than militants back in Germany. He only took issue with Labriola on two points: firstly, Labriola conceded that the general strike might have a different application in Germany than in Italy, given the 'semi-absolutist' conditions in Germany. But, for Michels, this was no argument against a general strike strategy in Italy: while Germany had universal (manhood) suffrage and a weak parliament, Italy had a very restricted franchise but a powerful parliament. Michels suggested that a general strike to expand the franchise in Italy could have a major impact. Michels also leant towards a voluntarist position on the long-term prospects of the strike, when it came to trying to assess the prospects of success of a mass strike. While it was impossible to guarantee that a strike would be successful in the short term, 'what will make the general strike an overwhelming success, and the proletariat invincible, in the long run, consists in the clear consciousness in the proletariat that they are in the right'. This consciousness of having right on their side, and the 'will' that emanates from this consciousness would be 'the only effective instruments in the struggle'. One only had to instil this consciousness of being in the right in the minds of the proletariat 'and the victory is already half won, on the political field'. Michels went further, describing the general strike as an innately 'revolutionary, rebellious, antilegalitarian' phenomenon. He suggested that a strong proletariat could use the general strike to enlarge the scope of its legal rights, but an even stronger proletariat would not need to confine itself to the sphere of legality. The anti-legalitarian means would outgrow initially the legalitarian ends to which it was applied.[94]

[91] Michels, 'La "giustizia" dello sciopero e il socialismo', p.236.
[92] Roberto [Robert] Michels, 'Sciopero Generale, Sindacalismo, Jena e Labriola', *Avanguardia Socialista*, III (2nd series), no.149, 21 October 1905, p.1.
[93] L'Avanguardia [A. Labriola], 'Dopo Jena. (Il congresso socialista tedesco)'. *Avanguardia Socialista*, III, no.147, 7 October 1905.
[94] Michels, 'Sciopero Generale, Sindacalismo, Jena e Labriola'.

SOCIALISM PLUS TEMPERAMENT   111

Michels also discussed the Jena Congress in relation to the Italian party's congress at Brescia, in an article for *Il Divenire Sociale*.[95] Once again, Karl Kautsky's name was brought into an Italian controversy. In the lead up to the Jena party congress, Kautsky was embroiled in a controversy with *Vorwärts*, still edited by Kurt Eisner, with whom Michels had come into conflict in 1903 over the Marburg run-off election controversy. *Vorwärts* brought up Kautsky's endorsement of Labriola's motion at the previous year's Bologna congress, using it to accuse Kautsky of collusion with 'semi-anarchist' positions, a charge which Kautsky vehemently refuted.[96] For Michels, the revisionist attack on Kautsky revealed 'the complete impotence of our parliamentary and bureaucratic party mechanism', turning 'the proud doctrine of Marxism into a Cinderella in practical terms'.[97] While Kautsky insisted in *Vorwärts* that he had in fact advised Labriola to change a few sentences that could be read as 'semi-anarchist', Michels unreservedly endorsed Labriola's Bologna motion concerning parliamentary reforms (and rejecting collaboration with bourgeois parties to achieve these). Michels also applauded a speech by Enrico Leone on the same theme, which Michels recalled as 'a true intellectual pleasure', which he often took pleasure in recollecting.[98] (Leone, for his part, praised Michels' critical commentary on Jena that was published in *Le Mouvement Socialiste*.)[99] Michels reiterated his central argument, that 'reforms do not damage the bourgeois system'.[100] Michels closed his article, however, by proclaiming the sense of isolation and disunity that those on the left of the movement felt: 'we, the Marxists, the revolutionaries, and syndicalists'. Michels thus proclaimed himself at one with the syndicalists, albeit on his own terms, which he ventured to define in a footnote: 'I consider as syndicalism the general tendency to shift socialist tactics away from the political-bourgeois field of parliamentarism and onto the economic-proletarian field, with a frank and open socialist belief in direct action and bringing the force of the class to bear.' Michels concluded by appealing that if Kautsky were being logical, he would declare himself on the far left, along with the revolutionary syndicalists (as it was, Kautsky aligned himself with the 'centre-left' in Italy, as in Germany).[101] Michels was also less concerned about being associated with anarchism than Kautsky was. In 1907, the anarchist journal *Il Pensiero*, edited by Pietro Gori and Luigi Fabbri, re-published an article on German Social

---

[95] Robert Michels, 'Attorno alla mozione di Brescia—Verso le nuovo assisi del Partito', *Il Divenire Sociale. Rivista di Socialismo Scientifico*, Anno I, no.21, 1 November 1905, pp.325–30, including Roberto [Robert] Michels, 'Kautsky e i rivoluzionari italiani', pp.326–9.

[96] Karl Kautsky, 'Noch einmal die unmögliche Diskussion', *Vorwärts*, no.216, 15 September 1905, 1. Beilage, with rejoinders by the *Vorwärts* editor in footnotes throughout the article.

[97] Michels, 'Kautsky e i rivoluzionari italiani', p.326.

[98] Michels, 'Kautsky e i rivoluzionari italiani', pp.327–8.

[99] Enrico Leone to Michels, n.d. [1905/06], in ARM/FLE; also in Volpe, *Carteggio*, pp.143–4.

[100] Michels, 'Kautsky e i rivoluzionari italiani', p.328.

[101] Michels, 'Kautsky e i rivoluzionari italiani', p.329.

112   ROBERT MICHELS, SOCIALISM, AND MODERNITY

Democracy by Michels first published in Gustave Hervé's *La Guerre Sociale*.[102] A note by the editors indicated that Michels was, as readers of the paper would already know, a revolutionary socialist, not an anarchist. But if his views differed somewhat from those of Fabbri and Gori, they were still deemed to be of interest to their readers. While Michels was dismissive of the number and influence of anarchists in Germany, his critique of parliamentary compromises and of patriotism would have been congenial. Elsewhere, Michels criticized the exclusion of anarchists from the International, while working-class reformists who did not subscribe to the idea of the primacy of the class struggle were allowed to participate. Michels saw some merit in the proposal of 'our friend Luigi Fabbri, who is without the slightest doubt the intellectual leader of the anarchists in Italy' that the anarchists and militant socialists should form an alliance, excluding anarchist individualists on the one hand and social democratic reformists inclined to class compromise on the other.[103] Michels subsequently assisted Fabbri in placing a manuscript with the *Archiv für Sozialwissenschaft und Sozialpolitik*.[104] Michels was happy to count anarchism that was committed to a radical concept of class struggle as part of the socialist movement and he regarded the theoretical differences between Marx and Bakunin as minor, claiming that the differences between the two were 'mainly only differences in temperament and divergence in questions of tactics and organisation'.[105]

One thing that still separated Michels from syndicalists, despite his belief in direct action, frank socialist convictions, and class struggle, was that he did not regard unions as better expressions of the will of the working class than political parties. In early 1906, Michels took up the question of the problematical relations between socialist political parties and workers' unions in an essay for *Il Divenire Sociale*, in which he distanced himself from radical critics of the nature of the political party *per se* (e.g. Ernest Lafont).[106] Michels sought to argue that the weaknesses that were manifesting themselves in the labour movement were less the result of divisions between 'reformism' and 'rivoluzionarismo' or of an

---

[102] Roberto [Robert] Michels, 'Il partito socialista tedesco dopo le elezioni', *Il Pensiero*, V, no.7, 1 April 1907, first published as Robert Michels, 'Un antipatriote allemande aux antipatriotes français', *La Guerre Sociale*, 1, no.13, 13–19 March 1907.

[103] Robert Michels, 'Le prochain congrès socialiste international', *Le Mouvement Socialiste*, no.188, July 1907, pp.38–46, here pp.39–40; also published in Italian as 'Il prossimo congresso socialista internazionale', in *Il Divenire Sociale*, III, no.15, 1 August 1907, pp.227–31 (omitting the middle section which dealt exclusively with the German Social Democratic Party). Michels dismissed differences over parliamentary participation as of secondary importance only.

[104] E. Jaffé to Michels, 9 February 1908, ARM/FLE; Luigi Fabbri to Michels, 18 December1907, Luigi Fabbri Archive, IISG.

[105] Robert Michels, Review of Ettore Zoccoli, *L'anarchia. Gli agitatori, le idee, i fatti*, in *Kritische Blätter für die gesamten Sozialwissenschaften*, Jg.III, Heft 10, 1907, pp.503–4.

[106] Roberto [Robert] Michels, 'Discorrendo di socialismo, di partito e di sindacato', *Il Divenire Sociale. Rivista di Socialismo Scientifico*, Anno II, no.4, 16 February 1906, pp.55–7. See the discussion of the differences between Michels and the proponent of French CGT-style syndicalism: Lafont in D'Alterio, *La capitale dell'azione diretta*, pp.95–7.

incompatibility between 'syndicalism' and the 'party', rather they resulted from what Michels termed 'the flagrant contradiction between socialist doctrine and the tactics of socialists'. This contradiction manifested itself in the actions of socialist leaders with respect to militarism and to their attitudes towards the existing state, which Marx had defined as the executive committee to defend the interests of the ruling classes. Michels cited both Bebel's advocacy of practical army reforms (such as new uniforms), and the support of Italian socialists for a reorganization of the army along with Bissolati's opposition to anti-militarist propaganda.[107] These inconsistencies between socialist theory and the practice of socialist leaders had its root, 'as everyone knows', 'in the opportunism of day-to-day politics, in the frenzied pursuit of votes upon votes', as if the 'accumulation of an infinite quantity of zeroes' could induce the ruling minority to cede power and allow the creation of a socialist society.[108] According to Michels, the socialist party had become decrepit (he did not distinguish here between Germany and Italy), having succumbed to the most bourgeois parliamentary prejudices. However, his proposed remedy was not to abandon the political party but to seek to bring about its rejuvenation through a revolutionary syndical movement, which would go back to the motion of the Brescia congress on the general strike and use it as the platform for a regenerated labour movement. 'Alongside a tired and neutral syndicate, there is correspondingly a hermaphrodite party. Create the political and revolutionary syndicate, and the party will follow you.'[109]

The editor of *Il Divenire Sociale*, Enrico Leone, was not convinced by Michels' reasoning, which Leone saw as seeking too much to square the circle in its account of relations between unions and party. In a partial dissent from Michels' account of these relations, Leone wrote: 'The important thing is to suppress this dualism between two souls.'[110]

Michels' sympathies for the syndicalist wing of the Italian labour movement were on display in a highly critical account of the Rome party congress written for a German readership.[111] Michels declared that 'Italian socialism finds itself without question in a crisis.'[112] There had been the threat of an open split in the party at the Rome Congress (7–8 October 1906), which had been averted by the efforts of the party centre ('integralists'), led by Enrico Ferri and Oddino Morgari. Unity had been preserved, but the ensuing compromise resolution saw the party centre

---

[107] Michels, 'Discorrendo di socialismo, di partito e di sindacato', p.56.
[108] Michels, 'Discorrendo di socialismo, di partito e di sindacato', p.56.
[109] Michels, 'Discorrendo di socialismo, di partito e di sindacato', p.57.
[110] Enrico Leone, 'Postilla', in *Il Divenire Sociale. Rivista di Socialismo Scientifico*, Anno II, no.4, 16 February 1906, pp.57–8, quotation p.58. Giorgio Volpe, *Da disillusione socialista*, p.101, argues that Michels' article underestimated the changes under way which were widening the divisions between revolutionary syndicalists and the socialist party.
[111] Robert Michels, 'Der italienische Parteitag zu Rom', *Die Neue Gesellschaft*, 2.Jg., Bd.3, 24 October 1906, pp.46–8 (dated Rome, 16 October).
[112] Michels, 'Der italienische Parteitag zu Rom', p.46.

moving closer to reformism 'in the eyes of many'.[113] Michels sketched the background of the conflict for his German readers, providing them with a description of the main conflicting factions. The reformists included some outstanding leaders and parliamentarians, and enjoyed strong support among 'the masses of agricultural labourers'. The reformists favoured collaboration between classes, and rejected revolutionary terminology, and were not even opposed in principle to participation in a ministry. The syndicalists were 'led by an elite of young university lecturers from southern Italy (Labriola, Leone, Loncao), joined by some old workers' leaders, who have maintained intransigent positions (Lazzari). They are the paedagogues of socialism.' Their 'highest goal' is the 'awakening and maintenance of the opposition between the class-conscious proletariat and the existing class society as a whole complex'. Despite participation in elections, they were opposed to parliamentarism. The syndicalists advocated shifting the labour movement's emphasis to revolutionary syndicates and unions, in part to avoid the pitfalls of bourgeois parliamentarism and professional politics.[114] In another report on the congress for a German paper, Michels concluded that while current prospects favoured the party's reformists, he remained confident that Italian socialism would recover from the 'bath in the swamp of government politics', and the 'infantile disorder of ministerialism' and would return to a policy based on the concept of class struggle.[115] In a debate with the French syndicalist Edouard Berth in early 1907, Michels argued that German and Italian socialist parties needed revolutionary syndicalists within the movement, as these 'guaranteed the preservation of a remnant of a revolutionary base'. Conversely, syndicalists had to remain within the parties in Italy and Germany, or they would atrophy outside the party.[116] The split between revolutionary syndicalists and the socialist party, and the departure of the syndicalist wing from the PSI was, however, already under way.[117]

Michels grew closer both politically and personally to the Italian radical syndicalists during 1906, especially after he attended the party congress in Rome in October. Michels had again spoken at an Italian congress as a German socialist observer, carrying greetings from the German party. His short address was a plea for party unity in the face of the demands of the class struggle, saying: 'the mountain we are climbing is much bigger than we had believed'.[118] Enrico Leone wrote to Michels (addressing him as 'Egregio Amico'), to share with him the project of

[113] Michels, 'Der italienische Parteitag zu Rom', p.67.

[114] Michels, 'Der italienische Parteitag zu Rom', pp.66–7.

[115] R.M. [Robert Michels], 'Aus der italienischen Sozialdemokratie', *Rheinische Zeitung*, no.292, 15 December 1906.

[116] Robert Michels, 'Controverse socialiste', *Le Mouvement Socialiste*, no.184, March 1907, pp.278–88 (quotation p.288).

[117] Volpe, *La disillusione socialista*, pp.102–25.

[118] Partito Socialista Italiano, *Resiconto Stenografico del IX Congresso Nazionale (Roma, 7-8-9-10 Ottobre 1906*, Rome, 1907, p.54.

creating a single national syndicalist paper for the whole of Italy, which subsequently appeared as *Lotta di classe* ('the class struggle').[119] Michels' correspondence with Arturo Labriola took on a much warmer tone from this time on, with Labriola even spending Christmas with Robert and Gisela Michels in Turin in 1907.[120] Despite the warm personal relations between Michels and these prominent Italian syndicalists, his support for them, and for the left wing of Italian socialism more generally, was mainly limited to writing for journals and newspapers: he did not play an active part in party organization or agitation in Italy, as he had in Germany from 1903 to 1905. By late 1906, Michels' writings on Social Democracy were becoming increasingly academic, and he also included work on the Italian socialist movement in his contributions for scholarly journals such as the *Archiv für Sozialwissenschaft und Sozialpolitik*.

In 1905/6, Michels published a book-length series of articles on Italian socialism for the *Archiv für Sozialwissenschaft und Sozialpolitik*, entitled 'Proletariat and Bourgeoisie in the Socialist Movement of Italy'.[121] He complemented this series with a very lengthy review of the literature on the history of the Italian Socialist Party, including a discussion of Werner Sombart's work.[122] In this article, Michels predicted that the Italian Socialist Party would split.[123] Despite the academic nature of this review article, Michels still showed a degree of nostalgia for the early, idealistic years of Italian socialism, 'when in virginal purity and innocence, still unmarked by parliamentary-statesmanlike disappointments, it wanted to storm the heavens'.[124]

Michels' series of studies of the Italian socialist movement reflected some of his characteristic preoccupations, especially on the role of middle-class recruits to socialism and the need for their idealism. At the very beginning of his study, Michels began by stressing the indispensable necessity for the participation of elements from the bourgeoisie (educated young men of bourgeois origin) in awakening the Italian socialist movement.[125] Michels distanced himself from Marxian explanations of the rise of the Italian labour movement, writing that the evident idealism of academic youth in Italy defied economic, historical materialist explanation, it could 'only be explained psychologically and historically'.[126]

---

[119] Leone to Michels, October 1906 [?], ARM/FLE.; Volpe, *Carteggio*, p.147.

[120] Volpe, *Carteggio*, pp.122–8; original letters from Labriola to Michels from October 1906 to December 1908 in ARM/FLE (only one side of the correspondence survives).

[121] Robert Michels, 'Proletariat und Bourgeoisie in der sozialistischen Bewegung Italiens', *Archiv für Sozialwissenschaft und Sozialpolitik*, Bd. 21, 1905, pp.347–416; Bd. 22, 1906, pp. 80–125, 424–86, 664–720. Published in book form: Roberto [Robert] Michels, *Il proletariato e la borghesia nel movimento socialista italiano*, Turin, 1908 (reprint New York, 1975). The book version was 'revised, corrected, and considerably augmented', p.7.

[122] Robert Michels, 'Literatur. Zur Geschichte des Sozialismus', *Archiv für Sozialwissenschaft und Sozialpolitik*, 23, 1906, pp.786–843.

[123] Michels, 'Literatur', p.804.   [124] Michels, 'Literatur', p.818.

[125] Michels, 'Proletariat und Bourgeoisie in der sozialistischen Bewegung Italiens', Bd. 21, pp.347–9.

[126] Michels, 'Proletariat und Bourgeoisie in der sozialistischen Bewegung Italiens', p.357; see also p.358.

116 ROBERT MICHELS, SOCIALISM, AND MODERNITY

Michels criticized Marx's negatively connoted characterization, in his polemics against Bakunin and his followers, of the early Italian socialist movement as dominated by *déclassé* bourgeois. This criticism had been echoed by Marx's 'epigones' (including Kautsky). In response to these criticisms, Michels stressed the need to consider the motives of the *voluntarily* 'déclassé': for a bourgeois to voluntarily join the workers' movement is 'proof of a high sense of sacrifice and the most profound loyalty to conviction'.[127] Michels discussed at length the extent to which the Italian socialist movement in its early stages had been dominated by bourgeois intellectuals, who continued to be strongly represented in the parliamentary caucus. In its early stages, the party had been a 'party of the educated', which had attracted the support of 'flower of Italy's *Geistesaristokratie* (aristocracy of the spirit, or of the mind)'.[128] One reviewer of the book version of Michels' article series, also writing in the *Archiv für Sozialwissenschaft und Sozialpolitik*, was moved to pose the question of why a party led by the flower of the country's intellectuals was not the most successful of its type in Europe.[129]

Citing Werner Sombart on the high proportion of non-workers in the leading ranks of Italian socialism, Michels resorted to his 'psychological' explanation, attributing it to the 'active part played by the heart and the imagination' in Italian socialist agitation.[130] In the Italian book version of Michels' article series he added a whole chapter on a comparison of 'the psychology of the Italian bourgeoise' compared with its German counterpart, which gave a clearly more favourable account of the Italian middle classes. They were described as imbued with a more democratic temper and less preoccupied with titles and other badges of rank and states than the German *Bürgertum*.[131]

Michels did explore data on the social composition of the party, discussing the statistics on occupations of Italian party members from 1903, although some of his chosen examples, for example comparing Marburg and Rimini, were idiosyncratic (neither town had much industry, with skilled workers from small concerns playing a prominent role, although Rimini had more bourgeois members than Marburg).[132] Again, however, Michels supplemented his social analysis with an appeal to national psychological factors:

> In this, the greater degree of *social* freedom and *political* emancipation, united with the psychological characteristics of the Italian national character, we find

---

[127] Michels, 'Proletariat und Bourgeoisie in der sozialistischen Bewegung Italiens', pp.360–3, quotation p.363; see also p.367.

[128] Michels, 'Proletariat und Bourgeoisie in der sozialistischen Bewegung Italiens', p.385.

[129] Michele Berardelli, Review of *Proletariato e borghesia nel movimento socialista italiano*, in *Archiv für Sozialwissenschaft und Sozialpolitik*, 27 (neue Folge), 1908, pp.848–51, here p.850.

[130] Michels, 'Proletariat und Bourgeoisie in der sozialistischen Bewegung Italiens', Bd. 21, p.386.

[131] Michels, *Proletariato e borghesia nel movimento socialista italiano*, pp.284–322.

[132] Michels, 'Proletariat und Bourgeoisie in der sozialistischen Bewegung Italiens', Bd. 21, pp.407, 416.

the primary reason for the phenomenon that the socialist party in Italy, alongside the strong industrial and agrarian working masses, which provide it with its strong base, also includes considerable sections of certain strata of the educated bourgeoisie.[133]

Turning to questions of party organization and strategy, Michels wrote: 'Every socialist party must be a movement of action, according to its immanent principle', with the revolutionary objective of transforming the economic base of society.[134] Michels' agonistic and idealist approach to Italian socialism was once again the thread that ran through his sociological analyses of the party. Again and again, Michels emphasized the ethical nature of Italian socialism, writing: 'The particular characteristic of Italian socialism consists in its *ethical stamp*'. Every socialist party, according to Michels, 'is in itself a party of ethics'. Socialist parties were are always characterized by a 'truly overflowing wealth of ethical factors'—these included a sense of obligation towards one's own class, called solidarity, and 'self-sacrificing striving for the shining goal of a classless ideal'.[135] This was especially true of Italy, where 'the grounding in thought of the socialist struggle in Italy is essentially taken from ethics'.[136] Even the revolutionary left socialists in Italy, such as the followers of Arturo Labriola, who mock the sentimental idealism of 'ethical socialists', were themselves ethically motivated.[137] In the Italian book version of the article series, Michels responded to Edouard Berth's criticisms of his emphasis on moral factors, writing: 'Moral idealism, for a workers' movement that is conscious of itself, is the source of all good. In the social movement, it is the sole guarantee of courageous and disinterested action.'[138]

The particular ethical character of Italian socialism was partly a matter of national character. Michels suggested that 'every country has a socialism *sui generis proprii*'—in accordance with its own nature.[139] In part, Michels returned to the role of the university-educated bourgeois intellectuals in the party leadership, who were less motivated by material interests than were the masses.[140]

Writing of the emerging conflict between the revolutionary and reformist wings of the party, Michels deplored the way in which the two sections of the party had become dragged into mutual recriminations over the bourgeois origins

---

[133] Michels, 'Proletariat und Bourgeoisie in der sozialistischen Bewegung Italiens', p.416.

[134] Michels, 'Proletariat und Bourgeoisie in der sozialistischen Bewegung Italiens', Bd.22, p.80.

[135] Michels, 'Proletariat und Bourgeoisie in der sozialistischen Bewegung Italiens', p.670; emphases in the original.

[136] Michels, 'Proletariat und Bourgeoisie in der sozialistischen Bewegung Italiens', p.671.

[137] Michels, 'Proletariat und Bourgeoisie in der sozialistischen Bewegung Italiens', p.672. See also Michels, *Proletariato e borghesia nel movimento socialista italiano*, p.278, with reference to Labriola himself.

[138] Michels, *Proletariato e borghesia nel movimento socialista italiano*, pp.393–4n1. See also Michels' 1907 essay: 'Il fattore morale nel movimento operaio', *Il Grido del Popolo*, XVI, no.32, 3 August 1907.

[139] Michels, 'Proletariat und Bourgeoisie in der sozialistischen Bewegung Italiens', Bd. 22, p.667.

[140] Michels, 'Proletariat und Bourgeoisie in der sozialistischen Bewegung Italiens', pp.674–5.

118 ROBERT MICHELS, SOCIALISM, AND MODERNITY

of their respective leaders. With this, the sense of decency within the party had sunk to an unprecedented low level.[141] While blaming the reformists for starting this unedifying fight, Michels also distanced himself from his friend and ally Arturo Labriola's proposal for a purely proletarian party (reverting in a sense to the Partito Operaio of the 1880s). Michels considered this proposal a 'theory of political suicide'.[142] In the Italian book version, Michels even argued that purely proletarian organizations were more susceptible to corruption (citing American examples).[143] Michels reiterated his belief in the ethical value of bourgeois recruits to socialism, elevating them in his choice of metaphor almost to a messianic status: 'as long as leading the struggle on the side of the oppressed is still syn-onymous with wearing a crown of thorns, the bourgeois who have come to social-ism will still have useful functions to fulfil.'[144] Bourgeois elements only became dangerous, Michels argued, when the party leaves the path of principle and seeks compromise with opponents and with government. Principled members would then be led to resign and go to anarchism or other radical alternatives, and the party would start to attract more dubious elements. Michels cited Bebel at the 1904 Amsterdam International Socialist Congress: 'From the socialist point of view the dangers threatening the socialist parties do not lie in their bourgeois splinters, but in the opportunism of their methods.'[145] Michels concurred that the threat for the party lay in the opportunism of the reformist wing, although given the Italian electoral laws and the restrictive franchise which excluded many of the lower classes from voting, Michels considered that an overemphasis on parlia-mentarism was less likely in Italy than in some other countries.[146]

Michels contrasted the organization of the German Social Democratic Party, with its 'mighty army of officials', with the less developed organization of the Italian Socialist Party. While this had some disadvantages for the Italian party, it had the major advantage that Italian party did not have an 'ossifying...profes-sional officialdom', with all of its negative consequences. The Italian party remained less bureaucratized and less subject to careerism—party intellectuals were all motivated by altruism and ideals, not by material incentives.[147] In the 1908 Italian book version, Michels suggested that party organization was some-how at odds with the Italian national character: 'As is well-known, the genus *zoon politikon*, Italian variety, abhors organisation'. He contrasted this with the

---

[141] Michels, 'Proletariat und Bourgeoisie in der sozialistischen Bewegung Italiens', pp.684–7. See also pp.691–4.

[142] Michels, 'Proletariat und Bourgeoisie in der sozialistischen Bewegung Italiens', p.702.

[143] Michels, *Proletariato e borghesia nel movimento socialista italiano*, pp.376–7.

[144] Michels, 'Proletariat und Bourgeoisie in der sozialistischen Bewegung Italiens', Bd. 22, p.703.

[145] Michels, 'Proletariat und Bourgeoisie in der sozialistischen Bewegung Italiens', pp.703–4, quota-tion p.704.

[146] Michels, 'Proletariat und Bourgeoisie in der sozialistischen Bewegung Italiens', pp.424, 716–17.

[147] Michels, 'Proletariat und Bourgeoisie in der sozialistischen Bewegung Italiens', pp.712, 713.

American party organization described by James Bryce as well as with countries such as Germany.[148]

Michels attended the International Socialist Congress in Stuttgart in August 1907 as a delegate of the Italian syndicalist movement, and was a member of the committee examining the relationship between party and trade unions, but there are no traces of any of his contributions in the records of the congress.[149] Michels did, however, take part in the deliberations of the caucus of the Italian delegates, in which he advocated a strong anti-militarist position, and sought to hold the Germans to the same line. According to the account in the Italian socialist newspaper *Avanti!*, in the discussion over the Italian delegates' credentials, Michels was recognized as a representative of the syndicalist faction despite his own disclaimer that he was not actually a syndicalist, describing himself rather as a member of the 'far left of the party'.[150]

Michels arrived in Turin in late 1907, to take up his lectureship in economics.[151] Here his colleagues included Achille Loria, the economist and reformist socialist, who espoused an evolutionary gradualist approach to socialism; the criminologist Cesare Lombroso, also a moderate socialist, with whom Michels was already friendly; and the conservative sociologist and elite theorist Gaetano Mosca. Michels' correspondence with Mosca is particularly deferential, as befitted Mosca's eminence and status as a senator. Arthur Mitzman states that a few months after his arrival in Turin, 'Michels withdrew from membership in the Italian Socialist Party to concentrate on his lectures and on an article for the Archiv' (referring here to the article on 'The Oligarchical Tendencies of Society'). Michels was by now 'a disillusioned syndicalist', according to Mitzman.[152] Allowing for the fact that Michels' adherence to syndicalism was always somewhat qualified, to say the least, and was largely platonic by 1907, confined more to the realm of ideas than to political activism, Michels' move to Turin in late 1907 certainly seems to mark a caesura, and a shift from committed and often intensely partisan political journalism to a more distanced academic and often critical treatment of the Italian socialist movement. In his article series for the *Archiv* on Italian socialism, Michels had praised the flourishing syndicalist periodical scene. In the Italian book version, writing just a year later, in September 1907, Michels

---

[148] Michels, *Il proletariato e la borghesia nel movimento socialista italiano*, p.15.

[149] Secrétariat du Bureau Socialiste International, ed., *VIIe. Congrès Socialiste International tenu à Stuttgart du 16 au 24 août 1907*, Brussels, 1908, pp.67, 106–7; cf. the German version: *Internationaler Sozialisten-Kongreß in Stuttgart, 18. bis 24. August 1907*, Berlin, 1907. The other representative of the Italian syndicalists was Franz Weiss. Clearly, the Italian syndicalists did not have the resources to go to Stuttgart themselves, and had to rely on friendly German proxies.

[150] 'VII Congresso socialista internazionale—Riunione della sezione italiana', *Avanti!* Anno XI, no.8256, 22 August 1907.

[151] The letter of appointment from the education ministry is dated 31 December 1907. ARM/FLE, Documenti personali.

[152] Arthur Mitzman, *Sociology and Estrangement: Three Sociologists in Imperial Germany*, New York, 1973, p.310.

120 ROBERT MICHELS, SOCIALISM, AND MODERNITY

noted that little remained of that flourishing.[153] Michels' article on the oligarchical tendencies of society, while principally aimed at German Social Democracy,
explicitly stated that syndicalists and trade unions were not immune from the
oligarchical tendencies immanent in large organizations. Michels cited the role of
the union leadership in calling off the general strike in Turin in October 1907,
against the wishes of the rank and file.[154]

Michels' contributed his last article to a syndicalist periodical in September
1908, his only contribution to the Italian socialist press that year, in the form of a
commentary on the state of the Italian socialist movement, published in the form
of an open letter to Enrico Leone in Leone's *Il Divenire Sociale*. In the open letter,
Michels counselled against disunity in the Italian labour movement, stressing that
the advantages of unity outweighed the differences between syndicalists and
reformists, even if there were genuine differences between the groups that needed
airing internally. Nor did Michels wish to see the socialist party left solely in the
hands of those seeking to bourgeoisify it. In a conciliatory vein, Michels argued
that there was a spectrum of opinion, within the reformist wing of socialism, that
included some constructive elements.[155] Michels counselled that there was a need
for realism about the attainability of socialist objectives in the near future, stressing above all the immaturity of the proletariat in Italy, which was not equipped to
take power even if that unlikely event should occur ('whether by a victorious general strike or by a vote of the famous majority plus one in parliament makes little
difference'). The proletariat was still completely dependent on the leadership of
intellectuals. At the same time, the Italian party was on its way to becoming a
democratic party with a pro-worker complexion. Michels saw this development
as deeply problematical, partly because of the workers' immaturity, and partly
because of the profound difference, an 'abyss', even, in Michels' term, between
democracy and socialism. Michels saw syndicalists as providing a vital counter-
balance to the development towards democracy, citing Sombart on the 'anti-
democratic essence' of syndicalism—its merit lay in its scepticism towards such
systems. Democracy was necessary for the maturity of the proletariat, but it could
not solve the social question. Michels even stated that 'democracy is noxious
(*nociva*) without the presence of *syndicalists*'.[156] For Michels, syndicalists constituted the essential avant-garde of the socialist party, as they had the keenest sense
of the importance of the class struggle. The youthful and energetic ranks of the
syndicalists 'represent the oxygen that is essential for the poorly nourished body

---

[153] Michels, 'Proletariat und Bourgeoisie in der sozialistischen Bewegung Italiens', Bd. 22, p.715n82;
Il proletariato e la borghesia nel movimento socialista italiano, p.378n2.

[154] Robert Michels, 'Die oligarchischen Tendenzen der Gesellschaft. Ein Beitrag zum Problem der
Demokratie', *Archiv für Sozialwissenschaft und Sozialpolitik*, Vol.27 (new series), 1908, pp.73–135, here
pp.107, 121.

[155] Roberto [Robert] Michels, 'Appunti sulla situazione presente del socialismo italiano', *Il Divenire
Sociale. Rivista di Socialismo scientifico*, Vol.IV, no.18, 16 September 1908, pp.294–6, here p.294.

[156] Michels, 'Appunti sulla situazione presente del socialismo italiano', p.295; emphasis in original.

SOCIALISM PLUS TEMPERAMENT   121

of the socialist army. To put it another way, in even more expressive terms, the syndicalist tendency is the male part of socialism'.[157] In his reply to Michels, Leone took issue with his psychological (and pessimistic) analysis of the Italian working class.[158] By this time, Leone and Michels were increasingly in disagreement over the prospects for syndicalism.[159]

This article is a crucial corrective to interpretations of Michels that depict him as a disappointed adherent of pure, direct democracy. If it came to a choice between democracy and socialism, Michels would choose socialism, which he associated with action, struggle, high ethical demands, and indeed virility. Michels never endowed democracy *per se* with such positive connotations. If he was becoming disillusioned, it was because the socialist parties were becoming less active, less combative, and, in his eyes, less virile. This article may well have served as Michels' farewell to syndicalism.

As Michels devoted himself increasingly to more academic engagement with the socialist movement, he followed up his book on the proletariat and bourgeoisie in Italian socialism with a slimmer book on the history of Marxism in Italy.[160] Like the first book, it consisted mainly of work previously published in the *Archiv für Sozialwissenschaft und Sozialpolitik*.[161] In these articles, Michels relied on 'the fruit of years of occupying himself with the widely spread outgrowths of Marxism in Italy', as he put it in his review of the literature.[162] Michels' 'historical-critical introduction to the history of Marxism in Italy' is a somewhat personality-driven narrative account, and occasionally anecdotal, with Michels clearly capitalizing on his years of association with the Italian labour movement. While Michels drew heavily on his own archive and on his recollections of encounters with contemporary eyewitnesses and participants, the essay ultimately reveals an increasing distance from Marxism. Michels referred to Marx's personal faults, especially his authoritarian traits, and his tendency to attack his rivals unfairly, and played down the significance of the ideological differences between followers of Marx and Bakunin in Italy.[163] Socialism had developed in Italy with-

---

[157] Michels, 'Appunti sulla situazione presente del socialismo italiano', p.296.
[158] Enrico Leone, 'Postilla', *Il Divenire Sociale. Rivista di Socialismo scientifico*, Vol.IV, no.18, 16 September 1908, pp.296–7.
[159] D'Alterio, *La capitale dell'azione diretta*, p.129n253.
[160] Roberto [Robert] Michels, *Storia del marxismo in Italia*, Rome, 1909.
[161] Robert Michels, 'Historisch-kritische Einführung in die Geschichte des Marxismus in Italien', *Archiv für Sozialwissenschaft und Sozialpolitik*, 24, 1907, pp.189–258; 'Die italienische Literatur über den Marxismus', *Archiv für Sozialwissenschaft und Sozialpolitik*, Bd.25, 1907, pp.525–71. The latter served as the bibliography for the Italian book version, being reproduced largely unchanged, except for a supplement with a list of important publications from 1907 to 1910. This consisted of only seven titles, including four by Arturo Labriola and one by Enrico Leone (*La revisione del marxismo*, 1909). Michels, *Storia del marxismo in Italia*, pp.xxxix–xl.
[162] Michels, 'Die italienische Literatur über den Marxismus', p.525.
[163] Michels, 'Historisch-kritische Einführung in die Geschichte des Marxismus in Italien', pp.196–7, 213–14. In the Italian book edition, Michels took issue with Plekhanov, Sombart, and Loria who had constructed 'an äbsolute antithesis' between Marx and Bakunin. Michels, *Storia del marxismo in Italia*,

122 ROBERT MICHELS, SOCIALISM, AND MODERNITY

out much knowledge of Marx, drawing on Italian traditions of political thought reaching back to the Renaissance.[164] Marx's reception took off after his death in 1883, when the first Italian translations of his work started appearing, and Italian socialism entered what Michels saw as its heroic period in the 1890s.[165] Unfortunately, in Michels' view, Turati, under the influence of Anna Kuliscioff, had then started to promote a watered-down version of Marxism.[166] In the 1909 Italian version, Michels found more space for the Italian critics of Marxism, including Gaetano Mosca, named as among those 'who put in doubt the feasibility of his [Marx's] centralized system of state "collectivism"', and Carlo F. Ferraris, who was among critics who 'counterpose the importance of ideal and ideological factors to the exaggeration of the economic factor'.[167]

Of particular interest, given his close relations with the individuals concerned, are Michels' observations on the Italian social anthropological school of thinkers within the socialist movement:

> Most important was the decisive influence that Marxism exercised over the new criminological-anthropological school. Those who one-sidedly emphasized anthropological factors in human development, the adherents of the theory of the 'born criminal' could not become Marxists. But Marxism had such a powerful influence on these circles, that it brought them to recognize the social factor and even led the most distinguished representatives of the school to socialism: Ferri, Niceforo, Florian, Franchi, Cosentini, and even the founding father Cesare Lombroso himself, joined the socialist party.[168]

Further, Michels wrote:

> Other so-called Marxists turned out, on closer inspection, to be simply Darwinists. We have already had occasion to note the extent to which Italian socialism was mixed with Darwinism. After the accession of the great criminologist Enrico Ferri to the workers' party (in 1893), the already very strong anthropological element in Italian socialism received new nourishment. Without unfortunately having studied Marx thoroughly, with the result that his

---

pp.65–6n1. He also added to his criticisms of Marx and Engels and their views on Italian socialism in the Italian book, p.95.

[164] Michels, 'Historisch-kritische Einführung in die Geschichte des Marxismus in Italien', pp.224, 226ff.

[165] Michels, 'Historisch-kritische Einführung in die Geschichte des Marxismus in Italien', pp.226–7, 232–3.

[166] Michels, 'Historisch-kritische Einführung in die Geschichte des Marxismus in Italien', p.233.

[167] Michels, *Storia del marxismo in Italia*, p.93.

[168] Michels, 'Historisch-kritische Einführung in die Geschichte des Marxismus in Italien', pp.239–40. In the Italian book version, Michels added 'biological' to 'anthropological': *fattori antropologici e biologici*. Michels, *Storia del marxismo in Italia*, p.92.

SOCIALISM PLUS TEMPERAMENT   123

doubtless correct fundamental idea was not always completely successfully realized, Enrico Ferri attempted to reconcile Marx with Darwin....In Italy, Arturo
Labriola and Turati's disciples came vigorously into conflict with him. Even
today, Ferri and his friends are generally denied recognition as Marxists.[169]

Michels attributed the influence of 'anthropological Marxism' in the Italian party
'to the general feeling of Italians for eclecticism' as well as the prestige that Ferri
personally enjoyed.[170] Despite his critical gloss on Italian 'anthropological
Marxism', Michels himself was prone to resort to referencing ethnic characteristics, including in this essay, as his discussion or Italians' innate eclecticism
illustrates.

In the 1909 Italian book version of his essay, Michels reflected that Marx was
becoming dethroned in the 'official' Italian party, with no successor to the throne
in sight. Only the now relatively marginalized syndicalists still held to Marx's
doctrine of the class struggle.[171] However, what Michels himself meant by
Marxism was not always free from eclecticism. *Storia del marxismo in Italia*
somewhat expanded the treatment of the influence of Georges Sorel and his
French syndicalist associates (Hubert Lagardelle and Edouard Berth) in Italy,
characterizing this school of syndicalists, which influenced Arturo Labriola and
Enrico Leone, as a synthesis of Marx with Proudhon, Bakunin, Bergson, and
Nietzsche.[172] At the same time as the Sorelians introduced these heterodox elements into syndicalism, Michels credited Arturo Labriola, in his opposition to
Turati, with representing the 'regeneration of Italian Marxism through Marx',
in contrast to the 'opportunistically flattened-out Marxism' of Turati. Unlike
the situation in Germany, where there was a conflict between 'orthodox' and
'revisionist' Marxism, in Italy there were theoretical disputes between a right-
wing and a left-wing revisionism.[173] For Michels, the vital core of Marxism was
the agonistic commitment to active class struggle, not a historical materialist
philosophy. Once again, Michels cited

the hordes of bourgeois intellectuals, who in Italy, as the Italian expression had
it, had married the cause of the workers [were] are a far too vital proof for the
high importance of moral factors in social life, for one to thoughtlessly fixate on
[a one-sided economistic historical materialism] as an explanation.[174]

---

[169] Michels, 'Historisch-kritische Einführung in die Geschichte des Marxismus in Italien', pp.241–2.
[170] Michels, 'Historisch-kritische Einführung in die Geschichte des Marxismus in Italien', p.242.
[171] Michels, *Storia del marxismo in Italia*, p.148.
[172] Michels, *Storia del marxismo in Italia*, pp.117–18.
[173] Michels, 'Historisch-kritische Einführung in die Geschichte des Marxismus in Italien', p.250.
On this point, see also Michels' review of Enrico Leone, *L'economia sociale in rapporto al socialismo*, in
Archiv für Sozialwissenschaft und Sozialpolitik, 27 (new series), 1908, pp.852–4.
[174] Michels, 'Historisch-kritische Einführung in die Geschichte des Marxismus in Italien', p.251.

124   ROBERT MICHELS, SOCIALISM, AND MODERNITY

In a largely friendly review of Michels' short book in the *Archiv für Sozialwissenschaft und Sozialpolitik*, Arturo Labriola endorsed Michels' key findings, especially the absence of an orthodox Marxist school in Italy. (In Labriola's view, there was no such thing as orthodox Marxism, except in the imagination of a small group of Russian socialists.) Labriola also concurred with Michels on the essentially idealist nature of Marxism, and expressed a voluntarist and agonistic interpretation of Marxism close to Michels' own:

> Marxism was not only born out of idealism, it is also its logical continuation. Its quintessence is idealist. Its supreme fundamental principle is epistemological. It preaches action in the sense that the human being is only able to recognize that which he himself has created; for him revolution is the necessary means to the end of social creation. Its final goal is transcendental, since it quite fundamentally goes beyond that which the presently existing society can offer.

Labriola claimed that syndicalism was the rightful heir of this essence of Marxism.[175]

Michels' academic writings on Italy were by no means confined to studies of socialism and the labour movement. For example, in 1908 he contributed a general essay on 'demographic-statistical studies on the history of development in Italy' to the relatively conservative German social science journal *Jahrbuch für Gesetzgebung, Verwaltung und Volkswirtschaft in deutschen Reiche*, known as Schmoller's *Jahrbuch* after its founder Gustav Schmoller. Michels sounds a critical note here on Italian socialism even when he referred to the party's support for raising literacy rates in order to enable more workers to attain the qualifications for the right to vote: he characterized this effort as being motivated by 'parliamentary opportunism'.[176] A more distanced and academic stance vis-à-vis the labour movement is also in evidence in a review of recent Italian literature on social questions in the *Archiv* in the same year. There is an element of continuity, however, with Michels reiterating his old notion of the ethical nature of the strike (especially in Italy). Taking issue with the argument that nearly all strikes arose from wage demands of the workers, Michels emphasized that in Italy in particular the 'ethical motives of strikes' (for example, solidarity with unfairly disciplined colleagues or support for women experiencing harassment from employers) were very common.[177]

---

[175] Arturo Labriola, Review of Michels, *Storia del marxismo in Italia*, in *Archiv für Sozialwissenschaft und Sozialpolitik*, 33, 1910, pp.925–9 (absence of orthodoxy, p.926; quotation, p.928; syndicalism as rightful heir of Marxism, p.929). By this time, Labriola had also withdrawn from active involvement in the Italian Socialist Party. Marucco, *Arturo Labriola e il sindacalismo rivoluzionario*, pp.187–201.

[176] Robert Michels, 'Demographisch-statistische Studien zur Entwicklungsgeschichte Italiens', in *Jahrbuch für Gesetzgebung, Verwaltung und Volkswirtschaft in deutschen Reiche (Schmollers Jahrbuch)*, Vol.XXXII (new series), 2, pp.95–126, here p.122.

[177] Robert Michels, 'Italienische sozialstatistische und sozialpolitische Literatur', *Archiv für Sozialwissenschaften und Sozialpolitik*, Bd.27 (N.F.), 1908, pp.526–45, here p.534. Similarly, in an

SOCIALISM PLUS TEMPERAMENT   125

In 1908 Michels also published a translation of Enrico Ferri's 1902 brochure *Il metodo rivoluzionario*. Significantly, the translation appeared in a series of 'the main works of socialism and social policy' published by C.L. Hirschfeld in Leipzig and edited by Professor Georg Adler of the University of Kiel, a long-standing 'bourgeois' expert on the socialist movement and social policy, who maintained a critical distance from German Social Democracy.[178] Michels appears to have written to Adler with a list of Italian socialist works that might be suitable for the latter's series, including works by Arturo Labriola, Carlo Pisacane, Bakunin, and Antonio Labriola. Adler considered the works by Arturo Labriola and Pisacane to be too lengthy, and Antonio Labriola insufficiently original in terms of Marxist theory. Bakunin was rejected as Adler wanted an Italian socialist work to fill a gap in his series.[179] It could be viewed as a case of Michels' knowledge of, and old connections to, the labour movement being utilized to cement his credentials in academia. In Germany, only a few socialists, notably Eduard Bernstein, crossed the ideological and class trenches and published in both socialist and bourgeois venues. Michels' introduction, which constituted a third of the slender volume's length, covered some familiar ground: Michels referred to Italian national charac-ter as providing an explanation for the country's early reception of socialist ideas;[180] he stressed the importance of non-working-class intellectuals in the rise of Italian socialism;[181] and he stressed the ethical element in Italian socialism.[182] On Ferri himself, Michels wrote: 'The entry of this eminent intellectual into the workers' party belongs, along with the entry of the famous anthropologist Cesare Lombroso, whose favourite student Ferri was, to the most significant moments in the history of this party which does not want for converts.' At the same time, Michels' approbation for Ferri was not unqualified: the brochure which Michels was presenting to his readers was 'far from the best theoretical treatise of Italian socialism' in recent times. Ferri's work would have to compete with writings by Antonio Labriola, Arturo Labriola, Benedetto Croce, Ivanoe Bonomi, and others. But it was significant in that it was the major statement on socialist tactics by the most prominent representative of the tendency in the party which had been

---

article on Italian trade unionism for Johannes Conrad's reference work, *Handwörterbuch der Staatswissenschaften*, ed. Johannes Conrad et al. (3rd edn), Jena, 1909, Bd.4, Michels stressed the ethical motives and ethical choice of the means of struggle in Italian rural workers' unions (*leghe*); p.1206. His views on the particularly ethical character of Italian political life were further expounded in Robert Michels, 'Der ethische Faktor in der Parteipolitik Italiens', in *Zeitschrift für Politik*, Bd.3, no.1, 1910, pp.56–91.

[178] Ferri, *Die revolutionäre Methode*, with an introduction by Michels, 'Die Entwicklung der Theorien im modernen Sozialismus Italiens', pp.7–35. Michels also added extensive notes to Ferri's text.

[179] Georg Adler to Michels, 31 July 1907, ARM/FLE.

[180] Michels, 'Die Entwicklung der Theorien im modernen Sozialismus Italiens', pp.7–9, 13.

[181] Michels, 'Die Entwicklung der Theorien im modernen Sozialismus Italiens', pp.9, 21, 27, 29–30.

[182] Michels, 'Die Entwicklung der Theorien im modernen Sozialismus Italiens', pp.13–14, 19.

126 ROBERT MICHELS, SOCIALISM, AND MODERNITY

dominant since 1904.[183] Furthermore, Michels conceded that Ferri's 'anthropo-logical socialism' needed to be supplemented with a consideration of economic factors, but he did not go any deeper into this in his own introduction.[184]

Michels' academic publications continued to display an increasing critical distance from the Italian socialist movement, and from Marxism. In a lecture given at the University of Turin in December 1908 which Michels subsequently published in the liberal journal *La Riforma Sociale*, Michels discussed the tendency of *homo economicus* to engage in cooperation, but he specifically excluded from the scope of the lecture the question of the desirability and feasibility of 'that complex of ideas and postulates which is generally known under the name of socialism'. However, Michels did acknowledge that there were a growing number of scholars with sceptical views on these points, including his distinguished colleague Gaetano Mosca.[185] The following year, he contributed an article to an Italian economics journal critiquing the Marxian concept of 'immiseration'. In this essay, Michels wrote about socialists and Marxists in the third person. He considered that Marx's theory of immiseration as an economic law had been falsified by historical developments, partly because of the effects of labour movement organization, but he allowed that it could still have some psychological validity (as workers felt themselves increasingly to be relatively worse off than the upper classes).[186]

In October 1909, Michels gave a speech to the Camera del Lavoro in Turin, which he published not in a socialist periodical but in the academic journal *Rivista Italiana di Sociologia*. In the speech, he diagnosed a 'psychological crisis of socialism'. In Michels' view, socialism and the international labour movement were suffering from a simple of crisis of nerves.[187] In view of the sclerotic tendencies of socialist political parties, Michels wrote that the 'man of science' could only fervently welcome the young theory of syndicalism, but this theory too could assume the rigid forms of a new church.[188] While remaining critical of the reformist trade unionists for their indifference to socialist ideas and their tendency to opportunism, he also questioned the ideas of more radical syndicalists like Edouard Berth, cautioning that unions were subject to the same laws of

---

[183] Michels, 'Die Entwicklung der Theorien im modernen Sozialismus Italiens', p.34. Michels' characterization of Ferri's influence here was already outdated by the time the translation appeared. Ferri resigned from the editorship of the party paper *Avanti!* in January 1908 and he rapidly became marginalized in the party thereafter. Andreucci, 'Enrico Ferri', pp.347–8.

[184] Michels, 'Die Entwicklung der Theorien im modernen Sozialismus Italiens', pp.34–5.

[185] Roberto [Robert] Michels, 'L'uomo economico e la cooperazione', *La Riforma Sociale*, Vol.XX (series 3), year XVI, March–April 1909, pp.186–212. (Lecture to the Corso Libero di Economia Politica alla Reale Università di Torino, held 1 December 1908). Reprinted in Roberto [Robert] Michels, *Potere e oligarchie. Organizzazione del partito ed ideologia socialista (1900–1910)* (ed. Ettore A. Albertoni), Milan, 1989. Pagination here follows the Albertoni publication. Here p.471.

[186] Roberto [Robert] Michels, 'Delucidazioni sulla teoria dell'immiserimento', *Giornale degli Economisti e Rivista di Statistica*, Vol.39, series 2, no.5–6, November–December 1909, pp.417–53.

[187] Roberto [Robert] Michels, 'La crisi psicologica del Socialismo', *Rivista Italiana di Sociologia*, Anno XIV, May–August 1910, pp.365–76, pagination here from offprint (copy in ARM/FLE): here p.3.

[188] Michels, 'La crisi psicologica del Socialismo', p.5.

organization (and the deleterious effects of organization and representative structures) as political parties—syndicalism was therefore no panacea for the problems besetting the labour movement.[189] Michels drew on his essay on the fundamentally conservative character of party organization, arguing that socialism was not immune to the 'necessary and fatal' problem of organization and thereby oligarchy.[190] Michels even voiced scepticism concerning the syndicalist concept of the general strike: the examples to date had been disappointing in practice, and he expressed concern that if a general strike were successful, it might bring to power a proletariat that was not yet mature enough to exercise power. Michels went so far as to suggest: 'In fact, given the complete immaturity of the proletariat in all fields of human activity, the consequences of an immediate and current triumph of the workers could only be a complete disaster.' The maxims of Pareto and Mosca would be vindicated—workers would only dethrone the existing oligarchy to set up a new one.[191] On a positive note, in conclusion, Michels stated that revolutionary syndicalism did still bear an element of idealism: 'it carries in its breast the sacred fire of youth'. Syndicalism represented a synthesis of Marx's scientific conception of socialism and the class struggle, and an ethical conception rejected by Marxism. However, Michels argued that syndicalism still lacked understanding of the psychological factor.[192] In Michels' eyes, the value of syndicalism lay in its embodiment of an idealist and ethical conception of politics, and its commitment to action and struggle. However, Michels no longer entertained the possibility that a syndicalist general strike might lead to socialism, as the workers were not ready to rule, and they would only create another oligarchy if it did.

As Michels withdrew from engagement with Italian socialist politics, the reformists whom he had so often flayed for timidity and willingness to compromise had the last laugh. On 16 February 1911, Anna Kuliscioff wrote to her partner and comrade Filippo Turati:

> Today Michels was here, and I can't tell how amazed I was to have found in this virtual syndicalist of two years ago a good German professor, slightly philistine and very petit bourgeois in his political views. Also, according to him, socialism is finished not only in Italy but in the whole world.[193]

---

[189] Michels, 'La crisi psicologica del Socialismo', pp.6–7, 9.

[190] Michels, 'La crisi psicologica del Socialismo', p.10, citing Michels' own 'Der konservative Grundzug der Partei-Organisation', *Monatsschrift für Soziologie*, Jg.1, April 1909, pp.228–36; May 1909, pp.301–16.

[191] Michels, 'La crisi psicologica del Socialismo', p.13.

[192] Michels, 'La crisi psicologica del Socialismo', p.14.

[193] Filippo Turati and Anna Kulisicioff, *Carteggio. Vol. III/1: 1910–1914*, ed. Franco Pedone, Turin, 1977, p.408.

4

Michels and French Socialists and Syndicalists

Robert Michels' involvement with French socialism has been less thoroughly researched than his activity in Germany and Italy. It might be divided into three overlapping phases—as historian, as witness and critic from the outside, and as participant in the discussions of the revolutionary syndicalist section of the French socialist movement, in particular through his involvement with the journal *Le Mouvement Socialiste* as a regular contributor. Michels also had associations with individual figures on the French Left, notably with the radical anti-militarist Gustave Hervé. Michels' engagement with French socialists and syndicalists is also of broader historiographical interest, as it has been cited by Zeev Sternhell in support of his controversial argument on the supposedly left-wing origins of fascism. In this argument Michels serves as a key link between revolutionary syndicalism and later fascist ideology.[1] On closer examination, this link is more problematical: Michels' identification with syndicalism was never unequivocal, and his ideological views hardly developed in a straight line from syndicalism to being an adherent of Mussolini.

In 1907, in an exchange with Karl Diehl in the *Archiv für Sozialwissenschaft und Sozialpolitik*, Michels summed up his credentials as an expert on French socialism:

> I certainly agree with Diehl that it is difficult to follow the different tendencies especially within French socialism, above all for someone who has not conducted his studies on the spot there. But this writer has, apart from studies in libraries and archives on this topic, carried out studies on French socialism over some months in Paris (in autumn 1904 and in winter 1906), has lived in constant personal contact with the leaders of the different tendencies in French socialism and has often had the opportunity, for example in the Ecole des Hautes Etudes Sociales (Hôtel des Sociétés Savantes) to communicate his findings not only on the German, but also on the French labour movement, to an expert French audience, without meeting with contradiction, as far as he is aware.[2]

---

[1] See especially Zeèv Sternhell, with Mario Sznajder and Maia Asheri, *The Birth of Fascist Ideology*, trans. David Maisel, Princeton, NJ, 1994.
[2] Robert Michels, 'Kontrareplik', *Archiv für Sozialwissenschaft und Sozialpolitik*, Bd.24, 1907, pp.470–1.

Robert Michels, Socialism, and Modernity. Andrew G. Bonnell, Oxford University Press. © Andrew G. Bonnell 2023.
DOI: 10.1093/oso/9780192871848.003.0005

MICHELS AND FRENCH SOCIALISTS AND SYNDICALISTS   129

Robert Michels was proud of his part-French family heritage, the source of his affinity with the Latin peoples that was such a key part of his personal identity. He had attended the Französisches Gymnasium in Berlin and had shone in French in his *Abitur* (the German matriculation examination). His doctoral dissertation had been on Louis XIV, for which he undertook research in French archives. As Michels began his planned scholarly career as a historian, he published a number of essays on the early history of French socialism as well as Italian, even if contemporary Italian socialist literature started to claim a greater share of his attention. He published a series of reviews and edited documents on the history of French (and Italian) socialism for Eduard Bernstein's periodical *Documente des Socialismus*.

Perhaps a legacy of Michels' study of the France of Louis XIV for his dissertation was an essay on the utopian communism (albeit of an authoritarian and monarchistic variety) of François de Salignac de la Mothe-Fénélon (1651–1715), as sketched in Fénélon's didactic novel *Les aventures de Télémagne* ('the adventures of Telemachus', the son of Odysseus). Michels had to concede that Louis XIV was right in calling Fénélon a 'bel esprit chimèrique' ('a fanciful wit'), but he considered the publication of Fénélon's book a 'courageous deed', nonetheless.[3]

Michels also contributed a translation of Louis Blanc's socialistic political programme, written on the eve of the February revolution of 1848. In his commentary, Michels stressed the extent to which socialistic ideas were endorsed by a number of figures from the bourgeois republican milieu, showing the formidable influence of socialist ideas at that time.[4] One of Louis Blanc's supporters in 1848, François Vidal, was the subject of an essay by Michels in *Documente des Socialismus*. Vidal seems to have appealed to Michels as a 'warm-hearted idealist, who likes to bring out the ethical elements in human character'. If Vidal essentially sought only to carry out Louis Blanc's ideas, 'his temperament, different by nature, was able to lend them another shape'.[5] This emphasis on the ethical dimension of socialism was one that chimed with Michels' own conception of socialism as a mark of a superior ethical way of life.

Michels returned to Louis Blanc and the 1848 revolution in France in an article on 'the right to work' that he contributed to the journal *Ethische Kultur* in 1903. While Michels discussed the gap between socialist conceptions of the 'ateliers nationaux' (the 'national workshops' set up during the 1848 revolution in France) and their realization, he presented a positive view of the work of Louis Blanc and the radical worker Albert (Alexandre Martin). Michels saw the great achievement

---

[3] Robert Michels, 'Ein kommunistischer Entwurf am Hofe Ludwig XIV', *Documente des Socialismus*, Vol.2, no.14–15, 1902, pp.92–5, quotations pp.93, 95.

[4] Robert Michels, 'Das Programm der Socialdemokraten Frankreichs am Vorabend der Revolution von 1848', *Documente des Socialismus*, Bd.1, 1902, pp.230–1.

[5] Robert Michels, 'François Vidal und die Arbeitscommission des Luxembourg', *Documente des Socialismus*, Bd.1, 1902, pp.261–7, quotation p.267.

130 ROBERT MICHELS, SOCIALISM, AND MODERNITY

of the Luxembourg commission for the workers as having provided a common platform for representatives of all political tendencies and schools of thought which supported social reform. Michels cited Blanc's claim that two months of the commission had been enough to bring forward the arrival of complete justice in society by perhaps half a century.[6]

Turning to contemporary French socialist politics: in 1902, writing in the Italian socialist newspaper *Avanti!*, Michels saw France as a dire example of how disunity could weaken the movement of the proletariat (the branches of French socialism would only be formally united in the Section Française de l'Internationale Ouvrière (SFIO) in 1905):

> The example of France, where tendencies theoretically no more different from each other than the Ferrian and Turatian [wings of Italian socialism], or Bernsteinian and Kautskyan [wings of German Social Democracy]!—are waging a bitter and implacable war against each other in a way that renders any common action impossible.[7]

At around the same time, Michels also queried the sentimental attachment of some French socialists (among supporters of Jean Jaurès) to small land-holdings, despite socialist collectivism in theory.[8]

In September 1903, Michels took part in the Dresden party congress of the Social Democratic Party, at which the party leader August Bebel lent his weight to the party left's critique of the revisionist tendency. As discussed in Chapter 2, Michels acted as a partisan of the left in this debate, critical of the conduct of the party newspaper *Vorwärts* under the editorship of Kurt Eisner, even if aspects of Michels' own position would actually have been at odds with the position of the party left, had his views been subjected to closer scrutiny. After the Dresden congress, with its symbolic triumph over revisionism and reformism, Michels travelled to Paris, ostensibly to conduct historical research, but he also planned to give talks to German, French, and Italian socialist groups while he was there.[9] On this occasion (October 1903), Michels met the prominent French Marxist (and son-in-law of Karl Marx) Paul Lafargue (for a Sunday lunch), and Edouard Vaillant (a prominent representative of the left wing of French socialism), Louis Dubreuilh and Alexandre-Marie Bracke. He also made the acquaintance of the

---

[6] Dr Robert Michels, 'Das Recht auf Arbeit. Historisches zur sozialen Frage', *Ethische Kultur*, Jg.XI, Nr.42, 17 October 1903, pp.329–30, quotation p.330.

[7] Roberto [Robert] Michels, 'Fra due congressi. Imola e Monaco', *Avanti!*, Anno VI, no.2097, 8 October 1902.

[8] Robert Michels, Review of Gerolamo Gatti, *Agricoltura e Socialismo. Le nuove correnti [d]ell' economia agricola*, in *Documente des Socialismus*, Vol.2, 14–15, 1902, pp.62–4, here p.63.

[9] 'Aus dem Kreise Marburg-Kirchhain', *Mitteldeutsche Sonntags-Zeitung*, no.45, 8 November 1903.

MICHELS AND FRENCH SOCIALISTS AND SYNDICALISTS 131

French socialist activist Charles Rappoport, obtaining introductions to Rappoport and others from Karl Kautsky.[10]

In France, Michels had the opportunity to observe the participation of French socialists in the French bourgeois coalition government. On balance, Michels' evaluation, as conveyed in the Magdeburg *Volksstimme*, was negative: he saw the contributions of Alexandre Millerand and Jaurès to the defence of the (bourgeois) democratic republican state form as positive, but limited. On the other hand, and here Michels used the French example for an implied critique of the German revisionists, the fixation on day-to-day work in parliament led to the 'final goal' of socialism becoming lost to view, and the French socialists found themselves having to share responsibility for outright reactionary and oppressive decisions of the coalition government, with the result that the left wing of the party was breaking away.[11] Writing from Paris, Michels reported finding advantages and disadvantages of the French bourgeois republic (bearing in mind that Michels criticized the German party for failing to campaign more strongly for their republican constitutional views); Michels saw the Third Republic as an improvement on Imperial Germany's constitution, but still not genuinely democratic. Jaurès could rely on applause from bourgeois republican deputies when he held abstract speeches on ethics, but he met harder resistance when he tried to put more concrete proposals into practice. Michels stressed that the French socialists should not let themselves be side-tracked by the chance of getting a vice-presidency in the Chamber of Deputies.[12]

A month later, in January 1904, Michels welcomed the expulsion of Millerand from Jaurès's French Socialist Party. Michels welcomed the end of the experiment of the socialist minister ('His Excellency Minister comrade Millerand'), as he considered the example of Millerand's ministry to have had serious negative effects on the international socialist movement ('for years it has weighed on international socialism like a nightmare and has sown a veritable Pandora's crop of evil poisonous seeds in the widest of circles'). Millerand had clashed with Jaurès when the former voted against a disarmament bill moved by the Radical-socialist deputy Hubbard on 25 November, and thereby found himself voting against all other socialist deputies in the Chamber. Michels was sceptical about the chances of

---

[10] See Jean-Luc Pouthier, 'Roberto Michels et les syndicalistes révolutionnaires français', *Cahiers Georges Sorel*, no.4, 1986, pp.39–60, here p.42; Michels to Karl Kautsky (postcard), 22 October 1903 (from Paris), International Institute for Social History (IISH), Amsterdam, Archief Kautsky K D XVII, 535; Kautsky to Michels, 24 October 1903, in Archivio Roberto Michels in Fondazione Luigi Einaudi (ARM/FLE), Turin.

[11] Robert Michels, 'Die Teilnahme an der Macht', *Volksstimme* (Magdeburg), no.304, 31 December 1903.

[12] Rober Michels, 'Durch Spottlieder gemildert!', *Volksstimme* (Magdeburg), Jg.14, Nr.286, 8 December 1903, p.1. Jaurès had been elected vice-president of the Chamber in January 1903, a step criticized by the left wing of the French socialist movement. Harvey Goldberg, *The Life of Jean Jaurès*, Madison, Milwaukee, and London, 1968, p.296.

132   ROBERT MICHELS, SOCIALISM, AND MODERNITY

Millerand's expulsion bringing about a renewal of Jaurès's party: Jaurès and his supporters moved against Millerand not to cleanse the party, but in an act of self-defence, trying to save what credibility they could in the eyes of their voters, according to Michels. Michels described Millerand as the 'intellectual progenitor of all shadings of "practical revisionism"' in the international labour movement, and Millerand's departure from the party was therefore a major symbolic blow to 'opportunism' in Germany, Italy, and elsewhere.[13] At the same time, Michels was critical of Jaurès, who was playing down any suggestions by French left-wing socialists that the defeat of revisionists at Dresden had implications for revisionist and reformist tendencies in France, insisting on the significance of the difference between Germany's imperial constitution and France's democratic republic.[14] Jaurès characterized imperial Germany as 'halfway between Western liberalism and Eastern barbarism'.[15] In Michels' view, Jaurès was sowing confusion in the French labour movement, and making too many concessions in order to stay as part of the government coalition. Instead of conducting 'socialist class politics', Michels wrote, Jaurès believed in 'salvation by the power of government alone'.[16]

In addition to his articles in the German Social Democratic press, Michels expanded on his critique of Jaurès in letters to Kautsky. Kautsky thanked Michels and congratulated him on evidently not having wasted his time in Paris. Kautsky wrote to Michels that he could see some greatness in Jaurès, who was no common careerist (*Streber*), but that Jaurès had allowed himself to be dragged down by 'highly dubious elements' such as Millerand. 'Now he finally seems to want to free himself from them', Kautsky wrote, giving rise to the hope that 'Jaurès will play a great role in the political life of France yet'.[17] Michels responded, characterizing Jaurès as 'more a poet than a politician', and as excessively optimistic by nature, who needed to be disillusioned by some harsh reaction against his politics from outside the socialist party, in order that he learn some hard lessons. Interestingly, Michels argued that the German 'national character' was intrinsically more susceptible to revisionism than the French; only the more favourable climate for 'bourgeois democracy' in France and the dominant personality of Jaurès enabled socialist revisionism in France to prosper more than in Germany. If a more accommodating government ruled in Germany, Michels suggested, the German party would be overrun with epigones of Jaurès.[18] Michels continued to see Jaurès

---

[13] Robert Michels, 'Das Ende vom Liede Millerand', *Volksstimme* (Magdeburg), Jg. 15, Nr.8, 10 January 1904, pp.1–2. On Millerand's expulsion, see Leslie Derfler, *Alexandre Millerand: The Socialist Years*, The Hague and Paris, 1977, pp.241–5.

[14] Goldberg, *The Life of Jean Jaurès*, pp.311–12; Derfler, *Alexandre Millerand*, p.241.

[15] Jean Jaurès, 'L'inevitable', *La Petite République*, 12 September 1903, in Jean Jaurès, *Oeuvres, Tome IX. Bloc des gauches 1902–1904*, ed. Gilles Candar, Vincent Duclert, and Rémi Fabre, Paris, 2016, p.385.

[16] Robert Michels, '"Schulbuben"-Kritik', *Volksstimme* (Magdeburg), No.5, 7 January 1904 (leading article, p.1).

[17] Kautsky to Michels, 8 January 1904, ARM/FLE.

[18] Michels to Kautsky, 10 January 1904, IISH Archief Kautsky K D XVII, 536.

MICHELS AND FRENCH SOCIALISTS AND SYNDICALISTS   133

as a manifestation of a transnational wave of revisionism in the socialist movement, which he criticized in the Italian syndicalist *Avanguardia Socialista* as based on an overoptimistic and illusory view of society, which denied the reality of class conflict. Michels wrote scathingly of Jean Jaurès' ill-founded (even 'infantile') optimism regarding the prospect of peaceful collaboration across class divisions.[19] Michels' view of Jaurès would later soften, as he came to compare Jaurès's stance on anti-war resolutions at the Socialist International congresses favourably with the circumspect position of the German party on this issue.

By end of 1904, Michels' involvement in French socialism entered a new phase when he started his association with *Le Mouvement Socialiste*, where his article on 'The dangers of the German socialist party' appeared in December. He began by quoting Jaurès's critical remarks about the German party at the International Socialist Congress at Amsterdam. For Jaurès to accuse the German party of opportunism, was, Michels argued, like a thief giving evidence in a case of theft, but he believed the attacks had a kernel of truth.[20]

This was a severe critique of the German Social Democratic Party, which Michels declared to be lacking in '*the courageous will to action*, the *revolutionary ferment*'.[21] Michels offered a number of explanations for the passivity of the German Social Democratic Party: unlike the French socialists, they faced a united bourgeois bloc; Germany lacked a strong revolutionary tradition, and the factor of 'race': the passive, slow, ponderous German national character.[22]

Michels became a regular contributor to the syndicalist journal *Le Mouvement Socialiste* and a regular correspondent with the French revolutionary syndicalist Hubert Lagardelle. Michels' correspondence with Lagardelle (of which only Lagardelle's letters survive) points to some of the limits of Michels' involvement with French syndicalism, however. Lagardelle greeted Michels' collaboration with the journal enthusiastically, all the more so because the Italian syndicalists Arturo Labriola and Walter Mocchi had told him that Michels 'largely shared our points of view'. Somewhat paradoxically, Lagardelle had a contrasting view of the national conditions that favoured political radicalism—while Michels blamed German backwardness for the insufficient radicalism of the German party, Lagardelle suggested that German conditions were more conducive to radicalism than a more democratic state, which tended to dissolve radicalism. Despite this, Lagardelle wrote to Michels, the German party was getting bogged down in parliamentarism, and was overrun with reformists '[Alfred] Südekum & Co. and

[19] Roberto Michels, 'A proposito di socialismo illusorio', *Avanguardia Socialista*, anno II, no.88, 6 August 1904.
[20] Robert Michels, 'Les dangers du Parti socialiste allemande', *Le Mouvement Socialiste*, no.144, 1 December 1904, p.193. Michels' contributions *to Le Mouvement Socialiste* have also been reprinted in Robert Michels, *Critique du socialisme. Contribution aux débats au début du XXe siècle*, ed. Pierre Cours-Salies and Jean-Marie Vincent, Paris, 1992.
[21] Michels, 'Les dangers du Parti socialiste allemande', p.193.
[22] Michels, 'Les dangers du Parti socialiste allemande', p.199.

134   ROBERT MICHELS, SOCIALISM, AND MODERNITY

other clowns'. 'Only a strong revolutionary syndicalist current can save socialism', Lagardelle exclaimed, and urged Michels to join *Le Mouvement Socialiste* in this venture, and to help spread revolutionary syndicalism in Germany.[23] Michels' response to Lagardelle clearly evinced a degree of sympathy with Lagardelle's project, even though he distanced himself from the German anarcho-syndicalist Raphael Friedeberg. While Michels tended to agree with some of Friedeberg's criticisms that the German party was not demonstrating sufficient revolutionary *élan*, he was sceptical of the prospects of building a revolutionary syndicalist movement in Germany. Nonetheless, Lagardelle encouraged Michels to put him in touch with any potentially like-minded comrades in Germany, to whom copies of *Le Mouvement Socialiste* could be sent, with a view to building a truly international movement of 'revolutionary revisionists'.[24] Michels did oblige with a list of potential contacts, as well as sending Lagardelle the article on the state of the German party.[25]

A year after the cordial beginning of the correspondence between Michels and Lagardelle, Lagardelle seems to have been slightly chagrined by the fact that Michels expected to be paid for his contributions to *Le Mouvement Socialiste*. (Michels did not hold any paid party post, such as editor of a Social Democratic Party newspaper, which he could well have done—as already seen, Rosa Luxemburg had once offered her services to help him find an editorship.) Lagardelle protested that French journals were generally impoverished, lacking in both funds and subscribers—an indication that *Le Mouvement Socialiste* was not sustained by any mass readership base. Indeed, Lagardelle lamented that the subscribers had disappeared, apparently scared off by the journal's revolutionary, anti-militarist, and anti-patriotic stance, and that the ordinary readership was too small to sustain a normal journal. Lagardelle subsidized the journal out of his own pocket, and drew no pay as editor, nor did most contributors receive an honorarium— available funds were essentially reserved to compensate the foreign contributors. Lagardelle added that *Le Mouvement Socialiste* could not call on the treasury of a rich political party, like the German *Die Neue Zeit*, nor was it backed by 'millionaire Jews' like (according to Lagardelle) Jaurès's *Humanité*. (*Le Mouvement Socialiste*'s financial situation would worsen during 1906, partly because of lawsuits against it.) At the same time, Lagardelle was already pronouncing the failure of the newly united SFIO in his letter to Michels:

> In France, official socialism, the reunited electoral socialism of Guesde and Jaurès, is disintegrating faster than could have been predicted. It is the end of the

---

[23] H. Lagardelle to Robert Michels, 17 October 1904, ARM/FLE. This correspondence is also published in Willy Gianinazzi, 'La démocratie difficile à l'ère des masses. Lettres d'Hubert Lagardelle à Robert Michels (1903–1936)', *Mil neuf cent*, no.17 (Intellectuels dans la République), 1999, pp.103–48.

[24] H. Lagardelle to Robert Michels, 23 October 1904, ARM/FLE.

[25] H. Lagardelle to Robert Michels, 28 March 1905, ARM/FLE.

socialist party as far as it represents a movement of social transformation. The electoral kitchen is only of interest to that association of subaltern officers in search of jobs or seats, and all their discussions are to do with the recipe of the electoral sauce.

The trade union movement, on the other hand, was vigorous and in conflict with the government.[26]

In the course of 1905, Michels was also contributing to the Italian syndicalist journal *Il Divenire Sociale* (edited by Enrico Leone): the journal also published during that year articles by Berth, Griffuelhes (several articles), Lagardelle, and Sorel. In mid-1905, Michels' article on the German Free Trade Unions Congress in Cologne for *Le Mouvement Socialiste* showed him as identifying with revolutionary syndicalism as found in France and Italy. He contrasted this revolutionary syndicalism, based on class struggle, with English-style trade unionism, based on the pursuit of limited improvements in pay and conditions, and argued that the German trade unions were following the latter tendency. Michels wrote here of revolutionary syndicalism: 'It is the organizer of social war, against all peace, all compromise, all diplomacy, thus constituting the eminently necessary counter-weight to the parliamentarism of the Party. It only knows the struggle, and only lives in struggle.' Michels praised the revolutionary syndicalism of France and Italy as an 'admirable example', in contrast to the German trade union movement:[27] in the former, he saw 'revolutionary conceptions, anti-legalitarian, even anti-étatist, which grow in the same proportion as the audacity of the class enemies.'[28]

Michels had already struck a syndicalist note in his report on the Ruhr miners' strike for *Le Mouvement Socialiste* in April 1905. The leaders of the unions had been 'pusillanimous' before the outbreak of the strike. Since the last major Ruhr strike in 1889, the German labour movement had pursued the 'most civilised form of class struggle', parliamentary action, which had of course changed nothing. Michels wrote that the bourgeois parties were sufficiently realistic not to be taken in by the radical rhetoric of parliamentarians, and had not been intimidated by it. Finally, the workers had called on the union leaders to declare a strike, for Michels: 'Depressing proof of what a long period of *worker bureaucratism* can do

[26] Lagardelle to Michels, 31 October 1905, ARM/FLE. Lagardelle's reference to rich Jews financing Jaurès's *L'Humanité* is not the only anti-semitic remark in Michels' correspondence with this group of French syndicalists. Edouard Berth wrote to Michels that the Dreyfus case had ended in 'the insolent triumph of the Jews', adding 'I am not antisemitic by nature, I don't need to tell you that', but he believed that the French bourgeoisie was now dividing into two camps 'the clerical and the Jewish', and the latter was now in the ascendant: 'the Jewish or Jewified, Masonic, free-thinking, even socialist, bourgeoisie is now triumphant, and for anyone with some taste that really does not feel good!' Berth to Michels, 20 November 1906, ARM/FLE.

[27] Robert Michels, 'Le congrès syndical de Cologne', *Le Mouvement Socialiste*, No.149, 1 July 1905, pp.313–21.

[28] Michels, 'Le congrès syndical de Cologne', p.321.

136 ROBERT MICHELS, SOCIALISM, AND MODERNITY

to make the masses forget how to decree their own actions'.[29] Michels criticized the demand articulated in a chain of Social Democratic Party meetings for a nationalization of the Ruhr mines as showing an *étatisme* that displayed 'the total lack of Marxist spirit in the daily political life of German Social Democracy'.[30] Not only that, the strike leaders showed a failure to appreciate the '*psychological factor in any strike movement*', being more concerned with the state of the strike funds than with the mood of the workers.[31] Michels concluded that, after the strike: 'The masses are convinced that the parliamentary, neutralist and legalitarian tactics of their chiefs are bankrupt, and at their cost'.[32] He rejected the respect for legality that one found among German union leaders, exclaiming: let the bourgeois fear the strong arms of the workers!

Michels' sympathies were not exclusively shared with French syndicalists, however. As in Italy, he saw no need to distance left-wing socialism or syndicalism from anarchists of an equally radical temper. He wrote a largely sympathetic review of Augustin Hamon's anarcho-socialist *Socialisme et anarchisme. Etudes sociologiques et définitions*.[33] Michels had already made a point of praising Hamon's *Humanité Nouvelle* upon its reappearance in 1903, commending the journal to readers of the bourgeois reform-movement journal *Ethische Kultur*.[34]

Michels subsequently spent a couple of months in Paris in early 1906, where he got to know Lagardelle and Edouard Berth better, and also made the acquaintance of the leader of the Confédération générale du travail (CGT) Victor Griffuelhes and the leading exponent of French Marxism, Jules Guesde.[35] By this time, he had also started to correspond with Georges Sorel, who had already identified himself in a communication to Bernstein's *Documente des Socialismus* as among the 'thinking socialists' associated with the journal *Le Mouvement Socialiste*.[36] Around the time of Michels' 1906 visit to Paris, Sorel was taking part

[29] Robert Michels, 'La grève générale des mineurs de la Ruhr', *Le Mouvement Socialiste*, 152, 1 April 1905, pp.481–9, here p.481; emphasis in original.
[30] Michels, 'La grève générale des mineurs de la Ruhr', p.484.
[31] Michels, 'La grève générale des mineurs de la Ruhr', p.488.
[32] Michels, 'La grève générale des mineurs de la Ruhr', p.489.
[33] Robert Michels, Review of Augustin Hamon, *Socialisme et anarchisme. Etudes sociologiques et définitions*, in *Dokumente des Sozialismus*, Vol.V, 12, 1905, pp.537–8 (coincidentally, the last issue of Bernstein's journal before it ceased publication for financial reasons). On Hamon's chequered political career from anti-semitism to various forms of anarchism, which he then left behind to join the Socialist Party, see the brief biographical sketch by Justinien Raymond and Yves Le Floch, 'Augustin Hamon', in M. Enckell et al., eds., *Les anarchistes. Dictionnaire biographique du mouvement libertaire francophone*, Ivry-sur-Seine, 2014, p.238.
[34] Robert Michels [in rubric: Streiflichter:], 'Die Humanité Nouvelle und eine Ansprache an Zuchthäusler', in *Ethische Kultur*, Jg.XI, Nr. 50, 12 December 1903, pp.397–8.
[35] On Griffuelhes, see Bruce Vandervort, *Victor Griffuelhes and French Syndicalism, 1895–1922*, Baton Rouge and London, 1996; on Guesde, Jean-Numa Ducange, *Jules Guesde. L'Anti-Jaurès?*, Paris, 2017.
[36] 'Anfragen und Nachweise', *Documente des Socialismus*, Vol.3, 3, 1903, p.144. There is a large body of literature on Sorel. A good place to start is Jack J. Roth, *The Cult of Violence: Sorel and the Sorelians*, Berkeley, CA, 1980.

MICHELS AND FRENCH SOCIALISTS AND SYNDICALISTS   137

in the regular Sunday afternoon get-togethers of the *Mouvement Socialiste* circle at Lagardelle's home.[37] Michels himself was invited to take part in these gatherings. Only a few letters from Sorel to Michels are extant, although one letter from Sorel to Michels in December 1905 indicates that Sorel saw in Michels an ally against the 'official' socialists whom Sorel viewed as trying to destroy *Le Mouvement Socialiste* and his own writing career.[38]

Around this time, Michels wrote a lengthy review article for the *Archiv für Sozialwissenschaft und Sozialpolitik* on recent literature on socialism in which he offered a commentary on the state of the socialist movement in France.[39] In terms that directly echoed Lagardelle, Michels regarded the unity of the recently 'unified' French socialists as 'very precarious in its nature', because the union had been based on opportunistic, external considerations of electoral tactics, rather than a true unity of ideas. In the same essay, Michels characterized the syndicalists around the journal *Le Mouvement Socialiste*, whose theoreticians included Lagardelle, Berth, and Sorel, as the most significant among the socialist groups outside the unified party.[40]

While in Paris, Michels gave a lecture to French workers in the Palais du Travail, Belleville, Paris, on 21 February 1906 on the occasion of the Morocco crisis. He subsequently published the lecture in the German 'localists'" newspaper, *Die Einigkeit*, in the form of a series of articles on the danger of war and the German labour movement. The rationale for publishing it in German was to counter what Michels claimed were misrepresentations of his speech in *Vorwärts* and in the *Korrespondenzblatt* of the General Commission of Free Trade Unions, among other German labour movement papers.[41] Michels' lecture was held against the background of the Morocco crisis and the threat of war between Germany and France. Michels professed his alarm at the inactivity of the leadership of the German labour movement, especially of the Free Trade Unions, in the face of this danger. His lecture, Michels explained, was designed to try to explain this inactivity to French workers, and to dispel any misunderstanding that the German union leaders were driven purely by old-fashioned 'patriotism'.[42] In these articles, Michels heavily criticized the German Free Trade Unions for their lack of socialist ideology and party-political neutrality, contrasting them unfavourably

---

[37] Giovanni Busino, 'Lettres de G. Sorel à L. Einaudi, E. Rods et R. Michels', in *Cahiers Georges Sorel*, no.1, 1983, pp.71–95, here p.82.

[38] Letter from Sorel to Michels, 13 December 1905, in *Cahiers Georges Sorel*, no.1, 1983, p.83.

[39] Robert Michels, 'Literatur. Zur Geschichte des Sozialismus', *Archiv für Sozialwissenschaft und Sozialpolitik*, 23, 1906, pp.786–843, on France, see pp.802ff.

[40] Michels, 'Literatur, p.803.

[41] Michels, 'Kriegsgefahr', *Die Einigkeit*, no.21, 26 May 1906. On this speech, see also Robert Michels, 'Polémiques sur le Socialisme allemande', *Le Mouvement Socialiste*, no.176, 15 July 1906, pp.234–7, in which Michels also responds to criticisms from the German workers' reading club in Paris, and Otto Pohl, *Vorwärts*' Paris correspondent.

[42] Michels, 'Kriegsgefahr', 26 May 1906.

138   ROBERT MICHELS, SOCIALISM, AND MODERNITY

with the French CGT, which maintained a commitment to class struggle. Michels sought to explain to French workers this regrettable lack of ideological commitment. Victor Griffuelhes' unsuccessful peace mission to Berlin during the Morocco crisis had failed because of the ideological 'neutrality' of the German trade union leaders, not, Michels insisted, because of any innate patriotism of the German working class.[43]

A discordant note was sounded in Michels' relations with his French syndicalist comrades in early 1907. Edouard Berth published a critical commentary in *Le Mouvement Socialiste* on a long article Michels wrote for the *Archiv für Sozialwissenschaft und Sozialpolitik* on the social base of the Italian labour movement. Berth argued that party representative organization necessarily meant 'treason, deviation, *embourgeoisement*'.[44] Michels concurred with Berth, but argued that Berth was mistaken in arbitrarily singling out representative structures in political parties for this criticism—were not trade unions also based on the same fundamental principle, 'the principle of representation'? For Michels, the problem that needed to be resolved was '*to find a means of countering the inherent defects of all organisation, that is all representation*'. This was where Michels essentially parted company theoretically with syndicalists, even while he continued to express sympathy for their revolutionary temperament—based on his knowledge of the trade union movement in Germany, which was even more wedded to reformism and to building up its own organizational structures than the Social Democratic Party, Michels did not believe that a focus on unionism rather than political organization was a remedy for the maladies of the Second International. If any form of organization or representation was potentially suspect, this would apply to the CGT or the German Free Trade Unions as much as to the political parties that were pursuing a parliamentary strategy. Michels went on to argue that Berth's explanation for the strength of syndicalism in France was lacking in historical depth: 'Syndicalism, in France, is a historical fact. It is explained not so much by the innate revolutionary sentiment of the French proletariat as by the weakness in French life that the role of the *party* has always had.' This was in marked contrast to Germany or Italy, where the party had preceded the trade unions. In France, the party had been weak and fragmented after the suppression of the Paris Commune. Michels wrote: 'In France, the great mass of the proletariat is not intimately attached to the party.'[45]

---

[43] Michels, 'Kriegsgefahr', IV, *Die Einigkeit*, no.24, 16 June 1906. On Griffuelhes' mission to Berlin, described by Jolyon Howorth as a 'humiliating failure' due to the refusal of the German Trade Union leadership to cooperate with Griffuelhes' proposal for a joint political strike, see Vandervort, *Victor Griffuelhes and French Syndicalism*, pp. 109–10.

[44] Edouard Berth (under rubric: Revue Critique), 'Prolétariat et Bourgeoisie dans le movement socialiste italien', *Le Mouvement Socialiste*, XX, no.182, September–December 1906, pp.164–70, quotation p.165.

[45] Robert Michels, 'Controverse socialiste', *Le Mouvement Socialiste*, no.184, March 1907, pp.278–88, here pp.285–6, 287; emphasis in original.

After receiving Michels' article containing these comments for *Le Mouvement Socialiste* in January 1907, Lagardelle was taken aback by the sharpness of Michels' response to Berth, describing Michels' article as 'bien méchante' (very unkind), and querying the need for such aggressive formulations as Michels used. At the same time, noting that Michels had just secured a lectureship at the University of Turin, Lagardelle looked forward to Michels acting as a link between the *Mouvement Socialiste* group and the Italian revolutionary socialists around Arturo Labriola in Milan, hoping that they could form a common front at the 1907 International Socialist Congress in Stuttgart.[46] On 3 April 1907, a gathering of revolutionary syndicalists took place in Paris, which included Lagardelle, Berth, Arturo Labriola, and Boris Kritschewsky. In his address to the gathering, Michels saluted French syndicalism, comparing it positively with English trade unionism or the politically 'neutral' German unions: 'Its importance lies in the grand union of the class and the idea'. French syndicalism embodied the revolutionary socialist idea.[47] However, Michels did not resile from his critique of Berth, returning to it in his major 1908 essay for the *Archiv* on oligarchical tendencies in society. Citing his exchange with Berth, Michels argued that French trade unionism was showing increasing signs of oligarchical tendencies, referring to Griffuelhes' attack on critics from the radical left such as Gustave Hervé.[48]

After 1907, the *Mouvement Socialiste* group went into a decline. Already in November 1906, Berth had confided in Michels (who had written asking him for a copy of his review article on Michels' essays on the Italian socialist movement): 'The situation for the *Mouvement* is not brilliant'. Not only did the socialist party look askance at the journal, but leading trade unionists like Griffuelhes now preferred to write for Jaurès's *Humanité*, rather than *Le Mouvement Socialiste*. The journal was increasingly isolated and its continuing publication was somewhat precarious.[49] The break first with Sorel, then with Berth, in 1908–9 heightened the political and intellectual isolation of Lagardelle and his journal. In March 1909, Lagardelle wrote to Michels, with whom he continued to correspond, that he was in a 'période triste', with syndicalism and socialism in France 'in disarray'. Sorel had broken with the *Mouvement* five months previously, and Berth had just followed. Lagardelle bitterly complained that Sorel and Berth had both 'fallen

---

[46] Lagardelle to Michels, 12 January 1907, ARM/FLE.

[47] Robert Michels, 'Le syndicalisme et le socialisme en Allemagne', *Le Mouvement Socialiste*, no.188, July 1907, pp.58–63, here p.59.

[48] Robert Michels, 'Die oligarchischen Tendenzen der Gesellschaft. Ein Beitrag zum Problem der Demokratie', *Archiv für Sozialwissenschaft und Sozialpolitik*, Vol.27 (new series), 1908, pp.73–135, here pp.107–8.

[49] Berth to Michels, 20 November 1906, ARM/FLE. There appears to be a break of over a year in Berth's letters to Michels after this one, confirming that Berth was offended by the polemical nature of Michels' response to his review article. Giorgio Volpe, ed., *Il carteggio fra Roberto Michels e i sindacalisti rivoluzionari*, Naples, 2018, includes Michels' correspondence with Sorel and Lagardelle (in Italian translation), but for some reason omits the correspondence with Berth.

140 ROBERT MICHELS, SOCIALISM, AND MODERNITY

prey to the worst kind of intellectualisms', admiring 'the little abstract formulae that they had fabricated'. Once again, the *Mouvement* was out of money, and having difficulties with its publisher, and it was also running out of contributors, and Lagardelle begged Michels for an article on German or Italian topics.[50] By this time, Michels was publishing much less in socialist journals, and was focusing more on academic journals, in particular the *Archiv für Sozialwissenschaft und Sozialpolitik*, under the influence of Werner Sombart and Max Weber, but he did send Lagardelle one more article.[51]

During 1907, Michels established contact with the French anti-militarist and radical socialist Gustave Hervé, who had recently served time in prison for his anti-militarist and revolutionary propaganda activity. In February of that year, Hervé's paper *La Guerre Sociale* published an excerpt from Michels' article in *Le Mouvement Socialiste* on the German Social Democratic Party after the Mannheim congress, noting that Michels' credentials as a socialist activist added weight to his forceful criticisms of the party.[52]

Apparently in response to an invitation from Hervé, Michels sent *La Guerre Socialiste* a more pointed version of a commentary already published in the Italian journal *La Riforma Sociale*, on the meaning of the 1907 German elections for the German Social Democratic Party, addressed to 'Chers camarades de la Guerre Sociale'. Michels criticized the German Social Democrats for their timidity in failing to combat German nationalist election propaganda with a more forthright insistence on anti-patriotism, in the spirit of Marx's dictum that 'the proletariat has no fatherland'. Michels also referred to the dangers of parliamentary success, which could have led to compromise with the party's enemies had it not been for the electoral setback for the Social Democrats.[53] The militant anti-patriotism and anti-militarism expressed in Michels' article was in tune with Hervé's views on these issues. Michels' contact with *La Guerre Sociale* quickly came to the attention of the Prussian police, who were hyper-sensitive to anti-militarist propaganda of the sort practised by Hervé.[54] (On the other hand, Michels' links with Hervé have

---

[50] Lagardelle to Michels, 13 March and 1 April 1909, ARM/FLE.

[51] Robert Michels, 'La politique étrangère et le Socialisme', *Le Mouvement Socialiste*, 25, January–June 1909, pp.321–33.

[52] 'Jugement sur la social-démocratie allemande', *La Guerre Sociale*, 1, no.9, 13–19 February 1907. On Hervé, see Gilles Heuré, *Gustave Hervé. Itinéraire d'un provocateur*, Paris, 1997; Michael B. Loughlin, 'Gustave Hervé's Transition from Socialism to National Socialism: Continuity and Ambivalence', *Journal of Contemporary History*, 38, 4, 2003, pp.515–38. Loughlin notes the convergence between Hervé's views and Michels' criticisms of German Social Democracy on pp.520–1. On *La Guerre Sociale*, see Heuré, *Gustave Hervé*, pp.107–26, also the introduction to the anthology edited by Raoul Vilette, *La guerre sociale. Un journal 'contre'*, n.p., 1999, pp.9–18 (which also reprints Michels' article cited here on pp.111–13).

[53] Robert Michels, 'Un antipatriote allemande aux antipatriotes français', *La Guerre Sociale*, 1, no.13, 13–19 March 1907.

[54] Landesarchiv Berlin (LAB). A. Pr. Br. Rep. 030 Tit.95, No.16386: Akten der Abteilung VII-4 des Königlichen Polizei-Präsidiums zu Berlin, betreffend den Schriftsteller, Professor Dr Robert Michels 1903–1917, Bl.2.

MICHELS AND FRENCH SOCIALISTS AND SYNDICALISTS   141

mostly gone unnoticed by researchers on Michels, as the standard Michels bibliographies omit his contributions to *La Guerre Sociale*).

Michels found himself sharing much in common with Hervé's anti-militarist principles, chastising German Social Democrats for opposing the anti-militarism of their French comrades, and emphasizing the illogicality of national identities. Michels parted company with Hervé only in arguing that anti-militarism in a single country was not enough—the anti-militarist *élan* of French socialists, which Michels admired, would be in vain if the German socialists did not follow suit, and here Michels believed the omens were not promising, with Karl Liebknecht finding himself relatively isolated in his radical anti-militarist agitation. Michels also praised the 'tenacity and good sense of our comrade Edouard Vaillant', contrasting it favourably with the attitude of most German Social Democrats.[55]

Michels contributed *to La Guerre Sociale* again in May 1907, with a short article devoted to the question of whether there were revolutionaries in Germany. He concluded that there *were* revolutionaries in Germany, but that, taken as a whole, the German Social Democratic Party was far from revolutionary. 'There is little wanting for it to be solely a Millerandist party. There is already more than one Millerand in its ranks…'. There were party radicals, but they could not yet see how serious the decay of the party was becoming through the advance of the reformists.[56]

Michels' contacts with *La Guerre Sociale* continued, with the paper printing an interview with Michels following the International Socialist Congress in 1907. Michels complained that the venue had been badly chosen for a congress that had to decide on effective ways to combat militarism: the legal restrictions that prevailed in Germany (such as the restrictions on *lèse-majesté*) inhibited free debate, and the Germans as the host party were relatively backward when it came to the question of anti-militarist agitation. Michels feared that the need to accommodate German views on anti-militarist agitation had a negative effect on the more advanced French delegation, which had been willing to take a stronger anti-militarist position.[57] After the German party congress at Essen in 1907, Michels also expressed his concern in *Le Mouvement Socialiste* that the concessions to patriotism made by the Germans were encouraging opportunistic elements elsewhere to distance themselves from anti-militarist agitation: 'It is clear, for example, that that part of the French socialists who oppose Hervé's propaganda or the anti-militarism of the CGT draw particular inspiration from German practice

---

[55] Robert Michels, 'Le prochain Congrès socialiste international', *Le Mouvement Socialiste*, no.188, July 1907, pp.38–46, quotation on Vaillant, p.46. Around this time, Michels' friend Werner Sombart also contrasted the 'élan' and 'capacity for enthusiasm' of French socialists with their German counterparts. Friedrich Lenger, *Werner Sombart. 1863–1941*, Munich, 1994, p.152.

[56] 'L'Allemagne est-elle révolutionnaire', *La Guerre Sociale*, 1ère année, no.21, 8–14 May 1907.

[57] 'Nos interviews. Stuttgart. Opinion de Robert Michels, membre de la Social-Démocratie', *La Guerre Sociale*, 1ère Année, no.40, 18–24 September 1907.

142 ROBERT MICHELS, SOCIALISM, AND MODERNITY

and use it as a brake to prevent any forward progress'.[58] In Michels' file in the Berlin political police records, a note based on information received from Rome in June 1908 suggested that Michels' writing for Hervé's paper *La Guerre Sociale* may have continued into 1908.[59] But no further contributions to the paper by Michels have been identified. Just as Michels' contacts with *Le Mouvement Socialiste* started to atrophy as he settled into his academic career in Turin, so too he seems to have let drop his active links with Hervé (who spent most of 1908 in prison, his second term of incarceration as a result of his anti-militarist agitation).

However, Michels continued to praise Hervé's anti-militarism and anti-patriotism as an antidote to the opportunism of mainstream Social Democracy, from which he was more or less openly estranged by 1908. In 1910, writing in the *Archiv für Sozialwissenschaft und Sozialpolitik*, Michels gave the German translation of Hervé's anti-militarist tract *Das Vaterland der Reichen* ('the rich men's fatherland') a favourable review, commending Hervé's radical break with opportunism of official Social Democratic parties on questions of militarism and nationalism.[60] While convinced anti-militarism was a consistent element in Michels' writings, apparently fuelled by a visceral aversion to the military which he acquired during his own military service in Germany, Michels' sympathies with the French syndicalists and radical socialists otherwise seem to have been motivated less by theoretical considerations, and more by his perceptions of an affinity with their temperament and ethical principles, with their cultivation of a sense of revolutionary *élan*. As Pino Ferraris has suggested, and as Michels' exchange with Berth indicates, it is far from clear that Michels could be described as a syndicalist, as far as his attitude to the role of trade unions is concerned.[61] Indeed, as noted in Chapter 3, Michels distanced himself from syndicalism at the very moment he represented the Italian syndicalists at the Stuttgart International Socialist Congress in 1907.

Given the later intellectual trajectory of Lagardelle, Berth, Sorel, and Michels himself from left to right, it is not surprising that the circle around *Le Mouvement Socialiste* has been of great interest for Zeev Sternhell's work on the 'left-wing intellectual origins of fascism'.[62] However, a reading of Lagardelle's correspond-

---

[58] Robert Michels, 'Le patriotisme des socialistes allemands et le congrès d'Essen', *Le Mouvement Socialiste*, année X, no.194, 15 January 1908, pp.5–13, quotation p.12.

[59] LAB, A Rep. 030, Nr.16386, Bl.2.

[60] R.M. [Robert Michels], Review of Gustave Hervé, *Das Vaterland der Reichen*, in *Archiv für Sozialwissenschaft und Sozialpolitik*, 30 (new series), 1910, pp.582–4, here p.582.

[61] Pino Ferraris, *Saggi su Roberto Michels*, Camerino, 1993, pp.58–9, 172–5.

[62] Zeev Sternhell, *Neither Right nor Left: Fascist Ideology in France*, trans. David Maisel, Berkeley, Los Angeles, CA, London, 1986; Sternhell, with Sznajder and Asheri, *The Birth of Fascist Ideology*, which includes a focus on the syndicalists of *Le Mouvement Socialiste* and Michels. On the 'Sternhell debate', see David D. Roberts, 'How Not to Think about Fascism, and Ideology, Intellectual Antecedents, and Historical Meaning', *Journal of Contemporary History*, 35, 2000, pp.185–211; Michel Dobry, *Le mythe de l'allergie française au fascisme*, Paris, 2003; Serge Berstein and Michel Winock, eds., *Fascisme français? La controverse*, Paris, 2014; and Brian Jenkins, ed., *France in the Era of Fascism*,

ence with Michels suggests that Sternhell's attention to *Le Mouvement Socialiste* may be out of proportion to the journal's actual influence, given its increasingly exiguous subscription base, and Lagardelle's increasing isolation.[63] Michels and Sorel were also intellectuals without any real constituency in the labour movement at the time of their links with the journal. It misses the fact that Michels did not transition directly from radical left to far right, rather he moved to more bourgeois liberal positions by 1914.[64] It also occludes other intellectual influences on Michels, such as the elite theory and social-anthropological biologistic ideas prevalent in Italian social thought in the period, or Michels' intellectual debt to the crowd psychology formulated by Gustave Le Bon (discussed below). In French revolutionary syndicalism, like its Italian counterpart, Michels found a socialism with added temperament and *élan* that he missed among the more sober German comrades—a temperament that resonated with his own French origins and affinity for the Latin peoples. For Michels, temperament was always ethnically coded. While his anti-militarism was sincere and genuine, his relationship with revolutionary syndicalism in both France and Italy was more vicarious, and was limited by his profound scepticism towards trade unionism in general.

New York and Oxford, 2005, which includes an essay by Sternhell, reflecting on some of the criticisms of his work.

[63] See Pouthier, 'Roberto Michels et les syndicalistes révolutionnaires français'.

[64] A point made by Timm Genett, *Der Fremde im Kriege. Zur politischen Theorie und Biographie von Robert Michels 1876–1936*, Berlin, 2008.

PART II
MICHELS, MODERN IDEAS, AND MOVEMENTS

5

Feminism and the Sexual Politics of a New Century

Robert Michels is not usually remembered as a feminist, and does not generally feature in histories of the early-twentieth-century feminist movement.[1] However, like many male intellectuals of his time, from Ibsen a generation earlier to contemporaries such as Max Weber, Michels was particularly interested in the 'woman question', feminism, and the implications of changing sexual mores as a feature of modern society. He wrote frequently on women's issues, contributed to a wide (indeed, abnormally wide) range of feminist publications, from Clara Zetkin's left-Marxist *Die Gleichheit*, to *Die Frau*, on the moderate right wing of the German feminist movement, and published a book of essays on the 'sexual question' in 1911, the same year as his better-known main work on *Political Parties*; and, like that work, it appeared in several languages. He was active in the radical feminist 'sex reform' group, the Bund für Mutterschutz (League for Protection of Mothers), and supported his wife's involvement in feminist activities, Gisela Michels-Lindner. Timm Genett has even written: 'The struggle for equal rights for women in both private and public life is a central concern in Michels' political writings'.[2]

Feminism

In his very first scholarly journal article, published in the Italian periodical *La Riforma Sociale*, Michels dealt with the 'woman question' in Germany, identifying it as perhaps the most important of the social questions currently under discussion in that country.[3] Michels perceived the root of the problem in Germany as lying in the low esteem in which women were held there. Michels cited figures from August Bebel's work on *Woman and Socialism* on the dramatic increase of

---

[1] An exception to the tendency to neglect this aspect of Michels' work is Pino de Ferraris, *Saggi su Roberto Michels*, Camerino, 1993, pp.232–62; see also Andrew G. Bonnell, 'Robert Michels, Max Weber, and the Sexual Question', *The European Legacy*, Vol.3, 6, 1998, pp.97–105; Timm Genett, *Der Fremde im Kriege. Zur politischen Theorie und Biographie von Robert Michels 1876–1936*, Berlin, 2008, p.44.

[2] Genett, *Der Fremde im Kriege*, p.60.

[3] R. [Robert] Michels, 'Attorno ad una questione sociale in Germania', *La Riforma Sociale. Rassegna di scienze sociali e politiche*, Vol.19, ii, 8, 1901, pp.775–94.

Robert Michels, Socialism, and Modernity. Andrew G. Bonnell, Oxford University Press. © Andrew G. Bonnell 2023.
DOI: 10.1093/oso/9780192871848.003.0006

women's work in industry in Germany, while also pointing to statistics on their much lower pay rates compared with men's. Michels also found German women less well-organized than in many industrialized countries. The lot of the female rural labourer was miserable in the extreme, poorly paid and worse housed, and the life of waitresses, female shop assistants, and seamstresses was no better, with pay so low that it forced many women into prostitution. There was also a specifically bourgeois variant of the 'woman question': in Germany women of the middle classes had become excluded from any useful occupation, so that they tended to give themselves over to distractions. Michels did not censure the freedoms which young middle-class women were starting to enjoy in their social life, rather he regretted that girls' education in Germany was still too backward for them to make the best use of their relative liberty. The imbalance between men's status and that of women, with men freer to seek sexual fulfilment outside marriage, and men's tendency to choose younger women as wives, led to the problem of the spinster, or old maid ('*alte Jungfer*')[4]—a stock figure of fun in the humorous papers, but a cruel social reality for many, given the limited choices available to women. Michels called for better educational and professional opportunities for women, which would lead to the likelihood of more equal, more companionate marriage. He quoted the poet Ernst von Wolzogen: 'Races of heroes are only born from marriages well-matched in every respect.'[5] A reform of marriage would thus have eugenic benefits as well. Michels also cited Wolzogen in an article for the Italian feminist journal *Unione Femminile* that dealt with the figure of the 'old maid' and women's professional opportunities, in which he argued that the cruel lot of the 'old maid' within bourgeois society was one of the forces driving women into loveless and unhappy marriages. Such 'cold and calculated marriages do great harm to that instinct of elective affinity that Darwin called natural selection', which raises the question of whether such social conditions, in Michels' eyes, should be viewed as dysgenic.[6]

Michels dwelt at some length on the obstacles to women's participation in higher education in Germany, comparing the situation there unfavourably with other countries. Michels's own *alma mater*, the University of Halle, had been relatively progressive by German standards in opening its doors to women in the 1890s, but it witnessed a backlash from male medical students against the enrolment of women in 1899.[7] Michels went on to discuss the extent to which the new German Civil Code (*Bürgerliches Gesetzbuch*) of 1900 represented some reform, albeit rather limited, in the area of women's rights in marriage. He was

---

[4] The German term quoted in the Italian text.
[5] Michels, 'Attorno ad una questione sociale in Germania', p.9 [pagination of offprint]. Michels cites Wolzogen from Arthur Kirchhoff, *Die Akademische Frau*, Berlin, 1897, p.340.
[6] Roberto [Robert] Michels, 'La questione della Zitella e della donna professionista', *Unione Femminile*, 2, 19–20 October 1902, pp.144–6, here p.144.
[7] Michels, 'Attorno ad una questione sociale in Germania', pp.10, 11 [pagination of offprint].

FEMINISM AND THE SEXUAL POLITICS OF A NEW CENTURY 149

particularly critical of the Code's restrictive provision for divorce. Ultimately, Michels believed, the responsibility for the relative lack of progress in women's rights in Germany rested with the apathy of most German women, although he noted that the German Social Democratic Party had consistently campaigned for women's equality: it was 'the sole champion of the proletarian woman question'.[8] In addition, a bourgeois feminist movement was stirring: the Bund deutscher Frauenvereine (BDF) claimed 70,000 members, and its lobbying had contributed to what ameliorations there had been in women's rights in the new Civil Code. On the whole, however, the women's suffrage that had already become a reality on the other side of the world in New Zealand and South Australia was still a remote prospect in imperial Germany.[9]

In the course of 1902, Michels contributed to several different feminist journals. In May, for example, he wrote a warmly positive review article on *Das Weib und der Intellectualismus* by the German-Italian socialist feminist Oda Olberg (or Olberg-Lerda) for the Viennese *Dokumente der Frauen*, edited by Marie Lang.[10] Michels went out of his way to reassure the bourgeois feminist readers that, even though Olberg-Lerda was an adherent of the radical wing of the Italian socialists, her socialism was hardly obtrusive in her book, which was a rebuttal of claims of the alleged mental inferiority of women.[11] Olberg-Lerda's principal target was Professor Paul Julius Möbius of Leipzig, author of a treatise on 'The Physiological Feeble-Mindedness of Woman',[12] but she also drew other proponents of misogynistic ideas of women's natural inferiority and susceptibility to degeneration into her line of fire, including Cesare Lombroso. Elsewhere, too, Michels rejected biologistic explanations for women's subordinate position in society, which he regarded as the sociological and historical product of women's economic and intellectual subordination, especially through their dependent role in the family, and not to be accounted for by theories of women's 'innate weakmindedness'.[13] On the contrary, as social conditions changed, Michels believed that women were becoming physically and intellectually more and more men's equals, and were on the way to becoming morally men's equal through the experience of work and, in many cases, through struggle for equal rights in the workplace.[14]

---

[8] Michels, 'Attorno ad una questione sociale in Germania', p.17.

[9] Michels, 'Attorno ad una questione sociale in Germania', pp.17–18.

[10] Dr Robert Michels, 'Das Weib und der Intellectualismus', *Dokumente der Frauen*, VII, 4, 15 May 1902, pp.106–14. Michels also published a shorter version of the review in *Das freie Wort*, Jg.2, no.5, 5 June 1902, p.160.

[11] Michels, 'Das Weib und der Intellectualismus', p.107.

[12] P.J. Möbius, *Über den physiologischen Schwachsinn des Weibes*, Halle a.S., 1901. This slender work went through several editions.

[13] Dr Robert Michels, 'Die Frau als Streikende im Lohnkampf', *Die Frau*, Jg.10, Nr.12, September 1903, p.754.

[14] Michels, 'Die Frau als Streikende im Lohnkampf', p.752.

150   ROBERT MICHELS, SOCIALISM, AND MODERNITY

The following month, Michels contributed another article for the *Dokumente der Frauen*, on the beginnings of socialist organization among severely exploited Italian female rural labourers. The article is written from a socialist standpoint, referring to the class conscious self-organization of the labouring countrywomen, but stresses the claim of the women's organization to the sympathies of more well-off women, on the grounds of its principled moral goals.[15] Michels also contributed a couple of book reviews to the *Dokumente der Frauen*, including a review of a pamphlet by the socialist feminist Clara Zetkin, in which Michels praised the acuteness with which Zetkin diagnosed the extent to which different feminist groups posed demands which accorded with the economic circumstances of their respective classes, and welcomed Zetkin's aim of reforming the structure of the family (to include more participation of fathers in the raising of children).[16] Again, Michels attempted to formulate a favourable presentation of socialist ideas for a non-socialist readership.

Michels did not confine himself to reviewing Clara Zetkin's writings in bourgeois feminist journals; in April 1902, he contributed the first of what was to become a number of articles to Clara Zetkin's *Die Gleichheit*, dealing with legislation for the protection of women workers in Italy, writing as someone wholly identifying himself with the cause of the socialist party.[17] In one of his subsequent articles for *Die Gleichheit*, on the women's movement in Italy, Michels made one of his characteristic ethnographic generalizations: that Italian men did not tend to make Italian women feel their subordinate position as much as German men did, with the result that bitter 'anti-male' feminists were unknown in Italy (unlike in Germany, apparently).[18] Of perhaps more significance for readers of *Die Gleichheit*, familiar with the deep division between socialist and middle-class feminism in imperial Germany, was Michels' observation that the division between bourgeois and proletarian women's movements in Italy was less clear-cut than in any other country. That was not to say, Michels quickly clarified, that the proletarian women's movement was full of admixtures of bourgeois elements: 'that would be an *Unding* (something outrageous)'. Rather, the bourgeois women's movement was strongly influenced by proletarian elements, in so far as whenever women from the upper classes became involved in seeking to improve social conditions, they found themselves following the initiatives of socialist feminists.[19] Michels' series of articles on the history of the proletarian women's movement in

[15] Dr Robert Michels, 'Ein italienisches Landarbeiterinnen-Programm', *Dokumente der Frauen*, VII, 6 15 June 1902, pp.159–66.

[16] Dr Robert Michels, Review of Clara Zetkin, *Geistiges Proletariat, Frauenfrage und Socialismus*, in *Dokumente der Frauen*, Bd.7, Nr.9–10, 1 and 15 August 1902, p.276.

[17] Dr Robert Michels, 'Der Kampf um das Arbeiterinnenachutzgesetz in Italien', *Die Gleichheit*, Jg.12, no.9, 23 April 1902, pp.68–9.

[18] Dr Robert Michels, 'Die Frauenbewegung in Italien', *Die Gleichheit*, Jg.12, no.17, 13 August 1902, p.130.

[19] Michels, 'Die Frauenbewegung in Italien'.

FEMINISM AND THE SEXUAL POLITICS OF A NEW CENTURY   151

Italy (which appeared over several months in 1903) paid tribute to the work of pioneering socialist feminists like Anna Maria Mozzoni and Anna Kuliscioff.[20] While essentially a historical narrative of the evolution of Italian socialist feminism, Michels' own opinions on women's emancipation come through clearly: Michels consistently shows approval for the most thorough-going emancipatory programme in terms of women's economic, political, and legal situation, and in terms of rights to equality and freedom in marriage, sexual life, and reproduction. Thus Michels criticized a resolution of the party congress of the Partito Operaio in Bologna in 1888 for supporting women's entitlement to equal rights in the economic sphere, in the workplace, but failing to press for equal civil rights.[21] Michels endorsed the programme of the Lega Socialista Milanese of 1891, led by Filippo Turati and influenced by Anna Kuliscioff as far as its advocacy of women's equal rights in the sphere of family and reproduction was concerned: the programme demanded the abolition of the old-style patriarchal family, the secularization of marriage, legalization of divorce, and free sexual relations ('out of conviction, not out of frivolity'). The programme argued that sexual relations and marriage based on the complete equality and the free choice of both partners were in the interest of both individual happiness and of '*social progress* and finally also in the gradual *improvement of the species*.' However, Michels regretted that the programme qualified its advocacy of equality for women in the professions, calling for the right of women to enter '*almost all professions and social positions*'.[22] Michels then recounted how the self-sacrificial conduct of women of both the urban and rural proletariat in the early 1890s obliged male socialist leaders to view women's activism with more respect.[23] By 1895, Michels was pleased to report, the Italian socialist party recognized in principle the need for the full 'equality of women in political terms and in family law', a recognition accompanied by the publication of an Italian edition of August Bebel's *Woman in Socialism* ('still today one of the most read books in Italian libraries').[24] By August 1903, Clara Zetkin was

---

[20] Dr Robert Michels, 'Rückblick auf die Geschichte der proletarischen Frauenbewegung in Italien', *Die Gleichheit*, Jg.13, 1, 1 January 1903, pp.2–3; no.2, 14 January 1903, pp.11–13; no.5, 25 February 1903, pp.36–8; no.8, 8 April 1903, pp.58–60; no.11, 20 May 1903, pp.83–5; no.17, 12 August 1903, pp.131–4.

[21] Michels, 'Rückblick auf die Geschichte der proletarischen Frauenbewegung in Italien', no.2, 14 January 1903, p.12.

[22] Michels, 'Rückblick auf die Geschichte der proletarischen Frauenbewegung in Italien', no.5, 25 February 1903, p.37 (emphasis in original). See also no.8, 8 April 1903, p.58.

[23] Michels, 'Rückblick auf die Geschichte der proletarischen Frauenbewegung in Italien', no.5, 25 February 1903, pp.37–8.

[24] Michels, 'Rückblick auf die Geschichte der proletarischen Frauenbewegung in Italien', no.11, 20 May 1903, p.83. See also Dr Robert Michels, 'Die Ehescheidung in Italien', *Leipziger Volkszeitung*, Jg.10, no.33, 10 February 1903, in which Michels endorses those Italian socialist activists who campaigned for a divorce law in Italy; Robert Michels, Review of Guido Podrecca, *Il divorzio*, in *Ethische Kultur*, Jg.XI, Nr.19, 9 May 1903, p.151.

152   ROBERT MICHELS, SOCIALISM, AND MODERNITY

addressing Michels and his wife as personal friends, as well as regarding Michels as a comrade on the radical left of the Social Democratic Party.[25]

At the same time as he cultivated Zetkin and wrote for the socialist *Gleichheit*, Michels contributed a number of articles to Helene Lange's bourgeois liberal journal *Die Frau* on women in the Italian labour movement. In March 1902, he contributed a survey of the movement of Italian women workers, beginning by noting that although Italian women enjoyed somewhat more freedom in some respects than their German counterparts (for example, gaining the right to attend university about two decades earlier), the number of bourgeois women active in the feminist movement was still small. Michels went to some lengths to justify the reasonableness of Italian working women's support for the socialist party. He also stressed the high moral level of organized women workers in Italy.[26] This article was followed by a two-part essay on the campaign for protective legislation for women workers, an essay which Gertrud Bäumer, Helene Lange's right hand in the management of the journal, encouraged Michels to submit.[27] Michels attributed the slowness of social reform measures on the part of the Italian state to the 'lateness of the emergence of a class conscious and strong proletariat in Italy' (using Marxian language that readers of *Die Frau* might have been unaccustomed to read in their journal).[28] The fact that the Italian socialist party had begun to raise the demand for protective legislation for women workers Michels attributed to a great extent to the Russian-born Anna Kuliscioff, 'doubtless one of the most striking figures which international socialism has produced'. Not only was Kuliscioff endowed with 'wonderful physical loveliness…, a splendid Nordic teint, clever steel-blue eyes, and…blonde pigtails falling long down her shoulders, so that one compared her with a Pre-Raphaelite Madonna', she also possessed 'an incredibly sharp mind'. Kuliscioff was a 'genuinely Russian type'.[29] Together with her partner, the reformist socialist Filippo Turati, Kuliscioff was responsible for a bill to protect women workers in 1900,which won the support of the Italian feminist movement (90 per cent of whom Michels reckoned to be of the democratic camp politically, in any case) against the opposing government proposal.[30] The law that eventuated in 1902 was a compromise between the

[25] See Clara Zetkin to Robert Michels, postcard of 10 August 1903, ARM/FLE.
[26] Dr Robert Michels, 'Die Arbeiterinnenbewegung in Italien', *Die Frau*, Jg.9, no.6, March 1902, pp.328–36. In an example of auto-plagiarism, Michels borrowed passages from this article verbatim for his essay 'Der italienische Sozialismus auf dem Lande', for *Das freie Wort*, Jg.2, no.2, 1902.
[27] R. [Robert] Michels, 'Der Kampf um die Arbeiterinnenschutzgesetzgebung in Italien', *Die Frau*, Jg.9, H.9, June 1902, pp.513–18, 612–18. Gertrud Bäumer to Gisela Michels, 26 March 1902, ARM/FLE.
[28] Michels, 'Der Kampf um die Arbeiterinnenschutzgesetzgebung in Italien', p.513.
[29] Michels, 'Der Kampf um die Arbeiterinnenschutzgesetzgebung in Italien', p.514. Writing later, in his book *Storia del marxismo in Italia* (Rome, 1909, p.229), Michels could not resist stressing Kulisicioff's beauty, even citing Lombroso's anthropological assessment of her appearance (diametrically opposite to the criminal type).
[30] Michels, 'Der Kampf um die Arbeiterinnenschutzgesetzgebung in Italien', p.613.

FEMINISM AND THE SEXUAL POLITICS OF A NEW CENTURY   153

Kuliscioff-Turati bill and the government's, with a maximum twelve-hour day for women above 15 years of age (which had to be interrupted by breaks), and improved health requirements and factory inspection measures. For Michels, the reform act was a 'moral victory for the Left', one which he claimed would be the start of a long era of social reform in Italy.[31]

Gertrud Bäumer seems to have sought to cultivate Michels as a potentially useful ally, seeking to get him to review the latest volume of Lange's and Bäumer's *Handbuch der Frauenbewegung* in the *Frankfurter Zeitung*.[32] He contributed another article to the journal in October 1902, which vividly described a children's strike, carried out by young girls (aged mostly 9 to 14) working in tailors' workshops in Milan. The young girls went to the Milan *camera del lavoro* for assistance in formulating their industrial demands of their employers (mostly their mistresses in the workshops), and gained further help from the local women's union (Unione Femminile), whose leading figures Ersilia Majno-Bronzini and Elisa Boschetti Michels claimed to be among his friends. In the article, Michels stressed not only the girls' exploitation at the hands of their mistresses, whom he characterized as capitalists in a sense, despite their also belonging to a stratum of the fourth estate. He also stressed the moral danger in which many of the children found themselves, vulnerable to sexual exploitation.[33] It is not clear if he thought that the more pro-capitalist readers of *Die Frau* would respond more to the sexual moral scandal than the mere fact of severe economic exploitation. Michels also wrote a report for *Die Frau* on the (mainly behind-the-scenes) role of Italian socialist women in the Italian Socialist Party's congress at Imola, which was full of admiration for both the leaders of the Italian socialist women's movement, such as Anna Kuliscioff, and the rank and file, like the striking rice-growers (*risaiole*) of Molinella.[34] A similar note of admiration for Italian socialist women dominates Michels' article for the Viennese *Neues Frauenleben* on the economic struggle of women cigar-makers in Florence. Expressing his 'admiration' in the face of the evidence of 'women's steadfastness and women's courage to face sacrifice', Michels declared that Italy was the home of the 'New Woman'—'not the intellectual, educated' version (becoming familiar in bourgeois feminist discourse) but 'the intelligent proletarian' variety.[35]

In the context of the politically divided German women's movement, Michels verged on promiscuity in his willingness to contribute to periodicals representing almost the entire range of feminist opinion, a fact which the progressive liberal

[31] Michels, 'Der Kampf um die Arbeiterinnenschutzgesetzgebung in Italien', pp.616–18.
[32] Gertrud Bäumer to Robert Michels, 22 July 1902, ARM/FLE. On Bäumer, see Marie Luise Bach, *Gertrud Bäumer. Biographische Texte und Texte zu einem Persönlichkeitsbild*, Weinheim, 1989.
[33] Dr Robert Michels, 'Ein Kinderstreik', *Die Frau*, Jg.10, 1, October 1902, pp.16–19.
[34] Dr Robert Michels, 'Die sozialistischen Frauen Italiens auf dem Kongress zu Imola', *Die Frau*, Jg.10, no.3, December 1902, pp.152–5.
[35] Dr Robert Michels, 'Ein Kapitel aus den Kämpfen der Florentiner Cigarrenarbeiterinnen', *Neues Frauenleben*, Jg.15, no.3, March 1903, p.15.

154   ROBERT MICHELS, SOCIALISM, AND MODERNITY

feminist, Minna Cauer, coolly drew to his attention in September 1902 when he offered to write for the progressive feminist journal *Die Frauenbewegung* ('the women's movement'). Cauer responded that she had read Michels' articles in both *Die Frau* and *Die Gleichheit* with interest, although she felt his assessment of the bourgeois feminist movement in Germany, as far as she could judge from *Die Gleichheit*, was not entirely accurate. She went on to write:

> I do not therefore know what tendency you prefer to represent; naturally I do not demand that you commit yourself to a party or a tendency, however both *Die Frau* and *Die Gleichheit* are opponents of our progressive tendency. *Die Frau* represents the conservative, indeed almost the reactionary standpoint within the bourgeois women's movement, *Die Gleichheit* the *exclusively* social democratic view, i.e. it recognizes *on principle* nothing outside itself, and thus worships the dogma of infallibility.

Cauer invited Michels to send her articles so that she could form a clearer opinion of whether his work would actually be suited for *Die Frauenbewegung*, protesting politely that the opposing positions suggested by the location of his previous articles made it hard for her to judge. In case Michels was actuated by mercenary motives, she warned him that her journal could not promise 'golden fruits. Our honorarium is 4–5 Marks per column.'[36] Michels' need to support himself and a young family by his writing, and maintain a standard of living appropriate for someone pursuing an academic career, may indeed have been a motive for his seeking such diverse outlets for his work.

Michels managed to get Cauer, who was one of the most fervent advocates of women's suffrage, to accept a contribution on the question of women's right to vote, and to run it as the leading article in a December 1902 issue of *Die Frauenbewegung*. Michels took the opportunity of the appearance of an article in *Das freie Wort* questioning German women's readiness for the vote to argue for the pressing and immediate need for women's suffrage. This was not an uncontroversial position at this time, even within the German women's movement, with many moderate German feminists regarding agitation for women's suffrage as premature and overly radical, and it was only at the beginning of 1902 that a legal loophole had been discovered to allow the formation of a German Association for

---

[36] Minna Cauer to Michels, 3 September 1902, ARM/FLE. Minna Cauer had an acute sense of the differences between the 'radical' progressive wing of the bourgeois feminist movement, of which her journal *Die Frauenbewegung* was the principal mouthpiece, and the more conservative majority of the BDF on the one side and the Social Democratic women's movement on the other. See Ute Gerhard, *Unerhört. Die Geschichte der deutschen Frauenbewegung*, Frankfurt, 1996, pp. 218–19; Dietlinde Peters, 'Minna Cauer', in Henrike Hülsbergen, ed., *Stadtbild und Frauenleben. Berlin im Spiegel von 16 Frauenporträts*, Berlin, 1997, p.166. For Helene Lange's retrospective depiction of the differences between her and the progressive wing of the bourgeois women's movement represented by Cauer and Anita Augspurg, see Helene Lange, *Lebenserinnerungen*, Berlin, 1927, pp.223–6.

FEMINISM AND THE SEXUAL POLITICS OF A NEW CENTURY   155

Women's Suffrage.[37] While Michels conceded that the likelihood of the immediate introduction of women's suffrage in Germany was slight, he took the view that any open discussion of the topic would contribute to progress: 'especially... in a much read periodical with an educated readership with a modern outlook', he wrote, not flinching from a degree of flattery.[38] While it was true, Michels argued, that under existing social conditions women were generally more susceptible to reactionary influences than men (from church, state, and social and economic forces), this was not innately women's fault, but the fault of false education and male dominance in society. Even if the immediate introduction of women's suffrage strengthened reactionary parties in the short term, which Michels assumed was not in the interests of any of his readers, it would nonetheless be of benefit to the 'progress of humanity', and thoroughly necessary for the 'achievement of democratic and social goals'.[39] The vote for women was a necessary step towards the '*democratization of the masses*'. Only receipt of the right to vote would qualify women for its exercise, and the political contest for women's votes would quickly give them the necessary experience. Michels also sought to reassure the progressive liberal readers of *Die Frauenbewegung* that the material conditions and 'class consciousness' of the 'great mass of proletarian women' would render them immune to the blandishments of clerical and reactionary political interests.[40] The article seems to have been well-received by the readership of *Die Frauenbewegung*, according to a letter from Minna Cauer to Gisela Michels, in which Cauer assured Michels' wife that she had heard only positive reactions to the piece.[41]

Michels continued to publish in *Die Frauenbewegung* in the following year, with a leading article in February 1903 on the origins of the 'women question' as a social question. Michels criticized the extent to which the educated elite sought to either deny the existence of social questions or to dismiss them as purely materially motivated. Michels stressed that social movements had a moral-cultural and ideal dimension as well as material motives. He also defined a 'social question' as one that arises when the 'masses' are made conscious of the injustice of their situation by a numerically small conscious minority.[42] A few months later, Michels also published an article on 'Woman's Dilemma in Love' in *Die Frauenbewgung*.[43] Michels thus managed to publish in both the Marxist *Gleichheit* and the progressive

---

[37] Gerhard, *Unerhört*, pp.124, 171–2, 223–4.

[38] Dr Robert Michels, 'Frauenstimmrecht—schon heute eine Notwendigkeit', *Die Frauenbewegung*, Jg.8, no.23, 1 December 1902, p.177.

[39] Michels, 'Frauenstimmrecht'.   [40] Michels, 'Frauenstimmrecht', p.178.

[41] M. Cauer to Gisela Michels, 20 December 1902, ARM/FLE. The article received a favourable notice in the Viennese feminist periodical *Neues Frauenleben*, Jg.14, no.12, December 1902, p.22. Michels subsequently also contributed to the latter journal.

[42] Dr Robert Michels, 'Entstehung der Frauenfrage als soziale Frage', *Die Frauenbewegung*, Jg.9, no.3, 1 February 1903, pp.17–18.

[43] Dr Robert Michels, 'Das Dilemma des Weibes in der Liebe', *Die Frauenbewegung*, Jg.9, no.11, 1 June 1903, pp.82–4.

156 ROBERT MICHELS, SOCIALISM, AND MODERNITY

liberal *Frauenbewegung* even when the two journals (or their respective editors) were engaged in sometimes vitriolic polemics against each other.[44] However, in his essays for *Die Gleichheit*, he wrote from the standpoint of a convinced socialist, going so far as to pen flights of lyricism such as:

> Everywhere, things were stirring. On all sides, the broad masses of the hungering proletariat began to breathe. The great sun of socialist world liberation had shone and done wonders where even the great sun of the southerly heavens had been powerless. The goddess of Hope had awakened, and was waving to her sons.[45]

In his essays from the same period for bourgeois feminist journals, on the other hand, Michels sought to persuade mainly non- (or anti-)socialist readers of the reasonableness of the demands of the Italian labour movement, and of the moral integrity and intellectual stature of Italian socialist feminists. This approach, seeking to mediate between socialists and bourgeois feminism, at least when writing for bourgeois feminist journals, was no doubt assisted by the fact that Michels was mostly writing about Italy, and was thus already in the role of an interpreter or mediator, explaining a foreign movement to a German audience. In 1903, Michels contributed an essay on Social Democratic women to the *Frauen-Rundschau*, praising the socialist feminists across the ideological spectrum from Clara Zetkin on the left to Lily Braun on the right, and directly addressing the differences between socialist and bourgeois feminism. The only country where there was not a clear divide between bourgeois and socialist feminism, in Michels' view, was Italy, because of the state's preparedness to concede feminist demands such as admitting women to positions in universities and equal status for men and women schoolteachers. In all other countries, however, socialist feminists viewed bourgeois women's organizations as fated to fall short of the 'final goal' of the women's movement—complete equality—as long as the latter failed to address basic economic and social conditions affecting working women. 'What, for example, is the benefit to the proletarian woman of the admission of women to the career of university lecturer?', Michels asked. He argued that: 'The salvation of

---

[44] See, for example, Klara Zetkin, 'In eigener Sache', *Die Gleichheit*, Jg.13, no.13, June 1903, pp.101–2; and, in the same issue of *Die Frauenbewegung* as Michels' article 'Das Dilemma des Weibes in der Liebe', 'Große Gesichtspunkte', *Die Frauenbewegung*, Jg.9, no.11, 1 June 1903, pp.81–2. Michels continued to offer contributions to *Die Frauenbewegung*, in 1903/4, but Minna Cauer pleaded lack of space, given a substantial backlog of material and the need to give priority to matters of current importance. M. Cauer to Robert Michels, 7 April 1903; 8 January 1904, ARM/FLE.

[45] Michels, 'Rückblick auf die Geschichte der proletarischen Frauenbewegung in Italien', no.5, 25 February 1903, p.38.

FEMINISM AND THE SEXUAL POLITICS OF A NEW CENTURY   157

woman will have to stand in a logical and historical connection with the victory of the socialist idea, even if it does not directly coincide with the latter in time.'[46] Michels soon came up against the limits within which he could advocate socialist views within bourgeois feminist journals. Michels found his article on women's participation in strikes in Italy, which he submitted to *Die Frau*, was cut by the editor.[47] Gertrud Bäumer explained that Michels' article had contained 'sharply partisan' expressions, which did not fit in with the 'character of our journal'. Bäumer characterized *Die Frau* as neutral towards the party-political attitude of its contributors, but 'the obverse of this attitude is that we strictly avoid any advocacy of party point of view, even if only in the form of expression'. Thus, terms like 'emancipation of the proletarians' and 'entrepreneurs of the worst sort' were deleted. Bäumer added that the expression ' "total slavery" [*Ganzsklaverei*] of woman' contradicted 'the conception of the historical development of the women question that we have always advocated'.[48] Bäumer's conception of political neutrality did not prevent *Die Frau* from publishing contributions by Helene Lange and herself that advocated nationalist and pro-imperialist positions, for example Lange's endorsement in 1900 of the navy expansion programme.[49] Michels' justification of the notion of class struggle and rejection of German national chauvinism seem all the more incongruous beside such published opinions of *Die Frau*'s editors.

Michels tested the limits of Bäumer's and Lange's tolerance again the following year in a lengthy two-part article on women in the Italian *camere di lavoro*. The underlying theme of the article (which contained a rich amount of empirical data from Italian sources) was clearly the need for 'class solidarity' among Italian working women,[50] and the benefits of this solidarity in raising the material and cultural level of women workers so that they became part of the movement to which the future belonged, as Michels prophesied in a slightly purple conclusion.[51] Michels showed an awareness of the problem of the double burden for women in industrializing societies: they had to work long, tiring hours as wage-earners, only to return home to the traditional duties of the housewife.[52] However, his description of women affected by industrialization was not exactly empathetic: 'Out of the nothing-but-a-housewife [modern industrial society] kneads

---

[46] Dr Robert Michels, 'Die politische Tätigkeit der sozialdemokratischen Frauen', *Frauen-Rundschau*, Jg.4, no.21, 1903, pp.1045–8, here p.1045.

[47] Michels, 'Die Frau als Streikende im Lohnkampf', pp.752–8.

[48] Gertrud Bäumer to Michels, 9 August 1903, ARM/FLE.

[49] Helene Lange, 'Flottenbewegung und Friedensbewegung', *Die Frau*, 1900, p.323, cited in Gerhard, *Unerhört*, p.288. Bäumer and Lange were politically close to the position of Friedrich Naumann's National Social Party, combining advocacy of social reform with nationalist and imperialist foreign policy views.

[50] Dr Robert Michels, 'Die italienische Frau in den camere di lavoro', *Die Frau*, Jg.11, Heft 6, March 1904, p.369.

[51] Michels, 'Die italienische Frau in den camere di lavoro', April 1904, p.428.

[52] Michels, 'Die italienische Frau in den camere di lavoro', March 1904, p.367.

158   ROBERT MICHELS, SOCIALISM, AND MODERNITY

with its sooty hands at first just the dull and stupid woman factory worker [öde blöde Fabrikarbeiterin]'—but, he continued, this was just a step towards the creation of a 'higher type of woman'.[53] From being a mere cog in the machine, working women could change from having lives of 'dull vegetating away' to that of 'the joyful struggle for life' thanks to the experience of organization in the labour movement, to which the local *camera del lavoro* (which Michels went on to describe in detail) was often the first point of contact.[54] In addition to the economic struggles of the *camere di lavoro*, Michels stressed their work in 'the moral and intellectual elevation of their members'.[55]

Gertrud Bäumer wrote to Michels apologizing for the delay in publishing the article, but *Die Frau* wished to avoid too one-sided an emphasis on Italian affairs, and thus allowed for a gap between Michels' contributions, and the first part of the article covered perhaps somewhat too much material as far as the interests of the readers of *Die Frau* were concerned. While Bäumer allowed much of Michels' socialist phraseology to stand in the final version of the article, she decidedly took issue with Michels' suggestion that the readers of *Die Frau* would be unlikely to identify with 'simple working women'. Bäumer wrote that as Helene Lange was the chairwoman of the Allgemeine deutsche Kassirinnenverein (General German Association of Women Clerical Workers), she could not allow such an aspersion on German women white-collar workers to stand in her journal. Such a suggestion of narrow-minded class egoism would be unfair to German female clerical workers, even if, as everywhere, there were some members of the association with backward views. Judging by the absence of such a phrase in the published version, Michels duly modified the article.[56]

While Michels tested the limits of bourgeois feminists' openness to socialist views, he was also prepared to criticize male dominance within the working class, as reflected for example, in alcohol abuse among working-class men.[57] He also criticized some Italian socialists who viewed the campaign for the introduction of a divorce law as a diversion from more unambiguously socialist goals. For Michels, not only did the socialist movement need to claim for itself any progressive developments in 'science and moral education', it was also necessary to acknowledge that there were unhappy marriages in the proletariat, too.[58] Michels was also critical of the timidity of the draft divorce law proposed by two Italian

---

[53] Michels, 'Die italienische Frau in den camere di lavoro', March 1904, p.367.
[54] Michels, 'Die italienische Frau in den camere di lavoro', March 1904, pp.367–8.
[55] Michels, 'Die italienische Frau in den camere di lavoro', March 1904, p.369.
[56] Bäumer to Michels, 29 January 1904, ARM/FLE.
[57] Robert Michels, 'Zum Problem der Arbeiterhäuser', *Deutschland. Monatsschrift für die gesamte Kultur*, Jg.2, no.12, September 1903, p.747n.
[58] Michels, 'Die Ehescheidung in Italien'. See also Robert Michels, 'Landleute, Kinder und Frauen', *Neues Frauenleben*, Jg.17, 6, June 1905, pp.9–11, which deplored the subjugation of women in southern Italy; Michels' Review of Guido Podrecca, *Il divorzio*, p.151; Robert Michels, 'Eine Psychologie der sozialistischen Bewegung', *Leipziger Volkszeitung*, no.8, 4 January 1905.

FEMINISM AND THE SEXUAL POLITICS OF A NEW CENTURY 159

socialist members of parliament, which even lagged behind the recently adopted new German Civil Code.[59] A few years later, in his translation of Enrico Ferri's treatise *Il metodo rivoluzionario*, Michels took issue with Ferri's remark that the only divorce a working-class woman needed was a divorce from (material) misery, Michels wrote in a note: 'A remarkable claim. Working-class women also know a sexual question. Here Ferri falls victim to the greatest possible exaggeration that adherents of the so-called materialist view of history have ever been guilty of'.[60] Writing in *Die Gleichheit* on the occasion of the thirty-fourth edition of Bebel's *Die Frau und der Sozialismus*, Michels was pleased to note that with the exception of a 'small remnant of mostly foreign socialists'—here Michels named Cesare Lombroso, Enrico Ferri, and Ernest Belfort Bax as the most important in this company, the recognition of women's equality and equal rights was now seen as an essential tenet of socialism. Michels cited Bebel's words: 'There is no liberation of humanity without the social independence and equality of the sexes'.[61]

Michels also gave positive coverage to bourgeois feminists in some of his contributions to *Die Gleichheit*. In May 1904, Michels contributed a review essay on the latest volume (part IV) of the *Handbuch der Frauenbewegung* ('handbook of the women's movement') edited by Helene Lange and Gertrud Bäumer, in which he paid tribute to the 'thorough expertise' and 'richness of ideas', which made them, along with the social work pioneer Alice Salomon, 'the most outstanding pioneers of the moderate women's movement in Germany'.[62] Michels was pleased to acknowledge that Richard Wilbrandt's volume in the handbook series was cognisant of the difference between the situation of women from the upper classes, for whom the right to exercise a profession was a desired freedom, and proletarian women, for whom the 'right to work' was of purely academic interest, as they had to take on wage work and experienced it as a great burden. Michels noted with satisfaction that Wilbrandt recognized that the lot of working-class women was 'in the first place a component of the question of the workers, and can only be solved with this'.[63] Michels also noted Wilbrandt's observation that parts of the bourgeois women's movement had not always recognized the distinction between the classes of women when it came to the 'right to work', although Michels considered the feminist movement in Italy to suffer less from this problem, given the prominence of socialist women in it.

---

[59] Robert Michels, Review of Apostino [*recte* Agostino] Berenini and Alberts [*recte* Alberto] Borciani, *Progetto di legge pel divorzio*, in *Documente des Socialismus*, Vol.3, 8, 1903, p.352.

[60] Enrico Ferri, *Die revolutionäre Methode*, trans. Dr Robert Michels, Leipzig, 1908, p.79n1.

[61] Robert Michels, 'Der vierunddreissigste Bebel', *Die Gleichheit*, Jg.14, no.15, 13 July 1904, pp.113–15, here p.115. On Bebel's 'men's feminism', see Anne Lopes and Gary Roth, *Men's Feminism: August Bebel and the German Socialist Movement*, Amherst, NY, 2000.

[62] Dr Robert Michels, 'Die deutsche Frau im Beruf', *Die Gleichheit*, Jg.14, no.11, 18 May 1904, pp.82–4, quotation p.82. The volume in question was authored by Robert and Lisbeth Wilbrandt.

[63] Michels, 'Die deutsche Frau im Beruf', p.83.

160 ROBERT MICHELS, SOCIALISM, AND MODERNITY

At the women's conference that preceded the 1904 Bremen Social Democratic Party congress, Michels openly advocated collaboration between socialist and bourgeois feminists, arguing that German Social Democratic women should have agreed to participate in the recent international women's congress held in Berlin that was hosted by the bourgeois BDF.[64] As noted in Chapter 2, Michels argued that German Social Democrats worked together with bourgeois parties in the Reichstag all the time, so the socialist women should not have been deterred from working with bourgeois women's groups and might have exercised a positive influence on the international congress. Even the fact that the women's congress sent a delegation to pay respects to the Empress and Chancellor von Bülow should not have bothered the Social Democratic women: 'Parliament also sends delegations to the Kaiser'.[65] As noted in Chapter 2, this earned Michels a sharp rejoinder from Luise Zietz, who pointed to the fact that some bourgeois feminists advocated not equal franchise for all women, but an extension of existing discriminatory, property-based franchise laws for the benefit of women of the upper classes: the 'ladies' franchise'. Zietz also rejected the analogy with parliament, where parties competed with one another for seats. The Berlin women's congress was closer in nature to a liberal party congress, and socialists did not seek to participate in those.[66] Clara Zetkin also took issue with Michels' speech, stressing the class-bound limitations of the bourgeois feminist movement, in which the relatively progressive elements were a minority. Disagreeing with Michels' suggestion that Social Democratic women could have exercised a positive influence on the international women's congress, Zetkin declared: 'The iron armour of class prejudice cannot be broken by speeches'.[67] Michels felt the need to try to clarify 'misunderstandings' of his speech in a personal statement after Zetkin's response.[68]

It is worth pausing again to note the incongruity of Michels' militantly anti-revisionist position at the main Bremen congress, in which he rejected class compromise and overreliance on parliamentarism, and insisted on a fundamentally republican standpoint. At the same time, at the women's conference, he advocated cross-class collaboration, and cited parliamentary cooperation between parties in support of this argument. He also played down the significance of the bourgeois women's homage to the Empress, in contrast to his usual uncompromising

---

[64] On the congress, see Gerhard, *Unerhört*, pp.210–13.

[65] *Protokoll über die Verhandlungen des Parteitages der Sozialdemokratischen Partei Deutschlands. Abgehalten zu Bremen vom 18. bis 24. September 1904*, Berlin, 1904, p.342–4. Slightly different wording but substantially the same transcript in *Hamburger Echo*, no. 221, 20 September 1904, 2. Beilage; *Vorwärts*, no.221, 20 September 1904, 3. Beilage.

[66] *Protokoll Bremen 1904*, p.344.

[67] *Protokoll Bremen 1904*, p.348. A brief news report on the conference in *Vorwärts* also highlighted Zietz's and Zetkin's rejection of Michels' arguments on the international women's conference. 'Dritte Konferenz der socialistischen Frauen', *Vorwärts*, no.220, 18 September 1904. Incidentally, Michels was not the only male delegate to take part in the women's conference.

[68] *Protokoll Bremen 1904*, p.349.

FEMINISM AND THE SEXUAL POLITICS OF A NEW CENTURY   161

insistence on socialist republicanism. Michels does not seem to have reflected on the conflict between his emphasis on class conflict in the one arena and his advocacy of cross-class conciliation in the other, a conflict which Zetkin, for her part, sharply articulated. It would be overly reductive to explain this in terms of Michels' financial interest in continuing to publish in bourgeois feminist journals. Rather, Michels seems to have viewed the male political arena as one dominated by conflict and struggle, while the arena of working for the advancement of women was more open to collaboration and conciliation. These implicitly gendered political spheres each had their own logic. For Michels, both spheres were arenas in which one could take ethically advanced and progressive positions, without him reflecting on the theoretical tensions that arose in the process.[69]

Michels' position at the Bremen women's conference (and its rejection) was noted by the Viennese feminist journal *Neues Frauenleben* in its brief report on the Social Democratic women's congress. The *Neues Frauenleben* expressed the view that the arguments of 'our esteemed contributor' should be given more consideration in future by his socialist women comrades.[70]

Michels' advocacy of cooperation between socialist and bourgeois feminists also found expression in the fact of his contribution to Hermann Hillger's *Illustriertes Frauen-Jahrbuch* ('illustrated women's yearbook') in 1904, an enterprise associated with Helene Lange, but which gained contributors from a broad spectrum of the German women's movement. The yearbook was characterized by the *Neues Frauenleben* as showing a 'progressive, liberal' complexion, with contributors including Wilhelmine von Gehren, Helene Lange, Dr Anna Gebuer, Gertrud Bäumer, Anna Pappritz, the prominent pacifist author Bertha von Suttner, Auguste Fickert, Dr Käthe Schirmacher, and Paola Lombroso (Michels was the only male included in this list.) The contributions of Minna Cauer (on 'New Tendencies in the German Women's Movement') and Adele Gerber (on 'The Servant Question') were counted as radical by the Austrian journal.[71] Interestingly, Michels is counted here among the liberals rather than the radicals, despite his essay being on 'The Social Democratic Woman'.

Michels presented the contrast between the bourgeois and Social Democratic women's movements in the following terms in his yearbook contribution:

---

[69] Jean H. Quataert notes that while Michels acknowledged a number of reasons for the relatively low membership of the Social Democratic Party by the wives of male members, he did not acknowledge the significance of gender roles in the attitudes of members as a factor. Jean H. Quataert, *Reluctant Feminists in German Social Democracy, 1885–1917*, Princeton, NJ, 1979, p.157.

[70] A.F. [Auguste Fickert], 'Deutschland', in *Neues Frauenleben*, Jg.16, no.10, October 1904, p.12. The same issue contained an article by Dr Robert Michels, 'Gewerkschaftlich-Politische Zusammenhänge in der Arbeiterinnenbewegung Italiens', in *Neues Frauenleben*, Jg.16, no.10, October 1904, pp.3–6.

[71] L.K. [Leopoldine Kulka], review of *Hillger's Illustriertes Frauen-Jahrbuch 1904*, in *Neues Frauenleben*, Jg.16, no.5, May 1904, pp.17–18, here p.17.

162 ROBERT MICHELS, SOCIALISM, AND MODERNITY

The bourgeois women's movement strives for the equality of women in legal and political terms on the basis of the presently existing constitutional and property relations. The Social Democratic women's movement, which also recognizes these goals, considers their achievement, however, to be utopian for as long as the present system of economic and social privilege of particular classes, strata and cliques would destroy over and over again any freedom and equality which woman might achieve with man.[72]

The bourgeois women's movement was defined largely by the strata it represented:

The bourgeois women's movement is just that: bourgeois, that is, it is consciously concerned with the interests of the woman from upper and middle strata, and to some extent also with those of women from strata which come very close to the proletariat (teachers, lower female public servants, etc.). Consequently, it also fights for the woman worker, but only in her capacity as woman, not, however, for the woman worker as the member of a propertyless class, or only in so far as it does not conflict with the interests of the propertied.[73]

However, Michels went on, now identifying with the socialist position instead of just expounding on it, the class struggle did not cease when it came to women (although he felt it necessary to add that 'class struggle' was not an invention of the Social Democratic Party, nor even of the state, but of 'our whole historical and economic development'). Therefore, alongside their common interests as women, 'bourgeois and proletarian women as members of the two opposed classes struggling for [possession of] the state at the same time had opposite interests'.[74] Thus the different economic situations and 'scientific understanding of the economic laws' resulted in a sharp distinction between the proletarian and the bourgeois women's movements.[75] Michels was still keen to point out the common ground between the two, however: the Social Democratic Party was still the only one in Germany to include the full emancipation of women in its party programme, something reflected in the programmes of socialists in other countries as well.[76] As an indication of the equal status of women within socialist parties, Michels noted the accomplishments of Henriette Roland-Holst (an editor of the Dutch socialist theoretical journal *De Nieuwe Tijd*), Clara Zetkin, Rosa Luxemburg ('a woman of an unusually keen analytical mind and unconquerable desire for

[72] Dr R. [Robert] Michels, 'Die sozialdemokratische Frau', in Hermann Hillger, ed., *Hillger's Illustriertes Frauen-Jahrbuch 1904*, Berlin, Eisenach, Leipzig, 1904, col.809–16, here col.809.
[73] Michels, 'Die sozialdemokratische Frau', col.810.
[74] Michels, 'Die sozialdemokratische Frau', col.810–11.
[75] Michels, 'Die sozialdemokratische Frau', col.811.
[76] Michels, 'Die sozialdemokratische Frau', col.811–12.

FEMINISM AND THE SEXUAL POLITICS OF A NEW CENTURY   163

knowledge'), Anna Kuliscioff in Italy, the late Eleanor Marx-Aveling, the prominent Russian Social Democrat Vera Zasulitch, and Angelica Balabanoff.[77] Michels also paid tribute to prominent socialist women writers and intellectuals: Beatrice Potter-Webb, the Lombroso sisters: Paola Lombroso-Carrera and Gina Lombroso-Ferrero, Lily Braun, and others.[78] Michels followed with a very short survey of socialist women's organization in Germany (noting the effects of reactionary laws of association in most of Germany), France, Italy, and Austria.[79]

Michels' involvement with mainstream feminist journals tapered off after his Bremen confrontation with Luise Zietz and Clara Zetkin. While his disillusion-ment with German Social Democracy set in after what he perceived to be the weakness of the party in dealing with revisionism at Bremen, his advocacy of cooperation with middle-class feminists had also been rebuffed by the party's women leaders. In subsequent years, especially after the legalization of women's political organizations by the new Reich Law of Association in 1908, the main-stream BDF would drift more to the right (as more conservative and religious groups joined), and the gulf between socialist and bourgeois feminism continued to widen.[80] At the same time, Michels increasingly turned his attention to the sex reform movement and the small radical feminist group in the Bund für Mutterschutz (League for the Protection of Mothers).

The Sexual Question

Robert Michels' very first literary efforts reflected the concern of modernist intel-lectuals at the start of the twentieth century with new ways of understanding of sexuality, and a reform of society's mores relating to sex.

Writing articles on theatre for the short-lived Turin cultural journal *La Commedia* in 1901, Michels showed himself to be a partisan of such contempor-ary writers as Frank Wedekind and Arthur Schnitzler, whose frank depictions of sexual matters had run foul of conventional middle-class opinion and the German states' censorship. Michels took particular aim at the moral double standards of the German bourgeoisie when it came to sexual matters. Michels also cited the naturalist playwright Hermann Sudermann's *Die Ehre* ('honour'), which aroused antagonism because it 'fights against the exploitation of poor girls by rich men and shows how ridiculous chivalrous and medieval honour have now become'. The same playwright's *Heimat* ('home') 'attacks the prejudices and the malignant

---

[77] Michels, 'Die sozialdemokratische Frau', col.812.
[78] Michels, 'Die sozialdemokratische Frau', col.813.
[79] Michels, 'Die sozialdemokratische Frau', col.813–16.
[80] Richard J. Evans, 'Liberalism and Society: The Feminist Movement and Social Change', in Richard J. Evans, ed., *Society and Politics in Wilhelmine Germany*, London, and New York, 1978, pp.186–214.

164   ROBERT MICHELS, SOCIALISM, AND MODERNITY

consequences of the old morality'. Schnitzler's *Liebelei* ('dalliance') 'condemns the dalliances of the heartless upper-class men who constitute high society'. Many of the same bourgeois gentlemen who profess outrage at the immorality of such plays happily accept vulgarities in French farces, but they resist being confronted with such issues in more serious drama.[81]

In Michels' 1902 article for *La Riforma Sociale* dealing with the 'woman question' in Germany, he took issue with German claims that Germans were morally superior to the French, citing comparative statistics on illegitimacy and statistics on the incidence of venereal disease among German students.[82] He also considered the extent to which the new German Civil Code of 1900 regulated sexual matters, finding that it still allowed a husband to compel his wife into involuntary sexual relations, and he cited August Bebel in support of the view that sex within marriage could still often be legally an act governed not by mutual affection but by the economic need of a woman to provide for herself by selling her body. Michels' discussion of marriage also cited the psychologist and noted 'sex reformer' Magnus Hirschfeld (from Hirschfeld's 1900 book *Cultur und Ehe*).[83]

Michels chose the somewhat unlikely venue of Ludwig Woltmann's *Politisch-Anthropologische Revue* for a critical review of a misogynistic book on the 'Sexual Struggle' by an Italian author Pio Viazzi. Michels characterized Viazzi's work as 'an encyclopaedia of sexual life framed in scientific terms, from the point of view of a thoroughly male pessimism', which combined August Strindberg's theory of the demonic nature of women with 'Schopenhauer's unhealthy contempt for women', along with Lombroso's anthropological conception of women's inferiority.[84] Viazzi argued that women had succeeded in exploiting the male's greater sex drive to achieve control over men. Despite these 'ultra-masculinist theories', Viazzi was in agreement with the women's rights movement (and evidently Michels) on three points: greater sexual freedom for women, greater freedom in the choice of profession, and an improvement in women's education (even if Viazzi saw the last point as a means of strengthening male influence over women).[85] Michels took issue with Viazzi's arguments about women's inherent inferiority: in particular, Michels made fun of Viazzi's argument that women's love of colourful display was analogous to the customs of a primitive people by pointing to the splendour and colour of army officers' uniforms of various modern nations.[86] This example of subversive wit was an unusual note in a journal normally frequented by earnest

---

[81] Roberto [Robert] Michels, 'Il dramma moderno tedesco', *La Commedia*, I, no.9, 7 April, pp.1–2, quotations p.1. See also Roberto [Robert] Michels, 'La "pochade" in Germania', *La Commedia*, I, no.7, 24 March 1901, pp.2–3.

[82] Michels, 'Attorno ad una questione sociale in Germania', pp.1–2 of offprint [pp.775–6].

[83] Michels, 'Attorno ad una questione sociale in Germania', p.14.

[84] Dr Robert Michels, Review of Pio Viazzi, *La lotta di sesso*, in *Politisch-Anthropologische Revue*, Jg.2, 6, September 1903, p.530.

[85] Michels, Review of Pio Viazzi, *La lotta di sesso*, p.530.

[86] Michels, Review of Pio Viazzi, *La lotta di sesso*, p.531.

FEMINISM AND THE SEXUAL POLITICS OF A NEW CENTURY 165

völkisch race theorists and skull-measurers. Michels nonetheless concluded by respectfully describing Viazzi's book as a serious and erudite work that represented a significant contribution to a question that was still in much need of clarification.[87] Michels' criticisms of misogynistic and anti-feminist writings found a more natural home in the reformist journal *Ethische Kultur*, where he mocked the naiveté of a conservative Catholic Italian writer who tried to invoke the name of Goethe in support of a tract against any reform of divorce law, as if Goethe had been a pillar of conventional religious morality.[88]

Michels also sought to expand on his views on the sexual question in progressive feminist journals, placing an article on 'Woman's Dilemma in Love' in *Die Frauenbewegung*. The essay began boldly by querying the excessive social value placed on motherhood. Mothers would be forgiven any failing, including neglect of their husbands, if they only showed love for their children, even in the case of children born out of wedlock. At this point, the editor of *Die Frauenbewegung* felt constrained to add a reality check with the note that 'unfortunately the unmarried mother seldom receives forgiveness'.[89] Michels complained that women spending too much time on their children were insufficiently available for their husbands, adding that it was even worse in the case of intellectually active women, as the male was then deprived of a partner in his intellectual life as well: 'The man's co-worker, the social policy expert, the art historian, or whatever else she may be, experiences on account of her children a loss, if not in intellectual strength, at least in the possibility of employing it'.[90] It is easy to see this as a reflection of Michels' own domestic situation, in which his own wife and 'co-worker', the 'social policy expert' Gisela Michels-Lindner, was just about to have another baby. The article which starts off as a bold challenge to conventional notions of the overriding importance of motherhood for women, soon slides into a male complaint about the wife paying him less attention, but is somewhat saved for feminism in the last third of the piece, in which Michels takes up a suggestion of Clara Zetkin's, that males should re-think the domestic division of labour, and play a greater role themselves in raising their children, although Michels conceded that this would not be equally possible for all men under current social conditions.[91]

Michels took on the subject of motherhood again a year later, this time in Zetkin's *Gleichheit*, in his review of the reference work on women's occupations by Richard and Lisbeth Wilbrandt, Michels took issue with Richard Wilbrandt's emphasis on the woman's instinctive desire for motherhood as the strongest

---

[87] Michels, Review of Pio Viazzi, *La lotta di sesso*, p.532.
[88] Dr Robert Michels, 'Goethe als Eideshelfer gegen die Ehescheidung', in *Ethische Kultur*, Jg.XI, Nr.2, 10 January 1903, p.13.
[89] Michels, 'Das Dilemma des Weibes in der Liebe', p.83.
[90] Michels, 'Das Dilemma des Weibes in der Liebe', p.83.
[91] Michels, 'Das Dilemma des Weibes in der Liebe', p.83.

166 ROBERT MICHELS, SOCIALISM, AND MODERNITY

motive in women's personal lives: Michels, on the other hand, asserted that the erotic dimension, 'die Erotik', was in the first place a goal in itself for women also.[92] The excessive esteem accorded to motherhood was a product of women's limited options in the workforce. A large percentage of women, Michels believed, even if they were economically independent through the exercise of a profession, would always prefer the greater security of marriage to the economic uncertainties of the workplace, especially while married women were accorded a higher social status than unmarried working women. Michels complained that: 'Every third-rate *"Hausfrau"* in Germany enjoys more social standing in her caste than the most significant woman philologist'. The whole institution of marriage, with the dominant assumption of the male as the sole breadwinner, needed a more radical reform than Wilbrandt could contemplate. The abolition of marriage for money would only be possible if marriage were transformed into a 'bond between man and woman, which—as far, of course, as is physically possible—places the same rights and the same duties on both parties'.[93]

Michels endorsed what he presented as the standard socialist view on marriage: that a reform of marriage in a way that guaranteed the legal emancipation of women would require that marriage lost 'its present character as a marriage of property for the purpose of propagating inherited wealth'. He also shared the view that 'the vice of prostitution, that tears at our people's life' was not primarily an ethical question, to be solved by better moral education, but an economic one.[94] In an essay on August Bebel's *Die Frau und der Sozialismus* on the occasion of its thirty-fourth edition, Michels noted not only Bebel's survey of the history of women in different societies, and their future role in socialist society, but he also noted that Bebel addressed the 'famous age-old question of whether the woman has a right to the enjoyment of love, and rightly gives the answer that only such a senseless social order as capitalism with all its consequences could refuse this incontestable natural right'.[95]

Michels sought to go beyond his literary and often *feuilleton*-istic essays on the theme of sexual issues, contributing an article for the Marxist theoretical journal *Die Neue Zeit* on the question of morality in early 1903. This more theoretically ambitious article stressed that concepts of morality varied from one historical period to another, and between classes and cultures.[96] He chose as his particular focus the social regulation of sexuality. Michels contrasted the natural modesty of the working-class woman with the way in which 'the woman from the propertied and educated classes' exhibited her flesh at social occasions ('Arms and shoulders,

---

[92] Michels, 'Die deutsche Frau im Beruf', p.83.
[93] Michels, 'Die deutsche Frau im Beruf', p.83.
[94] Michels, 'Die sozialdemokratische Frau', col.809–10.
[95] Michels, 'Der vierunddreissigste Bebel', p.114.
[96] Robert Michels, 'Beitrag zum Problem der Moral', *Die Neue Zeit*, 21. Jg., Bd.1, 1902–1903, pp.470–5.

FEMINISM AND THE SEXUAL POLITICS OF A NEW CENTURY   167

and usually the breast down to the vicinity of the nipples—the technical term for these body parts is included in the general name "neck"—are bare').[97] Michels also gave the example of 'bridal morality', with the strict requirement among the upper classes for pre-marital 'purity' on the part of the bride. Custom prescribed that the young couple could only experience sexual intercourse on a prescribed day and after public celebration, 'without any transitional stages, that is, in a fairly brutal fashion'. Michels contrasted this with the situation among the proletariat, where it was accepted that an engaged couple could cohabit, and even if children appeared before marriage, in most cases this was not stigmatized.[98] Michels argued that the chosen examples showed that morality among the lower classes was both more natural than, and essentially superior to, that of the upper classes, those in the 'capitalist sphere of thought'.[99] Michels cast a quick glimpse at differences in morality between countries (a comparison not flattering to Germany), only to conclude that differences in outlook between classes were increasingly more important than those between the bourgeoisies of different countries (despite the hollow claims of bourgeois 'patriots' to moral superiority over other peoples).[100]

Michels expanded on his remarks on the brutality of bourgeois bridal customs, with some gusto, in a full-length article sent to the feminist journal *Die Frauen-Rundschau* (*The Women's Review*, formerly entitled *Dokumente der Frauen*), then under the new editorship of Helene Stöcker. This article pilloried bourgeois 'bridal morality' as 'the most frail, the most rotten, and the most abnormal' aspect of what he considered to be a generally 'frail, rotten and abnormal' moral condition in contemporary society.[101] Michels stressed what he regarded as the brutality of the wedding ritual, with the young couple treated as sexless beings, until the time they are thrown together on the designated wedding night, with sometimes traumatic results. He went through what he presented as the barbarous details of the ritual (for example, the need to avoid timetabling the wedding night during the bride's menstrual period) to underline his point, even comparing the bridal couple with beefsteaks being prepared for serving up. In such a context, the 'exhibition' of the bridal couple in the church Michels thought even more 'cynical' than their showing in the registry office. 'At the end of a long series of

---

[97] Michels, 'Beitrag zum Problem der Moral', p.471.
[98] Michels, 'Beitrag zum Problem der Moral', pp.471–2.
[99] Michels, 'Beitrag zum Problem der Moral', p.472.
[100] Michels, 'Beitrag zum Problem der Moral', pp.472–4.
[101] Robert Michels, 'Brautstandsmoral. Eine kritische Betrachtung', *Das Magazin für Litteratur*, Jg.72, 1. Juniheft 1903, p.99. Michels published an Italian version of the article in the anarchist journal *Il Pensiero*, edited by Pietro Gori and Luigi Fabbri, the following year, a close translation of the German original, keeping the same figures of speech. Roberto [Robert] Michels, 'La morale dei fidanzamenti', *Il Pensiero*, Anno II, No.14, 1 August 1904, pp.206–8. There is also a later version published in French: 'La morale des fiançailles', *L'Humanité Nouvelle*, Vol.3, 1, 1906, pp.90–6.

168 ROBERT MICHELS, SOCIALISM, AND MODERNITY

humiliations they are thrown into each other's arms like animals'.[102] Michels proposed less rigidly regulated courtship customs, which would allow a relationship to evolve naturally, and to the mutual satisfaction of the partners, as a more humane, healthy, and morally superior alternative to the prevailing bourgeois conventions.[103] Helene Stöcker initially responded favourably to Michels' submission of the article to the *Frauen-Rundschau* (although she later claimed she had not fully deciphered the manuscript), but a few months later she had second thoughts. Michels' article was so drastic and confrontational in its form and expression, Stöcker explained to the author, that it would be counter-productive, alienating more women readers than it would win over. If Michels were reluctant to tone down the writing, she advised him to submit it to the *Magazin für Litteratur* instead, which Michels duly did. The *Magazin* was quick to publish the 'bridal morality' article. Stöcker did not act out of personal prudery in rejecting the article—she was soon to become one of the most prominent figures in the 'sex reform' movement organized in the *Bund für Mutterschutz*, and she regarded Michels as an ally in that cause. However, in making her judgement of the possible negative impact of Michels' prose and iconoclastic argumentation on women readers, as she explained to Michels, she had already had some experience of such reactions. As it was, Stöcker's radical views on sex reform would be a contributing factor in her departure from the editorship of the *Frauen-Rundschau* by the end of 1903.[104]

Michels' critique of bourgeois marital customs was further developed in an article for *Ethische Kultur* in July 1904, which was also reprinted almost simultaneously in the *Frankfurter Zeitung*, one of Germany's foremost liberal daily newspapers. In an exercise in micro-sociology, Michels took as an object of analysis a brief engagement announcement. In addition to contrasting the pride with which the bridegroom advertised himself as a *Rittergutsbesitzer* (owner of a knightly landed estate) with the reticence of the bride's wealthy bourgeois parents to name her father's profession, Michels also read the engagement notice as a document of women's unequal position. The parents announced the transaction, as if she were an object for sale, passing from the father's hands to the groom's: 'We are dealing here', Michels wrote, 'with a relic of barbaric forms of expression from the era of *patria potestas*.' Even if contemporary brides might have a say in whom they marry, the language of social convention had not been reformed, with the result that the bride was placed in an inferior position to the groom

---

[102] Michels, 'Brautstandsmoral', pp.101–2.   [103] Michels, 'Brautstandsmoral', pp.102–3.

[104] Helene Stöcker to Michels, 3 December 1902; 13 May 1903, ARM/FLE. On the article, see the lengthy discussion in Genett, *Der Fremde im Kriege*, pp.55–7. While Genett emphasizes the emancipatory feminist critique of misogynistic social conventions, he does not note that the essay was effectively unpublishable in most feminist journals, even those with the most progressive editors. On Stöcker and the *Frauen-Rundschau*, see Christl Wickert, *Helene Stöcker 1869–1943. Frauenrechtlerin, Sexualreformerin und Pazifistin*, Bonn, 1991, pp.51–2; Stöcker to Michels, 17 February 1904, ARM/FLE.

FEMINISM AND THE SEXUAL POLITICS OF A NEW CENTURY   169

from the start, and the 'artificially produced double morality of man and woman' was perpetuated.[105]

Michels repeatedly advocated higher standards of sexual morality on the part of men, to be promoted by reform of social institutions and bourgeois customs. In September 1903, he commented on a newspaper article on women being verbally sexually harassed on the streets of Berlin. This 'lascivious sexuality of men, which cannot even be held in check on the open street, is mainly the fruit of the completely perverse education of youth that is customary in our schools and homes'. Sexually segregated upbringing should, Michels advocated, be replaced by a comradely co-education.[106] In a short note he contributed to *Ethische Kultur*, Michels noted a case in which a man knowingly infected with syphilis had been charged with causing bodily harm to a sexual partner. Michels deplored the fact that married men who likewise knowingly exposed their wives to infection escaped prosecution, and argued that doctors should be required to report cases of venereal disease where there was a danger that a husband (or husband-to-be) might infect his wife.[107] In another article in *Ethische Kultur*, Michels cited a story from the Italian socialist newspaper *Avanti!* on a murder committed out of jealousy. The socialist paper refused to speak of a 'crime of love', defining love as the opposite of the vanity, desire for revenge, and jealousy shown by the murderer. Michels himself defined love as 'a superlative of friendship, comradeliness and community of ideas, mixed with a healthy love of the senses [*mit gesunder Sinnesliebe*].'[108]

When Helene Stöcker and Adele Schreiber, along with Ruth Bré, formed the *Bund für Mutterschutz*, to improve the legal situation and welfare of unmarried mothers and their children, Michels was one of the league's supporters, as were Max Weber and Werner Sombart, along with prominent liberals such as Friedrich Naumann and Anton Erkelenz, noted doctors including Alfred Blaschko and Iwan Bloch, and feminists such as Hedwig Dohm, Minna Cauer, Lily Braun, and Marie Stritt. This somewhat eclectic grouping soon experienced a split, with the group around Bré adopting a Social Darwinist, racial hygienic, and rural romantic orientation, leaving the organization, which under Stöcker and Schreiber coupled its agitation for practical welfare reform with propaganda for a new, left-libertarian approach to questions of sexual morality.[109] Michels remained a

---

[105] Dr Robert Michels, 'Die Analyse einer Verlobungskarte', *Ethische Kultur*, Jg.XI, No.27, 4 July 1903, p.211; reprinted in *Frankfurter Zeitung und Handelsblatt*, no.183, 4 July 1903.

[106] Dr R. [Robert] Michels [under the rubric: Streiflichter], 'Die öffentliche Sicherheit der Frauen auf der Straße', in *Ethische Kultur*, Jg.XI, no.39, 26. September 1903, pp.310–11.

[107] R.M. [Robert Michels], 'Bestrafung geschlechtlichen Verkehrs Geschlechtskranker', in *Ethische Kultur*, Jg.XI, Nr.28, 11 July 1903, p.223.

[108] R. [Robert] Michels, 'Was heißt "Liebe"?', in *Ethische Kultur*, Jg.XI, Nr.28, 11 July 1903, p.222.

[109] See Helene Stöcker's programmatic call for a new morality, strongly inspired by Nietzsche: Helene Stöcker, 'Von neuer Ethik', *Mutterschutz. Zeitschift zur Reform der Sexuellen Ethik*, Jg.II, no.1, 1906, pp.3–11. Also Maria Lischnewska, 'Die Mutterschutz-Bewegung in Deutschland', *Neues Frauenleben*, Jg.XIX, no.1, January 1907, pp.1–4. On the Bund für Mutterschutz, see Richard J. Evans, *The Feminist Movement in Germany 1894–1933*, London and Beverly Hills, CA, 1976, pp.115–43; Ann

170 ROBERT MICHELS, SOCIALISM, AND MODERNITY

supporter of the *Bund für Mutterschutz*, publishing in its eponymous journal and its successor *Die Neue Generation*, and featuring on the League's advertised list of educational speakers. Some of Michels' articles in the league's journal were included in his 1911 essay collection *Grenzen der Geschlechtsmoral*, in which progressive feminist views sit oddly alongside Michels' self-consciously gallant observations of sexual mores in different countries. Max Weber, incidentally, was not entirely comfortable with Michels' embrace of the cause of sex reform (nor for that matter, was Marianne Weber, who aligned herself with the more conservative liberal wing of BDF—the umbrella organization of the German women's movement). Weber soon withdrew his support from the Bund für Mutterschutz, writing to Michels: 'The specific Mutterschutz gang is an utterly confused bunch. After the babble of Stöcker, Borgius, etc. I withdrew my support. Crass hedonism and an ethics that would benefit only men as the goal of women…that is simply nonsense'.[110] The more conservative branch of the women's movement, represented by *Die Frau* and Gertrud Bäumer and Helene Lange, had immediately distanced itself from the Bund für Mutterschutz at its inception.[111]

Michels had maintained a friendly correspondence with Helene Stöcker after she left the *Frauen-Rundschau* at the beginning of 1904, and was a recipient of Stöcker's circular letter in March 1905 inviting contributions to the journal of the Bund für Mutterschutz. He was clearly quick to seize the opportunity and submitted an article on 'The Prostitute as the "Old Maid" of the Proletariat', which canvassed the economic reasons for the differences between bourgeois and working-class sexual mores, and which appeared in the second issue of the journal.[112] Stöcker welcomed Michels' contribution, expressing the hope that it would 'shake people up a bit'.[113] Michels contrasted the phenomenon of the 'old maid' in bourgeois families with the relative absence of unmarried older women in the working class (with the exception of some female domestic servants).[114] Michels argued that the same social and economic conditions that deprived some bourgeois

---

Taylor Allen, 'Mothers of the New Generation: Adele Schreiber, Helene Stöcker, and the Evolution of a German Idea of Motherhood, 1900–1914', *Signs*, Vol.10, 3, 1985, pp.418–38, also Allen's *Feminism and Motherhood in Germany, 1800–1914*, New Brunswick, 1991, chs.9–10; Amy Hackett, 'Helene Stöcker: Left-Wing Intellectual and Sex Reformer', in Renate Bridenthal, Atina Grossmann, and Marion Kaplan, eds., *When Biology Became Destiny: Women in Weimar and Nazi Germany*, New York, 1984, 109–30; Wickert, *Helene Stöcker*, pp.53–4, 61–83; Edward R. Dickinson, *Sex, Freedom, and Power in Imperial Germany, 1880–1914*, Cambridge and New York, 2014, especially chs.9–12.

[110] Max Weber to Michels, 11 January 1907, in Max Weber, *Briefe 1906–1908*, Tübingen, 1990, (=Gesamtausgabe, Abt. II/5), p.211. See also Joachim Radkau, *Max Weber. Die Leidenschaft des Denkens*, Munich and Vienna, 2005, pp.481–3. Werner Sombart, although initially also a supporter of the Bund, dismissed its call for a 'new ethics' as 'the ethics of old women on heat', which he found 'repugnant'. Friedrich Lenger, *Werner Sombart. 1863–1941*, Munich, 1994, p.159.

[111] See the hostile comments reproduced in *Mutterschutz*, I, Heft 1, 1905, p.40; I, Heft 8.

[112] Dr Robert Michels, 'Die Dirne als "alte Jungfer" des Proletariats und die Prostitution', *Mutterschutz*, Jg.I, 2, 1905, pp.58–65.

[113] Stöcker to Michels, 20 June 1905, ARM/FLE.

[114] Michels, 'Die Dirne als "alte Jungfer"', p.58.

FEMINISM AND THE SEXUAL POLITICS OF A NEW CENTURY   171

women of the opportunity to have sex lives, forced many proletarian women into sex without choice through prostitution. Prostitution degraded both sexes, but Michels rejected attempts at abolishing prostitution that failed to attack the underlying economic causes of prostitution. Michels' article is somewhat impressionistic and relies on generalizations without citing sources or statistics. He spends a substantial part of the essay discussing male needs, which are taken as a given. In addition to low wages, he argues that another cause of prostitution was an 'overproduction of women', with more women reaching adulthood than men.[115] He also makes the observation that a third of prostitutes in England were foreigners, partly because English industry paid higher wages than was the case in France or Germany, but also partly because 'English girls are less able to withstand the rigours of the prostitute's profession'.[116]

Michels followed his *Mutterschutz* article on prostitutes and old maids with another contribution to the journal in 1906 entitled 'Erotic Forays' ('Erotische Streifzüge'), in which he compared sexual customs in Germany and Italy, and offered his impressions of 'love life in Paris'.[117] Michels contrasted the public displays of physical affection of German couples with the way in which such displays were strictly kept private in Italy.[118] Michels displayed a clear aesthetic preference for the way of life of Italians and French people as opposed to cruder and more gross German habits. He then went on to discuss prostitution in Paris, suggesting that 'prostitution in France is on a morally superior level to prostitution in Germany'.[119] Michels described what he considered to be the greater self-respect of Parisian prostitutes, except the very lowest sort. Paris had depraved street whores on the boulevards, like every city, he said, but they differed from German cities in the phenomenon of the *petite femme* of the Latin Quarter: the female companion of Parisian university youth.[120] Sounding a touch nostalgic for his own student days in Paris (where he had lived while doing research for his dissertation), Michels described the comradely, equal relationships between girls of the Latin Quarter and their student *copains* (chums), and inserted his own reminiscences of a girl called Marcelle.[121] In contrast to the aesthetically unappealing *Dirnentum* (prostitution) found in Germany, Michels found a certain 'idealism' in the Parisian *bohème*, where *grisettes* might take pride in a platonic relationship with a male friend, a relic of France's more refined culture.[122] Michels wrote that

---

[115] Michels, 'Die Dirne als "alte Jungfer"', p.62. On the concept of the 'surplus woman' in imperial Germany, see Catherine L. Dollard, *The Surplus Woman: Unmarried in Imperial Germany, 1871–1918*, New York and Oxford, 2012. Dollard provides a critical discussion of Michels' and Stöcker's discussion of the phenomenon of the *alte Jungfer* on pp.148–50. As Dollard puts it (p.149), Stöcker depicted the *alte Jungfer* as 'a symptom of a decrepit society in need of change'.
[116] Michels, 'Die Dirne als "alte Jungfer"', p.64.
[117] Dr Robert Michels, 'Erotische Streifzüge', *Mutterschutz*, II, Heft 9, 1906, pp.362–74.
[118] Michels, 'Erotische Streifzüge', pp.362–6.   [119] Michels, 'Erotische Streifzüge', p.366.
[120] Michels, 'Erotische Streifzüge', pp.366–9.   [121] Michels, 'Erotische Streifzüge', p.370.
[122] Michels, 'Erotische Streifzüge', p.372.

172 ROBERT MICHELS, SOCIALISM, AND MODERNITY

only faulty education and an unfortunate economic system had turned these women into 'what one designates as prostitutes [*Dirnen*]', but that in France many such women preserved a modicum of human dignity in their relationships.[123]

Michels obviously felt the need to qualify his expansive remarks on the Parisian *demi-monde*, concluding:

> At this point, in a periodical such as *Mutterschutz*, and with a writer such as myself, it is hardly necessary to state that we do not in any way consider the type of the free *hetaera*, as we have tried to describe it in the preceding lines, to be the ideal type of woman in the future or even in the present....every kind of prostitution is reprehensible and we must earnestly strive to do everything in our power to turn this from a current phenomenon into a historical one, in the process of transforming our economy.[124]

Despite this obligatory criticism of prostitution in general, the dominant tone of Michels' article is redolent of a worldly male guide to the pleasures of Paris, a kind of sexual Baedeker for the male connoisseur.

Michels sent a copy of this article to Max Weber, with whom he had been corresponding regularly throughout 1906. Weber's response to the article was somewhat reserved, suggesting that Michels overidealized Parisian prostitutes while being unfair to their German counterparts, who had their own kind of ethics. Rather pointedly, Weber wrote: 'You yourself are a moralist, from head to toe, of course, more farsighted than the "philistine"—why don't you admit it?' Weber pointed out that bourgeois norms around pre-marital sex had varied historically—'my eldest uncle came into the world a month after the wedding, and his father was in the Lützow Freikorps [against Napoleon]', and Weber himself had been able to travel with his then fiancée without restrictions. However, Weber defended the need for moral norms in principle. Weber referred to his decision to leave the Bund für Mutterschutz, asking Michels: 'What are you doing with these petit-bourgeois philistines run amok?'.[125]

During 1906, Weber's wife Marianne, then 'a leading figure in the moderate women's movement in Baden',[126] was embroiled in a controversy with the then-BDF president Marie Stritt.[127] Stritt had aligned herself with some of the more radical elements in the BDF, who in turn aligned themselves with the arguments

---

[123] Michels, 'Erotische Streifzüge', p.373.   [124] Michels, 'Erotische Streifzüge'.

[125] Weber to Michels, 11 January 1907, in Weber, *Briefe 1906–1908*, pp.210–11.

[126] Evans, *The Feminist Movement in Germany*, p.150.

[127] For a detailed account of this controversy, which identifies Marianne Weber as an exponent of a progressive liberal 'cultural Protestantism' in the debates over new sexual morality, see Edward Ross Dickinson, 'Dominion of the Spirit over the Flesh: Religion, Gender and Sexual Morality in the German Women's Movement before World War I', *Gender & History*, Vol.17, 2 August 2005, pp.378–408. Marianne Weber herself eventually became president of the by then increasingly conservative BDF in the Weimar Republic.

for a reform of sexual morality advocated by the Bund für Mutterschutz, on questions including not only improved access to contraception and sex education, but also legalization of abortion.[128] In her book *Ehefrau und Mutter in der Rechtsentwicklung* ('wife and mother in the development of law'), Marianne Weber took issue with writers whose theories seemed to amount to sexual libertinage, and 'among other things, [she] refuted the socialistic theories about the development of marriage.'[129] In 1907, Marianne Weber returned to the controversy, giving a lecture at Adolf von Harnack's invitation to the Protestant Social Congress on 'Sexual-Ethical Questions of Principle', in which she stated the Webers' 'shared ethical convictions', strongly defending the ethical foundations of monogamous marriage.[130] The views articulated by Marianne Weber had been tested in 'innumerable discussions' in the Webers' circle of friends and acquaintances, especially among the younger generation, of whom Michels was a prominent example. Marianne Weber wrote: 'the controversy over the new morality of happiness was of universal concern. The Webers had to take a stand on it in countless confidential conversations.'[131]

Max and Marianne Weber were not the only associates of Robert Michels to reject the kind of sex reform advocated by the Bund für Mutterschutz. The socialist feminist Clara Zetkin also disparaged the league. In January 1906, Clara Zetkin asked Michels if he or his wife could write an article for *Die Gleichheit* on the new Italian social insurance legislation for the protection of mothers. Zetkin briefly referred to the German Social Democratic women's organization's policies regarding social legislation for the protection of mothers and children. Zetkin added, tartly: 'We have nothing to do with the *Bund für Mutterschutz* and consider it practically the most insignificant enterprise of bourgeois reformers.'[132] It is not clear whether Zetkin was aware that Michels was already a contributor to the journal of the *Bund für Mutterschutz*.

Undeterred, Michels continued to write for *Mutterschutz* (later renamed *Die Neue Generation*). In 1907, he criticized the point of view of 'today's official socialism' in regard to the problem of the relations between the sexes, in terms which clearly

---

[128] The difficulty—even for educated and relatively emancipated women—in getting access to information about contraception, and to actual contraceptives, is illustrated by Gisela Michels-Lindner's query addressed to Oda Lerda-Oberg in late 1903, after the birth and death in infancy of her second son. Oda Lerda-Oberg to Gisela Michels-Lindner, 21 December 1903, ARM/FLE.

[129] Marianne Weber, *Ehefrau und Mutter in der Rechtsentwicklung. Eine Einführung*, Tübingen, 1907; Evans, *The Feminist Movement in Germany*, pp.150–1. See also Wolfgang Schwentker, 'Passion as a Mode of Life: Max Weber, the Otto Gross Circle and Eroticism', in Wolfgang J. Mommsen and Jürgen Osterhammel, eds., *Max Weber and his Contemporaries*, London, 1989, p.487; Marianne Weber, *Max Weber: A Biography*, ed. Harry Zohn, New York, 1975, p.373.

[130] Marianne Weber, *Max Weber*, p.373; Schwentker, 'Passion as a Mode of Life', p.487. On the role of Harnack and the Protestant Social Congress as a forum for these debates, see Dickinson, 'Dominion of the Spirit over the Flesh', pp.392–3.

[131] Marianne Weber, *Max Weber*, p.373.

[132] SAPMO/BA Berlin, NY4005/90, Clara Zetkin to Michels, 17 April 1906. There is also a copy of this letter in the International Institute for Social History, Amsterdam, Iring Fetscher Collection.

174   ROBERT MICHELS, SOCIALISM, AND MODERNITY

distanced himself from Zetkin's insistence on the primacy of economic factors: 'Today's official socialism has apparently solved the problem of relations between the sexes with a hypothesis: today's woman is oppressed and, and two postulates follow from this: complete equality of women and men before the law and economic independence. But this solution cannot be satisfactory on its own'.[133] Michels went on to critique the misogynistic writings of the English socialist (and author of the anti-feminist tract, *The Legal Subjection of Men* (1896)) Belfort Bax, with particular reference to Bax's critique of August Bebel's writing on the oppression of women. Michels exposed Bax's critique of arguments for women's emancipation as confused and reliant on poor anecdotal evidence. The critique of Bax may well have originated in an article that Michels offered to contribute to *Die Neue Zeit* early in 1902, in which case it represents another example of Michels' assiduous re-use and recycling of his own writings.[134] He also incorporated a discussion of Pio Viazzi's book *La lotta di sesso*, which he had already reviewed in the *Politisch-Anthropologische Revue* in 1902 (see above), comparing it with Bax's tract.

Subsequently, later in 1907, now writing as a *Privatdozent* from the University of Turin, Michels developed his thoughts about human dignity and the institution of marriage. Here Michels was less equivocal than in his reviews of Pio Viazzi in his insistence on the inequality inherent within marriage:

> Within the present form of marriage, the feeling of human dignity—in its specifically female manifestation... described as the dignity of women—must atrophy. Since it is not based on the rights of a free contract, the act of marriage—which under some circumstances can include free contract among its causal factors—represents the conclusion of the free contract, and presupposes a so-called marital duty and eliminates every individual right to and over one's own self, and comprehends the whole complexity of sexual life between man and woman not under psychological let alone ethical points of view but from the standpoint of a financial credit transaction. Marital obligation is the duty of payment in the manner of the issuing of a bond, taken over from the business world. It must necessarily destroy physical and moral values, which belong to the most valuable exponents of our cultural life.

For Michels, the subordination of individual autonomy in the most intimate sphere of life to a legally binding obligation was an infringement on human dignity, which ethically superior people could not require. Michels invoked the

---

[133] Dr Robert Michels, 'Streifzüge zum Problem des Geschlechtskampfes' [unter Rubrik 'Literarische Berichte'], in *Mutterschutz*, Jg.3, no.4, April 1907, pp.172–80, here p.173.

[134] IISH Nachlass August Bebel, 135. Michels to Bebel, 27 February 1902. Michels had since made Bax's personal acquaintance, on a visit to England in 1905. See ARM.FLE, *busta* Belfort Bax.

FEMINISM AND THE SEXUAL POLITICS OF A NEW CENTURY   175

judgement of 'the most enlightened, genuinely moral minds of Europe' in support of this point of view.[135] Most of Michels' article was given over to a review of the newly published Italian novel *Una donna* ('a woman'), published under the pseudonym Sibylle Aleramo. The novel describes the fate of a north Italian woman from a wealthy house who goes to work in southern Italy, where her desire for independence is met with incomprehension by the 'Orientals' in the backward community she lives in. She becomes a victim of rape, and is bound to marry the rapist. She then discovers the truth about why her mother was unhappy (as a result of ill-treatment by her father). Most of the article consists of a synopsis of the plot, about woman's unhappy fate and subjugation in marriage. Michels concluded from his reading of the novel that it had 'unravelled the problem of marriage in all its depths', asking: 'Who will still wish to deny that the present form of marriage is in need of reform?'.[136] This manner of drawing sweeping conclusions from selected literary or anecdotal evidence was characteristic of Michels' writings on the sexual question.

Michels returned to the defence of the 'new sexual ethics', which he proclaimed to be gradually dawning, and the fight against its main enemy, hypocrisy, in a leading article for the re-named journal of the Bund für Mutterschutz, *Die Neue Generation* ('the new generation') in 1909.[137] Michels wrote an article outlining what he considered to be borderline ethical questions, to demonstrate 'gradations of honourable conduct', in order to show the limitations of conventional morality in such matters as the legal categories of legitimate and illegitimate births. (Equal rights for children born 'illegitimate' was one of the original demands of the Bund für Mutterschutz.) However, in this article Michels conflated ethical questions with legal categories: 'The law only knows rigid norms and closes its eyes to all intermediate phases', for example, under the law there were registered prostitutes and decent women.[138] As an example of the 'intermediate gradations of morality' that might be encountered in real life, Michels cited an Italian prostitute he had once met ('who offered her, incidentally quite meagre, charms to fine gentlemen in a room in the middle of a large Italian town, but only "by recommendation"'), who insisted that she was a decent woman ('io sono una donna onesta'), as she did not allow her clients to acknowledge her on the street.[139]

Michels' anecdotal evidence in this article was, he related, derived 'from my own experience, coming from social and sexual-ethical curiosity'. For example, he related that he had personally interviewed several seamstresses in workshops in

---

[135] Privatdozent Dr Robert Michels (Turin), 'Frauenelend und Menschenwürde', *Mutterschutz*, Jg.3, no.12, December 1907, pp.483–9, quotation p.483.
[136] Michels, 'Frauenelend und Menschenwürde', pp.484 (southerners as 'Orientals'), here p.489.
[137] Prof. Dr Robert Michels, 'Die Zwischenstufen der Ehrbarkeit', *Die Neue Generation*, Jg.5, no.9, 14 September 1909, pp.351–9, here p.351.
[138] Michels, 'Die Zwischenstufen der Ehrbarkeit', p.352.
[139] Michels, 'Die Zwischenstufen der Ehrbarkeit', p.353.

176 ROBERT MICHELS, SOCIALISM, AND MODERNITY

Turin who worked as prostitutes on the side, while maintaining respectable appearances in the eyes of their family and even their fiancés.[140] Michels cited his friend, the anthropologist Alfredo Niceforo, and an unnamed young novelist in Rome, who spoke of similar seamstress workshops in Rome, 'in which the young girls "amuse themselves", earn money, and yet still manage to keep the capital they need for a marriage later on, their virginity'.[141] Michels also referred to examples of middle-class girls in Rome going dancing during the day ('in certain ball-rooms') and allowing men sexual liberties (up to a point) for money.[142] Michels suggested that just as such cases defied simple categorization concerning the women's professions, the distinctions of conventional sexual morality were also arbitrary, and to be superseded by new sexual ethics.

This argumentation did not impress Max Weber, to whom Michels had sent a copy of the article, as was his wont. Writing to Gisela Michels-Lindner (congratulating her on her own new book on local government enterprises in Italy), Weber generously praised an article that Michels had placed in the *Zeitschrift für Politik*,[143] but took issue with the piece on 'gradations of honourable conduct' in *Die Neue Generation*. Weber wrote: 'You know as well as I do—as he ultimately does himself—that he is a "moralist" from head to toe', and went on to ask: 'why does such an ethicist (moralist) make concessions to libertinism and in such [libertine] company make fun of those like himself?'. Weber complained that Michels' essay constructed spurious distinctions, and conflated questions of morality with social convention. He rejected Michels' arguments that women such as Parisian waitresses who engaged in part-time prostitution represented a 'hard nut for moralists to crack'. Weber wrote: 'Even the "white slaves" of our society have *both* their *conventional* rules—arising from the sociological conditions of their existence, *and* their "ethics", with which they are grounded in whatever remains of their human dignity that their fate still allows them to develop'.[144]

Earlier in 1909, Weber had written to Michels urging him to adopt more regular work habits, and to go to bed earlier at night. Weber was incredulous when Michels informed him that he was going to visit Paris for a rest, suggesting that the 'charms' of Paris were hardly conducive to resting. Weber warned Michels against the danger of a nervous breakdown (such as Weber himself had suffered):

---

[140] Michels, 'Die Zwischenstufen der Ehrbarkeit', pp.354–5.
[141] Michels, 'Die Zwischenstufen der Ehrbarkeit', p.355.
[142] Michels, 'Die Zwischenstufen der Ehrbarkeit', pp.355–7.
[143] Robert Michels, 'Der ethische Faktor in der Parteipolitik Italiens', in *Zeitschrift für Politik*, Bd.3, no.1, 1910, pp.56–91.
[144] Max Weber to Gisela Michels-Lindner, 25 December 1909, in Max Weber, *Briefe 1909–1910*, Tübingen. 1994 (Gesamtausgabe Abt. II/6), pp.349–50. The case that Michels referred to as a 'hard nut for moralists' was not in fact a waitress, but an artists' model, who used her work earnings to maintain male lovers. Michels, 'Die Zwischenstufen der Ehrbarkeit', p.358n.

FEMINISM AND THE SEXUAL POLITICS OF A NEW CENTURY 177

Believe me, I know the Bohemian *charm* of your 'intensive' way of life, but anyone who wishes to continue to live that life at *your* age needs to be alone in the world, and must be able to leave it—voluntarily or involuntarily—at any moment when the inevitable collapse occurs, without having to be accountable to anyone.

Weber recommended that a quiet stay in a lonely German forest, without working, would be better for Michels' nerves than the delights of Paris.[145]

As his wife Marianne recalled, Weber's views on the sexual question were constantly being tested in this period, partly by discussions with younger associates like Michels, partly by the difficult relationships within his own family circle (especially those involving Else Jaffé and his brother Alfred Weber). Arthur Mitzman has identified a certain 'retreat from ascetic rationalism' and from the values of his Calvinist background in Weber's last years, which he linked to the complications in Weber's personal life in this period.[146] However, while Marianne Weber, in her biography of Max Weber, noted some evolution in his attitude towards the behaviour of others around him, she emphasized that he nonetheless maintained an unshaken 'belief in the irreplaceable significance of norms'.[147] Joachim Radkau, in his biography of Weber, has written of Weber's rejection of August Bebel's *Woman in Socialism*, particularly of Bebel's critique of bourgeois marriage and the emphasis on the need to satisfy natural drives: 'The Webers...saw themselves confronted by a united front of sexualism, naturalism, materialism, and socialism'.[148] Weber's aversion to the new sexual ethics and to Freudian ideas of natural sex drives was expressed in drastic terms in a letter to Else Jaffé, in which he explained his rejection of an article by the Austrian psychoanalyst Dr Otto Gross on 'Psychologism since Nietzsche and Freud', which Gross had submitted to the *Archiv für Sozialwissenschaft und Sozialpolitik*: while conceding that Gross's approach to psychoanalysis might be in its infancy, Weber wrote, 'there is in my opinion no need that these apparently unavoidable nappies have to be laundered in our *Archiv*'. On the other hand, 'Sombart's Morgen or Mutterschutz will serve them up as a delicacy'.[149]

When Michels' *Political Parties* appeared at the end of 1910, Weber took Michels to task for his reference to the origins of the bourgeois marriage lying in the need of the male head of family to ensure that his offspring were legitimate

---

[145] Weber to Michels, in Weber, *Briefe 1909–1910*, p.124.

[146] Arthur Mitzman, *The Iron Cage: An Historical Interpretation of Max Weber*, New York, 1970, pp.277–92; see also Radkau, *Max Weber*, pp.484–94, 556–72; and the essays in Sam Whimster, ed., *Max Weber and the Culture of Anarchy*, Basingstoke and New York, 1999.

[147] Marianne Weber, *Max Weber*, p.387.   [148] Radkau, *Max Weber*, p.93.

[149] Max Weber to Else Jaffé, 13 September 1907, in Weber, *Briefe 1909–1910*, pp.393–403, quotation p.396. *Der Morgen* was a cultural journal co-edited by Sombart and Hugo von Hofmannsthal. See Friedrich Lenger, *Werner Sombart 1863–1941. Eine Biographie*, Munich, 1995, pp.154–65. Michels was also a contributor to *Der Morgen*. Sombart's friendship with Michels extended to discussions of 'the great topic of erotica'. Werner Sombart to Robert Michels, 14 February 1907, ARM/FLE.

178   ROBERT MICHELS, SOCIALISM, AND MODERNITY

heirs to his property, arguing that the opposite was the case: the need for a formal marriage arose out of the interest of the wife and her clan that her children, as opposed to those of slaves or concubines, would be heirs to the family fortune.[150] Here Weber could draw on his own work on 'Agrarian Conditions in Antiquity' (published in 1909), in which his comparative studies of ancient civilizations included consideration of the evolution of family structures in Mesopotamia, Egypt, Israel, the Hellenistic world, and Rome. With some variations, these studies argued that unlimited patriarchal authority had been progressively limited by the introduction of marriage contracts and laws, which provided married women with greater security.[151]

Michels continued to be active in the Bund für Mutterschutz, not only as a contributor to its journal, but also as a lecturer. The league advertised a list of speakers and topics in its journal, and Michels featured from 1909 until the outbreak of the First World War, mainly lecturing on Italian topics, but also on 'la recherche de paternité' ('investigating paternity'), the 'ethical boundaries of sexuality', and divorce.[152] Michels also found a forum for his views on sex reform in the new feminist journal *Frauen-Zukunft*, in which he published an article on 'neo-Malthusianism'.[153] Edward Ross Dickinson has summed up 'neo-Malthusianism' as a 'loosely organised' movement, 'which argued that the use of contraception was a necessary and entirely laudable means of avoiding individual poverty and social immiseration'.[154] Michels endorsed neo-Malthusianism, arguing that while the joys of parenthood were instinctive and natural (even if he viewed the joys of fatherhood as necessarily a diminished version compared with those of motherhood), putting a child into the world should be considered a serious responsibility, one that is all too often the result of thoughtless sexual acts. The need to limit reproduction was often an economic necessity, especially among the 'poorer classes of the population'.[155] Even in an economically comfortable bourgeois marriage, there was a case for contraception: too frequent births could also lead to high infant mortality, and the ruin of the mother's health. Furthermore, too frequent births could also have other ill effects, for example,

---

[150] Robert Michels, *Zur Soziologie des Parteiwesens in der modernen Demokratie*, Lepzig, 1911, p.13; Weber to Michels, 21 December 1910, Weber, *Briefe 1909–1910*, p.755. See also Weber's comments in *Verhandlungen des Zweiten Deutschen Soziologentages vom 20.-22. Oktober 1912 in Berlin*, Tubingen, 1913, p.189; Radkau, *Max Weber*, p.86.

[151] Max Weber, *The Agrarian Sociology of Ancient Civilisations*, London, 1976, pp.94, 131f, 143f, 250f. Weber also attributed to the rise of Christianity in late antiquity a major role in elevating the masses of the unfree 'from the status of "speaking tools" to the plane of humanity', not least by providing slave families with 'firm moral guarantees' (p.410). Cf. also the section on 'The Religious Status of Marriage and of Women', in Weber, *Economy and Society*, Vol.1, Berkeley, 1978, pp.604–7.

[152] 'Rednerliste des Deutschen Bundes für Mutterschutz', *Die Neue Generation*, Jg.5, 10, 14 October 1909, p.460; Jg.10, 8/9, 14 August 1914, p.467.

[153] Prof. Dr Robert Michels, 'Neomalthusianismus', *Frauen-Zukunft*, Vol.1, 1, 1910, pp.42–55.

[154] Dickinson, *Sex, Freedom, and Power*, p.46. See also James Woycke, *Birth Control in Germany, 1871–1933*, London and New York, 1988, pp.36–8, 54, 135, 163.

[155] Michels, 'Neomalthusianismus', pp.42–3.

FEMINISM AND THE SEXUAL POLITICS OF A NEW CENTURY 179

affecting the woman's capacity to engage in sexual relations with her husband (who might then be more inclined to engage in adultery).[156] Michels added the consideration that women with large families had less time to develop their mental gifts.[157] However, he then returned to the theme of the male's sexual needs: there were detrimental consequences for a marriage when a child is conceived and born immediately after marriage. The woman's initiation to sex was immediately overtaken by the cares and responsibilities of motherhood (with the consequence of more sexual abstinence for husband, especially if he had to work at home, as Michels mostly did in the first years of his marriage). Michels wrote: 'motherhood cheats the man of many of his finest hopes—I am referring here always to the first years of marriage for young husbands—and spoils the already existing qualities of his wife for him'.[158] Michels argued that the ability to separate sexual enjoyment from reproduction was a sign of social and cultural progress, writing:

The physical act of sexual love—originally a means to end and still esteemed exclusively as such by orthodox Christians of all confessions, vegetarians, and white-haired moralists—has gradually from one of the most essential phenomena of the animal psyche become an end in itself with the progressive emancipation of the human being. We must have the courage to confess that we love love and ecstasy for their own sake.[159]

For Michels, the so-called 'moral imperative' to confine sex exclusively to its reproductive purpose was itself 'brutal and immoral', arguing: 'erotic culture is therefore in this sense ethical culture'. Contraception was ethically responsible behaviour, more ethical than thoughtlessly producing children whom one might not be able to feed or look after.[160] Michels did refer to the social and economic consequences of overpopulation, and the fact that neo-Malthusianism's opponents included nationalist and militarists, fixated on the size of future armies.[161] The main emphasis of his article, however, was on neo-Malthusianism as both a sign and an enabler of a more advanced civilization, which allowed more room for individual autonomy and self-expression. Michels wrote: 'The civilised human being has the right to his self. This right includes the right to progeny, to determine the number of progeny, and to have no progeny'. Neo-Malthusianism was

[156] Michels, 'Neomalthusianismus', p.43. At this point, one remembers Gisela Michels-Lindner's plea to Oda Lerda-Oberg for advice on contraception (see above, n128). Gisela had five children in relatively quick succession, two of whom died in infancy.
[157] Michels, 'Neomalthusianismus', p.44.   [158] Michels, 'Neomalthusianismus', pp.44–6.
[159] Michels, 'Neomalthusianismus', pp.46–7.   [160] Michels, 'Neomalthusianismus', p.47.
[161] Michels, 'Neomalthusianismus', p.50.

180   ROBERT MICHELS, SOCIALISM, AND MODERNITY

only unnatural in the sense that all culture was unnatural: 'Neo-Malthusianism signifies a victory of human reason over animal unreason.'[162]

In 1911, the same year as his major work on *Political Parties* appeared, Michels gathered many of his articles on the sexual question into a volume called *Die Grenzen der Geschlechtsmoral. Prolegomena, Gedanken und Untersuchungen* ('the boundaries of sexual morality: prolegomena, thoughts, and investigations'), published by the Frauenverlag (Women's Publishing House).[163] The book included Michels' essays on 'erotic forays', 'gradations of honourable conduct', prostitutes and 'old maids', 'bridal morality', neo-Malthusianism, and women and intellectual life, along with new material written for the book. The mixture of new material and older essays, written over several years, and the wildly eclectic range of sources on which Michels drew, gave the work a somewhat unsystematic character, which is openly conceded in the foreword, in which he describes the book as a 'site for the collection of a small crowd of select important questions, which have made a rendezvous there and now play around in it'.[164] Michels also emphasized that the work, given its concern with 'boundary areas', dealt more with open questions than answers, and warned that it was not written for readers who adhered to any moral dogma, be it 'Christian-Bible-believing, Darwinian-Häckelian, libertarian or libertine'.[165]

The work was divided into four main parts: 'General Boundary Questions of the Erotic', 'Extramarital Boundary Problems', 'Premarital Boundary Problems', and 'Marital Boundary Problems'. Michels began by emphasizing the natural power of the sex drive, likening it to the natural need to satisfy hunger; however, he distanced himself from a reductive naturalism, arguing that human culture consisted of the progressive overcoming of the limitations of a 'state of nature', and he stressed that the difference between sex and the satisfaction of hunger was the involvement of another person, which made the sex act subject to the Kantian categorical imperative forbidding the exploitation of another person.[166] While compulsion or exploitation were ethically reprehensible, Michels wrote: 'Sexual hunger satisfied in voluntary love, including in free love, does not contradict the basic principles of ethics'.[167]

---

[162] Michels, 'Neomalthusianismus', p.54. As Timm Genett points out, 'Michels' thoughts on sexual liberation and autonomy in the erotic sphere rest on a linear view of history, which interprets the progress of civilization as an accumulation of gains in freedom.' Genett, *Der Fremde im Kriege*, p.49.

[163] The Frauenverlag (Munich and Leipzig) also published the journal *Die Frauen-Zukunft*. An English translation appeared in 1914 under the title *Sexual Ethics: A Study of Borderland Questions*, London and Felling-On-Tyne, 1914, in the 'Contemporary Science Series' edited by Havelock Ellis.

[164] R. [Robert] Michels, *Die Grenzen der Geschlechtsmoral. Prolegomena, Gedanken und Untersuchungen*, Munich and Leipzig, 1911, p.ix.

[165] Michels, *Die Grenzen der Geschlechtsmoral*, pp.ix–x.

[166] Michels, *Die Grenzen der Geschlechtsmoral*, p.17.

[167] Michels, *Die Grenzen der Geschlechtsmoral*, p.18.

FEMINISM AND THE SEXUAL POLITICS OF A NEW CENTURY   181

Timm Genett has characterized Michels' *Grenzen der Geschlechtsmoral* as 'more than an indictment [of conventional mores] in the cause of sex reform. The youthful discontent with the prevailing culture of sexuality becomes for Michels the midwife for a new discipline: "the science of love" [*Liebeswissenschaft*], more precisely, a *sociology of sexuality*'.[168] This is a somewhat generous assessment of the degree of methodological rigour evident in Michels' often anecdotal and impressionistic essays. Michels' book cites Cesare Lombroso and Christian von Ehrenfels, a professor of philosopher in Prague who advocated polygyny (men being allowed to have multiple wives), at least partly on the grounds of racial hygiene,[169] but otherwise his sources are largely literary, spiced with his own observations and reminiscences. There is no discussion of, let alone critical engagement with, other contemporary writers on sexual issues, such as Freud, Krafft-Ebing, or Magnus Hirschfeld.

Max Weber's response to Michels' book was reserved. While greeting the book's appearance, and describing it is 'charming', he complained that Michels' (largely negative) characterization of marriage suffered from an inadequate framing of the question, and that the book's personal and polemical qualities imposed limitations on the work. Weber wrote: 'the real problems start just where you stop'.[170] Weber, for one, did not seem to regard the book as founding a new branch of sociology.

A couple of weeks after this exchange of letters with Michels, Weber visited the Michels family in Turin in April 1911. Weber was somewhat taken aback by the Michels' frankness in sexual matters with their children—the eldest child, their 6-year-old daughter Manon, performed a game called 'adultery'. However, as Weber wrote to his wife Marianne, 'when I suggested she might become an actress, M[ichels] and wife were both (morally) *outraged*'. Weber found that Robert Michels 'had obviously become politically *very* resigned'. The two men continued their discussion on the topic of Michels' new book: 'Naturally, long discussions on the *erotic*. More on this verbally (not very much that was new). "The awareness, that one can *make conquests*, keeps one *young*. Therefore no 'marriage', i.e. no *renunciation* of feeling 'young'." I had a few things to say on this, as you can imagine'.[171] Michels' awareness of his ability to still make conquests comes through occasionally in his letters to Gisela around this time. In August 1912, on a visit to Britain, he recounted an 'adventure', meeting a woman who

---

[168] Genett, *Der Fremde im Kriege*, p.52; emphasis in original.
[169] On Ehrenfels, see Dickinson, *Sex, Freedom, and Power*, pp.263–5.
[170] Weber to Michels, 7 and 11 April 1911, in Max Weber, *Briefe 1911–1912* (=Gesamtausgabe II/7, i), Tübingen, 1978, pp.171–2, 178, quotation p.172 (7 April). Another, apparently lengthy, letter from Weber to Michels dealing with the book does not seem to have survived.
[171] Max Weber to Marianne Weber, 22 April 1911, in *ibid.*, pp.199–200, quotation on p.200. Emphases in original. On the relationship between Michels and Weber and their respective views on the sexual question, see also the discussion in Radkau, *Max Weber*, pp.361–7.

182   ROBERT MICHELS, SOCIALISM, AND MODERNITY

'*partout* wanted to have a child from me'.[172] It is worth noting in this context that Michels had the benefit of a handsome appearance and an imposing physical presence, being tall, blond, and blue-eyed, with an impressive moustache. A contemporary description of him related: 'Michels impresses one to start with; a man of six feet three inches or thereabout generally does; and when allied with magnificent physique one gets the impression of mental attributes in proportion, the effect is telling'.[173] The Austrian pacifist author Bertha von Suttner was also struck by Michels' 'tall, handsome appearance'.[174]

Timm Genett has suggested that Michels' texts in *Die Grenzen der Geschlechtsmoral* can be read as a key to his political thinking.[175] According to Genett, these essays, which he classifies as radical feminist, reveal a fundamental ethical standpoint in Michels' work. Michels' ethical approach to politics, based on the Kantian categorical imperative, stressed the importance of individual autonomy, self-realization, equal rights, and a positive attitude to social progress and modernity in general. Genett stresses Michels' affirmative attitude to modernity, contrasting it with the cultural pessimism of many of his contemporaries. Michels' 'contributions to the sexual revolution' of the early 1900s are linked to the broader context of bourgeois youth revolt and generational conflict in turn-of-the-century Germany, which saw calls for a newer, more authentic moral code.[176]

Genett's analysis of Michels' views on feminism and the sexual question has some merit: Michels' involvement in the Bund für Mutterschutz, and his contributions to the organization's journal, placed him in the avant-garde of the bourgeois feminist and sex reform movements of the early 1900s in Germany. But Genett's depiction of Michels' male feminism as exemplary and of contemporary relevance requires qualification in a number of respects.

Genett touches only lightly on some of the incongruities in Michels' male feminism: for example, Michels' occasional anecdotal excursions in his essays into the world of prostitution from the perspective of the gentleman customer. While Michels rejected the bourgeois double standard in sexual mores as a matter of principle, it re-emerges occasionally in the man-of-the-world tone of some of his more *feuilleton*-like essays. Here, Michels' 'male feminism' often tips over into

---

[172] Robert Michels to Gisela Michels-Lindner, 7 August 1912, ARM/FLE. Part of the letter has been blacked out and made illegible (possibly by Michels' daughter Manon, who originally had the custody of Michels' papers). Another postcard from Robert Michels to Gisela, 9 February 1912, refers to an 'adventure', which signified that he was 'not yet an old man' (also partially blacked out).

[173] G.S. Grose, 'The Right Road for Socialism: Special Interview with Dr Robert Michels', *The Socialist. Official Organ of the Socialist Labour Party*, Vol.III, no.35, July 1905, p.5. Michels kept his blond hair and imposing figure even late in his life. His 1935 Italian passport gives his height as 1.95 metres. ARM/FLE, Documenti Personali: Passport, Kingdom of Italy, 5 August 1935.

[174] In a diary note dated 15 January 1914, in Bertha von Suttner, *Lebenserinnerungen*, ed. Fritz Böttger, Berlin, 1969, p.541.

[175] Genett, *Der Fremde im Kriege*, p.44.   [176] Genett, *Der Fremde im Kriege*, p.50.

FEMINISM AND THE SEXUAL POLITICS OF A NEW CENTURY   183

masculine libertinism, which takes an essentializing view of male sexual desire as a given force of nature, which women need to accommodate. In *Die Grenzen der Geschlechtsmoral*, Michels discussed sexual violence initially in relation to sexual play and rape fantasies. He relates that a 'highly educated and thoroughly decent woman' once confessed to him her fantasy of being raped by her husband.[177] He even argues that women were partly to blame 'in some way' for rape, except for 'cases of absolute defencelessness', such as incapacitating illness or wounds, or attacks by armed gangs. Michels argued that, apart from such extreme cases, rape was always at least partly a result of women's learned cowardice and helplessness.[178] Genett refers to this passage as one which many readers might consider 'heretical', 'even today', and seeks to explain it by arguing that Michels was measuring behaviour against a new, heroic ideal of humanity, which in a Nietzschean fashion would overcome the weakness inculcated by social convention.[179] It is nonetheless difficult to accommodate Michels' statements on sexual violence within a feminist framework.[180]

A notable omission in Michels' book—and in all of his writings on sexual issues—is any acknowledgement of the existence of homosexuality and the contemporary movement for the rights of homosexuals. To make this point is not to seek to judge Michels' work by the social standards of the twenty-first century. At the start of the twentieth century, there was a very lively public debate about the reform of the penal code which (under paragraph 175) criminalized male homosexuality.[181] Even if it was not seen as a central concern of the Social Democratic Party, it was nonetheless a debate in which Social Democrats also participated, and which featured in the Social Democratic publications with which Michels was very familiar. In 1895 in *Die Neue Zeit*, Eduard Bernstein expressed support for the decriminalization of homosexual acts between males.[182] In 1898, August Bebel had signed Magnus Hirschfeld's petition for the reform of paragraph 175 of the German Penal Code, and initiated a parliamentary debate on the topic from the floor of the Reichstag.[183] As Magnus Hirschfeld's Wissenschaftlich-humanitäres Komitee (Scientific-Humanitarian Committee) lobbied for the

---

[177] Michels, *Die Grenzen der Geschlechtsmoral*, pp.79–80.

[178] Michels, *Die Grenzen der Geschlechtsmoral*, p.90.

[179] Genett, *Der Fremde im Kriege*, p.79.

[180] Dickinson (*Sex, Freedom, and Power*, p.260) also points to the problematical nature of Michels' comments on rape, although his citation here is slightly imprecise. Michels' statement that it is sometimes difficult for a male to tell whether 'the resistance that the girl puts up to his desire is genuine or fake' is on p.84 of *Die Grenzen der Geschlechtsmoral*, not p.80. In a similar vein, see also Professor Dr Robert Michels, 'Vom Wesen der Koketterie', *Die Neue Generation*, Jg.8, 1, 14 November 1912, which describes how women can unconsciously provoke men.

[181] See Dickinson, *Sex, Freedom, and Power*, ch.7.

[182] Dickinson, *Sex, Freedom, and Power*, p.142; see Eduard Bernstein, 'Zur Beurtheilung des widernormalen Geschlechtsverkehrs', *Die Neue Zeit*, Jg.13, 2, 1894/95, pp.228–33. Bernstein, writing from London, was partly responding to the trial of Oscar Wilde.

[183] Robert Beachy, 'The German Invention of Homosexuality', *Journal of Modern History*, Vol.82, 4, December 2010, p.824.

184   ROBERT MICHELS, SOCIALISM, AND MODERNITY

abolition of paragraph 175, it generally found support from the Social Democratic press and periodicals.[184] Against this background, Michels' silence on homosexuality in a book of nearly 200 pages on the 'boundaries of sexual morality' is noteworthy. One of the few references to homosexuality to be found in Michels' writings is in fact hostile: in his 1908 book on *Proletariat and Bourgeoisie in the Italian Socialist Movement*, he gives a long list of abuses and oppressive conditions in imperial Germany, from discrimination against socialists in universities, and discrimination against Jews, to the abuse of army recruits, and includes among these abuses the fact that 'in noble regiments homosexuals more or less go unpunished'.[185] In a review of Napoleone Colajonni's *Latini e Anglo-Sassoni* (Latins and Anglo-Saxons), Michels referred to homsexuality as 'the latest abnormality in the field of sexuality', and cited approvingly Colajonni's reference to Italians' consternation at the activities of German and English homosexual vacationers in the region around Naples. He also defended Magnus Hirschfeld's research into homosexuality among Berlin students only on the basis that such research was necessary to 'combat the abnormality' (a rare reference to Hirschfeld by Michels, which oddly misrepresents him).[186]

Michels was also sometimes prone to using highly gendered language. While gendered language was common and not regarded as unusual even by most feminists in this period, Michels had an occasional penchant for quite drastic formulations, for example his reference to socialism as a youth trying to force open the bridal chamber of power.[187] In 1932, looking back on his early years as a socialist in Germany, Michels was to boast of Mussolini taking up a phrase he coined, namely, that 'German Social Democracy resembled a giant that, despite his size, couldn't make a virgin pregnant', and he declared that he 'gradually came to view democracy in the light of a cult of incompetence and as possessed of a base fear of all manly responsibility'.[188] There is sometimes a swaggering machismo that comes through in Michels' prose, which is also incongruous given the claims sometimes made about his male feminism.

Genett's discussion of Michels' involvement in the feminist and sex reform movement is also rather thinly contextualized. As already noted, Michels confounded some contemporary feminists by contributing to feminist newspapers and periodicals across the political and ideological spectrum from Clara Zetkin's

---

[184] Dickinson, *Sex, Freedom, and Power*, p.176.

[185] Roberto [Robert] Michels, *Il proletariato e borghesia nel movimento socialista italiano*, Turin, 1908, p.319. This passage on the defects of imperial Germany did not feature in the original articles published in the *Archiv für Sozialwissenschaft und Sozialpolitik*.

[186] Robert Michels, Review of Napoleone Colajonni, *Latini e Anglo-Sassoni*, in *Kritische Blätter für die gesamten Sozialwissenschaften*, Jg.II, Heft 7, Juli 1906, p.328.

[187] Robert Michels, 'Die deutsche Sozialdemokratie im internationalen Verbande. Eine kritische Untersuchung', *Archiv für Sozialwissenschaft und Sozialpolitik*, 25, 1907, p.284.

[188] Robert Michels, 'Eine syndikalistisch gerichtete Unterströmung im deutschen Sozialismus (1903–1907)', in Max Adler et al., eds., *Festschrift für Carl Grünberg*, Leipzig, 1932, p.350.

Marxist *Die Gleichheit*, to the progressive liberal *Frauenbewegung*, to the more conservative-liberal *Die Frau*, as well as supporting the Bund für Mutterschutz, which was rejected by more conservative feminists and Zetkin alike. In the divided, intensely polarized scene of feminist politics in Wilhelmine Germany, such public ideological promiscuity could hardly be sustained for long. As suggested above, Michels' irenic approach to the ideological fault-lines within German feminism also stands in contrast with his militant espousal of class conflict between men during his radical socialist phase, which may indicate that he harboured a deeply gendered categorization of political struggles.

6

Intellectuals, Masses, and Leaders

Two new sociological concepts came into circulation at the end of the nineteenth century: 'intellectuals' and 'the masses'. These concepts increasingly gathered weight in social and political discourse in the early twentieth century: the emergence of 'the masses' as a potential political actor, and not just as an amorphous social construct, was a fundamental issue for modern politics, one that posed particular problems for European elites accustomed to a politics of 'notables', characterized by intra-elite accommodations and the continuing subordination of the 'common people'. In the late nineteenth century, conservatives such as Bismarck in Germany and Disraeli in Britain had widened the (male) franchise in order to outflank and undercut their liberal rivals. However, once the mass electorate had come into being, urbanization and the evolution of working-class consciousness eroded traditional deference to aristocratic elites, and the management of the mass electorate posed increasing problems for those in power. Arguably, the clash between a new organized mass politics of the left, in the form of the socialist labour movement, and attempts by old and new right-wing elites to create a counter-mobilization of other social groups outside the elites themselves, was one of the main factors shaping Europe's twentieth-century 'age of extremes' (to borrow Hobsbawm's term).

Intellectuals

As if to contrast with the increasing prevalence of the concept of the 'masses', the beginning of the twentieth century also saw the formation of the concept of the 'intellectual': a term which came to have both a descriptive function, referring to a particular social group, and a normative one: 'intellectuals' were a group with a mission, however that mission was defined. By common consent, 'intellectuals' first entered the lexicon as a noun in early 1898, in the context of the Dreyfus affair in France. Clemenceau referred in January of that year to the 'intellectuels' who had rallied to the support of an idea, and a week later, the anti-Dreyfusard Maurice Barrès threw the term back with a scornful characterization of 'the protest of the intellectuals', thereby successfully popularizing the term. Despite its pejorative and polemical use in the Dreyfus affair by the right, the literary

Robert Michels, Socialism, and Modernity. Andrew G. Bonnell, Oxford University Press. © Andrew G. Bonnell 2023.
DOI: 10.1093/oso/9780192871848.003.0007

INTELLECTUALS, MASSES, AND LEADERS   187

defenders of Dreyfus came to embrace the term 'intellectuals' as denoting not just a social category, but a vocation.[1]

If the origin of the word 'intellectual' can be identified with unusual precision, the emergence of a new social group defined by academic training or intellectual and literary activity, which did not see itself as integrated into normal bourgeois life, had already been evident in both France and Germany in the years preceding the Dreyfus affair. While some young university-educated men became frustrated at the shortage of employment suited to their qualifications and talents, and gravitated to the 'cultural pessimism' of the right, others identified themselves with the proletariat, and sympathized with socialism.[2] Controversy arose in the labour movement over the role of the new stratum of intellectuals in a workers' movement.[3] In 1895, Karl Kautsky devoted a series of articles in *Die Neue Zeit* to the question of the intelligentsia and social democracy.[4] Kautsky began by stating that, at least at one level, the question of whether the workers' party should admit intellectuals had already been resolved in the affirmative in *The Communist Manifesto* and by the fact that the party's founding figures (Marx, Engels, Lassalle) had themselves been intellectuals.[5] However, he continued to analyse the complications posed by the social situation of the intellectuals. While Kautsky perceived a strong feeling of discontent growing among intellectuals, only individual intellectuals would be able to embrace socialism, as the stratum of intellectuals, especially those in elite professions, were too accustomed to social privilege and the pursuit of professional (rather than class) interests.[6] Shlomo Sand has suggested that the debate over Marxism and intellectuals was relatively marginal in 'post-revolutionary' France compared with 'pre-revolutionary' Germany and Italy.[7] There was, however, a strong strand of anti-intellectual rhetoric among the radical syndicalists around *Le Mouvement Socialiste*, articulated by Georges Sorel,

---

[1] Pascal Ory and Jean-François Sirinelli, *Les intellectuels en France. De l'affaire Dreyfus à nos jours*, Paris, 1992, pp.5–7, and ch.1; Michel Winock, *Le siècle des intellectuels*, Paris, 1997, part I.

[2] In the case of Gernany, see the discussion of the so-called 'geistiges Proletariat' (intellectual proletariat) in the early 1890s in Helmut Scherer, *Bürgerlich-oppositionelle Literaten und sozialdemokratische Arbeiterbewegung nach 1890*, Stuttgart, 1974, pp.33–9; for the equivalent discussion in France, see Shlomo Sand, 'Le marxisme et les intellectuels vers 1900', in Madeleine Rebérioux and Gilles Candar, eds., *Jaurès et les intellectuels*, Paris, 1994, pp.207–8.

[3] See Christophe Prochasson, *Les intellectuels, le socialisme et la guerre, 1900–1938*, Paris, 1993, pp.24–42; Sand, 'Le marxisme et les intellectuels vers 1900', pp.203–22; Ulrich von Alemann, Gertrude Cepl-Kaufmann, Hans Hecker, and Bernd Witte, eds., *Intellektuelle und Sozialdemokratie*, Opladen, 2000, section I.

[4] Karl Kautsky, 'Intelligenz und Sozialdemokratie', *Die Neue Zeit*, Jg.13, 2, 1894/5, pp.10–16, 43–9, 74–80.

[5] Kautsky, 'Intelligenz und Sozialdemokratie', p.12. Interestingly, as Sand points out (in 'Le marxisme et les intellectuels vers 1900', p.206), Kautsky's essay also appeared translated into French in 1895 in the journal *Le Devenir Social*, reflecting an interest in the question in French socialist circles as well.

[6] Kautsky, 'Intelligenz und Sozialdemokratie', pp.43, 80.

[7] Sand, 'Le marxisme et les intellectuels vers 1900', pp.205–6.

188   ROBERT MICHELS, SOCIALISM, AND MODERNITY

Hubert Lagardelle and Edouard Berth (despite the journal's relative lack of a working-class mass base).[8]

As already noted in Chapter 3, when Michels came into contact with Italian socialism, he was immediately struck by the prominence of intellectuals in the party's ranks. Writing on his impressions of the 1902 Italian socialist party congress at Imola, Michels related:

> It was at first striking, what a huge percentage of the participants consisted of intellectuals; lawyers and university lecturers are, as well known, no rarity in the Italian socialist party, which is not only the party of the manually working classes, i.e. the so-called proletariat, but at the same time that of the highest circles of educated persons.[9]

Michels particularly noted the high number of educated bourgeois among Italian socialist members of parliament.[10] In addition to Michels' Italophile sentiments in general, and his sense of affinity with 'Latins' based on his family background, it seems to have been the ability of Italian intellectuals to combine successful university careers with political activism in the socialist party that attracted Michels to involvement in the Italian party. The more highly organized German party, with its cadres of skilled workers turned party functionaries, had less need of intellectuals to be the spokespersons of the socialist movement. At Imola, Michels was particularly impressed by the radical intellectuals around Enrico Ferri on the party's left—considering that the left had the advantage in terms of the quality of its intellectuals, while the reformist right had the greater quantity of intellectuals on its side.

Indeed, in an article for Clara Zetkin's *Die Gleichheit* in 1903, Michels cited an 1893 survey conducted by the periodical *La Vita Moderna* that purportedly showed that, with thirty exceptions, 'the entire world of scholars and artists' in Italy sympathized with socialism. (It is not clear how *La Vita Moderna* arrived at this figure, of course.) At that time, the prominent scholarly magazine *La Nuova Antologia* could almost have been called 'a Marxist discussion paper'. Universities were full of Marxist professors, and distinguished scholars and authors like Enrico Ferri and Edmondo De Amicis became adherents of the socialist movement.[11]

---

[8] Sand, 'Le marxisme et les intellectuels vers 1900', pp.210–19; Prochasson, *Les intellectuels, le socialisme et la guerre*, pp.32–5.

[9] R.M. [Robert Michels], 'Eindrücke vom Kongress der italienischen sozialistischen Partei in Imola', *Schwäbische Tagwacht*, no.226, 29 September 1902.

[10] On this, see Carl Levy, 'Introduction: Historical and Theoretical Themes', in Carl Levy, ed., *Socialism and the Intelligentsia, 1880–1914*, London and New York, 1987, p.14. Levy notes that 88 per cent of Italian socialist members of parliament in 1903 were university graduates, compared to only 16 per cent of German Social Democratic Party deputies.

[11] Dr Robert Michels, 'Rückblick auf die Geschichte der proletarischen Frauenbewegung in Italien', *Die Gleichheit*, no.8, 8 April 1903, p.59.

INTELLECTUALS, MASSES, AND LEADERS 189

Michels' overdrawn picture of a largely socialist Italian intelligentsia served at least in part to highlight the exclusion of socialist intellectuals such as himself from German universities.

The Italian labour movement had not always been so welcoming of bourgeois intellectuals, as Michels recorded in an essay on the history of the Partito Operaio (labour party) founded in Milan in 1882 as an exclusively working-class party. For Michels, the exclusion of intellectuals from the ranks of a socialist party was an 'infantile disease' in the early years of the Italian labour movement.[12] Michels was openly condescending about the results of the exclusion of educated intellectuals from the party, citing the founding proclamation from the first issue of the party paper *Fascio Operaio* with the comment: 'Even outwardly, this essay, which I have deliberately translated as literally as possible, is characteristically proletarian. Alongside a regrettable lack of clarity of ideas, it demonstrates a poorly educated use of language which betrays itself in an awful plethora of stylistic infelicities and lapses in logic.'[13] The Partito Operaio was for Michels, 'despite its many errors' in both 'theory and practice', a step on the way to the united socialist party which by 1891 represented a successful marriage of manual workers and brain workers (*Kopfarbeiter*).[14] Michels' essay on the Partito Operaio puts into perspective any suggestion that Michels idealized the proletariat as the subject of history in the Marxian sense: for Michels, the ideals of socialism always needed intellectuals to articulate them and provide theoretical leadership to the workers. Furthermore, workers owed intellectuals a debt of gratitude given the selfless way in which idealistic intellectuals fought for workers' rights.[15]

By 1904, Michels expressed a more critical view of the role of intellectuals in the Italian socialist party. After the (in Michels' view) inconclusive party congress in Bologna, he lamented the rising influence of revisionism in Italy, Germany, and France. In Italy, he linked this influence to the dominance in many of the economic organizations of the working class over many years of

revisionist 'intellectuals'—for unfortunately it is seldom in Italy that workers are taken on as officials in workers' organisations, less because of a lack of the necessary capacities, as because of an excessive respect that still prevails for the good coat of the '*Signori*' and the '*Avvocati*', who are as plentiful as the sand on the seashore and know how to present themselves.

---

[12] Dr Robert Michels, 'Eine exclusiv proletarische Bewegung in Italien im Jahre 1883', *Documente des Socialismus*, Vol.4, 2, 1904, pp.64–9, here p.64.

[13] Michels, 'Eine exclusiv proletarische Bewegung in Italien im Jahre 1883', p.67.

[14] Michels, 'Eine exclusiv proletarische Bewegung in Italien im Jahre 1883', p.69. See also Robert Michels, 'Die Entwicklung der Theorien im modernen Sozialismus Italiens', introduction to his translation of Enrico Ferri, *Die revolutionäre Methode*, Leipzig, 1908, p.27.

[15] Robert Michels, Review of Eugenio Ciacchi, *Cosè la camera del lavoro?*, *Documente des Socialismus*, Bd.1, 1902, p.381.

190   ROBERT MICHELS, SOCIALISM, AND MODERNITY

Michels suggested that it was such revisionist 'intellectuals' who had taken over *Avanti!*, the party's principal newspaper, for a period, and who had helped to promote ministerialism in the party.[16] In part, Michels' complaint was that it was the *wrong* intellectuals who had been gaining influence, but he was also moving towards a more critical sociological analysis of the social composition of the functionaries gaining control of socialist parties.

Michels did not, however, move to an *ouvrieriste* (worker-only) position, rejecting some syndicalists' arguments for exclusively proletarian organizations. He rejected the view that workers' syndicates could be more genuinely socialist than parties with more heterogeneous composition. In Michels' view, both parties and unions needed ideas and ideology (and, by extension, intellectuals). He argued: 'all socialism is ideology, based on economic and historical facts, yes, but ideology.' A union that sought to do without ideology and base itself on class alone 'would fall into the errors of English trade unionism and into the famous neutralism of the trade unions of Germany'. Such a union would embrace Catholics 'and other *authentic workers by profession but bourgeois by mentality*' and would thus cease to be an instrument of the emancipation of the working class. Not proletarian birth, but with the right set of ideas in one's head made one a socialist.[17]

In his book-length series of articles on 'Proletariat and Bourgeoisie in the Socialist Movement of Italy' in the *Archiv für Sozialwissenschaft und Sozialpolitik* (1905/6), Michels also stressed that socialism (as 'ideological striving') was a question of accepting a certain programme, not a matter of class location. Socialism did not necessarily and logically depend on the existence of a 'modern proletariat'. But, on 'empirical-historical' grounds, he conceded that where there was no modern proletariat, socialism without a basis in economic interests would remain a 'hot-house flower': 'In our present times, so painfully averse to every paedagogical direction, economic mass egoism is of much greater efficacy than the act of will of idealism.'[18] Michels began his survey of the social bases of Italian socialism by emphasizing the contribution of young, educated bourgeois for the emergence of social revolutionary movements, citing Bakunin on this point. At the same time, Michels noted that the presence of such non-proletarian elements in the labour movement was often seen as a problem, rather than as a historical necessity.[19] By the time of writing, however, Michels noted that 'the leadership

---

[16] 'Einheit der Partei', *Hamburger Echo*, Jg.18, no.88, 15 April 1904.

[17] Roberto Michels, 'Discorrendo di socialismo, di partito e di sindacato', *Il Divenire Sociale. Rivista di Socialismo Scientifico*, Anno II, no.4, 16 February 1906, pp.55–7, quotations p.55.

[18] Robert Michels, 'Proletariat und Bourgeoisie in der sozialistischen Bewegung Italiens', *Archiv für Sozialwissenschaft und Sozialpolitik*, 21, 1905, pp.347–416; 22, 1906, pp.80–125, 424–86, 664–720; quoation here from 21, p.373.

[19] Michels, 'Proletariat und Bourgeoisie in der sozialistischen Bewegung Italiens', 21, p.347. According to Bakunin, the role of young educated bourgeois in the labour movement was not to lead

INTELLECTUALS, MASSES, AND LEADERS   191

and positions of trust in the party are overwhelmingly in the hands of bourgeois intellectuals.[20]

As noted in Chapter 4, Michels' account of the role of bourgeois intellectuals in Italian socialism was criticized by Edouard Berth in *Le Mouvement Socialiste*. Michels responded on this point that: 'The workers' movement would not know how to exist without a troop of intellectuals serving it as enlighteners.' Through no fault of their own, the workers' schooling had been way behind that given to the bourgeois, which conferred immense advantages on the latter. Michels went on:

> But the socialist worker needs a theory, and for theories, he needs theoreticians. Now history teaches us that proletarians (through no fault of their own) have not been able to provide *savants*. Poor Malon, an autodidact, but little learned, is proof of this. And he was the only worker theoretician. Marx, Saint-Simon, Engels, Lassalle, Bakunin, Kropotkin, creators of rejuvenating theories [*théories vivifiantes*], such as Lagardelle, Berth, Labriola, etc., in our times, are intellectuals [*intellectuels*]. For the workers' movement is absolutely powerless to dispense with intellectuals.

Michels argued that the history of socialism shows that intellectuals from bourgeois backgrounds—provided they embraced the cause of the proletariat, acted without ulterior motives, and were prepared to break all the bridges between themselves and a 'return into the camp of the enemy bourgeois', have not only been better equipped to resist the temptations of political accommodation, but have brought with them a greater fund of revolutionary ideas than the chiefs of the workers—who were 'in general, easy to corrupt'—but even more than the 'proletarian masses themselves, of whom history shows us, despite all, more weaknesses than strengths.'[21] Michels also stressed the high ethical quality of the socialist intellectuals, citing Edmondo de Amicis as a witness to the fact that only the 'highest degree of altruism' would lead a non-worker to enter the workers' party, in the face of so many penalties, professional and personal: 'The socialistically organized intellectuals are from the first to the last, selfless men.'[22]

Writing in 1906, Michels depicted Social Democracy as a movement of the persecuted. It consisted of 'intellectuals from the bourgeoisie who have joined it

the workers' movement or to be its prophet, but to help bring into clarity the still confused 'unconscious but mighty aspirations of the proletariat'; pp.348–9.

[20] Michels, 'Proletariat und Bourgeoisie in der sozialistischen Bewegung Italiens', 22, 1906, p.664. See also 21, 1905, p.391.

[21] Robert Michels, 'Controverse socialiste', *Le Mouvement Socialiste*, no.184, March 1907, pp.278–88, quotations p.283. The idea that intellectuals' mission of enlightening the working class was essential for socialism to develop was also expressed in R. [Robert] Michels, *L'Allemagne, le socialisme et les syndicats*, Paris, 1906 (offprint from *Revue Internationale de Sociologie*), p.3.

[22] Michels, 'Proletariat und Bourgeoisie in der sozialistischen Bewegung Italiens', 22, p.695; see also p.713.

192   ROBERT MICHELS, SOCIALISM, AND MODERNITY

[who] are virtually boycotted by the class from which they stem. In Prussia a special ministerial decree forbids them from lecturing positions at universities....Nor do workers fare better, who participate in the Social Democratic movement'.[23] As noted above, the everyday persecution of workers by employers is mentioned here almost as an afterthought after the reference to Michels' thwarted academic aspirations. After 1906–7, however, a greater distance is evident in Michels' references to intellectuals in the labour movement. By 1908, an increasingly disillusioned Michels still insisted on the immaturity of the Italian proletariat and its need to be guided by intellectuals, but he now made scathing comments about the fickleness of the latter, who were prone to switching from one ideological tendency to another.[24] In his 1908 long essay on the oligarchical tendencies of society, which in some respects served as a sketch for his larger work on *Political Parties*, Michels diagnosed two types of intellectuals, given the overproduction of intellectuals, who were unable to all find gainful employment:

> those who have been successful in finding themselves a living at the state trough, while the others consist of those who, in Scipio Sighele's words, have besieged the fortress without managing to gain admission. The first can be compared with a gang of slaves, who are always ready to defend the state which feeds them, whatever the issues at stake might be, partly out of class egoism, partly out of personal self-interest (for fear of losing their position). They should therefore be considered the 'most loyal pillars of the state'. The others, on the other hand, are the sworn enemies of the state; they are the eternally restless spirits, who lead the bourgeois opposition and who in part also take over the leadership of the revolutionary parties of the proletariat.[25]

Michels himself had been besieging the fortress of state employment in his unsuccessful quest for a professorship in Germany—his correspondence with Weber testifies to how long and assiduously he sought a German *Habilitation*, even after his offers from Turin and later from Basel. But he had previously framed his commitment to socialism in much more idealized terms.

In a review of Arturo Labriola's brochure *Riforme e rivoluzione sociale* in 1909, Michels drew attention to a statement by Labriola that it was 'the greatest misfortune for the workers that their leaders were bourgeois literati, who find satisfaction of some of their own subjective needs...in proletarian politics, and who force their own bourgeois means of struggle onto the proletariat (parliamentarism,

---

[23] Dr [Robert] Michels, 'Die Kriegsgefahr und die deutsche Arbeiterbewegung', *Die Einigkeit. Organ der Freien Vereinigung deutscher Gewerkschaften*, no.23, 9 June 1906.

[24] Roberto [Robert] Michels, 'Appunti sulla situazione presente del socialismo italiano', *Il Divenire Sociale. Rivista di Socialismo scientifico*, Vol.IV, no.18, 16 September 1908, pp.294–6.

[25] Robert Michels, 'Die oligarchischen Tendenzen der Gesellschaft. Ein Beitrag zum Problem der Demokratie', *Archiv für Sozialwissenschaft und Sozialpolitik*, Vol.27 (new series), 1908, pp.73–135, here p.85.

INTELLECTUALS, MASSES, AND LEADERS   193

scandals, freemasonry, atheism, narrow legalism)'. Labriola stressed that the main task facing modern workers was to promote the technical and intellectual capacity of the masses by all means.[26] Michels was no longer as invested as he had been a few years previously in defending intellectuals against criticism by syndicalists, but he still had a dig at Georges Sorel, suggesting that Labriola's work was superior to Sorel's, in part, because the northern French former civil servant had never attended a large public meeting and only knew 'the passions and suffering of the masses from books'.[27] Here Michels glossed over the fact that his own experience of workers' meetings had mostly been in the small university town of Marburg and its environs, where mass meetings rarely assumed unmanageable proportions.

Labriola's strictures notwithstanding, Michels continued to stress the dependence of the socialist movement on intellectual leaders and theoreticians from bourgeois and even aristocratic backgrounds, arguing that these were not only intellectually (given their better educational opportunities) but also morally superior to socialist leaders of proletarian origins. Part of the reason for this moral superiority was 'psychological'—the bourgeois socialist had to overcome his own background, a moment of crisis which required qualities such as 'abnegation and altruism'. The situation was very different for the ordinary worker, for whom a career in the labour movement represented an improvement in his conditions, hence the common phenomenon of 'embourgeoisement' of former workers functionaries which was such a major theme in Michels' *Political Parties*.[28]

In *Political Parties*, Michels insisted on the 'incompetence of the masses'. Their objective incapability to take political action in their own interest, especially as the business of politics became more professionalized and complex, resulted in their dependence on a stratum of leaders.[29] The masses also needed intellectuals to guide them, and at a time when the party was subject to discrimination and repression by the state apparatus, it attracted intellectuals whose break with their own bourgeois background meant that men of greater energy and revolutionary *élan* were prominent among the recruits to the cause of socialism.[30] With the growth of the Social Democratic Party, however, intellectuals could be found across the spectrum from the anarchist or revolutionary left to reformists and revisionists, and a backlash against the influence of intellectuals arose, including from upwardly mobile former workers.[31] Michels also noted the attraction of the Social Democratic Party for intellectuals of Jewish background, and the party's

---

[26] Robert Michels, Review of Arturo Labriola, *Riforme e rivoluzione sociale*, in *Jahrbuch für Gesetzgebung, Verwaltung und Volkswirtschaft im Deutschen Reich*, Jg.32, 1, 1908, pp.381–3, here p.382.
[27] Michels, Review of Arturo Labriola, *Riforme e rivoluzione sociale*, p.383.
[28] Roberto [Robert] Michels, 'La crisi psicologica del socialismo', *Rivista Italiana di Sociologia*, anno XIV, May–August 1910, pp.365–76 (quotation here p.12, pagination here from offprint).
[29] Robert Michels, *Zur Soziologie des Parteiwesens in der modernen Demokratie*, Leipzig, 1911, p.83.
[30] Michels, *Zur Soziologie des Parteiwesens*, pp.304–5.
[31] Michels, *Zur Soziologie des Parteiwesens*, pp.310–12.

194 ROBERT MICHELS, SOCIALISM, AND MODERNITY

indebtedness to Jewish intellectuals.[32] The latter were drawn to socialism in part by their experience of continued social discrimination, in part by their 'innate' internationalism.[33] Unfortunately, in Michels' view, the growth of the party and its associated organizations, such as cooperatives and mutual aid funds, increasingly offered intellectuals 'a good living and an influential position': 'As is always and everywhere the case, so too in democracy success means the death of idealism'.[34]

Masses

In 1895, Gustave Le Bon's *La psychologie des foules* (known in English simply as *The Crowd*) proclaimed the advent of the 'ERA OF CROWDS'.[35] The 'voice of the masses' was becoming 'preponderant' in politics, Le Bon wrote, as the popular classes formed syndicates, labour unions, and popular assemblies, imposing their will on governments: 'The divine right of the masses is about to replace the divine right of kings', a phenomenon viewed pessimistically by Le Bon in view of what he considered the limited capacity of crowds to engage in reasoning.[36] Frank Pfetsch argued that Michels' concept of the 'masses' followed that of Le Bon: 'Characteristic for both of them is the view of the masses as a purely psychological category', a category which takes on a negative ideological coloration.[37] There are grounds for seeing Michels as influenced by Le Bon and his crowd psychology, especially as he wrote *Political Parties*, even if Le Bon's influence was one among others in the formulation of Michels' views on politics and oligarchy (e.g. Sombart, Weber, the Italian social anthropologists). Not only did Michels cite Le Bon (approvingly) in his *magnum opus*, it appeared with the same publisher as the German translation of Le Bon's *The Crowd*, Klinkhardt of Leipzig, who promoted Michels' book as related to that of Le Bon.[38] When Michels' *Political Parties* appeared, he sent a copy to Le Bon, paying his respects to the French author, and seeking Le Bon's assistance with finding a French publisher.[39]

---

[32] Michels, *Zur Soziologie des Parteiwesens*, p.250.

[33] Michels, *Zur Soziologie des Parteiwesens*, pp.249–50.

[34] Michels, *Zur Soziologie des Parteiwesens*, p.255.

[35] Gustave Le Bon, *The Crowd*, introduced by Robert K. Merton, Harmondsworth, Middlesex, 1981, p.14 (capitalized in original). On Le Bon, see Benoît Marpeau, *Gustave Le Bon. Parcours d'un intellectual 1841–1931*, Paris, 2000; Robert A. Nye, *The Origins of Crowd Psychology: Gustave Le Bon and the Crisis of Mass Democracy in the Third Republic*, London and Beverly Hills, CA, 1975.

[36] Le Bon, *The Crowd*, pp.15–16, quotation p.16.

[37] Frank Pfetsch, *Die Entwicklung zum faschistischen Führerstaat in der politischen Philosophie von Robert Michels* (diss., Heidelberg), 1964, p.103.

[38] Jacket advertisements on original edition of Michels, *Zur Soziologie des Parteiwesens*.

[39] See ARM/FLE, correspondence, *busta* Gustave Le Bon. Le Bon replied that Michels' book contained good ideas but was too long, and would need to be shorter, and more succinctly written, for publication in French. Le Bon to Michels, 27 November 1911.

Michels engaged with the concept of 'the masses' in some of his earliest writings on social questions. He explicitly addressed the concept in an essay in 1902 for the Frankfurt periodical *Das freie Wort*.[40] Michels began by acknowledging the difficulty in precisely defining the term: the term was commonly understood to refer to 'the majority of uneducated and property-less'.[41] He found the definition of 'die Masse' in the recent *Geschichtsphilosophie* (*Philosophy of History*) of the historian Theodor Lindner (Michels' father-in-law) insufficient: Lindner defined 'die Masse' as 'the whole of all people living in any group'. Michels found this definition too broad, and criticized the use of the term because it failed to recognize that, for example, 'to name only a few significant men in today's Germany, Wilhelm II, von Liszt, Bernstein, Bebel are also parts of the "whole"', but would not necessarily be reckoned as belonging to 'the masses'. Michels thus arrived at a negative definition of the masses: the masses were the generality of the population (Michels cites Nietzsche's reference to the 'much-too-many'), not including the particularly influential individuals.[42] In the second half of the essay, Michels argued that: 'All progress in intellectual matters is owed to specific outstanding individuals',[43] however, progress in morality was only accomplished by the evolution of the collective in society. Individuals could not accomplish lasting change in the morality of a whole society, at least not on their own. Michels concluded by putting a positive valuation on the collectivity of the masses as the agents of moral progress, using Marxism as an illustration: 'Even the strictest Marxist recognizes that the replacement of the individualistic system by the socialist system can only occur through a step-by-step evolution'. He cited Enrico Ferri's statement that the transformation of society presupposed that the proletariat had already brought about a transformation of morality.[44] Michels thus accepted an elitist, semi-Nietzschean dichotomy between the masses and the outstanding individuals, but sought to reconcile this definition of the masses with an optimistic belief in the progress of the masses towards a better, socialist society. The only Marxist element in Michels' thinking here is a Bernsteinian emphasis on evolutionary social improvement (interestingly, Bernstein figures here as the first socialist among Michels' outstanding individuals, named even before the people's tribune, Bebel): the essay does not reflect a Marxian understanding of either class structure or of the dialectical nature of the development of class struggle.

The necessity for intellectuals, propagandists, and leaders to exercise a moral and paedagogical influence over the masses is a theme in some of Michels'

---

[40] Robert Michels, 'Begriff und Aufgabe der "Masse"', *Das freie Wort*, Jg.2, no.13, 5 October 1902, pp.407–12 (using the term 'die Masse' in its singular form).

[41] Michels, 'Begriff und Aufgabe der "Masse"', p.3 of offprint (in FLE).

[42] Michels, 'Begriff und Aufgabe der "Masse"', pp.4–5.

[43] Michels, 'Begriff und Aufgabe der "Masse"', p.5.

[44] Michels, 'Begriff und Aufgabe der "Masse"', p.8.

196   ROBERT MICHELS, SOCIALISM, AND MODERNITY

statements from this period.[45] Michels suggested that it was the role of the labour movement in Italy to 'civilize the masses', a task that was still incomplete in the south of the country.[46] He also suggested that it was challenging for 'the few real Marxists in the Italian [socialist] party' to reconcile the 'materialist view of history' with the importance of the 'moral factor in the education of the masses'.[47]

Interestingly, at around the same time as Michels' essay on the masses in *Das freie Wort*, the founder of the National Social Party, Friedrich Naumann, wrote an article for the *Politisch-Anthropologische Revue* on the impossibility of socialism from an anthropological and psychological point of view, based on the characteristics of the 'masses'—the industrial, urban masses—which formed the basis of the socialist movement. Naumann wrote that socialism presupposed a high degree of organization among the masses. The masses that socialism addressed itself to, however, were 'the ruled, the servants', who somehow had to be constituted as a collective political agent capable of exercising rule.[48] Naumann argued that the collective psychology of the urban working masses made it easier to organize them for a revolution, which would take an appeal to their passions and elemental sense of justice, than to organize them for 'long-lasting, regular state politics'.[49] Naumann posed a question that Michels would later take up: 'Who actually rules, when the masses rule?' In principle, everyone, but in practice: 'it is a relatively small number of representatives or officials, who look after the exercise of rule.'[50] In theory, these representatives were answerable to the mass, however, 'the larger the political subject becomes, the more extensive the involvement of the socialist party in the life of the state, the more the democratic control over the deputies becomes illusory'.[51] Over time, the social distance between the 'propertyless crowd' and the increasingly professional stratum of their representatives had to increase. This was a natural process, but would be felt to be 'a kind of injustice' and would lead to estrangement between representative party officials and their increasingly disengaged and disillusioned constituency.[52] Naumann ended with a critique of contemporary Social Democratic politics for failing to educate the masses to take greater political responsibility, particularly in foreign affairs— this was in keeping with Naumann's political objective, which was to reconcile the

---

[45] Robert Michels, 'Der italienische Sozialismus auf dem Lande', *Das freie Wort*, Jg.2, no.2, 1902 (offprint in FLE), p.13 of offprint.

[46] Dr Robert Michels, 'Die Frau als Streikende im Lohnkampf', *Die Frau*, Jg.10, Nr.12, September 1903, p.757.

[47] Robert Michels, Review of Giovanni Lerda, *Il socialismo e la sua tattica*, in *Documente des Socialismus*, Bd.1, 1902, p.434.

[48] Friedrich Naumann, 'Die psychologischen Naturbedingungen des Sozialismus', *Politsch-Anthropologische Revue*, Vol.I, no.7, 1902, pp.564–71, here p.565.

[49] Naumann, 'Die psychologischen Naturbedingungen des Sozialismus', p.569. Naumann added (p.570) that a revolution was nonetheless increasingly unlikely under the conditions of a modern industrial state.

[50] Naumann, 'Die psychologischen Naturbedingungen des Sozialismus', p.568.

[51] Naumann, 'Die psychologischen Naturbedingungen des Sozialismus', pp.568–9.

[52] Naumann, 'Die psychologischen Naturbedingungen des Sozialismus', p.569.

German working class with the monarchy and with an imperialist foreign policy.[53] Naumann's article is of interest not only as a contribution to the contemporary discussion on the role of the masses, but also because it anticipates much of Michels' argumentation in his later major work on political parties and the iron law of oligarchy. Given that Michels was familiar with the *Politisch-Anthropologische Revue*, and contributed an essay to the journal which appeared not long after Naumann's article,[54] it is highly probable that Michels read it, even if he still considered Naumann a political adversary in 1902. Michels referred to Naumann in mid-1903 as 'scrittore elegante, ma confusionario fuori concorso' ('an elegant writer, but unsurpassed at creating confusion').[55] The views of the editor of the *Politisch-Anthropologische Revue*, the former Social Democrat Ludwig Woltmann, on democracy and 'the masses' went even further than Naumann. Not only socialism, but democracy, was impossible because 'the people', the *demos*, were not as ideologues imagined them, but instead 'a mass, and includes a quantity of born slaves for whom being ruled by others offers a comfortable and beneficial arrangement'.[56]

In December 1902, in an article on women's suffrage for the progressive liberal feminist *Die Frauenbewegung*, Michels spoke of the 'democratization of the masses' as a high priority.[57] In a subsequent article for the same journal, Michels argued that a 'social question' only ever came into existence because of the work of a numerically small, conscious minority, who managed to enlighten 'the masses' about their situation:

> The oppressed classes, races, sexes etc. had admittedly been previously *aware* of a strong contrast between their situation and that of the ruling classes, etc, but they understood this condition to be something natural, 'God-given'. As soon, however, as the masses are enlightened and feel their condition to be oppressive and unjust, and furthermore come to realize that there is nothing or at least almost nothing natural and 'God-given', but that all is the work of human beings and can be pushed aside or at least changed in important aspects, then a social question arises.

However, this coming to awareness was always the work of a 'small minority'.[58]

---

[53] Naumann, 'Die psychologischen Naturbedingungen des Sozialismus', pp.570–1.

[54] Dr Robert Michels, 'Das unerlöste Italien in Österreich', *Politisch-Anthropologische Revue*, Jg.1, 9, December 1902, pp.716–24.

[55] Dott. Roberto [Robert] Michels, 'Democrazia e socialismo in Germania (Dopo le elezioni)', *Avanti!*, Anno VII, n.2375, 18 July 1903 (leading article).

[56] Cited in Wolfhard Hammer, *Leben und Werk des Arztes und Sozialanthropologen Ludwig Woltmann*, Mainz, 1979 (=diss. der Johannes-Gutenberg-Universität Mainz), p.82.

[57] Dr Robert Michels, 'Frauenstimmrecht—schon heute eine Notwendigkeit', *Die Frauenbewegung*, Jg.8, no.23, 1 December 1902, p.178.

[58] Dr Robert Michels, 'Entstehung der Frauenfrage als soziale Frage', *Die Frauenbewegung*, Jg.9, no.3, 1 February 1903, pp.17–18, quotation p.18.

198   ROBERT MICHELS, SOCIALISM, AND MODERNITY

During 1903–4, in the context of his engagement with the German Social Democratic Party, Michels tended to use more Marxian diction, referring more frequently to class than to the more amorphous concept of the 'masses'.[59] In the wake of his disappointment with the failure of the party to definitively break with revisionism at the 1904 Bremen party congress, he reverted to talking about the masses (and the need to educate them) in his critique of the party published in *Le Mouvement Socialiste*. Michels attacked the tendency of the party to fall prey to 'parliamentary opportunism'.[60] However, the strength of socialism lay not in parliament, but in the masses.[61] It was an illusion, Michels wrote, that the German party held the masses, in fact, the 'masses hold the party'.[62] Unfortunately, for reasons of electoral expediency, the Social Democratic Party had failed to campaign against religious superstition in the masses, and the official policy that religion was a 'private matter' allowed people with the most backward views into the party.[63] Michels concluded his long critical essay with the statement that the German party, for all its great past achievements, was marching towards 'une impasse', and it needed to remember once again its mission, which was to inspire 'the working masses' with an awareness of their human dignity and with a socialist consciousness: the main obstacle for socialism to overcome was the 'ignorance of the masses'.[64]

Michels was increasingly critical of the failure of the Social Democratic Party to educate the masses correctly during 1905, especially in his contributions to *Le Mouvement Socialiste*. He diagnosed an increasing passivity of the 'masses' as a result. Commenting on the Ruhr miners' strike, Michels lamented that the masses had unlearned how to act for themselves: 'Depressing proof of what a long period of *worker bureaucratism* can do to make the masses forget how to decree their own actions'.[65] After the 1905 Jena party congress, Michels complained of an absence of the spirit of self-sacrifice in the party, which had become 'too parliamentary and too optimistic'.[66] Michels wrote: 'One of our first and highest duties

---

[59] Robert Michels, 'Zur Ethik des Klassenkampfes', *Ethische Kultur*, Jg.XII, no.3, 1 February 1904, pp.21–2.

[60] Robert Michels, 'Les dangers du parti socialiste allemande', *Le Mouvement Socialiste*, no.144, 1 December 1904, pp.193–212.

[61] Michels, 'Les dangers du parti socialiste allemande', p.205.

[62] Michels, 'Les dangers du parti socialiste allemande', p.202. Here Michels partly echoes a statement made by August Bebel in the debates at the previous year's Dresden party congress, in Michels' presence: 'Anyone who wants to be a leader among us, must act as the party wishes, and not how he wishes. (Applause). He has to carry out what the mass is striving for, what it feels and thinks. They [the leaders] are the tools of the party, not the generals and commanders, who say: I go in front and you have to obey me.' *Protokoll über die Verhandlungen des Parteitages der Sozialdemokratischen Partei Deutschlands. Abgehalten zu Dresden vom 13. bis 20. September 1903*, Berlin, 1903, p.228.

[63] Michels, 'Les dangers du parti socialiste allemande', pp.202–3.

[64] Michels, 'Les dangers du parti socialiste allemande', p.212.

[65] Robert Michels, 'La grève générale des mineurs de la Ruhr', *Le Mouvement Socialiste*, 152, 1 April 1905, pp.481–9, here p.481; emphasis in original.

[66] Robert Michels, 'Le socialisme allemande et le congrès d'Iéna', *Le Mouvement Socialiste*, no.166–167, November 1905, pp. 281–307, quotation p.296.

INTELLECTUALS, MASSES, AND LEADERS   199

is to awaken the spirit of collective sacrifice in our masses.' If the party leaders resisted this task, it would be necessary to carry it out in defiance of them. Michels also alluded to the 'psychology of the masses', which he viewed as 'still in such a weak condition, that they always absolutely submit to their leaders'.[67]

In 1906, in the context of a discussion of Germany's imperialist foreign policy in relation to the Morocco crisis, Michels bemoaned 'the servile mentality of the German masses' ('mentalità servile delle masse germaniche'), which, coupled with the peculiarities of the German constitution, enabled the Kaiser to act in an autocratic fashion, although he did acknowledge the existence of opposition to militarism on the left of the Social Democratic Party.[68]

Turning to Italy, Michels found the Italian socialist party to be in a state of crisis after the 1906 Rome party congress. Referring to the socially heterogeneous base of the Italian socialist movement, Michels drew a contrast between the syndicalists on the left, 'led by an elite of young university lecturers from southern Italy (Labriola, Leone, Loncao), joined by some old workers' leaders, who have maintained intransigent positions (Lazzari)', who were. 'the paedagogues of socialism', and the reformist right, who included some outstanding leaders and parliamentarians, and who were supported by 'the masses of agrarian workers'.[69] While a split of the party was averted at the Rome congress, this was at the cost of a compromise resolution that saw the party centre moving closer to reformism 'in the eyes of many':

> The victory of the party centre over the right and the left is a victory of the mass idea, a victory of the party following, the victory of the idea that it would currently be not only a crime, but an act of stupidity, to drive apart the masses so painstakingly held together and to conduct politics off one's own bat.

Here, the masses appear as a dead weight limiting the party's freedom to adopt genuinely militant tactics and principles.[70]

As Michels became increasingly critical of socialist parties, his emphasis on the passivity and docility of the masses also increased. In his address to a gathering of European revolutionary syndicalists in Paris in April 1907, Michels stated that the weakness and timidity of the German party was partly a product of its bureaucratic organization, but there was also the factor of the ' "well-behaved" character of our masses', who were anxious to imitate the bourgeoisie, which could hardly

---

[67] Michels, 'Le socialisme allemande et le congrès d'Iéna', p.303.

[68] Roberto [Robert] Michels, 'Divagazioni sullo imperialismo germanico e la questione del Marocco', La Riforma Sociale, Anno XIII, vol.XVI (2nd series), 1906 (pagination of offprint in FLE), p.11.

[69] Robert Michels, 'Der italienische Parteitag zu Rom', Die Neue Gesellschaft, 2.Jg., Bd.3, 24 October 1906, pp.46–8, quotations p.46.

[70] Michels, 'Der italienische Parteitag zu Rom', p.48.

produce 'a psychology of moral revolt and the sense of the brutal opposition between classes'.[71] The organized masses within the party also tended to 'support [their leaders] passively and obey blindly'.[72] Writing in the German 'localist' syndicalist newspaper *Die Einigkeit*, Michels argued that the 'voting masses' which the German Social Democratic Party had succeeded in attracting had become a liability, as the party had become a captive of its heterogeneous electorate, who were far from all being convinced socialist revolutionaries: these masses hindered the party from energetic and bold action. Michels conceded that a political party could not call 'revolutionary popular movements' into being: 'these must grow independently out of the masses'.[73] The German voting masses were far from giving rise to a revolutionary movement, however. In his 1908 essay in response to Bernstein in *Sozialistische Monatshefte*, Michels looked back at the 1903 Dresden party congress and deplored the way in which the party radicals (amongst whom he had once numbered himself) had instrumentalized the dull allegiance of the 'masses' to tradition and their distrust of innovation:

> As is the case at every party congress of German Social Democracy, the great mass of the delegates in Dresden was neither revisionist nor *radical*. But the *radicals* understood how to get the grey mass of delegates to rebel against the revisionists, by grabbing them by their most essential characteristic, that is their *Misoneismus* [= aversion to innovation], or to put it more mildly, their deep-rooted sense of *tradition*.[74]

Such susceptible, grey masses were in need of leaders.[75] In Michels' view, there was no point in trying to analyse the different social bases of revisionism and radicalism in the labour movement. The debates took place between the intellectuals and the leaders, and the proletarian 'masses' simply responded instinctively to the battles between the leading minds at the top of the party.[76] The 'inert mass' of the party, accustomed to following Bebel 'in all his metamorphoses', had followed him in opposing revisionism at Dresden, and now followed him in a pro-revisionist course at the 1906 Mannheim congress.[77]

---

[71] Robert Michels, 'Le syndicalisme et le socialisme en Allemagne', *Le Mouvement Socialiste*, no.188, July 1907, pp.58–63, here p.61.

[72] Michels, 'Le syndicalisme et le socialisme en Allemagne', p.62.

[73] Robert Michels, 'Kriegsgefahr' III, *Die Einigkeit*, no.23, 9 June 1906.

[74] Robert Michels, 'Einige Bemerkungen zum Problem der Demokratie. Eine Erwiderung', *Sozialistische Monatshefte*, XIII, no.25, 17 December, 1908, pp.1615–21, here p.1616; emphases in original.

[75] Robert Michels, 'Die deutsche Sozialdemokratie', *Archiv für Sozialwissenschaft und Sozialpolitik*, 23, 1906, p.526.

[76] Michels, 'Die deutsche Sozialdemokratie', p.537.

[77] Robert Michels, 'Le socialisme allemand après Mannheim', *Le Mouvement Socialiste*, IX, no.182, 1907, pp.5–22, here pp.6n, 12, 13.

INTELLECTUALS, MASSES, AND LEADERS   201

Michels proceeded to generalize these observations of the malleability of the 'masses' into sociological laws. In his 1908 *Archiv* essay on the oligarchical tendencies of society, Michels argued that one of the main factors hindering the development of democracy was the indifference, in particular the political indifference, of the majority, and its need for leaders. Michels cited Alexandre Dumas *fils* as saying that all progress was the work on 1 per cent, resisted by the other 99 per cent.[78] The majority lacked interest or insight in matters affecting the common good.[79] It was 'glad if men could be found, who would carry out its business for it. The need to be led, mostly in connection with a flourishing hero worship, is boundless within the masses, including in the organized masses of the workers' parties'.[80] In his 1909 essay on the conservative tendency of all organization, Michels referred to the readiness of the 'masses' to delegate authority to a small number of leaders. Representation then meant that the will of the individual was designated the will of the masses. But the formation of a professional leadership cadre was 'the beginning of the end of democracy'.[81] This process was facilitated by the hunger for power of the leaders on the one hand and the 'need for leadership and indifference of the crowd' on the other:

The masses possess a profound urge towards personal hero-worship. In their primitive idealism they need secular gods, to him they attach themselves with a love that is all the more blind, the harder their lives become. Frequently, the need to look up to someone is the only *rocher de bronze*, which survives all transformations in their world view. The Saxon factory workers in recent years have turned from being pious protestants to Social Democrats. With this development a great transformation of values may have been connected. But in their living room they have only removed the obligatory portrait of Luther to put one of Bebel in its place.[82]

The natural tendency of the 'masses' towards inertia and indifference had been exacerbated by the conditions of capitalism, which had imposed on workers a grey, monotonous existence. Michels cited Werner Sombart as an authority on the desolate state into which 'the masses' work under capitalist conditions, a state in which 'all functions of the soul atrophied'.[83] Under these conditions, even the historically necessary idea of class struggle did not just awaken idealism among

---

[78] Michels, 'Die oligarchischen Tendenzen der Gesellschaft', here p.82.

[79] Michels, 'Die oligarchischen Tendenzen der Gesellschaft', p.83.

[80] Michels, 'Die oligarchischen Tendenzen der Gesellschaft', pp.83–4.

[81] Robert Michels, 'Der konservative Grundzug der Partei-Organisation', *Monatsschrift für Soziologie*, Jg.1, April 1909, pp.228–36; May 1909, pp.301–16, here p.234.

[82] Michels, 'Der konservative Grundzug der Partei-Organisation', p.303.

[83] Robert Michels, 'Das Proletariat in der Wissenschaft und die Ökonomisch-Anthropologische Synthese', in Alfredo Niceforo, *Anthropologie der nichtbesitzenden Klassen. Studien und Untersuchungen*, trans. and ed. Robert Michels and Adolph Köster, Leipzig and Amsterdam, 1910,

202   ROBERT MICHELS, SOCIALISM, AND MODERNITY

workers, but also 'other, regressive forces, which fill the ethicist with anxiety and give food of thought to the social paedagogue'—a large step away from Michels' earlier, overwhelmingly positive assessment of the ethical value of the class struggle.[84]

Leaders

Michels originally viewed the socialist movement as a combination of 'keen propaganda of the leaders and the selfless mutual support of the workers'.[85] By 1908–9 he had moved to a more frankly elitist position stressing the passivity and need for hero worship of 'the masses' and the self-interest and desire for power of the leadership group. However, even in his early socialist writings, in which Michels stressed the democratic nature of the workers' movement, there was a special place for the ethically superior individual whose education and intellectual qualifications helped to elevate the workers. On the twentieth anniversary of the death of Karl Marx, Michels wrote:

> Social Democracy represents a world view in which there is no place for a cult of personality, no veneration of saints. But that does not mean that we cannot gratefully remember and honestly admire the outstanding men who have put their lives in the service of the liberation of humanity from the rule of obsolete, but partly still surviving, institutions and economic systems.

In this context, Michels singled out the sacrifices made by well-educated young scholars from well-off backgrounds who choose to commit themselves to social democracy (like Marx and Michels himself).[86] Similarly, Michels' May Day profile of August Bebel for the Turin socialist paper *Il Grido del Popolo* began: 'Socialists do not know the glorification of their great men'. Personality cults were alien to socialism, but Michels immediately qualified that generalization in the case of a leader like Bebel.[87]

In the period in which he was closest to the Social Democratic Party's left Marxist wing (1903–4), Michels criticized Lassalle for having been too much the autocratic *generalissimo* of the party. Lassalle's errors were products of the time he

---

p.13. This section of Michels' introduction to Niceforo is lifted from his review of Werner Sombart, *Das Proletariat*, in *Archiv für Sozialwissenschaft und Sozialpolitik*, 27 (neue Folge), 1908, pp.835–7.

[84] Michels, 'Das Proletariat in der Wissenschaft', p.13; Michels, 'Zur Ethik des Klassenkampfes', pp.21–2.

[85] Robert Michels, 'Der Sozialismus in Italien', *Das freie Wort*, Jg.1, no.16, 20 November 1901, pp.492–8, quotation p.495.

[86] 'Was bedeutet uns Karl Marx?', *Mitteldeutsche Sonntags-Zeitung*, no.11, 15 March 1903 (leading article).

[87] Roberto Michels, 'Augusto Bebel', *Il Grido del Popolo*, XII, no.18, 1 May 1903, p.1.

INTELLECTUALS, MASSES, AND LEADERS   203

in which he lived, however, '*if, instead of crowds of admiring men of the people, he had had class-conscious and self-conscious proletarians, if instead of disciples blindly following him he had had critically thinking party comrades*, Lassalle would have become quite a different man.'[88] At this point, in August 1904, Michels was still adhering to an orthodox Marxian Social Democratic conception of leadership and party organization (at least in the context of a programmatic leading article for the Social Democratic press).

In the period in which he became increasingly disillusioned with organized socialism, Michels occupied himself with the elite theory of Gaetano Mosca and Vilfredo Pareto, and took up their arguments that state and party bureaucracies become instruments of the domination of a minority that makes up the political class.[89] Building on his reception of Mosca and Pareto, Michels' 1908 *Archiv* article on the oligarchical tendencies of society argued that the 'machinery of organization summons up major changes within the organized mass'. Any extensive organization required a degree of technical specialization among those directing it, with the result that ultimately leadership functions were transferred to a small group. (Here, Michels also cited Rosa Luxemburg in her brochure *Mass Strike, Party and Trade Union*).[90] Not only the 'technical indispensability' of the leaders, but the attitude of the masses, who were profoundly grateful towards these leaders was a main conservative factor promoting oligarchy.[91] The leadership cadre became a closed caste, and the leaders took on a dominating relationship towards the led.[92]

Michels supplemented his sociological analysis of the inherently oligarchical nature of organization with psychological remarks on the nature of leadership in his 1909 article on the conservative tendency of party organization.[93] Self-aggrandisement and lust for power were psychologically unavoidable among leaders, in Michels' view, and these tendencies were reinforced by the psychological need of the 'masses' to be led.[94] Nearly every party leader worth mentioning

[88] Dr R. [Robert] Michels, 'Ferdinand Lassalle', *Mitteldeutsche Sonntags-Zeitung*, Jg.11, no.35, 28 August 1904.
[89] Roberto Michels, 'L'oligarchia organica constituzionale. Nuovi studi sulla Classe Politica', *La Riforma Sociale*, Vol.XVIII, series 2, anno XIV, December 1907, pp.961–83. Reprinted in Roberto Michels, *Potere ad Oligarchia. Organizzazione del partito ed ideologia socialista (1900–1910)*, ed. Ettore A. Albertoni, Milan, 1989, pp.431–57.
[90] Michels, 'Die oligarchischen Tendenzen der Gesellschaft', here p.102. This article expands on Michels, 'L'oligarchia organica constituzionale'. There are points of contact between Michels' and Luxemburg's critique of the Social Democratic Party and the Free Trade Unions' organizational culture, with the significant difference that Luxemburg espoused a more dynamic view of the potential reciprocal relationship between leaders and the masses. There is, incidentally, no evidence of Michels' engagement with Lenin's ideas on party organization in this period, Michels' focus remaining essentially on socialism in western and southern Europe.
[91] Michels, 'Die oligarchischen Tendenzen der Gesellschaft', pp.112–13.
[92] Michels, 'Die oligarchischen Tendenzen der Gesellschaft', pp.114ff, 118ff.
[93] Michels, 'Der konservative Grundzug der Partei-Organisation'.
[94] Michels, 'Der konservative Grundzug der Partei-Organisation', p.303.

204   ROBERT MICHELS, SOCIALISM, AND MODERNITY

tended to identify the cause he represented with his own person, in a manner akin to Louis XIV's motto: 'l'état c'est moi'—'Le Parti c'est moi!'. A revolt of the masses against the oligarchy of the leaders was possible, but such a revolt could only succeed if the masses found a new and more powerful leader.[95]

Michels' increasing pessimism about the prospects of democracy was shared by Max Weber in this period, who also doubted that progress towards more democracy was possible, as opposed to better selection of leaders under conditions of democratic political competition.[96] Michels' views on the masses and leaders were partly formed in his intellectual exchanges with Weber and Werner Sombart, and influenced by the Italian elite theorists. However, his *Political Parties* also shows the influence of ideas of mass psychology derived from Gustave Le Bon. Even if there are relatively few direct citations from Le Bon (although enough to show Michels' familiarity with Le Bon's work on crowd psychology), the fundamental importance of categories such as the need of 'the masses' for leadership and their need for hero worship indicate Michels' increasing affinity with the work of Le Bon.[97] Le Bon had already insisted on precepts such as the instinctive need for masses, or crowds (*foules*) to follow a leader, the tendency of leaders to exercise domination over the led, and the importance of the prestige of a leader in winning the admiration of the crowd.[98] Le Bon was an incongruous source of inspiration for someone who had recently been a socialist activist. He was militantly anti-socialist as well as being a pessimist about democracy.[99] He also adhered to doctrines of racial hierarchy and was profoundly anti-semitic.[100] As will be discussed in Chapter 8, Michels himself was not immune to thinking in terms of ethnic and racial categories.

After he embraced Italian fascism, Michels moved on to embrace the idea of leadership over the masses: what had once been a regrettable functional necessity became a positive, even heroic, virtue. In a particularly fulsome tribute to Benito Mussolini, Michels, in the *Basler Nachrichten* in 1925, repeatedly invoked 'the masses': which it was Mussolini's destiny to master. Mussolini, Michels reiterated, was a Carlylean figure, one who was a 'prototypical example of the inner needs of the masses for *hero worship*... This party offers its leader, *il Duce*, absolute, blind trust and burning admiration.' Fortunately, in Michels' view, fascism had found in Mussolini a 'leader in the grand style', one whose gifts included boldness and 'an extraordinary power of suggestion towards the masses'. Michels invoked Weber's

---

[95] Michels, 'Der konservative Grundzug der Partei-Organisation', p.314.

[96] Joachim Radkau, *Max Weber. Die Leidenschaft des Denkens*, Munich and Vienna, 2005, p.121.

[97] Direct citations of Le Bon in Michels, *Zur Soziologie des Parteiwesens*, pp.154, 194, 253.

[98] Le Bon, *The Crowd*, pp.117–40.

[99] See Gustave Le Bon, *Psychologie du socialisme*, Paris, 1902, which equates socialism with barbarism that would bring tyranny in its wake, largely because of the psychology of the masses to which it appeals.

[100] Marpeau, *Gustave Le Bon*, pp.147–52; Marco Schütz, *Rassenideologien in der Sozialwissenschaft*, Berne, 1994, pp.105–46.

concept of charismatic leadership to characterize Mussolini, 'who has gained the power to rule not out of the accretion of tradition but through his own innate *dynamis*'. Michels, however, avoided drawing the logical conclusion from Weber's notion of charismatic leadership, that it would inevitably be replaced by routinization and bureaucratization, by keeping the focus on Mussolini's personal courage, dynamism, and avowedly Nietzschean resolution to 'live dangerously'. Thus Mussolini, despite the fact that a modern head of state had different obligations from that of a leader of warrior hordes ('of which the Fascist party was originally composed'), maintained the symbiosis with the masses from which he himself had sprung, despite the risks involved in exposing his person to the crowd: 'born of the masses, he is able to hold his own within the mass'. Michels' depiction of 'the masses' here is indeed 'Carlylean': the characteristics of the masses include, deep in their subconscious, 'the latent longing for the heroic type of the leader'.[101] In this unmediated symbiosis of leader and masses, there is of course no place for the intellectual, unless he chooses to applaud from the sidelines, in this case from Basel.

[101] Robert Michels, 'Mussolini und das gefahrvolle Leben', *Basler Nachrichten*, 23 November 1925, 2. Beilage zu Nr.323. The words 'hero worship' are in English in the original, a nod to Carlyle.

7

Internationalism, Patriotism, Nationalism

Robert Michels' writings on the complex of issues around nationalism, patriotism, and internationalism have continued to attract scholarly interest.[1] Timm Genett has distinguished four discrete phases in the evolution of Michels' thinking on nationalism: from 1902 to 1907, a republican patriotism with a cosmopolitan-internationalist dimension as far as external relations were concerned; 1907–13: a disillusioned analysis of nationalism aligned with his work on oligarchy and the sociology of political parties, stressing nationalism as an instrument of political domination; 1913–23: a period in which Michels' identification with his adoptive Italian nationality showed increasingly positive views on Italian patriotism and nationhood; and from 1923 on, when Michels' support of Mussolini's fascism increasingly coloured his writings on patriotism, with an increasing emphasis on nationalistic mythologies.[2] Heinrich August Winkler pointed to a trend away from critical thinking in Michels' writings on patriotism, from his trenchant criticism of the self-interested instrumentalization of patriotism when it suited the business interests of the bourgeoise (in 1913) to his 1929 treatise on patriotism, which replaced sociological analysis with anecdotal and folkloric retailing of national peculiarities. In Winkler's analysis, Michels was increasingly losing 'his critical impulses along with his analytical abilities'.[3]

---

[1] See in particular the recent work of Federico Trocini, *Tra internazialismo e nazionalismo. Roberto Michels e i dilemmi del socialismo di fronte alla Guerra e all'imperialismo (1900–1915)*, Rome, 2007; Federico Trocini, 'Da internazionalista a "italiano per elezione". Per un bilancio complessivo della riflessione di Roberto Michels sul tema della nazione', *Storia e Politica*, IV, 1, 2012, pp.60–84; Federico Trocini, 'Ubi Bene, Ibi Patria: Patriotism, Nationalism and Internationalism in Robert Michels' Reflection', in Massimo Pendenza, ed., *Classical Sociology Beyond Methodological Nationalism*, Leiden, 2014, pp.182–214. Somewhat problematically, Trocini argues that Michels' writings on nationalism show that he 'remained faithful to that absolute conception of democracy—founded on the Rousseauist paradigm of "uncontrasted sovereignty of the people"—by virtue of which he would repeatedly declare himself a fervent advocate of the nationality principle and of its main tool, the plebiscitary referendum', Trocini, 'Ubi Bene, Ibi Patria', p.195. This plays down Michels' decisive rejection of the viability of democracy in domestic politics by 1910. See also Duncan Kelly, 'From Moralism to Modernism: Robert Michels on the History, Theory and Sociology of Patriotism', *History of European Ideas*, 29, 2003, pp.339–63.

[2] Timm Genett, *Der Fremde im Kriege. Zur politischen Theorie und Biographie von Robert Michels 1876–1936*, Berlin, 2008, p.119.

[3] Heinrich August Winkler, 'Robert Michels', in Hans-Ulrich Wehler, ed., *Deutsche Historiker*, Göttingen, 1973, pp.450–1. Winkler is referring to Robert Michels, 'Zur historischen Analyse des Patriotismus', *Archiv für Sozialwissenschaft und Sozialpolitik*, 36, 1913, pp.14–43, 394–449 and *Der Patriotismus. Prolegomena zu seiner soziologischen Analyse*, Munich and Leipzig, 1929.

Robert Michels, Socialism, and Modernity. Andrew G. Bonnell, Oxford University Press. © Andrew G. Bonnell 2023.
DOI: 10.1093/oso/9780192871848.003.0008

INTERNATIONALISM, PATRIOTISM, NATIONALISM 207

There was, in fact, a strong situational component to Michels' writing on nationalism, patriotism and internationalism. From his earliest writings, Michels demonstrated an allergy to the nationalism that was on the march in Wilhelmine Germany. This allergy may have had a combination of sources—the aversion of his Francophile Rhineland background to the Prussian-dominated empire (an aversion which admittedly skipped a generation in the case of Michels' father), generational revolt against the repressive official culture of Wilhelmine Germany, and an aversion to German militarism fed by his own negative experiences of military service. On the other hand, Michels always evinced a warmer attitude to Italian nationalism, even when it took on more aggressive imperialist forms after 1910. For Michels, Italian nationalism, as represented by figures such as Mazzini and Garibaldi, was more democratic and fed by more positive national characteristics than its German counterpart.[4] Even while Michels' attitudes to nationalism, patriotism, and internationalism evolved as he moved away from an embrace of the concept of class struggle to a more elitist attitude, his strong aversion to German militarism remained a consistent feature of his writing.

Michels' almost visceral dislike of German chauvinistic nationalism is evident in one of his earliest essays, which also makes room for a specifically Rhenish form of patriotism. Writing on the then already half-forgotten Rhineland poet Wolfgang Müller von Königswinter in 1902, Michels disparaged Müller's nationalistic outpourings from the year 1870, celebrating the German victory over the French (they 'belong to the most frightful and thoughtless products of our "patriotic" poetry'), but he seems to have been more receptive to Müller's local Rhenish patriotism. Not only were Müller's works steeped in his Rhenish origins and the *joie de vivre* of the Rhineland's traditional way of life, but Michels also stressed that Müller was also among the Rhineland writers who sought artistically to emancipate their home region from the hegemony of Berlin as much as possible, albeit with little success.[5]

In an essay in May 1902 for *Das freie Wort*, Michels sought to distinguish between three different kinds of outlook: nationalism, national consciousness, and internationalism.[6]

---

[4] Trocini states that Michels viewed the Italian Risorgimento as carrying the potential of 'a fusion of socialism and patriotism'. Trocini, 'Ubi Bene, Ibi Patria', p.184.

[5] Dr Robert Michels, 'Ein rheinischer Poet', *Südwestdeutsche Rundschau*, Jg.2, no.9, 1 May 1902, pp.361–3, quotation p.361. On Rhinelanders' democratic spirit and opposition to Prussian bureaucracy and authoritarianism, see Roberto [Robert] Michels, 'La vittoria dei conservatori nelle elezioni germaniche del 1907. Appunti storici e statistici', *La Riforma Sociale*, Anno XIV, vol. XVII, 2nd series, 15 February 1907, pp.133–51; cited from the offprint, pp.7–8.

[6] Dr Robert Michels, 'Nationalismus, Nationalgefühl, Internationalismus', *Das freie Wort*, Jg.2, no.4, 20 May 1902, pp.107–11. Kelly, 'From Moralism to Modernism', p.341 dates Michels' engagement with the concept of patriotism from 1906, missing the earlier essays that included discussion of patriotism in discussions of nationalism and internationalism. Unfortunately, Kelly's article contains some factual inaccuracies, e.g. stating (p.342) that Michels taught as a *Privatdozent* at the University of Marburg during his time as a socialist activist there, which would not of course have been possible.

208   ROBERT MICHELS, SOCIALISM, AND MODERNITY

Michels defined nationalism (*Nationalismus*) as the desire to 'make one's own national group [*Volkstum*] the dominant one'. Nationalism was 'patriotism taken to extremes', with the distinction that Michels defined patriotism as 'mainly defensive' and nationalism as intrinsically aggressive. Michels complained that Germans generally failed to distinguish between patriotism and aggressive nationalism, whereas the English termed the latter 'jingoism' and the French 'chauvinism'.[7] Michels saw nationalism as taking on dangerous properties in countries like Germany, Russia, and Hungary, where ethnic minorities could become the targets of pressure to assimilate, a process characterized by intolerance and potential cruelty.[8] Michels saw 'national consciousness' as a phenomenon of a different kind, which was 'something completely healthy', for example in the case of Italian unification, in which national consciousness was a unifying factor among different populations with a common identity, and thus constituted a potential step towards 'a higher form of world order'. Again, Germany provided a negative example of the misuse of national consciousness through the state and through ultra-nationalist pressure groups like the Pan-Germans, who sought to force a specific version of German national identity onto 'completely indigestible Danes, French and Poles' within the borders of the Reich.[9] A healthy, non-aggressive national consciousness was thus something that could be found 'only among peoples who are too much forced into a defensive position to be able to proceed offensively themselves with any success. It is the struggle for life of small and oppressed minorities'. An example was *Italia Irredenta* in the Habsburg lands, and the ethnic minorities within the borderland regions of the German Reich.[10] Such a healthy, defensive national consciousness was compatible with Michels' third category, 'internationalism', which was, however, completely incompatible with nationalism. Internationalism, whether in its Catholic ('ultramontane') or socialist variant, placed other values above those of the nation. Internationalism, in Michels' view, represented 'the highest form of human co-existence'.[11] Michels went on to discuss the new book (or rather brochure, given its length of fifty-six pages) by Gumplowicz, *Nationalismus und Internationalismus im 19. Jahrhundert* ('nationalism and internationalism in the nineteenth century'). Michels praised

[7] Michels, 'Nationalismus, Nationalgefühl, Internationalismus', p.107. Michels did, however, pause to criticize the 'expressions of barbaric antisemitism' in France, currently experiencing the Dreyfus case.

[8] Michels, 'Nationalismus, Nationalgefühl, Internationalismus', pp.107–8.

[9] Michels, 'Nationalismus, Nationalgefühl, Internationalismus', pp.108–9. See also Robert Michels, Review of Ernst Hasse, *Deutsche Politik. 1. Bd. Heimatpolitik. 3. Heft. Deutsche Grenzpolitik*, in *Kritische Blätter für die gesamten Sozialwissenschaften*, Jg.II, Heft 10, October 1906, pp.444–6.

[10] Michels, 'Nationalismus, Nationalgefühl, Internationalismus', p.109. Michels subsequently contrasted the Poles and the Wends (or Sorbs) as examples of the importance of moral factors in history, arguing that the Poles had maintained their own national consciousness while the Wends had subordinated their identity to German nationalism. Robert Michels, 'Iets over de betrekking tusschen ethiek en klassenstrijd', *De Nieuwe Tijd*, Vol.10, 9, September 1905, p.603.

[11] Michels, 'Nationalismus, Nationalgefühl, Internationalismus', p.109; emphasis in original.

INTERNATIONALISM, PATRIOTISM, NATIONALISM 209

Gumplowicz's work, especially for its forthright expression of free thinking versus absolutism, even if he had some reservations about its lack of a clear distinction between 'nationalism' and 'national consciousness', and he found some fault with the factual content in Gumplowicz's work, especially concerning Italy.[12]

Michels' sympathy for the cause of *Italia irredenta* led to his first contribution to Ludwig Woltmann's *Politisch-Anthropologische Revue*, in December 1902, which dealt with the situation of the Italian minorities in the Habsburg Empire.[13] Michels reported that Austrian students had disrupted the inaugural lecture of an Italian professor in Innsbruck, while violent street fighting had broken out in Trieste as the result of a strike among Italian workers. The strike had turned from an 'economic struggle between capital and labour power into a political struggle between Italians and German officialdom'.[14] Michels took these outbreaks of unrest as the occasion to analyse the situation of the Italian minorities in Austria: these numbered approximately 800,000, making up 45 per cent of the population of Tirol, and a third of the population of Friaul (Friuli), and a much greater proportion of the city of Trieste, with significant Italian populations in Istria and Dalmatia. While materially the Italians in Austria may not have been poor, they were treated by officialdom in a manner 'most unworthy of such a great *Kulturnation*'. This, and historical memories of national independence in the past, nourished discontent with Habsburg rule. Italians felt drawn to the Italian nation by 'culture, race, outlook on life and language'.[15] Michels went on to write that Germans could not withhold sympathy from the Italians of *Italia irredenta*, 'for the reason alone, apart from everything else, because in many respects, despite the antagonism existing between them, they find themselves in a very similar position to the German-Nationals, who basically are indeed also striving for a reunification with the German Reich' (a tactical argument, perhaps, to appeal to the largely right-wing German nationalist readers of the *Politisch-Anthropologische Revue*).[16]

Michels argued that the Italians in Austria laboured under a number of disadvantages—one of the main obstacles to their national aspirations, indeed the 'Hauptfeind' (main enemy) of all Italians struggling for their nationality, was clericalism, the Catholic church holding fast to the Habsburg state.[17] The second greatest enemy of *Italia irredenta* in Austria was the German population, especially

---

[12] Michels, 'Nationalismus, Nationalgefühl, Internationalismus', pp.109–11. Genett ascribes considerable significance to Michels' subsequent correspondence with Gumplowicz, as far as the development of Michels' thought on nationalism was concerned. Genett, *Der Fremde im Kriege*, pp.122–32. See Ladislaus Gumplowicz, *Nationalismus und Internationalismus im 19. Jahrhundert*, Berlin, 1902.

[13] Dr Robert Michels, 'Das unerlöste Italien in Österreich', *Politisch-Anthropologische Revue*, Jg.1, 9, December 1902, pp.716–24.

[14] Michels, 'Das unerlöste Italien in Österreich', pp.716–17, quotation p.717.

[15] Michels, 'Das unerlöste Italien in Österreich', p.717.

[16] Michels, 'Das unerlöste Italien in Österreich', p.718.

[17] Michels, 'Das unerlöste Italien in Österreich', pp.718–19.

210   ROBERT MICHELS, SOCIALISM, AND MODERNITY

in Tirol, while the Italians in Trieste and on the Adriatic coast were coming under pressure from the growing Slavic population.[18] Although the Triple Alliance had meant that 'official Italy' had effectively disowned the Italians behind the Austrian imperial border, 'in the people the old Garibaldian love for a unification of Pan-Italy glowed more and more', encouraged by the Italian patriotic association 'Dante Alighieri' (Michels described the association as abandoned by the government, and opposed by the socialists for 'tactical reasons', but recently enjoying the strong support of the nationalist poet Gabriele D'Annunzio).[19] Michels concluded his article by asking the question, perhaps anticipating the suspicious response of the German *völkisch* nationalist elements in the *Politisch-Anthropologische Revue*'s readership: 'Is Germandom [*Deutschtum*] in any way threatened by the demands of the Italians?'. Michels hastened to answer the question in the negative: 'The Trentino is a self-contained territory, Italian through and through, and in the Triestino there is only a racial conflict with the Slavs'. Only the 'Austrian idea' was threatened by the political goals of *Italia irredenta*, and Michels quoted Bismarck's curt dismissal of the right for that idea to exist. Sooner or later, Michels predicted, the national question would have to be solved, whether simultaneously with the social question or not (of which, Michels added, it is only a part).[20] In a 1905 essay on Garibaldi, Michels stressed Garibaldi's republicanism and the compatibility of Garibaldi's commitment to national self-determination with internationalism. He quoted Garibaldi as describing himself late in life as a cosmopolitan, but one who would dedicate his life to the cause of *Italia irredenta* ('to deny the Italianness of Nice is to deny the light of the sun').[21]

At the same time as his 1902 essay on *Italia irredenta*, Michels, who was critical of German imperialism, criticized the Italian socialist Ettore Ciccotti's pamphlet attacking Italian expansionist foreign policy. Michels was unconvinced by Ciccotti's economic explanation for Italian expansionism, and found that Ciccotti had failed to demonstrate adequately his conclusion that socialism was the solution to all conflicts.[22] As he moved closer to socialism, Michels did, however, voice criticism of Italian colonialism in the 1890s, and praised the protests against it that took place in Italian cities in 1896.[23] Michels was aware of the risk of double standards in discussions of nationalism. In an essay in *Die Neue Zeit* on the 'problem of morality', Michels mocked German patriots, or rather chauvinists, for their

---

[18]   Michels, 'Das unerlöste Italien in Österreich', pp.719, 720.

[19]   Michels, 'Das unerlöste Italien in Österreich', p.723.

[20]   Michels, 'Das unerlöste Italien in Österreich', p.724. Genett (*Der Fremde im Kriege*, p.134) points out that Michels implicitly did not seem to think the national claims of Slavs in this region needed to be taken into consideration.

[21]   Robert Michels, 'Die Beziehungen Giuseppe Garibaldis zum Sozialismus', *Dokumente des Sozialismus*, Vol.V, 4, 1905; p.184.

[22]   Robert Michels, Review of Ettore Ciccotti, *Quale dev'essere il nuovo indirizzo della Politica Estera?*, in *Documente des Socialismus*, Bd.1, 1902, pp.529–30.

[23]   Dr Robert Michels, 'Die Friedensbewegung in Italien', *Die Frau*, Jg.10, Nr.8, May 1903, p.461.

hypocrisy and double standards. He quoted Theodor Lindner: 'Strong self-consciousness here is called national pride, elsewhere it is vanity or arrogance, holding fast to old customs is considered loyalty to the folk heritage here, elsewhere as backwardness.' Similarly, the Germans considered their cultural expressions of chauvinism to be evidence of healthy patriotism, while the patriotism of foreigners (Michels cited French nationalist author and activist Paul Déroulède's *Chants d'un soldat* as a work that was reviled by Germans as representing vulgar chauvinism).[24] Michels also contrasted the horror which was expressed in Germany over British atrocities in the Boer War with the willingness of the same German circles to justify repressive acts against Germany's Polish minority.[25]

As Michels increasingly wrote from the perspective of a socialist activist from 1903 on, he became a fervent advocate of internationalism, which he insisted was compatible with a properly understood patriotism. 'Internationalism does not mean that one has no fatherland', Michels wrote. 'One can be very attached to one's fatherland and still be a very good internationalist. Indeed, I would even go so far as to claim that the more one loves one's fatherland, the more one will also respect other peoples.'[26] Socialist internationalism did not entail the abolition of cultural difference. Using culinary examples, Michels stated that whether Italians preferred polenta and pasta and Germans potatoes was immaterial: socialism would improve living standards for both peoples, enabling them to eat more meat. Socialism was also opposed to any idea that differences between peoples should lead to hatred and bloodshed: 'With the progressive spread of socialism through the world, continental wars will also disappear, and in our grandchildren's history books, they will be spoken of as one speaks of the completely incomprehensible acts of a horde of cannibals'. Socialist internationalism did not rest on sentiment, but on 'historical necessity and economic insight', the insight into the fact that war served only the interests of militarism and the ruling classes. The German proletariat could not be emancipated without the emancipation at the same time of 'other nations at the same stage of cultural development'. A socialist society could not survive on its own, not only because of the threat of the 'bayonets of neighbouring monarchies' (an indication that Michels saw socialism and monarchy as essentially polar opposites—the reference is to the monarchical state form, not to the capitalist mode of production in the societies concerned), but also because of the impossibility of carrying out the 'regulation of production and consumption for which we strive' in a limited space. Michels concluded:

---

[24] Robert Michels, 'Beitrag zum Problem der Moral', *Die Neue Zeit*, 21. Jg., Bd.1, 1902–1903, p.473. Lindner was, incidentally, Michels' father-in-law.

[25] Michels, 'Beitrag zum Problem der Moral', pp.474–5.

[26] Dr Robert Michels, 'Der Internationalismus der Sozialdemokratie', *Mitteldeutsche Sonntags-Zeitung*, no.9, 1 March 1903.

212 ROBERT MICHELS, SOCIALISM, AND MODERNITY

But we socialists are not only international. We are also national, indeed, among all the Germans, we are the ones who love our people the most. For the fatherland does not consist so much in a piece of earth, let alone in a fat history book or a coloured flag. The fatherland is human flesh and blood, and the happiness of the people is a greater good than so-called expansion of the state's power externally. We fight for the happiness of the people, not just the social democratically-inclined parts of it. Socialism is a goal of humanity, not the goal of a sect.[27]

Michels expressed similar sentiments in a contribution to the Italian journal *La Vita Internazionale*, in which he emphasized the pacific and international nature of the socialist movement and the popular desire for peace, despite the push for war-readiness by the German elites. The Pan-German League represented a perversion of 'noble nationalism, an unhealthy and fantasizing tendency' and the pro-imperialist National Social leader Friedrich Naumann, although gifted, was a 'confusionario di prim'ordine' (a 'first-class creator of confusion').[28] Elsewhere Michels also warned against allowing the internationalism of Social Democracy to become a mere formula, invoked every few years at the international congresses: keeping socialist internationalism alive required vigilance, real collaboration, and a willingness to engage in mutual criticism.[29]

Michels' rejection of narrow nationalism and his Italophile sympathies were both evident in a 1903 contribution to *Ethische Kultur* on the International Latin Congress in Rome, which was attended by official representatives of the Latin nations of Europe and South America. Michels applauded the lack of narrow ethnic chauvinism at the congress, quoting with approval the words of the Italian minister Nasi, who appealed to the humanist traditions associated with the city of Rome. Michels approvingly quoted Nasi's statement: 'I believe that the formation of nationalities, this glory of the twentieth century, is only a stage on the path to a federation of all, which will guarantee all civilized peoples independence and peace'. Michels still subscribed to a vision of human progress, one in which nations were a step in the evolution towards a more cosmopolitan future. Michels added that, unfortunately, 'we do not in any way have today a sharp separation of individual nationalities, but still suffer heavily from "historically developed"

---

[27] Michels, 'Der Internationalismus der Sozialdemokratie'. Much of this essay was reiterated a year later in Robert Michels, 'Der Internationalismus der Arbeiterschaft', *Ethische Kultur*, Jg.12, no.15, 1 August 1904, pp.113–14. Michels updated the essay with a reference to the 1904 Amsterdam International Socialist Congress, which, in time, would become the embryo of 'the great international parliament of peace' (p.114).

[28] Dott. Roberto [Robert] Michels, 'Le elezioni politiche in Germania e la Pace', *La Vita Internazionale*, VI, no.15, 5 August 1903, p.463. For Michels' aversion to the Pan-German League, see his scathing review of a work by its leader Ernst Hasse in: Michels, Review of Ernst Hasse, *Deutsche Politik* (see note 9 above).

[29] Robert Michels, '"Schulbuben"-Kritik', *Volksstimme* (Magdeburg), No.5, 7 January 1904 (leading article, p.1).

INTERNATIONALISM, PATRIOTISM, NATIONALISM   213

"state"-formations on a dynastic basis and not on an ethical one', even if Michels believed that nationalities were on the way to developing more of an independent existence.[30] Michels would later stress the importance of *latinité* as a cultural ideal.

An example which Michels persistently criticized of the way in which the borders of undemocratic dynastic states cut across nationalities was the German Empire. The national minorities on either side of the German-Danish border, the non-Germans of Alsace-Lorraine, and the Poles and other Slavic minorities in the German east were all victims of such anti-democratic dynastic politics and the repressive and 'foolish' attempts by the German Empire to 'Germanize' peoples of different races.[31] In an article for *Ethische Kultur* in December 1903, dedicated to the ethical vindication of the socialist idea, Michels stated that national self-determination for peoples and tribes (*Völker* and *Stämme*) was the indispensable precondition for peace, and socialism was the precondition for such a solution of national questions, by removing the capacity of small ruling cliques to decide arbitrarily over questions of war and peace for entire peoples.[32] Michels spoke out within the Social Democratic Party (at the Bremen party congress in 1904) on the need for socialists to recognize the rights of national minorities within the borders of the Reich when debating the right of 'national self-defence'—national self-defence should not mean opposing the right to self-determination of the Poles in the eastern parts of the Reich, for example.[33]

In early 1904, Michels contributed an article to the *Magazin für Litteratur*, one of the foremost periodicals of literary modernism in Germany, on the theme of a 'Renaissance of Patriotism'.[34] Michels contrasted what he presented as genuine patriotism with the conventional 'hurrah'-patriotism of the German upper classes, exemplified by university students. (Michels cited a publication by his Marburg friend Ernst Thesing on student culture in support of his scathing view of students' beery expressions of jingoism.[35]) Michels defined patriotism as 'a feeling of the heart, which presupposes certain bonds of common life, language,

---

[30] R. [Robert] Michels, 'Durch Nationalität zur Internationalität', *Ethische Kultur*, Jg.XI, Nr.18, 2 May 1903, S.141–2. Nasi is mis-spelt as Rasi in the article, presumably a type-setting error.

[31] Dott. Roberto [Robert] Michels, 'Psicologia e statistica delle elezioni generali politiche in Germania (Giugno 1903)', *La Riforma Sociale*, Fasc.7, Anno X, vol.XIII, seconda serie, 15 July 1903, pp.541–67, 'foolish': quotation p.10 of offprint pagination.

[32] Dr Robert Michels, '"Endziel", Intransigenz, Ethik', *Ethische Kultur*, Jg.XI, no.50, 12 December 1903, pp.393–5; no.51, 19 December 1903, pp.403–4, here p.404.

[33] *Protokoll über die Verhandlungen des Parteitages der Sozialdemokratischen Partei Deutschlands. Abgehalten zu Bremen vom 18. bis 24. September 1904*, Berlin, 1904, p.206. In the same speech, Michels touched on the war in south-west Africa, opposing any support for the German war effort there, arguing that the resistance of the Herero people to German rule was justified; p.206.

[34] Dr Robert Michels, 'Renaissance des Patriotismus', *Magazin für Litteratur*, Jg.73, March 1904, pp.153–6.

[35] In Michels' view, jingoism was not confined to the German bourgeoisie. He also criticized England, including the English working class, for susceptibility to chauvinism and jingoism. Dr Robert Michels, 'Englands gegenwärtiger Kulturwert', *Politisch-Anthropologische Revue*, Jg.3, 1, April 1904, pp.53–63.

214 ROBERT MICHELS, SOCIALISM, AND MODERNITY

culture, a commonly experienced *history, not so much political history as literary, racial affinities*, as well as finally a *feeling of belonging*'.[36] Michels was also at pains to distinguish between attachment to a fatherland and allegiance to a particular dynasty. Michels contrasted his notion of the ideal of patriotism with the conventional chauvinism of the bourgeoisie to conclude that for a true 'renaissance of patriotism' to occur an ethical revolution would be necessary, transforming conditions in the country as a whole.[37]

Michels returned to the theme of patriotism in February 1905 in *Ethische Kultur*, in a two-part article which posited a typology of patriotism which was largely a list of manifestations of patriotism which Michels considered spurious or harmful, in order to contrast them with a healthy kind of love for the fatherland. Firstly, there was megalomaniac patriotism, the sort that saw only good in one's own fatherland while being unable to find any merit in another's country, and which provided the breeding ground for wars. Such national arrogance took the form of chauvinism or jingoism, and was impervious to any kind of objective scientific reflection. Secondly, there was what Michels called the 'pseudo-ethical form' of patriotism. This was to be found when national arrogance and self-interest was cloaked in claims of the prerogative of a nation with 'higher culture' to bring its culture to other, less developed peoples, as in the case of German colonialism in Africa in the present (Michels alluded to the war in Hereroland) and in Poland in the past. Against this justification for imperialism, Michels asserted an unqualified right of self-determination for every people: a 'higher culture did not give a people any right to subjugate or mistreat another'. From this perspective, the history of German unification provided no reason for national pride, as it was achieved through wars that involved breaches of law and justice.[38] Thirdly, Michels identified the 'fantastic form' of patriotism: the veneration of an idealized, abstract image of the nation, manifested in pompous ceremony and various forms of mystification of the fatherland, while ignoring the real social problems within the country: a barbed portrait of Wilhelmine cults of the nation. Fourthly, Michels cited the 'interested form' of patriotism, the form of patriotism espoused by the capitalist whose understanding of the national interest coincided with his own material interests (in contrast to the worker, who, in accordance with the Marxian definition of the proletarian, had nothing but his labour to sell). Michels

---

[36] Michels, 'Renaissance des Patriotismus', p.155; emphasis in original.

[37] Michels, 'Renaissance des Patriotismus'.

[38] Robert Michels, 'Die Formen des Patriotismus', *Ethische Kultur*, Jg.XIII, 3, 1 February 1905, pp.18–19. While Michels attacked colonialism as a source of conflict between peoples, he did not rule out colonialism if it were undertaken by a future socialist society. Such a society would be exporting a higher level of social development, and there would not be the danger of international conflict under socialism. Roberto [Robert] Michels, 'Il problema coloniale di oggi e di domani', *Il Divenire Sociale. Rivista di Socialismo Scientifico*, I, no.19, 1 October 1905, pp.307–8; see also Roberto [Robert] Michels, 'Il socialismo ed il problema coloniale', *Il Divenire Sociale. Rivista di Socialismo Scientifico*, I, no.22, 16 November 1905, pp.351–3.

also drew a distinction between monarchism and patriotism: monarchism was also an expression of particular (dynastic, aristocratic) interests. Fifthly, there was the atavistic form of patriotism—the form adhered to by a majority, while the minority were served by the 'interested form' of patriotism: the primitive satisfaction of believing one's own nation to be stronger than others', a primitive manifestation to which a self-professed *Kulturnation* was not immune.[39]

These forms of patriotism evoked a reaction among many who went to the opposite extreme: an abstract internationalism, that denied the reality of the nation as a product of 'racial psychology, climate and historical conditions'.[40] This denial of the nation was no less problematical, as the nation was a 'vital factor in cultural development', and an expression of a 'deep need, which the broadest masses feel in their heart of hearts'. Michels advocated the reconciliation of cosmopolitanism and patriotism in 'national and social internationalism'. This commenced with the acknowledgement of 'the influence of race, climate, as well as other economic, historical, moral and intellectual coefficients' in the production of real differences between peoples, constituting different 'popular physiognomies'.[41] It was natural for every people that had developed historically as a distinct community to wish to preserve its cultural integrity: this desire for the preservation of cultural integrity was true patriotism. In support of this argument Michels cited Ladislaus Gumplowicz's concept of 'democratic nationalism'. Michels also cited both the *Handbook for Social Democratic Voters* and Goethe in support of the notion that the true patriot was the one who wanted to make his nation a better and more enlightened place.[42]

By late 1905, Michels was increasingly dissatisfied with the adherence of the German Social Democratic Party to its internationalist principles, especially in the wake of the 1905 Morocco crisis. At the Jena party congress, Michels was critical of August Bebel's 'socialist patriotism' and his affirmation of the doctrine of support for national self-defence. For Michels, there was no difference between 'socialist' and 'bourgeois' patriotism when it came to the defence of the German nation, especially given that the German nation contained Polish, Danish, and French minorities within its borders.[43] Michels complained that the instinct of internationalism was still too weakly developed among German Social Democrats, 'especially among the leaders': 'War could have broken out without

---

[39] Robert Michels, 'Die Formen des Patriotismus', *Ethische Kultur*, Jg.XIII, 4, 15 February 1905, pp.26–8, here p.27. Michels also took aim at chauvinism in a subsequent article in *Ethische Kultur*: Dr Robert Michels, 'Entwickelung und Rasse', *Ethische Kultur*, Jg.XIII, 20, 15 October 1905, p.156.

[40] Michels, 'Die Formen des Patriotismus', *Ethische Kultur*, Jg.XIII, 4, p.27.

[41] Michels, 'Die Formen des Patriotismus', *Ethische Kultur*, Jg.XIII, 4, pp.27–8.

[42] Michels, 'Die Formen des Patriotismus', *Ethische Kultur*, Jg.XIII, 4, p.28.

[43] Robert Michels, 'Le socialisme allemande et le congrès d'Iéna', *Le Mouvement Socialiste*, no.166–7, November 1905, pp. 281–307, here p.290. Michels had already taken issue with Bebel's views on national self-defence in Robert Michels, 'Les dangers du parti socialiste allemande', *Le Mouvement Socialiste*, no.144, 1 December 1904, p.203.

216   ROBERT MICHELS, SOCIALISM, AND MODERNITY

finding the least obstacle from the three million socialist voters. In the hour of danger, this splendid collection of votes, this model bureaucratic organism which is German socialism, did not count: it was asleep.[44] Michels increasingly advocated a more radically anti-militarist position, as formulated by Gustave Hervé in France. Borrowing the title of Hervé's anti-militarist book, *The Fatherland of the Rich* (*Leur patrie*; in the German edition: *Das Vaterland der Reichen*), Michels invoked Marx's dictum that the proletarian has no fatherland, and argued that if faced with the threat of war, the response of the proletariat must be a 'general strike out of international humanity'.[45]

Michels' explanations for the failure of German Social Democracy to live up to its internationalist ideals evolved over time, reflecting his gradually increasing distance from the party. In early 1906, he still insisted that 'the German workers are international' in their sentiments, but that the party and the Free Trade Unions failed to prosecute anti-militarist agitation among the German working class with sufficient vigour out of concern for preserving organizations and treasuries.[46] Elsewhere, he blamed the German national character, with its 'passivity, penchant for blind discipline and respect for authority'.[47] In 1907, writing for Hervé's radically anti-militarist *La Guerre Sociale* (in an article entitled: 'A German Antipatriot to French Antipatriots'), Michels criticized the ideological timidity of the German party for failing to instil in the German workers Marx's lesson that patriotism and militarism were outgrowths of capitalism.[48] Michels was again roundly critical of what he regarded as confused ideas about patriotism within German Social Democracy in an article on 'Proletarian Patriotism' printed in the Essen *Arbeiter-Zeitung* in April 1907. The party's setback in the 1907 'Hottentot elections', he argued, had been the result of the party's failure to clearly enlighten the rank and file about the need to oppose official patriotism and chauvinism, and Michels again took issue with Bebel's justification of the right of national self-defence.[49]

Michels' disillusionment with the party was sharpened by the moderation of its position on militarism at the International Socialist Congress in Stuttgart in 1907.

---

[44]   Michels, 'Le socialisme allemande et le congrès d'Iéna', pp.297, 291.

[45]   Robert Michels, 'Das Vaterland der Reichen', *Mitteldeutsche Sonntags-Zeitung*, no.52, 1905. See also Michels' praise for Hervé's book in his review in *Archiv für Sozialwissenschaft und Sozialpolitik*, 30 (neue Folge), 1910, p.582, which draws on a more detailed appreciation by Michels in *Kritische Blätter für die gesamten Sozialwissenschaften*, Bd. II, 2, 1906, pp.77–9.

[46]   Dr [Robert] Michels, 'Die Kriegsgefahr und die deutsche Arbeiterbewegung', *Die Einigkeit. Organ der Freien Vereinigung deutscher Gewerkschaften*, no.25, Beilage, 23 June 1906.

[47]   R. [Robert] Michels, *L'Allemagne, le socialisme et les syndicats*, Paris, 1906 (offprint of article for the *Revue Internationale de Sociologie*), p.7.

[48]   Robert Michels, 'Un antipatriote allemande aux antipatriotes français', *La Guerre Sociale*, 1, no.13, 13–19 March 1907. This article was translated into Italian in the anarchist paper *Il Pensiero*: Roberto Michels, 'Il partito socialista tedesco dopo le elezioni', *Il Pensiero*, V, no.7, 1 April 1907.

[49]   Genosse [Robert] Michels, 'Proletarischer Patriotismus', *Arbeiter-Zeitung* (Essen), no.77, 5 April 1907, p.1 (leading article). In a similar vein, see Robert Michels, 'Die deutschen Sozialdemokraten und der internationale Krieg', *Der Morgen*, no.10, 16 August 1907, pp.299–304.

As a result of the German party's caution, the Second International passed only 'platonic declarations of their peaceful intentions', which fell short of Domela Nieuwenhuis's stronger resolutions calling for a general strike and a strike of the military in the event of war, largely thanks to German opposition to the latter.[50] In *Le Mouvement Socialiste*, Michels denounced the patriotism espoused by the German Social Democratic Party as a threat to the progress of the international socialist movement.[51] The 'uniquely parliamentary character' of German socialism was held responsible for the party's pandering to popular patriotism.[52] Given the particularly backward and ultra-militarist character of the imperial German state, the German party had a particular duty to be critical of their fatherland, but they were neglecting this duty.[53] Instead, the German socialist party declared its willingness to defend the fatherland—'a fatherland composed for the one part of provinces stolen from the Poles, the Danes and the French, and for the other part of capital stolen from the workers by the barons of industry and finance.'[54]

Against the background of the Morocco crisis, and the threat that Wilhelmine imperialism and sabre-rattling posed to peace, Michels gave a lecture to the Society for Ethical Culture in Berlin on 17 January 1906 that was subsequently published as 'Patriotism and Ethics: A Critical Sketch'.[55] Michels equated the dominant, typical forms of 'patriotism' in contemporary Germany with nationalism and chauvinism: 'at age two we proudly wear a cardboard spiked helmet, at three we already love "our Kaiser", at four we already sing the *Wacht am Rhein*', and so on until one joins a nationalistic student fraternity at 19. Such nationalism and chauvinism in turn lead to contempt and enmity for other nations, and thus to war and plunder.[56] The slogan 'Right or wrong, my country' (*sic*, English in original) was at the same time the peak of patriotic sentiment and the peak of a lack of ethical sentiment.[57] Posing the question, what is the *Vaterland*?, Michels allowed that affection for one's local birthplace or place of childhood memories may be natural (citing the Italian word *campanilismo* for this), but such local attachments were not identical with 'state patriotism in the grand style'. Michels argued that patriotism was not a product of the accident of birth, nor was it the product of 'blood' or race.[58] Germany was too racially heterogeneous for such a definition to be viable, considering the presence of Jews, descendants of

---

[50] Robert Michels, 'Die deutsche Sozialdemokratie im internationalen Verbande. Eine kritische Untersuchung', *Archiv für Sozialwissenschaft und Sozialpolitik*, Vol.25, 1907, p.186.

[51] Robert Michels, 'Le patriotisme des socialistes allemands et le congrès d'Essen', *Le Mouvement Socialiste*, Année X, no.194, 15 January 1908, pp.5–13, especially p.12.

[52] Michels, 'Le patriotisme des socialistes allemands et le congrès d'Essen', p.9.

[53] Michels, 'Le patriotisme des socialistes allemands et le congrès d'Essen', pp.10–11.

[54] Michels, 'Le patriotisme des socialistes allemands et le congrès d'Essen', pp.11–12.

[55] Dr Robert Michels, *Patriotismus und Ethik. Eine kritische Skizze*, Leipzig, 1906 (dedicated to the neo-Kantian Karl Vorländer). See the discussion of this lecture in Kelly, 'From Moralism to Modernism', pp.144–7.

[56] Michels, *Patriotismus und Ethik*, pp.10–11.   [57] Michels, *Patriotismus und Ethik*, p.11.

[58] Michels, *Patriotismus und Ethik*, p.13.

Huguenots, Danes, Poles, etc. 'Blood' or 'race' alone could not determine nationality or national feeling. (Significantly, Michels was not denying the existence of 'race' here, but was rather insisting on the non-congruence of racial boundaries and the boundaries of German nationality.[59]) To illustrate this point, Michels gave the example: in terms of 'race, approach to life, and feeling', a farmer in the Rhineland would have more in common with a French 'foreigner' across the border than with a distant east Prussian 'compatriot'.[60] (While Michels did not expressly say so here, the same would apply, perhaps *a fortiori*, for a Rhinelander of upper-middle-class, part-French origins, such as Michels himself.) As far as economic determinants of nationality were concerned, Michels pointed to the tendency of the capitalist order towards 'cosmopolitanism on the terrain of economics'. Both labour migration and capital investment crossed national borders.[61] Furthermore, capitalism produced differences between classes within national boundaries, rather than unifying them.[62] Most vigorously, Michels rejected any equation of patriotism with allegiance to the Hohenzollern dynasty. Current dynastic formations were historically contingent—the outcome of 'coercion, war, dynastic marriage', and were therefore arbitrary.[63] The current state, as the product of armed force, could not provide a moral basis for a justification of patriotism.[64] Having chipped away at the possible rational bases for patriotism, Michels concluded that patriotism lacked 'any real foundation'. It is a 'delusion [*ein Hirngespinst*], and not even a beautiful one', it was 'a phrase, under cover of which all manner of atrocities are committed'.[65] However, Michels did allow some ethical justification for patriotism, for example, in cases of resistance against rule by foreigners speaking a different language, mentioning specifically the cases of Poles in Posen and Italian *irredenta* in Trentino and Trieste as examples that should command the sympathies of any ethicist. Here, the factor of national culture was decisive, previously left out of his survey of patriotism.[66] The right to one's own language was sacrosanct, even if language alone did not constitute nationality.[67] For Michels, patriotism on its own was not sufficient, but it could be justified by the defence of a higher ideal of culture or progress, as in the case of the French Revolution.[68] Only culture, in the sense of some progress towards higher ethical principles in the interests of humanity as a whole, could make patriotism ethical. Such patriotism may even require one to wish the defeat of one's own country, if it is opposing such progress.[69] Michels espoused a kind of ethical *Kulturpatriotismus*, which depended on an ideal of human progress for its validity, but was not wholly voluntaristic. Race, life experience, and language (even if

---

[59] Michels, *Patriotismus und Ethik*, pp.14–15.
[60] Michels, *Patriotismus und Ethik*, p.15. [61] Michels, *Patriotismus und Ethik*, p.16.
[62] Michels, *Patriotismus und Ethik*, pp.17–20. [63] Michels, *Patriotismus und Ethik*, p.22.
[64] Michels, *Patriotismus und Ethik*, pp.23–4. [65] Michels, *Patriotismus und Ethik*, p.26.
[66] Michels, *Patriotismus und Ethik*, pp.27–8. [67] Michels, *Patriotismus und Ethik*, p.29.
[68] Michels, *Patriotismus und Ethik*, p.29. [69] Michels, *Patriotismus und Ethik*, p.30.

INTERNATIONALISM, PATRIOTISM, NATIONALISM   219

language was not solely determinant) could all contribute to an authentic sense of patriotism, which did not rely on existing state structures or national boundaries.

In his article series for the *Archiv für Sozialwissenschaft und Sozialpolitik*, Michels was again critical of ascribed and fixed notions of nationality: 'The nationality question is a nonsense in itself, in so far as one seeks to understand it as anything other than the right of a permanent plebiscite'. Michels referred to article 30 of the Declaration of Rights of Man and the Citizen, which guaranteed the eternal right of the people to revise their own decisions. The complexity of differentiation within any human society made national generalizations meaningless. Michels cited Heinrich Heine: 'General characteristics are the sources of all evils. It takes more than a generation to comprehend the character of a single person, and a nation consists of millions of individual people'.[70] However, in the Italian book edition, Michels went on to elaborate on this point at greater length, and qualified his earlier argument: 'Scientifically, it is undeniable that the combination of race, climate, economic, moral and intellectual conditions, have created differences between the different human groupings, or rather they have given each people its particular physiognomy, albeit transitory and ephemeral'.[71] Elsewhere, Michels stressed the illogicality of identifying with national states, but conceded that 'the people, including the proletariat, feel foreign oppression much more than native-born oppression'.[72] Michels continued to be critical of the coercive nationalism that would force people of diverse races and language into one national identity.[73] Michels' solution to nationality questions was the right of every ethnic group to decide which 'race or state' it wished to belong to: 'every population has the right to decide spontaneously which ethnic group it wants to belong to'.[74]

Even before he moved to Turin in 1907, Michels drew positive examples of patriotism from Italy and cited negative examples of nationalism and chauvinism from the German Empire. This polarity continued after Michels' move to Italy. In a 1908 essay on Alexander Herzen in Italy. Michels described Herzen's disgust at German attitudes towards Poles and others, and German disregard of the rights of other nationalities.[75] After being disappointed by his experiences of Germany and France, Herzen arrived in Italy: 'For the first and the last time in his life he

---

[70] Robert Michels, 'Proletariat und Bourgeoisie in der sozialistischen Bewegung Italiens', *Archiv für Sozialwissenschaft und Sozialpolitik*, 22, 1906, pp.665–6.

[71] Published in book form: Roberto [Robert] Michels, *Il proletariato e la borghesia nel movimento socialista italiano*, Turin, 1908 (reprint New York, 1975), p.269.

[72] Robert Michels, 'Le prochain congrès socialiste international', *Le Mouvement Socialiste*, no.188, July 1907, p.42.

[73] Roberto [Robert] Michels, 'Appunti sulla solidarietà', *La Riforma Sociale*, vol.20, series III, Anno xvi, no.5, September–October 1909, pp.661–73, here pp.12–13 (pagination of offprint).

[74] Robert Michels, 'La politique étrangère et le socialisme', *Le Mouvement Socialiste*, 25, January–June 1909, p.332.

[75] Roberto Michels, 'Le memorie di Herzen e l'Italia', *Nuova Antologia*, Anno 43, Vol.138, Fascicolo 887, 1 December 1908, p.360.

220   ROBERT MICHELS, SOCIALISM, AND MODERNITY

did not submit to melancholy and sadness after arriving at the destination of his travels'. The enthusiasm and willingness to self-sacrifice of the Italian youth, the physical beauty of the people—the new surroundings pleased him without any negative impressions. 'Above all, he was pleased at the moral qualities of the Italians'.[76] Following on from Herzen's observations, Michels distinguished between the nature of patriotism in Italy of the *Risorgimento* and patriotism in the 'French, English, or German sense'. Free from narrow chauvinism, the patriotism of Italians in this period had not been detached from egalitarianism and a sense of justice: 'The Italian patriotism of the *Risorgimento* consisted solely in wanting to chase foreigners from Italian soil, and not in wanting to seek military glory or to make conquests in foreign lands'.[77] Once Italy was free of foreign rule, Italians had no use for national animosities. Throughout the essay, Michels identified with Herzen's generalizations about national character, and he specifically endorsed Herzen's generally positive judgement on Italian national character.[78] While Michels insisted on the difficulty of arriving at an adequate scholarly definition of nations and nationalities, he was happy to engage in subjective generalizations about national psychology, based on his own observations, delivered in sometimes anecdotal fashion.[79] In these generalizations, Italian 'national character' tended to fare better than the German one, although Michels attested that both countries shared a 'physiological freshness' as young nations.[80]

In his final, in retrospect valedictory, article for *Le Mouvement Socialiste*, Michels expressed the point of view that all patriotism was inherently egocentric. Nations sought rights for themselves, not equal rights for all—even the previously benign Italian form of patriotism was showing signs of aggression. But he was now more pessimistic about the internationalism of the socialist movement, seeing the internationalism of workers and socialist parties as superficial, even though peace between nations was in the workers' own interest. Only an enlightened few were genuinely internationalist, and they had a huge task ahead of them to educate others.[81] Michels wrote: 'These days, internationalism only has a real value in the heads of a small minority of superior men'.[82] There is no doubt that Michels counted himself among this minority of superior men, and he was able to find reasons for this in his own biography:

[76] Michels, 'Le memorie di Herzen e l'Italia', pp.361–2, 363.
[77] Michels, 'Le memorie di Herzen e l'Italia', p.362.
[78] Michels, 'Le memorie di Herzen e l'Italia', p.367n1.
[79] Robert Michels, 'Zur Psychologie der Bourgeoisie in den verschiedenen nationalen Verbänden', *Monatsschrift für Soziologie*, Jg.1, July 1909, pp.473–4.
[80] Michels, 'Zur Psychologie der Bourgeoisie in den verschiedenen nationalen Verbänden', pp.580–2.
[81] Michels, 'La politique étrangère et le socialisme', pp.321–33.
[82] Michels, 'La politique étrangère et le socialisme', p.333.

INTERNATIONALISM, PATRIOTISM, NATIONALISM   221

Men whose lives have brought them into different conditions, and who have had the opportunity to put down roots in more than one country during their existence do not as a rule have the same 'pure' and indivisible patriotism as the petit bourgeois philistine [*Spiessbürger*] who has never left the walls of his local town.[83]

Moving away from his earlier identification with Marxism, Michels also now held that not only 'nation', but class too, were 'very relative concepts'.[84]

As mentioned at the start of the chapter, Michels remained consistent in his loathing of German militarism, which seems to have had a foundation in his own experience of military service.[85] He described in Clara Zetkin's *Die Gleichheit* in April 1903, how brutally militarism tore young men away from their just-begun professions, and from their circle of families and friends, in order to lock them up in 'that combination of penitentiary and madhouse', the barracks, for one to three years. Militarism took away women's menfolk, and subjected them to needless hardships and all manner of moral dangers ('the most revolting unnatural sexual temptations and other forms of corruption') in the barracks. Militarism, and its ugly twin brother, the expansion of the fleet ('Marinismus'), took millions of marks away from the people, taxing the basic necessities of life and spending money that could be used for the improvement of society for destructive purposes. Militarism was directed not only towards the preparation of wars, but also against the 'enemy within': i.e. the proletariat itself, whose sons, fathers, and brothers were drilled to put down any unrest among the 'wage slaves', as the deployment of troops against striking Ruhr miners showed. Michels exhorted the readers of *Die Gleichheit* to be uncompromising opponents of militarism, and to support Social Democracy in the coming Reichstag elections, to that end.[86]

Michels poured scorn on German chauvinists' calls for naval expansion in a brief review of a work of navalist propaganda for the journal *Ethische Kultur*. Michels characterized the naval propagandist as blind to all social conflicts in his own country, while trying to instigate national feeling on the part of a supposedly united 'people' against an external enemy. The book's treatment of England was also marked by 'blind hatred, that falsifies history' as far as its presentation of England was concerned.[87] Also for *Ethische Kultur*, Michels contributed a

---

[83] Robert Michels, Review of Giuseppe Romano-Catania, *Filippo Buonarotti*, in *Archiv für Sozialwissenschaft und Sozialpolitik*, 28 (neue Folge), 1909, p.812.

[84] Michels, 'Zur Psychologie der Bourgeoisie in den verschiedenen nationalen Verbänden', p.470.

[85] On the experiences of German Social Democrats in military service in imperial Germany, see Andrew G. Bonnell, *Red Banners, Books and Beer Mugs: The Mental World of German Social Democrats, 1863–1914*, Leiden, 2021, ch.5.

[86] R.M. [Robert Michels], 'Die Frau und der Militarismus', *Die Gleichheit*, Jg.XIII, no.9, 22 April 1903, p.70.

[87] Dr Robert Michels, Review of Ernst Teja Meyer, *Los von England!*, in *Ethische Kultur*, Jg.XI, Nr.3, 17 January 1903, p.23.

222 ROBERT MICHELS, SOCIALISM, AND MODERNITY

translation of a column by a young Italian worker, printed in the Turin socialist paper *Il Grido del Popolo*, which dealt with the destructive effects of a conventional patriotic and militarist education, recommending instead a teaching of history which revealed the real horrors of war.[88] Elsewhere, Michels presented a highly positive picture of the deeply anti-militarist nature of the Italian people, contrasting Italian anti-militarism favourably with the situation in Germany, or for that matter in France, preoccupied as it was with *revanche* for 1870–1.[89] Another note contributed by Michels to *Ethische Kultur* deplored the harshness of military justice, seeing it as evidence of a state 'in which external military discipline is ranked higher than logic and humanity'.[90] Michels also contributed a positive review of an anti-militarist pamphlet by the Portuguese sociologist Pinto Ribeiro, citing his core claim: 'Culture has the ultimate goal of making human beings. Militarism is dedicated to turning humans into beasts—that is, the exact opposite'.[91] A drastic example of the brutalization brought about by war was found by Michels in a memoir of the 1866 Austro-Prussian war, in which an officer recalls feeling peckish as he smelled the 'roasted' flesh of dead men and horses on the battlefield.[92]

One of the major themes in Michels' increasingly critical commentary on the German Social Democratic Party from the Bremen party congress in 1904 on was its failure to give sufficiently radical effect to its professions of anti-militarism.[93] Michels identified strongly with the anti-militarist propaganda espoused by Gustave Hervé, which was subject to state repression in Wilhelmine Germany.

Michels developed a critique of Wilhelmine German society and culture, which, as Timm Genett has suggested, in some respects anticipated the critical social history 'Sonderweg' interpretation of Hans-Ulrich Wehler and others.[94] For Michels, the German Empire was a case study in incomplete and flawed modernization, with a bourgeoisie lacking in political will for liberal reform and subservient to an anachronistic and feudal ruling elite. In the wake of the June 1903 elections, Michels wrote:

---

[88] R. [Robert] Michels, 'Geflügelverkäuferin und Geschichtsunterricht, eine Parabel', in *Ethische Kultur*, Jg.XI, Nr.24, 13 June 1903, pp.189–90. See also Robert Michels, 'Der innere Zusammenhang von "Schlachten" und "Morden"', in *Ethische Kultur*, Jg.XI, Nr.25, 20 June 1903, S.198 (citing Lombroso on the life story of a murderer).

[89] Michels, 'Die Friedensbewegung in Italien', pp.459–63.

[90] Dr Robert Michels, 'Disciplin?', in *Ethische Kultur*, Jg.XI, Nr.38, 19 September 1903, p.303.

[91] Dr R. [Robert] Michels, Review of Pinto Ribeiro, *Estudos e Panegyricos*, in *Ethische Kultur*, Jg.XI, Nr.46, 14 November 1903, p.367.

[92] Robert Michels [under the rubric: Streiflichter], 'Die Verrohung eine Begleiterscheinung des Krieges', in *Ethische Kultur*, Jg.XI, Nr.36, 5 September 1903, p.286.

[93] Dr Rob. [Robert] Michels, 'Bremer Erbschaften', *Mitteldeutsche Sonntags-Zeitung*, Jg.11, no.43, 23 October 1904. See also Michels, 'Les dangers du parti socialiste allemande', p.211; Michels, 'Die deutsche Sozialdemokratie im internationalen Verbande', pp.180ff, 189.

[94] Genett, *Der Fremde im Kriege*, pp.80–117, especially p.83.

The German bourgeoisie has been unable to conquer for itself the position which is due to it under modern industrialization. Weak, gossipy, and above all, verbose, it does not have sufficient courage to put an end to feudalism and to carry out its own emancipation as a class. Leaving the political supremacy without further ado to the nobility, it asks for nothing but the financial dominance over its country, and if possible over the world.[95]

Not only did the bourgeoisie surrender political dominance within the German state to the aristocracy, Michels argued that they accepted aristocratic hegemony in the sphere of values and social mores: 'our bourgeoisie...still finds itself consciously or unconsciously slavishly aping the "noblest of the nation".'[96] Elsewhere, citing an example of deference on the part of a highly successful merchant, who 'furthermore was descended from a so-called old patrician family of a Rhineland Hansa-town' (possibly an old acquaintance of the patrician Michels family of Cologne), to a *Rittergutsbesitzer* (proprietor of a knightly landed estate), Michels wrote:

Despite the fact that we have long been in an age of industrialism, here in Germany we are still far from managing to completely digest feudalism. The development of our social conditions has not been able to keep pace with economic progress. Economically we have long passed the period of the agrarian state, but socially and politically we are still stuck deep in its outlook. While in the socially more advanced countries, like England and America, indeed even in countries still economically far behind us like, for example, Italy, the industrial bourgeoisie has emancipated itself from feudalism, if not yet completely at least to a very high degree, und plays the role in state and society which the contemporary development of private capitalism assigns to it, in Germany the *roture* [commons] still does not yet enjoy equal social rights in fact. If they want to amount to anything at all socially, then this can only occur if they take on a feudal nature, i.e. to copy it as well as they can. And even then, the highest positions in the army, the navy, etc. are hermetically closed to them.

One of the thousand-and-one phenomena resulting from this pathological condition—the permanence of which is incidentally to be attributed to the political and social spinelessness of our German bourgeoisie—is also the higher regard in which agrarian capitalism stands by comparison with industrial and mercantile capitalism. The '*Rittergutsbesitzer*' even if, as in our case, he belongs to a parvenu family, is considered to be worth more than the man of commerce,

[95] Dott. Roberto [Robert] Michels, 'Psicologia e statistica delle elezioni generali politiche in Germania (Giugno 1903)', *La Riforma Sociale*, Fasc.7, Anno X, vol.XIII, seconda serie, 15 July 1903, pp.541–67, quotation on p.12 of offprint.
[96] Robert Michels, 'Brautstandsmoral. Eine kritische Betrachtung', *Das Magazin für Litteratur*, Jg.72, 1 June 1903, p.99.

224 ROBERT MICHELS, SOCIALISM, AND MODERNITY

indeed, while the former knowingly or unknowingly tends to show off his wealth, the latter feels an irrepressible embarrassment at the name 'merchant'.[97]

For Michels, an important starting point in trying to understand the German Reich was to realize that it was a flawed nation-state, holding as it did several discontented national minorities against their will. In an article on the 1903 Reichstag elections for the Italian syndicalist newspaper *Avanguardia Socialista*, Michels wrote:

> The brutal and warmongering policies of official Prussia have unfortunately resulted in the occupation of territories, which, in culture, race and language, belong to non-Germanic peoples. Thus we have the Danes in the North, the Poles and Lithuanians in the East, and in the West the French in Lorraine and the Frenchified Alsatians. All these peoples living 'in diaspora' have their own irredentist movements, which are crystallized in their respective political parties. This fact gives its own special character to German political life.[98]

Also in *Avanguardia Socialista*, Michels stressed that a key difference between German and Italian politics was the absence in Germany of a democratic, republican bourgeois left: 'we do not have any republican bourgeois party'.[99] Older vestiges of bourgeois republican traditions, for example in Michels' native Rhineland, had been suppressed or abandoned.[100] In an article for the left Social Democratic newspaper the *Leipziger Volkszeitung*, Michels compared the record of the bourgeois revolution in Germany unfavourably even with the Italian case: 'The bourgeois revolution in Italy has on the whole done a far better job of getting rid of feudalism than the movement of the German bourgeois philistines, which, for all its literary brilliance, has been pathetic.' In many respects, Italy benefitted from a more liberal political climate than Germany.[101]

As already noted, Michels viewed the German Reich as the most backward state in Europe, apart from Russia and Turkey.[102] He wrote in *Le Mouvement Socialiste*: 'Germany is still the country of the most extraordinary personal absolutism. Although industry has developed there to the point of constituting formidable

---

[97] Dr Robert Michels, 'Die Analyse einer Verlobungskarte', *Ethische Kultur*, Jg.XI, No.27, 4 July 1903, p.211; reprinted in *Frankfurter Zeitung und Handelsblatt*, no.183, 4 July 1903.

[98] Dott. Roberto [Robert] Michels, 'La tattica dei socialisti tedeschi alle elezioni generali politiche', *Avanguardia Socialista*, Anno II, no.28, 5 July 1903. See also Michels, 'Psicologia e statistica delle elezioni generali politiche in Germania', pp.7–10 of offprint.

[99] 'La tattica dei socialisti tedeschi alle elezioni generali politiche'; emphasis in original.

[100] Roberto [Robert] Michels, 'I progressi del repubblicanesimo in Germania', *Rivista Popolare di Politica, Lettere e Scienze*, Anno IX, No.15, 15 August 1903, p.400.

[101] Dr Robert Michels, 'Die Ehescheidung in Italien', *Leipziger Volkszeitung*, Jg.10, no.33, 10 February 1903. See also Dr Robert Michels, 'Die italienische Frau in den camere di lavoro', *Die Frau*, Jg.11, Heft 7, April 1904, p.426.

[102] Michels, 'Les dangers du parti socialiste allemand', p.193.

INTERNATIONALISM, PATRIOTISM, NATIONALISM 225

correspondence to England itself, it is not the common bourgeoisie which rules there, but the rural aristocracy'.[103] Michels went on to speak of the nobility's success in monopolizing the higher ranks of the army and the diplomatic service; the Prussian *Gesindeordnung* (master and servant code), which deprived rural labourers and domestic servants of elementary rights of association; the regime of mistreatment of army recruits, and the *lèse-majesté* laws. (Michels also did not forget to refer to the *lex Arons*, which barred socialists from teaching in any of the country's universities, despite the three million votes cast for Social Democracy.)[104] 'Our state', Michels wrote, 'is not, in effect, the state of a bourgeoisie in decadence [like France], it is still the feudal state of a barbaric age.'[105] In a similar vein, addressing a syndicalist gathering in Paris in April 1907, Michels pronounced that since the recent revolution in Russia, Germany was bringing up the rear of the civilized nations of Europe: 'We are not even dominated by the industrial and commercial bourgeoisie, the class type of the capitalist system, but by hordes of semi-barbarian country squires, the surviving expressions of a pre-capitalist and feudal regime. Germany today still resembles, *mutatis mutandis*, *ancien régime* France'.[106] Michels described imperial Germany as a 'police state which would be insupportable to men seized with liberty'. While the bourgeoisie in Germany reproached Social Democrats for their alleged lack of patriotism, 'our socialist action is patriotic in a sense, since we want to cleanse our country of the vestiges of the past'.[107] This usage of the word 'patriotism' was largely rhetorical in this instance, but it also points to the connection for Michels between genuine patriotism and self-determination.

Michels took part in the Second German Congress of Sociologists in Berlin in 1912, at which the principal theme was nations and nationality. Michels spoke on the 'historical development of the idea of the fatherland', giving a historical survey of the evolution of patriotism and nationalism.[108] As Duncan Kelly has suggested, Michels' historical analysis of patriotism has points in common with late twentieth-century 'modernist' accounts of nationalism, viewing the emergence of national identities as linked to the rise of increasingly centralized and ethnically unified modern states (notably England and France from the late seventeenth

---

[103] Michels, 'Les dangers du parti socialiste allemande', p.194.
[104] Michels, 'Les dangers du parti socialiste allemande', pp.194–5.
[105] Michels, 'Les dangers du parti socialiste allemande', p.199.
[106] Robert Michels, 'Le syndicalisme et le socialisme en Allemagne', *Le Mouvement Socialiste*, no.188, July 1907, pp.59–60, quotation p.60. See also Michels, 'Zur Psychologie der Bourgeoisie in den verschiedenen nationalen Verbänden', p.476: 'Germany...is not governed by the class of education or economic strength, but by hussar and Uhlan officers of aristocratic birth, by bureaucrats and diplomats with the title of Count'.
[107] Michels, 'Le syndicalisme et le socialisme en Allemagne', p.60.
[108] Professor Dr Robert Michels, 'Die historische Entwicklung des Vaterlandsgedankens', in *Verhandlungen des Zweiten Deutschen Soziologentages vom 20.–22. Oktober 1912 in Berlin*, Tubingen, 1913, pp.140–84. A revised and significantly expanded version of this paper was subsequently published as Michels, 'Zur historischen Analyse des Patriotismus', pp.14–43, 394–449.

226 ROBERT MICHELS, SOCIALISM, AND MODERNITY

century on).[109] Michels argued that patriotism was not an innate characteristic, but something that was learned or acquired, and pointed out that many people were in a position to choose from more than one available national identity, a choice that was typically limited by the actions of the state.[110] He particularly emphasized the significance of the French Revolution of 1789 as a catalyst for the development of a modern idea of patriotism.[111] This differed somewhat from Weber's view, with Weber being more inclined to locate the origins of nationality much earlier, in the middle ages.[112] Michels' account of the evolution of patriotism also took account of the effects of the rise of industrialization and the socialist critique of conceptions of patriotism by Karl Marx and Gustave Hervé, emphasizing particularly Hervé's view of the relative and constructed nature of national identity, and his 'dogma' of the 'negation of patriotism'.[113] However, Michels diagnosed a progressive decline of proletarian internationalism in the socialist movement, which he saw as resulting from a number of factors: democratic politics, which entailed the flattery of the masses and an appeal to patriotic sentiments; the tendency of socialist parties to pursue parliamentary methods, which resulted in increased identification with the state; rising education levels, providing workers with better access to national literature and a greater sense of belonging to the national culture; and increased labour migration, which sharpened workers' sense of national differences.[114] Finally, Michels noted the influence of imperialism on the working classes: especially in the case of 'privileged and organized English workers' who sought a share of the profits from imperial possessions and exports to the empire.[115]

At the same time as Michels noted the degree to which imperialism was undermining the internationalism of which he had previously been a fervent advocate, he also emerged as a defender of Italian imperialism following the Italian colonization of Libya in 1911. In an essay in the *Archiv für Sozialwissenschaft und Sozialpolitik*, Michels brushed aside moral objections to the Italian seizure of Libya, and argued that Italy had a 'genuine need for expansion', not so much for economic reasons, but because of the demographic imperative, in view of Italy's

---

[109] Kelly, 'From Moralism to Modernism', p.350. Surprisingly, though, there is little evidence that Michels engaged with the writings on nationalism or national questions of the Austro-Marxists such as Otto Bauer.

[110] Michels, 'Die historische Entwicklung des Vaterlandsgedankens', p.165.

[111] Michels, 'Die historische Entwicklung des Vaterlandsgedankens', pp.153–7.

[112] See Weber's comments in *Verhandlungen des Zweiten Deutschen Soziologentages*, p.190; Joachim Radkau, *Max Weber. Die Leidenschaft des Denkens*, Munich and Vienna, 2005, pp.530–1.

[113] Michels, 'Die historische Entwicklung des Vaterlandsgedankens', p.170–1.

[114] Michels, 'Die historische Entwicklung des Vaterlandsgedankens', pp.172–4.

[115] Michels, 'Die historische Entwicklung des Vaterlandsgedankens', pp.175–6. To some extent, this anticipates Lenin's critique of the labour aristocracy deriving profit from the spoils of imperialism. It would hardly fit the case of German Social Democracy, where the party opposed empire in part because of its expense to the nation and to workers who were taxed through indirect taxation to pay for the costs of Germany's colonies.

overpopulation which without colonial expansion would continue to result in the motherland losing part of its people every year through emigration. A secondary justification, although one that Michels argued should not be dismissed, was the issue of national prestige, with Italy shaking off the status of Cinderella among Europe's leading nations. Italy was 'the slave breaking his chains. The nation that has attained maturity and is at the same time struggling for self-respect and the recognition of its neighbours'.[116] Here, Michels came close to the 'national syndicalist' concept, espoused by the leader of the Italian Nationalist Association, Enrico Corradini, of Italy as a 'proletarian nation', a concept that forged a rhetorical bridge between syndicalists and nationalist advocates of imperialism.[117] Michels commenced a correspondence with Corradini in 1911, exchanging publications with him.[118] It is hard to imagine Michels ever finding common cause with the German ultra-nationalists of the Pan-German Association. His aversion to the Wilhelmine German brand of militarism and chauvinism was too ingrained. But as Michels left behind his affiliations with socialist internationalism, the identification with his adoptive nation became stronger. Michels had always found Italian nationalism, with its democratic and republican origins, more congenial than German nationalism, and he was willing to accompany its evolution even as it took on a more imperialist and bellicose trajectory.

---

[116] Robert Michels, 'Elemente zur Entstehungsgeschichte des Imperialismus in Italien', *Archiv für Sozialwissenschaft und Sozialpolitik*, 34, 1912, pp.55–120, 470–97; quotations, p.495. This was subsequently expanded to book-length form in R. [Robert] Michels, *L'imperialismo italiano*, Milan, 1914.

[117] See Franco Bozzi, 'L'imperialismo proletario italiano nel pensiero di Roberto Michels', in Gian Biagio Furiozzi, ed., *Le sinistre italiane tra guerra e pace (1840–1940)*, Milan, 2008, pp.122–45.

[118] See ARM/FLE, *busta* Enrico Corradini. On Corradini and the Italian Nationalist Association, see Alexander J. De Grand, *The Italian Nationalists and the Rise of Fascism in Italy*, Lincoln, NE, 1978.

8

Ethnicity and Race

Most of the standard treatments of Robert Michels' thought have paid scant attention to the salience of concepts of race and innate ethnic characteristics seen throughout Michels' works. Pino Ferraris pointed to the influence of Italian criminologists such as Lombroso and Enrico Ferri on the young Michels, and the extent to which their sociological analyses of the Italian peasantry contained a biological strand.[1] Erhard Stölting discerns a development in Michels' attitude towards Social Darwinism and eugenics, from a fundamental rejection of such positions to a view that accepted the need for enlightened intellectuals to overcome the intellectual and moral backwardness of the lower classes at least partially through eugenic means.[2] Timm Genett's *magnum opus* on Michels notes the influence of Lombroso's biologistic thinking on Michels, and notes that eugenic ideas can be traced throughout Michels' writing career, but he tends not to view racial and ethnic categories as fundamental for Michels' work.[3] Ideas of racial and ethnic difference play a consistent and important part in Michels' thought, however, even if they tended to be soft-pedalled in his writings for the German Social Democratic Party. This prevalence of race in Michels' views has yet to be subjected to a systematic analysis. Furthermore, the fact that the biologistic influences on Michels' thought came more from Italian sources rather than German is worth emphasizing in light of recent historiography which has increasingly focused on the significance of the evolution of racial thought in Italy on the emergence of Italian fascist ideology, in contrast to older literature which depicted racism as having been imported into Italian fascism from German Nazism.[4]

---

[1] Pino Ferraris, *Saggi su Roberto Michels*, Camerino, 1993, pp.20–1.

[2] Erhard Stölting, 'Robert Michels (1876–1936)', in Dirk Kaesler, ed., *Klassiker der Soziologie. Bd.1. Von August Comte bis Norbert Elias*, Munich, 2003, p.241. See also Olivier Bosc, 'Eugénisme et socialisme en Italie autour de 1900. Robert Michels et l'"éducation sentimentale des masses"', *Mil Neuf Cent*, 18, 2000, pp.81–108.

[3] Timm Genett, *Der Fremde im Kriege. Zur politischen Theorie und Biographie von Robert Michels 1876–1936*, Berlin, 2008, pp.178–84; on persistence of eugenic ideas, p.182.

[4] See Alizia S. Wong, *Race and the Nation in Liberal Italy, 1861–1911. Meridionalism, Empire, and Diaspora*, New York and Basingstoke, 2006; Maria Sophia Quine, 'Making Italians: Aryanism and Anthropology in Italy during the Risorgimento', in Marius Turda, ed., *Crafting Humans: From Genesis to Eugenics and Beyond*, Göttingen, 2013, pp.127–52; Adrian Gillette, *Racial Theories in Fascist Italy*, London and New York, 2002; Giorgio Israel, *Il fascismo e la razza*, Bologna, 2010; Patrick Bernhard, 'Blueprints of Totalitarianism: How Racist Policies in Fascist Italy Inspired and Informed Nazi Germany', *Fascism*, Vol.6, 2017, pp.127–62. For an influential formulation of the older thesis of the incommensurability of Nazi racism and Italian fascist conceptions of the 'New Man', see Renzo De

---

Robert Michels, Socialism, and Modernity. Andrew G. Bonnell, Oxford University Press. © Andrew G. Bonnell 2023.
DOI: 10.1093/oso/9780192871848.003.0009

ETHNICITY AND RACE   229

A number of influences can be discerned as possibly contributing to Michels' affinity with ideas of biological racism. In Halle, he had attended the lectures of Alfred Kirchhoff on Darwinism. Kirchhoff was a pioneer of geography as a university discipline at German universities, and was a proponent of an organic, holistic approach to geography that included a consideration of racial biology. For the more radical proponents of racial science, however, Kirchhoff's willingness to attribute causation to geographical and climatic factors diluted their emphasis on the primacy of racial difference as the driving factor in world history.[5] Another of Michels' Halle professors, the political scientist Johannes Conrad, was also open to considering the relevance of German adapters of Darwinism to the field of politics; in January 1900, Conrad joined the widely influential German popularizer of the theory of evolution, Ernst Haeckel, and Eberhard Fraas in launching an essay prize competition on the topic: 'What can we learn from the principles of evolutionary theory about the internal political development and legislation of states?'[6]

A second major influence was the prevalence of biologistic thinking in the social sciences among intellectuals in Turin, and the Italian social anthropological school more broadly. Michels was exposed to this several years before he became a colleague of the Turin professors Cesare Lombroso and Achille Loria. When Michels first visited Turin, he made the acquaintance of the famous psychiatrist and criminologist Lombroso, the pioneer of 'criminal anthropology', who sought to identify scientifically the biological preconditions of criminality. When Michels settled in Turin, he and his wife became close friends with the Lombroso family, and there is no doubt that, along with the economist Achille Loria, who strove to synthesize socialism with Darwinism, Lombroso was one of the intellectual leading lights of the pre-1914 Turin which Michels found so congenial.

Michels was introduced to Lombroso's methods as early as 1901, when Lombroso presented him with an offprint of his article 'On the shortness of the big toe in epileptics, criminals and idiots'.[7] In this article, which Michels retained in his papers, Lombroso sought exhaustively to test a colleague's hypothesis that there was a correlation between a short big toe, relative to the second, and criminality or mental abnormality. An examination of his collection of skeletons having

Felice, *Fascism: An Informal Introduction to Its Theory and Practice* (An Interview with Michael A. Ledeen), New Brunswick, NJ, 1976.

[5] See Fr. G., Review of A. Kirchhoff, *Mensch und Erde*, in *Politisch-Anthropologische Revue*, Vol.II, 6, 1903, p.532.

[6] Wolfhard Hammer, *Leben und Werk des Arztes und Sozialanthropologen Ludwig Woltmann*, Mainz, 1979 (=diss. der Johannes-Gutenberg-Universität Mainz), pp.18–19. One of the contestants was Ludwig Woltmann, who was unsuccessful. See Ludwig Woltmann, 'Die Preisrichter von Jena', *Politisch-Anthropologische Revue*, Jg.4, 1, April 1905, pp.48–51 for Woltmann's polemic against the judges' decision.

[7] Cesare Lombroso, 'Sulla cortezza dell'alluce negli epilettici, nei criminali e negli idioti', *Archivio di Psichiatria, Scienze Penali ed Antropologia criminale*, Vol.XXII, 4–5, 1901; offprint in Lombroso-Michels correspondence with dedication from Lombroso to Michels, ARM/FLE.

230 ROBERT MICHELS, SOCIALISM, AND MODERNITY

proven inconclusive, Lombroso examined the feet and measured the toes of 270 epileptics, a number of lunatics, and 399 thieves, prostitutes, and other offenders. (The confined populations of Turin must have become accustomed to unusual visitations from the distinguished professor of psychiatry.) The findings: male epileptics were twice as likely as 'normal' to have a short big toe, but this did not apply to women, for some reason; among criminals, 'there exists a difference, without doubt, but not to a very great extent'.[8]

Lombroso did not confine himself to charting the physiological (and physiognomic) peculiarities of the criminal classes: his scientific analysis also involved recourse to reified ethnic categories. For example, his analysis of the notorious murderer Alberto Olivo, in an article which Michels also received from the author, not only recorded his dysfunctional family background and a wealth of physiological data, as well as psychological observations, but also tried to draw conclusions from the mixed and apparently inherently volatile ethnic background of the killer. 'A noteworthy ethnic and morbid inheritance weighed on Olivo', Lombroso wrote. His father 'was of mixed Italian and Slavic origins, and with Spanish blood in his veins. His mother was Albanian crossed with Greek: clever, erotic, attractive, impulsive, subject to convulsions: died of cancer of the uterus at 38 years old.' Olivo therefore inherited a disposition to alcoholism and mental illness, on top of which 'the mixture of three races, Italian, Albanian, Greek and perhaps Spanish' also contributed to his criminal personality.[9] Lombroso partly attributed the persistence of backwardness in Italy's south to the racially mixed composition of the region's population.[10]

In his study of the history of the labour movement in Turin, Paolo Spriano argued that Lombroso's influence was pervasive among the circle of pro-socialist academics at the University of Turin in the early 1900s (a group of socialist intellectuals whose relationship with actual workers tended to be at a distance). This influence involved not only Lombroso's idealistic, humanitarian approach to socialism, and his positivistic approach to science, but also his tendency to biologistic thinking and reification of ethnic categories:

How many times do we find in the speeches and writings of the Torinese socialists the acceptance as a scientific 'fact' of the 'Latin' character of the Italian proletariat, especially that of the South, and this character being taken as an

---

[8] Lombroso, 'Sulla cortezza dell'alluce negli epilettici, nei criminali e negli idioti'.

[9] Cesare Lombroso, 'Il caso Olivo', *Archivio di Psichiatria, Medicina legale ed Antropologia criminale*, offprint (n.d.) in ARM/FLE, p.1 of offprint. Mary Gibson and Nicole Hahn Rafter write: 'Race is integrally woven into Lombroso's theory of atavism, which equates white men with civilization, and black, brown, and yellow men with "primitive" and "savage" societies.' Mary Gibson and Nicole Hahn Rafter, 'Editors' Introduction', to Cesare Lombroso, *Criminal Man*, Durham, NC, and London, 2006, p.17. On Lombroso, see also Mary Gibson, *Born to Crime: Cesare Lombroso and the Origins of Biological Criminology*, Westport, CN, and London, 2002; Delia Frigessi, *Cesare Lombroso*, Turin, 2003.

[10] Gibson and Rafter, 'Editors' Introduction', p.18.

ETHNICITY AND RACE   231

explanation of its anarchic and spontaneist excesses, and its alleged aversion to organization.[11]

Other scholars have referred to a 'medley of positivism and determinism, as in the case of sociologist Achille Loria', predominant in Italian socialist thought in the early 1900s.[12] This kind of thinking was no less prevalent when Michels arrived in Turin at the end of 1907, and became a colleague, associate, and friend of both Lombroso and Loria.

Michels addressed the issue of the relationship between Lombroso's thought and socialism in a review of a collection of Lombroso's essays on topical issues (*Il momento attuale*, 1904) for the left-Marxist newspaper the *Leipziger Volkszeitung*, Michels distinguished between an earlier Lombroso, whose work focused exclusively on physiological peculiarities of criminals and matters such as heredity and atavism, to the exclusion of social factors in the explanation of criminal behaviour, and who expressed anti-socialist political views, and a later Lombroso. The later Lombroso, influenced by the growth of the Italian socialist movement, his insights into the living conditions of Turin workers, and the intellectual contribution of his socialist student, Enrico Ferri, gravitated towards the Italian socialist party, becoming a representative of the party on the Turin city council in 1902, and subsequently making room for social factors in his writings on criminology. Michels stressed the evidence for Lombroso's democratic convictions in these essays, even if their composition pre-dated Lombroso's commitment to socialism: the essays showed Lombroso's opposition to militarism and his anti-clericalism, as well as showing scepticism about monarchism.[13]

Michels' acquaintance with Lombroso extended to his family. In an appreciation of Gina Lombroso-Ferrero's work on South America, Michels wrote, in terms that echoed Cesare Lombroso's negative judgements on race-mixing with backward elements:

---

[11] Paolo Spriano, *Storia di Torino operaio e socialista. Da De Amicis a Gramsci*, Turin, 1972, pp.46–7; cf. also Alain Goussot, 'Jaurès et les intellectuels italiens', in Madeleine Rebérioux and Gilles Candar, eds., *Jaurès et les Intellectuels*, Paris, 1994, pp.253–4.

[12] Ilaria Porciani and Mauro Moretti, 'The Polycentric Structure of Italian Historical Writing', in Stuart Macintyre et al., eds., *The Oxford History of Historical Writing*, Vol.4: *1800–1945*, Oxford and New York, 2011, p.235. See also Richard Bellamy, *Modern Italian Social Theory*, Stanford, CA, pp.59–60.

[13] Rob. [Robert] Michels, 'Cesare Lombroso als Politiker', *Leipziger Volkszeitung* (Feuilleton-Beilage), no.20, 25 January 1905. Michels had previously taken the feminist writer Adele Schreiber to task for asserting that the 'modern anthropological school' (i.e. of Lombroso) disregarded social factors in its theory of crime. Dr [Robert] Michels, Review of Adele Schreiber, *Kinderwelt und Prostitution*, *Ethische Kultur*, Jg.XII, 1, January 1904, p.7. See also Michels' review of Cesare Lombroso, *Il momento attuale* und *Problèmes du jour*, in *Archiv für Sozialwissenschaft und Sozialpolitik*, 29, 1909, pp.685–7, in which Michels highlights Lombroso's statement distancing himself from his earlier work which had linked revolutionaries to 'anthropologically inferior elements' (p.685). On Lombroso's sometimes conflicted relationship with socialism, see Frigessi, *Cesare Lombroso*, pp.262–71.

232   ROBERT MICHELS, SOCIALISM, AND MODERNITY

Of outstanding interest are the observations scattered through the work on Italian emigrants, who, as is well-known, carry out the function of bearers of culture in South America, and who in many places constitute the only healthy element of population in the midst of the not very numerous, and in part decadent, old Spanish and old Portuguese original white population, the mass of mixed-race people and the proletarian negroes and Indians, and who can therefore rightly be regarded as the yeast which South America will best make use of to shape its future, as it is already doing.[14]

As will be outlined below, Michels also engaged with, and translated, works by Lombroso's prominent students Enrico Ferri and Alfredo Niceforo, both of whom were exponents of 'social anthropology'. Moving outside socialist circles to conservative elite theory, Michels also took on some of the social biological assumptions underlying the work of Gaetano Mosca and Vilfredo Pareto, as he moved closer to their views on elites and oligarchy.[15]

The third major influence to which Michels was exposed in the field of racial theory was the journal *Politisch-Anthropologische Revue*, to which Michels became a contributor. Even bearing in mind Michels' promiscuity when it came to seeking outlets for his publications—a financial necessity for someone living by his pen (and attempting to support a family in a fashion befitting his social station as a future university professor), Michels' association with the journal deserves comment. The *Politisch-Anthropologische Revue* was founded in 1901/2 by the renegade Social Democrat Ludwig Woltmann.[16] Woltmann had (briefly) been on the revisionist wing of the Social Democratic Party and had been an exponent of a neo-Kantian 'ethical socialism'. By the time he started the *Politisch-Anthropologische Revue*, however, he had become alienated from the party, and, with the conspicuous exception of Michels, German Social Democrats kept their distance from the journal, which attracted a mix of German academic scholars interested in the interaction between racial factors and the new social sciences

---

[14] Robert Michels, Review of Gina Lombroso-Ferrero, *Nell'America Meridionale*, in *Archiv für Sozialwissenschaft und Sozialpolitik*, 31 (neue Folge), 1910, p.624.

[15] As pointed out decades ago by David Beetham, 'Michels and His Critics', *Archives Européennes de Sociologie*, Vol.22, 1981, p.83, although Beetham did not expand on this insight. Bellamy's reference to Michels as 'Mosca's pupil' is a little misleading in so far as Michels did not study under Mosca, and Mosca was one influence on Michels among others. Bellamy, *Modern Italian Social Theory*, p.135. However, Michels' correspondence with Mosca (a senior professor at Turin and a member of Italy's senate) is notably deferential and pays tribute to Mosca's intellectual importance. *Busta* Gaetano Mosca in Michels correspondence, ARM/FLE.

[16] On Woltmann, see the dissertation by Hammer, *Ludwig Woltmann*; Erhard Stölting, 'Die anthroposoziologische Schule. Gestalt und Zusammenhänge eines wissenschaftlichen Institutionalisierungsversuchs', in Carsten Klingemann, ed., *Rassenmythos und Sozialwissenschaften in Deutschland*, Opladen, 1987, pp.134–40; Marco Schütz, *Rassenideologien in der Sozialwissenschaft*, Berne, 1994, pp.191–225.

ETHNICITY AND RACE   233

and (increasingly) racial theorists and propagandists from the right-wing *völkisch* fringe.[17]

The fundamental basis of Woltmann's thought has been summed up in the sentence: 'The inequality of the human races is the driving force of world history'.[18] Among the races, according to Woltmann, the highest was the Nordic, which was the bearer of progress. In the programmatic introduction to the *Politisch-Anthropologische Revue*, Woltmann declared the pages of the journal independent of any philosophical doctrine or political party, but its tendency was clear enough in its declared goals: to promote theoretical knowledge of the 'natural doctrine of development' ('der natürlichen Entwickelungslehre'), relating to 'the causes and laws of organic change, adaptation, heredity, selection [*Auslese*], perfection, and degeneration, among plants and animals, as well as among humans'; the historical goal of studying the 'social and intellectual [*geistigen*] history of the human race from the point of view of organic natural history'; and the 'practical' goal, of promoting racial hygiene through a better understanding of the biological roots of contemporary social conflicts and concerns.[19] Woltmann himself wrote on recent developments in Darwinism, and the physical degeneration of the modern woman, in the first year of the journal. Other contributors in the journal's first year included Ludwig and Ladislaus Gumplowicz, the eugenicist Wilhelm Schallmayer (on natural and sexual selection among savage and highly cultured peoples),[20] and the doctor and social anthropologist Ludwig Wilser, to some extent Woltmann's mentor in racial theory (on selective human breeding, on a cultural history of racial instincts, and on Gobineau and his racial doctrine).[21] The founder of the National Social Party, Friedrich Naumann, contributed a short essay on the 'psychological natural preconditions of socialism' among the urban

---

[17] On neo-Kantian 'ethical socialism', see the anthology by Hans-Jörg Sandkühler and Rafael de la Vega, eds., *Marxismus und Ethik*, Frankfurt, 1974. On Woltmann's links with the Social Democratic Party, which seem to have ended some time after the 1899 Hannover party congress, see Eduard Bernstein, 'Ludwig Woltmanns Beziehungen zur Sozialdemokratie', *Politisch-Anthropologische Revue*, Vol.6, 1, April 1907, pp.45–53. On the divergence between Woltmann and the Social Democratic Marxist reception of Darwin, and Heinrich Cunow's critique of Woltmann, see Richard Saage, *Zwischen Darwin und Marx. Zur Rezeption der Evolutionstheorie in der deutschen und österreichischen Sozialdemokratie vor 1933/34*, Vienna, Cologne, Weimar, 2012, pp.121–9. Kevin Repp, *Reformers, Critics, and the Paths of German Modernity. Anti-Politics and the Search for Alternatives, 1890–1914*, Cambridge MA and London, 2000, p.302, comments that the *völkisch*-right contributors to the *Politisch-Anthropologische Revue* 'seem like strange allies for the Social Democrat Woltmann', but Woltmann was no longer a Social Democrat when he founded the journal.

[18] Hammer, *Ludwig Woltmann*, p.3.

[19] Ludwig Woltmann, 'Naturwissenschaft und Politik. Zur Einführung', *Politisch-Anthropologische Revue*, Vol.I, 1, 1902, pp.1–2.

[20] Hammer draws a distinction between Schallmayer's interest in eugenics, shared by Alfred Ploetz, and Woltmann's emphasis on racial inequality, which Schallmayer later rejected. See Hammer, *Ludwig Woltmann*, pp.4, 58.

[21] In 'Gobineau und seine Rassenlehre', *Politisch-Anthropologische Revue*, Jg.1, 8, 1902, pp.593–8, Wilser insisted on the 'healthy kernel' in, and richness of, Gobineau's thought, while taking issue with Gobineau's thesis of the Asian origins of the European '*Kulturvölker*'. Wilser and Woltmann endorsed Gobineau's notion of the higher racial value of the Nordic race.

234   ROBERT MICHELS, SOCIALISM, AND MODERNITY

masses (which, interestingly, anticipated themes of Michels' *Political Parties* of 1910/11).[22] Subsequently, the journal's contributors included such leading lights of *völkisch* ideology as the veteran anti-semitic publicist Theodor Fritsch, and the strident (indeed unhinged) proclaimer of Aryan supremacy, Jörg Lanz von Liebenfels,[23] along with a motley collection of skull-measurers and racial theorists, but also established scholars like the biologist Hans Driesch and Cesare Lombroso, the latter writing on the 'influence of race and freedom on genius' (albeit in response to a piece by Woltmann with which he disagreed).[24]

Michels' association with the *Politisch-Anthropologische Revue* has not received the attention it deserves, partly because the standard Michels bibliographies omit a number of his contributions to the journal, but partly because of the tendency of most writers on Michels (with some notable exceptions) to concentrate on his writings on elites and oligarchies in political parties and organizations to the exclusion of other elements in his thought.

As noted in Chapter 7, Michels' first contribution to the *Politisch-Anthropologische Revue*, in December 1902, dealt with a topic that was apparently more political in nature than biological: the situation of the Italian minorities, *Italia irredenta*, in the Habsburg Empire.[25] Michels argued that the approximately 800,000 Italians in the Tyrol, Friuli, Trieste, Istria, and Dalmatia were being treated by Habsburg officialdom in a manner most unworthy of such a great 'Kulturnation'. This, and historical memories of national independence in the past, nourished discontent with Habsburg rule. Italians felt drawn to the Italian nation by 'culture, race, outlook on life and language'.[26] 'Race' was thus identified as one factor of political significance, albeit coming after culture, and Michels does not attempt to set up a hierarchy of causal factors here. He does, however, approvingly quote the Spanish

---

[22] Friedrich Naumann, 'Die psychologischen Naturbedingungen des Sozialismus', *Politsch-Anthropologische Revue*, Vol.I, no.7, 1902, pp.564–71.

[23] J. Lanz-Liebenfels, 'Die Urgeschichte der Künste', *Politisch-Anthropologische Revue*, Vol.2, 2, 1903, pp.134–56. From the article's conclusions: '1. For anthropology the not at all surprising fact that the white race of the Aryans was mixed in the Mediterranean basin with the ape-like pygmy race, which originated in the African ape-centre, while towards the East it was most probably crossed with a similar pithecoid race advancing from the Sunda islands, on this see Dubois' Pithecanthropus of Java and the interesting essay of Szombathy. The small figure of the eurafrican and mongoloid race, its physical and mental characteristics, are explained by this fact, just as the phenomena of *Missgeburten* and embryonic development also of Aryan children. *Negroes and Mongols are*—in short—*the product of Aryan sodomy....*The Aryan has raised up humanity.... *To the Aryan belongs the earth!* (Rigveda IV]'; pp.152–3, 154, emphasis in original. It is not suggested that Michels was influenced by Lanz-Liebenfels, but the latter's writing illustrates how far into the racist far right the constituency of the *Politisch-Anthropologische Revue* extended.

[24] Cesare Lombroso, 'Der Einfluss von Rasse und Freiheit auf das Genie', *Politisch-Anthropologische Revue*, Vol.2, 12, March 1904, pp.948–50 (taking issue with Woltmann's claim that genius was a specifically Germanic phenomenon, arguing instead that it was a product of degeneration, and often of racial mixing, but also needed freedom to manifest itself). Unsurprisingly, there was a difference between German and Italian race theorists on the respective merits of the Germanic and Latin 'races'.

[25] Dr Robert Michels, 'Das unerlöste Italien in Österreich', *Politisch-Anthropologische Revue*, Jg.1, 9, December 1902, pp.716–24.

[26] Michels, 'Das unerlöste Italien in Österreich', p.717.

phrase 'la Musica de la sangre' ('music of the blood') to characterize the 'feeling of national belonging'.[27]

In the second year of the *Politisch-Anthropologische Revue*, Michels contributed a review of Pio Viazzi, *La lotta di sesso* ('the battle of the sexes').[28] Michels' critique of this misogynistic tract has already been discussed in Chapter 5. To some extent, Michels could be seen as going against the grain of the *Politisch-Anthropologische Revue*: both in defending the national claims of Italians against the Teutomane and Pan-German tenor of many of the journal's contributors (Michels emphasized the vitality of Italian intellectual life, as if to challenge the frequent claims of the decadence of the Latin peoples made by other contributors to Woltmann's *Revue*),[29] and in criticizing a misogynist tract in a journal whose contributors were fond of scientifically demonstrating the intellectual inferiority of women. Apart from a reference to Lombroso (on the highly developed feelings of modesty among the African Dinka people), Michels' review hardly engages with racial theory, despite the character of the journal being now well-established towards the end of its second year. However, Michels continued to associate himself with the *Politisch-Anthropologische Revue*.

In April 1904, an article by Michels on 'The Cultural Value of England in the Present' appeared in the *Revue*.[30] The article shows Michels in an impressionistic, essayistic mode, generalizing about national character. Michels cited the French historian Gabriel Monod on the global cultural importance of England, and cited Karl Marx, 'who knew more about prophesying than most', as describing England as the 'classical country of the capitalist mode of production', and therefore as the country in which the rest of Europe could glimpse its future.[31] However, Michels went on to argue, since Monod and Marx had formulated their views of England, 'the most elementary functioning of England's national character, at least in certain classes, has undergone such rapid further development, that the views of Marx and Monod on the state and value of English culture requite a careful new analysis and detailed revision'.[32] After reviewing some of the evidence for the 'cultural worth' of English civilization—the philanthropic influence that had supported emancipatory anti-slavery and national independence movements around the world (despite continuing oppression in Ireland), the constitutional guarantees of freedoms, and a 'long chain of social legislation'—Michels found that

---

[27] Michels, 'Das unerlöste Italien in Österreich', p.719.

[28] Dr Robert Michels, Review of Pio Viazzi, *La lotta di sesso*, in *Politisch-Anthropologische Revue*, Jg.2, 6, September 1903, pp.530–2.

[29] Michels, Review of Pio Viazzi, *La lotta di sesso*, p.530.

[30] Dr Robert Michels, 'Englands gegenwärtiger Kulturwert', *Politisch-Anthropologische Revue*, Jg.3, 1, April 1904, pp.53–63. Note that the same issue of the journal included an article by Ludwig Woltmann on 'Gobineau's Forerunners', W. Wilser on 'Indo-Germanic Problems', V. Haecker, 'Descent Theory and Bastardism', etc.

[31] Michels, 'Englands gegenwärtiger Kulturwert', pp.53–4.

[32] Michels, 'Englands gegenwärtiger Kulturwert', p.54.

236 ROBERT MICHELS, SOCIALISM, AND MODERNITY

England had become subject to crass 'racial egoism'(*Rassenegoismus*), expressed in militarism and jingoism, which had even affected the English working class.[33]

Considering that Michels was still politically aligned with the Marxist left of the German Social Democratic Party, two things are striking in this article: one is the readiness with which he lumps together Karl Marx's economic analysis of the development of capitalism in Britain as foreshadowing economic developments elsewhere in Europe and the world with Monod's entirely subjective assessment of the moral and cultural worth of English civilization. No less noteworthy was the way in which Michels, who might still be considered nominally a Marxist within Social Democratic circles, casually overturned Marx's economic analysis on the basis of his own subjective analysis of 'national character' as a factor with historical causal power of its own. Michels argued, plausibly enough, that industrial development had led to imperialism, which had in turn led to changes in the British national character. However, he did not close the circle of his argumentation by arguing that these changes in national character in turn had an impact on the development of the productive forces and relations of production which were the basis of Marx's analysis. Even though Michels ends his argument by suggesting that only a reawakening of the (now largely apolitical) English proletariat could restore 'the necessary moral equilibrium' that England 'needs for the regaining of its old cultural value',[34] his argument on the abstract and subjective plane of national character and cultural values departed far from Marx.

In April 1907, Michels was one of the many contributors and people associated with the *Politisch-Anthropologische Revue* to contribute a short tribute to Woltmann after his death on 30 January 1907 while swimming off the Riviera. This gave Michels an opportunity to clarify his relationship with the journal and the ideas it represented:

I openly confess that I was closer to the first period of scientific work of our scholar, too soon deceased, let us call it the Marxist-Darwinist or rather the social darwinistic period, than his second. And I confess equally frankly, that as much as Woltmann has achieved much of significance through his 'Political Anthropology', and as notable as its results doubtless are, its methods and aims seem to carry grave risks. Namely, and I am convinced that this is despite the purely scientific and dispassionate intentions of its proponents, through the essential emphasis of the idea of race in general and the theories of the predominance of the Nordic-Germanic racial elements in the upper strata of society and the intellectual leaders of all other cultured nations in particular, chauvinism, the mortal enemy of all true culture, has received new nourishment, and the world of scholarship abroad has in part been filled with mistrust. However, as

---

[33] Michels, 'Englands gegenwärtiger Kulturwert', pp.55ff.
[34] Michels, 'Englands gegenwärtiger Kulturwert', p.63.

already stated, this fact cannot in any way diminish the scientific value of the works of Woltmann, which consists above all in following in the footsteps of Gobineau and in working against the underestimation of the racial question, which is increasingly prevalent today in this era of idolatry of the state (*Statolatrie*).

I have unfortunately not been personally acquainted with Woltmann. As far as I have come to learn of him, I have been given the image of a man of a proud feeling of independence, which is a rarity in our epoch of organizational obsessions (*unserer organisationslüsternen Zeitepoche*), with no ambition but for the laurels that grew of their own accord on the tree of science, and who went his own way without regard for the caste spirit of academe. Therefore all who are dedicated to science, especially among the inhabitants of the German Reich, will have to doubly mourn the loss of such a man so early.[35]

Michels, as a practising cosmopolitan, who had been inoculated as a boy in Cologne against Borussified *Reichsdeutsch* chauvinism, could never identify with the Pan-German and German hyper-nationalism that frequently appeared in the *Politisch-Anthropologische Revue*. Nor could Michels, who took such pride in his affinity by descent and cultural preference with the Latin peoples, accept the notion of the primacy of the Nordic race as the essential bearer of all culture.[36] However, he explicitly praised Woltmann for further developing the racial theories of Gobineau, especially in an age in which the 'racial question' was so widely 'underestimated'. Michels saw not only Woltmann's personal example, as an independent scholar who turned his back on both academy and party to pursue his version of the truth, but also quite explicitly his racial ideas as an antidote to 'Statolatrie', the cult of the state, and to our 'epoch of organizational obsessions'.

That Michels did not regard racial biology as a sideline separate from his interests both in social science and in socialist politics, as early as 1904, is indicated by his review of a bibliographic yearbook on economics and social science edited by the Hungarian Ervin Szabò, in which he found fault with the omission of the *Politisch-Anthropologische Revue* from the otherwise quite comprehensive

---

[35] Robert Michels, contribution to 'Gedenkworte' for Ludwig Woltmann, *Politisch-Anthropologische Revue*, Vol.6, 1, April 1907, pp.84–5.

[36] Typically, contributors to the *Politisch-Anthropologische Revue* placed the Latin races below the Germanic, e.g. Dr Curt Bühring, 'Niedergang und Erwachen der lateinischen Rassen', *Politisch-Anthropologische Revue*, Vol.2, 2, 1903, pp.169–70: for Bühring (claiming Gobineau as an authority) the decline of the Latin states could be traced to the exhaustion of the thin active stratum of Germanic elements in these peoples: 'Whatever Italy and France achieve today, is still an act of Germanic racial blood' (p.170). Ludwig Woltmann himself claimed that most of Italy's major creative literary figures in modern times were of Germanic descent. Ludwig Woltmann, 'Die Herkunft der neueren Dichter Italiens', *Politisch-Anthropologische Revue*, Vol.4, 2, May 1905, pp.89–90. See also Ludwig Woltmann, *Die Germanen und die Renaissance in Italien*, Leipzig, 1905; Ludwig Woltmann, *Die Germanen in Frankreich*, Jena, 1907, discussed in Hammer, *Ludwig Woltmann*, pp.103–12.

238   ROBERT MICHELS, SOCIALISM, AND MODERNITY

reference work, at the same time as he noted the omission of the liberal reformist *Ethische Kultur* and the Italian journals *Rivista Popolare* and *Socialismo*.[37]

Michels' borrowings from race theory were not confined to his links with the *Politisch-Anthropologische Revue*. Michels made frequent generalizations about 'national (or ethnic) character' (*Volkscharakter*). In the socialist women's newspaper *Die Gleichheit*, he acknowledged that any generalization of a people numbering in the millions (or of a sex, for that matter) was fraught with difficulty. Nonetheless, he argued that it was still possible to identify a few salient characteristics of Italian women, provided one kept in mind the fact that there would always be exceptions to the rule. He regarded the characteristics of Italian women as partly the result of climate, partly of the history of the country.[38] The Italian, both male and female, was 'far more natural and simpler than the German woman'. Italian women were less prone to vanity over their social status. Italian men were not as prone as Germans to making women feel their subordinate position, with the result that Italian feminists were never 'anti-male' (unlike some German feminists, apparently). Another result of the greater naturalness of Italian women was, according to Michels, a greater readiness to defend themselves physically against assault compared with German women.[39] Michels expanded on his generalizations on Italian women in *Die Frau* in 1904, where he also referred to the awakening of the women's labour movement in Italy, stating that only 'organization', by opposing the worst excesses of exploitation of women's labour, had been able to 'avoid the complete degeneration of the race'.[40] Elsewhere, Michels employed racialist arguments to explain the peculiar difficulties that socialism encountered in Sicily, using terms strongly reminiscent of Lombroso's view on Sicilians' mixed 'racial' origins. The 'ethnic character' ('Volkscharakter') of the Sicilians, with its strong 'mixture with Oriental elements', displayed a tendency to 'childish-religious superstition and reverence for authority', that northern Italian socialists found alien. Michels considered it understandable, however, that 'the socialist idea, in accordance with different ethnic characteristics, might naturally realize itself in different ways in different races'.[41] In another article, Michels drew

[37] Roberto Michels, Review of Jules Mandellò, *Bibliographia economica universalis*. Repertoire bibliographique annuel des travaux rel. aux sciences économiques et sociales, 1ère année 1902, ed. Ervin Szabò, Brussels, 1903, in *La Riforma Sociale*, Anno XI, second series, Vol.XIV, no.3, 15 March 1904, p.256.

[38] Dr Robert Michels, 'Die Frauenbewegung in Italien', *Die Gleichheit*, Jg.12, no.17, 13 August 1902, p.130.

[39] Michels, 'Die Frauenbewegung in Italien'.

[40] Dr Robert Michels, 'Die italienische Frau in den camere di lavoro', *Die Frau*, Jg.11, Heft 6, März 1904, p.372.

[41] Dr Robert Michels, 'Rückblick auf die Geschichte der proletarischen Frauenbewegung in Italien', *Die Gleichheit*, no.8, 8 April 1903, p.59.

ETHNICITY AND RACE   239

a sharp contrast between the 'Graeco-Arabic Palermitans' and the 'Celto-Roman Torinese' as an explanation for the differences in their political behaviour.[42]

Michels touched on questions of race and ethnic identity in an article on Jewish ethnic identity and the extent of public respect given to Jews in April 1903. This was Michels' only article dedicated to the so-called 'Jewish question' and appeared in the *Jüdische Rundschau*, the official newspaper of the Zionist Union for Germany (Zionistische Vereinigung für Deutschland). Michels began by castigating those Jews who, for their own egotistical reasons, made a vain attempt to deny their Jewish ancestry and tried to blend into the Christian population. Citing the Zionist journalist and well-known popular author Max Nordau (author of the contemporary bestseller *Degeneration*), Michels denounced such attempts as doomed to fail, because of the impossibility of 'refugees from Israel' losing what Nordau called their 'distinctive physiognomy'. Jews who denied their membership of their tribe were destined to retain their 'innate particular tribal characteristics'. 'Ethnic-anthropological' metamorphoses did not happen overnight, and not even over a couple of generations. Michels drew an analogy between the ethnological differences between Jews and Gentiles, and the innate differences between men and women. In both cases, differences were innate and inescapable, but their collective value in both cases was the same. They were entitled to equal social esteem, even if their qualities resided in differing fields of moral existence of intellectual capacity.[43]

The Jews' right to equal social esteem was potentially undermined by those Jews who sought vainly to escape their Jewish heritage, as Michels put it in colourful terms:

Therefore even the person of Jewish descent can not only damn his race by word and deed—as cheap and humanly low as that is—but also deny it, as much as he will. Just as he early circumcised his children, he can now have his own name cut back, in order to arouse the ridiculous impression that he might have been born in the middle of the Teutoburg Forest. None of this will enable him to reduce the distinguishing signs of his race by a jot. And not only outwardly![44]

---

[42] Robert Michels, 'Ein Volksaufstand für einen diebischen Minister', *Volksstimme* (Frankfurt/M.), no.170, 24 July 1907, quoted in Genett, *Der Fremde im Kriege*, p.176. Similarly, Dr Robert Michels, 'Der italienische Sozialismus', *Aus der Waffenkammer des Sozialismus* (ed. *Volksstimme*, Frankfurt a.M.), Vol.9, July–December 1907, p.19, stresses the importance of the mixed racial composition of Sicily and southern Italy for understanding the course of the development of the socialist movement there. See also Dr Robert Michels, 'Ein Blick in den "Zukunftsstaat"' [II], *Mitteldeutsche Sonntags-Zeitung*, no.11, 15 March 1903, although at this time Michels stressed common socialist ideals prevailing over the racial differences.

[43] Dr Robert Michels, 'Judentum und öffentliche Achtung', *Jüdische Rundschau*, Jg.8, no.17, 24 April 1903, pp.151–3, here p.151.

[44] Michels, 'Judentum und öffentliche Achtung'.

240 ROBERT MICHELS, SOCIALISM, AND MODERNITY

Michels goes on to cite the characteristics of 'the essential nature of Semitism' set out in Guglielmo Ferrero's *L'Europa giovane* ('young Europe').[45] These characteristics are mostly positive: 'the ethical yearning to improve the world, the revolutionary impulse, the tendency to criticism, the selfless readiness for sacrifice for higher ideals', and finally, a peculiar kind of pessimism, that stood in contrast to some of the other features listed. These characteristics also helped to explain, as Michels, following Ferrero, outlined, why it was so hard for Jews to shed the racial distinctiveness that they had developed over a couple of millenia, without any 'mixture of blood' diluting this distinctiveness.[46] Michels added his own praise of the Jews, who had 'performed the highest cultural work' at a time when Germanic and Celtic people were still practising human sacrifice. Michels cited a long list of Jewish luminaries who had contributed to the progress of humanity: Spinoza, Marx, Lassalle, Bernstein, Lombroso, Heine (in that order), and several others.[47]

For Michels, those who acted as 'deserters' from their Jewish heritage, fully deserved the social contempt they encountered, when people continued to use the word 'Jew' in a derogatory way behind their back. While Michels listed a number of motives behind contemporary anti-semitism, he ventured to suggest that the force of contemporary anti-semitism would not have been as great if 'the great majority of the Jews had not themselves given it excellent nourishment. And this nourishment is: a lack of self-consciousness'. Michels indicated that he personally had no respect for baptized Jews (this may have been linked to Michels' aggressively secular outlook, which discounted the possibility of sincere conversions). People who set out 'to conceal what they are and to seem to be, what they are not', deserved no respect, in Michels' view. Such Jews contributed to anti-semitism themselves, and those anti-semites who were still decent people of finer feelings (Michels cited the Jewish writer Mathias Acher as an authority for the claim that such people existed among anti-semites) would not continue to cling to their prejudices if more Jews expressed self-respect as far as their ethnic heritage was concerned. Only when Jews proudly identified with their own national heritage and the contributions of great Jewish minds to culture and progress, only then would anti-semitism finally collapse into 'an extract of lunacy and delinquency'. Only a strengthening of Jewish national consciousness among Jews (and by 'national', Michels clearly means 'ethnic' and 'racial', as he does not refer to the Zionist homeland project) would lead to the overcoming of anti-semitism.[48]

---

[45] Cited as *L'Italia giovane* in Michels, 'Judentum und öffentliche Achtung', p.151, but correctly as *L'Europa giovane* in the note on p.152.

[46] Michels, 'Judentum und öffentliche Achtung', pp.151–2. Michels returned to Ferrero's positive characterization of Jews a few years later in Robert Michels, 'Proletariat und Bourgeoisie in der sozialistischen Bewegung Italiens', *Archiv für Sozialwissenschaft und Sozialpolitik*, 22 1906, p.111.

[47] Michels, 'Judentum und öffentliche Achtung', p.152.

[48] Michels, 'Judentum und öffentliche Achtung', p.153.

ETHNICITY AND RACE   241

Michels' essay makes troubling reading in a couple of respects: the ready assumption of an essential Jewish racial identity, and the claim that Jews (and their collective low self-esteem) were partly to blame for anti-semitism. That Michels places an overwhelmingly positive valuation on Jewish racial characteristics does not detract from the racial essentialism of his premisses. For the newspaper of the Zionist federation, the most welcome aspect of Michels' article, of course, was the polemic against the efforts of many German Jews to assimilate into Gentile society, efforts which Michels did not hesitate to depict as both futile (because of the impossibility of effacing racial characteristics) and essentially dishonourable.

In another essay published in 1903, Michels gave a brief, and dismissive, description of the anti-semitic parties in Germany as part of a survey of German politics in relation to the 1903 elections for the Italian review *La Riforma Sociale*. Michels' description of the anti-semitic parties as fragmented, mutually hostile, and claiming to represent the petite bourgeoisie, while in fact representing no-one, was accurate enough, and hardly surprising, coming from someone then in the Social Democratic Party. What is somewhat more surprising, indeed bizarre and inexplicable, is his assertion that nearly all the anti-semitic Reichstag deputies 'wage a race war against the Jews and...let themselves get paid lavish salaries by the latter. These are facts, which have been demonstrated a thousand times.'[49] Michels did, however, clearly voice his distaste for the anti-semites, with their 'speculation on the most bestial instincts of men, arousing race hatred'.[50]

In his 1906 lecture on 'Patriotism and Ethics', Michels used the example of Jewish minorities to argue against an exclusively racial definition of nationality, but not because racial differences did not exist. Jews were 'undoubtedly to be regarded as members of a different ethnological race from us', but should not be excluded from the nation, 'regardless of whether they are of the Mosaic faith or have been "Germanized" through baptism'. A strict racial definition of the nation would exclude Jews, as 'Semitic' German Jews were racially more closely related to French Jews than to other Germans. Germany was too racially heterogeneous for a definition of nationality based on 'blood' or 'race' to be viable, considering the presence of Jews, descendants of Huguenots, Danes, Poles, etc. (He even referred to the mixed descent of Germany's royal houses—even the Kaiser might have to fight on the side of the English in wartime if 'blood' descent was decisive.)[51] At this time, Michels still endorsed Marx's view that economics was a

---

[49] Dott. Roberto [Robert] Michels, 'Psicologia e statistica delle elezioni generali politiche in Germania (Giugno 1903)', *La Riforma Sociale*, Fasc.7, Anno X, vol.XIII, seconda serie, 15 July 1903, pp.541–67, quotation on p.13 of offprint.
[50] Michels, 'Psicologia e statistica delle elezioni generali politiche in Germania', p.19 of offprint.
[51] Dr Robert Michels, *Patriotismus und Ethik. Eine kritische Skizze*, Leipzig, 1906, p.14.

242   ROBERT MICHELS, SOCIALISM, AND MODERNITY

more important determinant of identity than race, but he still treated biological race as a real factor.[52]

Michels' combination of normative disapproval of anti-semitism and persistent essentialist views of Jewish racial identity is also apparent in his first substantial academic treatment of the German Social Democratic Party in the *Archiv für Sozialwissenschaft und Sozialpolitik* in 1906:

> The Jew finds himself disadvantaged in his career, he is as good as excluded from the judiciary, the officer corps, or government service. And yet an old and justi-fied feeling of moral outrage against the wrong done to their tribe lives on amongst the Jews [*im Judentum*]. Given the degree of idealism that inspires this race, governed by extremes as it is, this feeling of injustice is converted into an abhorrence of all injustice and is raised to the height of a revolutionary urge for sweeping improvement of the world. For the rest, the internationalism that is entirely innate in the logical minds of the Jews, which leads them to overcome with ease the obstacle of the reproach of Social Democracy's 'unpatriotic' nature.[53]

In the same article, Michels complained of the way in which the anti-semitic par-ties appealed to 'barbaric prejudices': 'The anti-semites of course try to exploit the barbaric racial prejudices, which are still rooted in our popular masses, by accus-ing *every* Social Democratic election candidate, with a name that could even half be construed as having a Semitic origin, of being Jewish—David, Michels, even Auer'.[54] Interestingly, in the same essay, Michels referred to the internal differen-tiation within the working-class base of Social Democracy, citing not only type of work, and differing wage levels, but also 'differences in the mixture of blood and of climate'.[55] In 1909, Michels referred to Jews as a race, and even suggested that, despite being dispersed among different states (and being unable to constitute a nation of their own), they might well be the only pure race in Europe.[56] In the same essay, he considered the question of whether the particular adaptability of the German bourgeoisie was partly due to the presence of gifted Jews in key sec-tors of the economy, as this was also a Jewish characteristic, before deciding that

---

[52] Michels, *Patriotismus und Ethik*, p.20. See also Michels' review of Alfonso Asturaro, *Il material-ismo storico e la sociologia generale*, in *Kritische Blätter für die gesamten Sozialwissenschaften*, Jg.II, 2, February 1906, pp.70–1.

[53] Robert Michels, 'Die deutsche Sozialdemokratie', *Archiv für Sozialwissenschaft und Sozialpolitik*, 23, 1906, p.520.

[54] Michels, 'Die deutsche Sozialdemokratie', p.519n69.

[55] Michels, 'Die deutsche Sozialdemokratie', p.539.

[56] Robert Michels, 'Zur Psychologie der Bourgeoisie in den verschiedenen nationalen Verbänden', *Monatsschrift für Soziologie*, Jg.1, July 1909, pp.469.

ETHNICITY AND RACE   243

the evidence for the Jewish influence on the character of the German bourgeoisie was inconclusive.[57]

As noted in Chapter 6, Michels carried his discussion of the role of Jews in Social Democracy over into his main work on *Political Parties*, where he devoted a section to the role of Jewish intellectuals in the party, and the party's indebtedness to Jewish intellectuals who were drawn to socialism by their experience of social discrimination, and in part by their 'innate' internationalism.[58]

Michels regarded racial differences as real and significant, even if in his socialist phase he tended to give primacy to economic factors and class, and sought to reconcile this belief in racial difference with internationalism. In 1904, writing on the International Socialist Congress in Amsterdam, Michels wrote that: 'The international socialists by no means seek to artificially destroy the existing national racial differences'.[59] Frontiers between countries might be the 'arbitrary products of diplomacy', but differences in language and race were real and natural, even if Michels stressed that '*these natural racial differences do not have to lead to mutual hatred and murderous bloodshed*'.[60]

In an article in *Ethische Kultur*, Michels argued that national differences were real, and the product of racial characteristics, among other factors. Some conventional forms of patriotism had evoked a reaction among many who went to the opposite extreme: an abstract internationalism, that denied the reality of the nation as a product of 'racial psychology, climate and historical conditions'. This denial of the nation was no less problematical, as the nation was a 'vital factor in cultural development', and an expression of a 'deep need, which the broadest masses feel in their heart of hearts'.[61] Michels advocated the reconciliation of cosmopolitanism and patriotism in 'national and social internationalism'. This commenced with the acknowledgement of 'the influence of race, climate, as well as other economic, historical, moral and intellectual coefficients' in the production of real differences between peoples, constituting different 'popular physiognomies'.[62] Michels' acceptance of the idea that national differences existed is reflected in his negative comments on the German national character; for example, his critique in *Le Mouvement Socialiste* of the tendency of the German

[57]   Michels, 'Zur Psychologie der Bourgeoisie in den verschiedenen nationalen Verbänden', August–September 1909, pp.576–8.

[58]   Robert Michels, *Zur Soziologie des Parteiwesens in der modernen Demokratie*, Leipzig, 1911, pp.249–50.

[59]   Robert Michels, 'Der Internationalismus der Arbeiterschaft', *Ethische Kultur*, Jg.12, no.15, 1 August 1904, p.113. Michels does, however, refer to differences in climate as the basis for differences in dietary habits between, for example, Italy and Germany.

[60]   Michels, 'Der Internationalismus der Arbeiterschaft'; emphasis in original. For a similar argument, see Robert Michels, 'Le prochain congrès socialiste international', *Le Mouvement Socialiste*, no.188, July 1907, pp.38–46.

[61]   Robert Michels, 'Die Formen des Patriotismus', *Ethische Kultur*, Jg.XIII, 4, 15 February 1905, p.27.

[62]   Michels, 'Die Formen des Patriotismus', pp.27–8.

244 ROBERT MICHELS, SOCIALISM, AND MODERNITY

Social Democratic Party towards passivity in the face of threats from the German state gave a number of possible reasons for the phenomenon: political, historical, and 'racial'—the passive, slow, and ponderous German national character.[63] Elsewhere, this time in an article published in Italy, Michels referred to 'the subordinate, docile and authoritarian nature of the Teutonic tribe. The average German feels a profound need to venerate, admire, prostrate himself, allow himself to be led by somebody.' In Italy, on the other hand, given the innate good sense and democratic sentiments of the Italian people, a ruler like Kaiser Wilhelm II would not last a fortnight. And, as already noted in Chapter 5, Michels believed that 'English girls are less able to withstand the rigours of the prostitute's profession' (than Frenchwomen or Germans).[64]

Writing for the readership of *Ethische Kultur* in late 1905, Michels explicitly rejected the idea that one could generalize about 'Germanic' or 'Latin' (*romanisch*) peoples.[65] However, Arthur Mitzman is too categorical in describing this article as a rejection of 'the silliness of the distinction between "*Romanen*" and "*Germanen*"' and of racial distinctions more generally, especially when this article is read in the context of Michels' other utterances about race. Michels did *not* reject the notion that race was a historically relevant factor, but argued that such supra-national collectivities were simply too large and too historically and culturally diverse to be the subject of generalizations: even within a nation, there were significant cultural differences between regions.[66] Michels did hedge a little, insisting that his comments were necessarily tentative and touched only on the surface of these issues, given the limits of space. The main aim of his article was to criticize German nationalist writers and historians who portrayed the Germanic peoples as the repository of all virtues. Not only was this too sweeping a generalization, it was mistaken to impute moral virtue to one people rather than another. Michels also pointed to the emergence of cross-national solidarity among the workers of 'Kulturländer', so that French and German workers were coming to see themselves as having more in common with each other than with compatriots from different classes. It was therefore all the more important to seek to avert a future war between Germany and France, which would be a crime.[67] Michels was happy enough to make generalizations about the innate national character of Italians and Germans to the advantage of the former, however, as can be seen in

---

[63] Robert Michels, 'Les dangers du parti socialiste allemande', *Le Mouvement Socialiste*, no.144, 1 December 1904, p.199. See also Robert Michels, 'La solidarité sociale en Allemagne', *Annales de l'Institut International de Sociologie*, Vol.XII, 1910, p.16 (of offprint).

[64] Dr Robert Michels, 'Die Dirne als "alte Jungfer" des Proletariats und die Prostitution', *Mutterschutz*, Jg.1, 2, 1905, p.64.

[65] Dr Robert Michels, 'Entwickelung und Rasse', *Ethische Kultur*, Jg.XIII, 20, 15 October 1905, pp.155–7; 21, 1 November 1905, pp.163–4.

[66] Arthur Mitzman, *Sociology and Estrangement: Three Sociologists in Imperial Germany*, New York, 1973, pp.292–3.

[67] Michels, 'Entwickelung und Rasse', p.164.

ETHNICITY AND RACE   245

his comment that 'Certainly the Italian peasant possesses a moral strength unknown to the peasants of Germany'.[68]

Michels even partly attributed the differences between the ideological strands in early Italian socialism to the 'racial' character of their founders. Giuseppe Mazzini, Mikhail Bakunin, and Benoît Malon represented very different human types: 'to begin with, in their national-racial character [*Schon völkisch*]....The difference in origins, race, social standing and temperament corresponded to the variety of their socialist views'. Bakunin, for example, was characterized by the combination of 'half-barbaric Russian prince' and 'sharp-edged disciple of Hegel'.[69] In the 1909 Italian book version, Michels commented on Marx's brutality as a polemicist and cited Alexander Herzen's opinion that this was due to 'an innate vice in the German race'.[70] Not surprisingly, this critical comment about the German race did not appear in the original *Archiv* publication. The *Archiv* article ended with an unusual (for Michels) note of German national pride, noting that the penetration of Marxism into Italian thought was a case of 'Germania docet' (possibly a genuflection to the national sensibilities of the *Archiv* and its co-editors Weber and Sombart).[71] However, in the Italian book version, Michels went on to add:

> that is, if one can ever call by the name of German science doctrines of a man who was of *Jewish-Semitic* blood (*di sangue **ebreo-semita***); who was born, grew up and became a man and a scholar in that environment between French and German which is the *Rhineland*; who lived more than half his life in *England*; who took a large part of his concepts from the French socialist school, and who was, in the final account, at least in theory, as steeped in internationalism as ever any other man of science before or after him.[72]

Michels applied a similar analysis to his friend Werner Sombart, in a profile for an Italian journal, attributing Sombart's personal characteristics to his mixed racial heritage ('due razze incrociate'), due to his family's part-French Huguenot

---

[68] Roberto Michels, *Il proletariato e la borghesia nel movimento socialista italiano*, Turin, 1908 (reprint New York, 1975), p.187. This comment did not appear in the original German version published in the *Archiv für Sozialwissenschaft und Sozialpolitik*. Note also the extended comparison of the psychology of the Italian and German bourgeoisie on pp.284–322, which credits Italians with more naturalness, a finer aesthetic sense, and a more democratic temper than Germans (also absent in the *Archiv* version). See also Michels' Review of Napoleone Colajonni, *Latini e Anglo-Sassoni*, in *Kritische Blätter für die gesamten Sozialwissenschaften*, Jg.II, 7, July 1906, pp.327–9, which endorses Colajonni's defence of Latins such as the Italians against Woltmann's exaggerated claims for the superiority of the Germanic peoples.

[69] Robert Michels, 'Historisch-kritische Einführung in die Geschichte des Marxismus in Italien', *Archiv für Sozialwissenschaft und Sozialpolitik*, 24, 1907, p.195. In the Italian book version (Roberto Michels, *Storia del marxismo in Italia*, Rome,1909, p.22), Michels uses the word 'razza' for *völkisch*.

[70] Michels, *Storia del marxismo in Italia*, p.22n.

[71] Michels, 'Historisch-kritische Einführung in die Geschichte des Marxismus in Italien', p.258.

[72] Michels, *Storia del marxismo in Italia*, p.159.

246   ROBERT MICHELS, SOCIALISM, AND MODERNITY

heritage: French in his 'vivacity of spirit', stylistic elegance, fine artistic sensibilities, and his ease in adapting himself to different environments; and 'most German' in his precise scientific method and the universality of his knowledge. Sombart had also benefitted greatly from spending a good deal of time in Italy, and had nearly become 'Italianized'.[73] The combination of French and German heritage and life in Italy were of course characteristics Sombart shared with Michels himself.

By 1908, Michels was publishing principally in 'bourgeois', non-socialist journals, and at around the same time he was willing to reverse his earlier priority of economic factors vis-à-vis racial factors and national characters. Now, Michels wrote: 'Political economy is a highly potent factor in the history of transformations of human life, but it would be pushing historical materialism to the absurd if one tried to deny that the national character of a people could not resist, up to a certain point, that same economic factor.'[74] At this time, Michels started to express sympathy for liberal advocates of Italian imperialism, such as Luigi Einaudi, whose 'large-scale capitalist and democratic spirit' he viewed as an expression of Italy's innate national vitality and regeneration, and of the 'ideal of the future of the Italian race.'[75]

Michels also engaged with the work of the Italian 'social anthropology' school, translating books by Enrico Ferri and Alfredo Niceforo, both of whom were former students of Lombroso, into German and publishing them with his own introductions. Ferri developed an attempt at a synthesis of Darwin, Spencer, and Marx.[76] Michels characterized the adherence of 'this distinguished intellectual' to socialism, Ferri had an established reputation as a criminologist before joining the Italian Socialist Party, 'together with the entry into the party of the famous anthropologist Cesare Lombroso, whose favourite pupil Ferri had been', as one of the 'most significant moments in the history this party which certainly is not lacking in conversions'.[77] Michels conceded that Ferri's 'anthropological socialism' needed to be supplemented by knowledge of economic factors.[78] Ferri's pamphlet was originally published in 1902 as an intervention in the dispute between the Italian party's left and right wings, and dealt mainly with political strategy. Michels' translation came at a time when Ferri had just given up the editorship of

---

[73] Roberto Michels, 'Economisti Tedeschi—Werner Sombart', *Nuova Antologia*, Anno 43, Vol.134, Fasc.871, 1 April 1908, p.418.

[74] Roberto Michels, 'La formazione di centri d'affari meni abitati nelle città moderne della Germania', *La Riforma Sociale*, vol.XIX, serie II, anno XV, 1908, pp.629–37, p.11 of offprint.

[75] Robert Michels [under the rubric: Kritische Literatur-Übersichten], 'Italienische sozialstatistische und sozialpolitische Literatur', *Archiv für Sozialwissenschaften und Sozialpolitik*, Bd.27 (N.F.), 1908, pp.536–7.

[76] F. Andreucci, 'Enrico Ferri', in Andreucci and Detti, eds., *Il movimento operaio italiano*, Vol.III, Rome, 1977, pp.342–8.

[77] Dr Robert Michels, 'Die Entwicklung der Theorien im modernen Sozialismus Italiens', introduction to Enrico Ferri, *Die revolutionäre Methode*, Leipzig, 1908, p.34.

[78] Michels, 'Die Entwicklung der Theorien im modernen Sozialismus Italiens', p.35.

the party newspaper *Avanti!* and was starting to distance himself from the party.[79] In his introduction to Ferri's book, Michels began by discussing 'racial psychological characteristics of the Italian people', highlighting Italians' 'feeling for independence and human dignity, pronounced individuality, lack of prejudice, enthusiasm'.[80] Italy's national division (along with the absence of an industrial proletariat on any large scale) had hindered the development of socialism in mid-nineteenth-century Italy, which Michels partially explained by stating: 'It is an empirical law, that in epochs of racial struggles [*Rassenkämpfen*], the class struggles cannot attain their full significance'.[81]

While Ferri's work dealt principally with questions of socialist tactics and strategy, social anthropology was much more to the fore in Michels' translation and edition of Alfredo Niceforo's *Anthropology of the Poorer Classes*.[82] Michels had previously reviewed Niceforo's study of the Italian peasantry for the *Archiv für Sozialwissenschaft und Sozialpolitik*. Michels described Niceforo's work, which was based on an analysis of a hundred skulls exhumed from a pauper's grave in a south Italian town (in the Molise), as

> one of the most interesting and notable monographs, which deal with the connections between anthropology and economy, and which substantiates the thesis of the anthropological inferiority of the poorer classes on the basis of a well-chosen case study and with the assistance of all the means available to modern science.[83]

Michels' only criticism of Niceforo's method of analysing skull shapes to determine the prevalence of a Mediterranean type was that he had not analysed a control group of skulls of wealthier people from the region, although he did pose the

---

[79] Andreucci, 'Enrico Ferri', pp.347–8.

[80] Michels, 'Die Entwicklung der Theorien im modernen Sozialismus Italiens', p.8.

[81] Michels, 'Die Entwicklung der Theorien im modernen Sozialismus Italiens', p.10.

[82] Alfredo Niceforo, *Anthropologie der nichtbesitzenden Klassen*, trans. Prof. Dr Robert Michels and Dr Adolph Köster, Leipzig and Amsterdam, 1910, with an introduction by Michels, 'Das Proletariat in der Wissenschaft und die ökonomisch-anthropologische Synthese'. On Niceforo, see Angelo Matteo Caglioti, 'Race, Statistics and Italian Eugenics: Alfredo Niceforo's Trajectory from Lombroso to Fascism (1876–1890)', *European History Quarterly*, Vol.47, 3, 2017, pp.461–89.

[83] Robert Michels, Review of Alfredo Niceforo, *Ricerche sui contadini. Contribute allo studio antropologico ed economico delle classi povere*, in *Archiv für Sozialwissenschaft und Sozialpolitik*, 27 (new series), 1908, pp.837–8. See also Robert Michels, Review of *Annales de l'Institut International de Sociologie*, edited by Réné Worms, Vol.XI (proceedings of the 6th Congress, held in London, July 1906), in *La Riforma Sociale*, year XIV, second series, Vol.XVIII, nos.9–10, September–October 1907, pp.996–7, which complained of the unsystematic nature of many of the contributions, but singled out Niceforo's approach, and his study of the 'Physical and mental differences between different social groups' for praise; and Robert Michels, Review of Alfredo Niceforo, *Forza e ricchezza*, in *Kritische Blätter für die gesamten Sozialwissenschaften*, Jg.III, Heft 1, January 1907, pp.29–30, which states that 'questions of race (Germanic, Celtic influences, etc.)' might play a greater role in the anthropological differences between social classes than Niceforo suggests.

248   ROBERT MICHELS, SOCIALISM, AND MODERNITY

question of how much of the physical condition of the poor was the effect or the cause of poverty.[84]

Michels' introduction to Niceforo's *Anthropology of the Poorer Classes* initially rejected any attempt to reduce social or economic phenomena to natural scientific explanations, stating that 'the inherent tendencies of nature are not transferable to the economy', and he criticized both Ernst Haeckel's attempts to apply biological explanations to social conditions and the Social Darwinism of Otto Ammon.[85] However, he went on to argue that, nonetheless, the disciplines were intimately connected: 'Today economic theory cannot manage any more without anthropology, without sociology in its broadest sense' (note the implicit equation of sociology 'in the broadest sense' with anthropology here).[86] Michels went on to state that the two disciplines, economics and the natural sciences, were now 'undoubtedly following the same fundamental tendency', which 'a gifted neo-Marxist, Enrico Leone' had identified as 'the dialectical principle of contradiction'.[87] Michels also cited Lombroso and his school, arguing that while Lombroso's biological explanation for criminality was initially too one-sided, excluding economic considerations, Lombroso had subsequently moved to a synthesis of anthropological and economic views of crime—while also moving towards socialism in his political views.[88] Of Lombroso's school, 'the most significant student of Lombroso, Enrico Ferri, went with flag flying into the camp of social democracy and since then is trying to work out a synthesis of Darwin-Spencer-Marx in his anthropological socialism'.[89] Niceforo's work was also a product of this intellectual tendency. Niceforo (himself a Sicilian) had established a reputation with a work arguing that southern Italians were innately (racially) inferior to northerners.[90] In Michels' words, Niceforo 'had arrived at a biological science, which one can also easily count among the social sciences'. Niceforo was 'the creator of a new branch of science, which he has christened the "Anthropology of the poor man"'.[91] Niceforo's scholarly territory was in the overlap between economics and anthropology. Michels argued that 'Niceforo's theories, based on his anthropometric investigations, brilliantly supported the doctrine of historical

---

[84] Michels, Review of Alfredo Niceforo, *Ricerche sui contadini*, pp.838, 839.

[85] Michels, 'Das Proletariat in der Wissenschaft und die ökonomisch-anthropologische Synthese', pp.18, 15–17.

[86] Michels, 'Das Proletariat in der Wissenschaft und die ökonomisch-anthropologische Synthese', p.22.

[87] Michels, 'Das Proletariat in der Wissenschaft und die ökonomisch-anthropologische Synthese', p.24. On Enrico Leone, see Luigi Marco Bassani, *Liberismo e marxismo nel pensiero di Enrico Leone*, Milan, 2005.

[88] Michels, 'Das Proletariat in der Wissenschaft und die ökonomisch-anthropologische Synthese', pp.24–5.

[89] Michels, 'Das Proletariat in der Wissenschaft und die ökonomisch-anthropologische Synthese', p.25.

[90] See Wong, *Race and the Nation in Liberal Italy*, pp.63–70.

[91] Michels, 'Das Proletariat in der Wissenschaft und die ökonomisch-anthropologische Synthese', p.26.

ETHNICITY AND RACE 249

materialism.' Both Marx and Niceforo had established 'the existence of two social worlds', Marx by economic analysis, defining the lack of an economic common interest between the poor and the rich, while Niceforo discovered that these were different anthropological-biological types, although Michels claimed that Niceforo saw these as in turn having economic causes.[92] The question arose from the discovery of the anthropological-biological inferiority of the lower classes: 'Is this intellectually and physically defective proletariat, as the studies of political-social anthropology reveal to us, ready for its emancipation as a class, and if we have to answer this question in the negative, what do we need to do, to make it ready?'[93] This question pointed towards eugenics as an approach to solving the 'social question', as opposed to the self-emancipation of the working class through political struggle.

Interestingly, Michels' edition of Niceforo was reviewed highly positively in the *Politisch-Anthropolische Revue*, which drew from the work the conclusion that

> Niceforo's exposition of the share of race [in the anthropological differences between classes] will be of particular interest here. Even if he does not agree with all conclusions of the anthropo-sociologists..., he still arrives at the finding: 'the influence of race in the formation of the lower classes is accordingly extant'.[94]

Michels' evolution towards increasing proximity to racial thought is also reflected in his review of the second edition of Ludwig Gumplowicz's work *Der Rassenkampf* (*Racial Conflict*) in 1910. Michels wrote:

> His [Gumplowicz's] theory of the ethnic impurity of the state and the immanent conflictual nature of all social groups annoyed the nationalists and, in a different direction, the socialists. Gumplowicz became the *bête noire* of both the state-supporters and the dreamers of harmony among those dedicated to the sciences. That has not changed much today. However, it is possible to say that, at least in the circles of those scholars who are *striving* for objectivity, the second edition will be looked at with very different eyes than was the case for the first. The path of development, which the class struggle on the one hand and the struggle of races and languages on the other hand, have displayed, has sharpened our vision in many ways and led us considerably closer to Gumplowicz, even if we do not join with

[92] Michels, 'Das Proletariat in der Wissenschaft und die ökonomisch-anthropologische Synthese', p.27.
[93] Michels, 'Das Proletariat in der Wissenschaft und die ökonomisch-anthropologische Synthese', p.28.
[94] G. Weiss, Review of Alfredo Niceforo, *Anthropologie der nichtbesitzenden Klassen*, trans. and intro. by Robert Michels, in *Politisch-Anthropolische Revue*, Jg.9, 4, July 1910, pp.212–13.

250 ROBERT MICHELS, SOCIALISM, AND MODERNITY

him completely. The present collection of writings may be considered a standard work by anyone who feels the need to engage with the problems of the time.[95]

At this time, the relationship between the nascent academic discipline of sociology and the increasingly assertive advocates of racial biology and associated fields such as proponents of racial hygiene was a highly contentious question. In the years from 1905 to 1907, Ferdinand Tönnies had engaged in a sustained and intensely critical attack on the eugenic ideas of Wilhelm Schallmayer after Schallmayer won the 1900 Krupp essay prize for a treatise on the application of the theory of evolution to the internal development of the state and state legislation. Tönnies attacked Schallmayer for his crude transposition of biological categories to social life.[96] There was something of an *éclat* at the first German Congress of Sociologists in Frankfurt in October 1910 when the advocate of racial hygiene Alfred Ploetz gave an address on 'The Concepts of Race and Society and some Related Problems'. Ploetz argued that society should be seen as a subset of the broader category of 'race', thereby claiming primacy for racial-biological factors over sociological ones. Also controversial were his advocacy of racial hygiene, including seeking to improve the race by eliminating the physically weakest elements, and his defence of racial discrimination and segregation, for example in the United States. His presentation met with vigorous disagreement, particularly from Tönnies and Max Weber. The controversy over the place of racial biology and racial hygiene in German sociology carried over into the second congress, in 1912.[97] Despite his objections to Ploetz's inflated claims for the study of racial biology and the objectionable social prescriptions in his presentation in Frankfurt, Weber was still open to considering the role that race played in social and economic life, and in 1911 he solicited an essay on 'Economy and Race' from Michels for his project to produce a major handbook of social science.[98] This essay finally appeared in 1923.[99]

[95] Robert Michels, Review of Ludwig Gumplowicz, *Der Rassenkampf*, in *Archiv für Sozialwissenschaft und Sozialpolitik*, 31 (N.F.), 1910, p.264.
[96] Sheila Faith Weiss, *Race Hygiene and National Efficiency: The Eugenics of Wilhelm Schallmayer*, Berkeley, Los Angeles, CA, and London, 1987, pp.108–12; for a particularly in-depth treatment of Tönnies' response to Schallmayer, see Cornelius Bickel, 'Tönnies' Kritik der Sozialdarwinismus. Immunität durch Philosophie. Die Auseinandersetzung mit der Krupp-Preisfrage von 1900', in Klingemann, ed., *Rassenmythos und Sozialwissenschaften in Deutschland*, pp.172–211.
[97] For Ploetz's lecture and the ensuing debate, see *Verhandlungen des Ersten Deutschen Soziologentages vom 19.-22. Oktober 1910 in Frankfurt a. M.*, Tübingen, 1911, pp.111–64. See also Dirk Kaesler, *Max Weber. Preuße, Denker, Muttersohn. Eine Biographie*, Munich, 2014, pp.652–62; with more emphasis on the issue of race and the Ploetz controversy than Dirk Kaesler, Joachim Radkau, *Max Weber. Die Leidenschaft des Denkens*, Munich and Vienna, 2005, pp.531–4; Repp, *Reformers, Critics, and the Paths of German Modernity*, pp.304–8.
[98] Weber to Michels, 7 and 11 April 1911, in Max Weber, *Briefe 1911–1912* (=Gesamtausgabe II/7, i), Tübingen, 1978, pp.171–2, 178.
[99] Robert Michels, 'Wirtschaft und Rasse', in *Grundriss der Sozialökonomik*, Vol.II/1, Tübingen, 1923, pp.124–87.

ETHNICITY AND RACE   251

In the meantime, Michels had developed his own project for a handbook of social sciences, and from the summer of 1913 on he sought to mobilize his extensive transnational intellectual networks for a work to be called *Handwörterbuch der Soziologie / Encyclopédie der Sociologie*, to be published by Veit & Co. of Leipzig. In addition to trying to get contributions from figures such as Gustav Schmoller, Georg Simmel, and Max Weber (all of whom declined), and contacts from his socialist period such as Karl Kautsky and Georges Sorel (who also declined), Michels followed up on his old association with the *Politisch-Anthropologische Revue* to collect contributions from racial theorists. The associate of the late Ludwig Woltmann, the advocate of 'racial hygiene' Alfred Ploetz, now editor of the *Archiv für Rassen- und Gesellschafts-Biologie*, readily accepted Michels' invitation to write on the subject of 'race', and indicated that he might also be able to contribute articles on eugenics and social anthropology. He also recommended Professor Eugen Fischer in Freiburg as an expert on the latter topic, and Friedrich (or Fritz) Lenz in Munich, 'one of the sharpest minds of the coming generation' on eugenics.[100] Fischer declined on the grounds of other commitments and pressing deadlines,[101] but Lenz responded enthusiastically and at length. Lenz was willing to write on up to twelve keywords, including 'political anthropology', which he defined as not confined to the ideas of Woltmann.[102] Rather, Lenz saw 'political anthropology' as 'the science of the social significance of the hereditary differences (therefore racial differences) of human beings. Then it can largely be treated together with social anthropology' (Lenz cited Eugen Fischer as endorsing this view).[103] Lenz also tried to clarify Michels' keywords 'Auslese' ('selection') and 'Zuchtwahl' ('natural selection'):

> *Selection (Auslese).* Here *natural selection (Zuchtwahl)* seems to me to be not the narrower but the broader concept, at least in so far as it refers to purely *biological* things. Preservation in natural selection is called selection, destruction in natural selection is called culling out (*Ausmerzung*): both go hand in hand together. Herr Dr Ploetz, whom I asked for advice, is of the same opinion.[104]

Lenz also commented on Gobineau and Nietzsche as proposed subject headings (among many others on which he provided comments), reducing Nietzsche to the status of an epigone of Gobineau: 'On *Gobineau*. As a successor to Gobineau *Woltmann* is above all to be considered, I would gladly treat him. On the other hand, *Nietzsche* largely stands on the shoulders of Gobineau, I would only discuss

---

[100] A. Ploetz to Michels, 12 January 1914, ARM/FLE.
[101] E. Fischer to Michels, 2 March 1914, ARM/FLE.
[102] F. Lenz to Michels, 3 March 1914 and 10 March 1914, ARM/FLE.
[103] Lenz to Michels, 10 March 1914.   [104] Lenz to Michels, 10 March 1914.

252   ROBERT MICHELS, SOCIALISM, AND MODERNITY

his influence under the heading "Gobineau". The keyword 'Ploetz', Lenz wrote, should be linked to 'eugenics', 'racial hygiene', 'Galton', etc.[105]

The involvement of the racial hygienists and 'political anthropologists' was to cause a serious disagreement between Michels and one of his most distinguished prospective authors, Ferdinand Tönnies. Michels asked Tönnies to write on the concept of class and its social significance.[106] Tönnies expressed his reservations about the handbook prospectus (which Michels enclosed in his letters to potential contributors) to Michels in his initial response to the invitation, but by the time he received the contract from Veit & Co. at the start of 1914, these reservations had escalated to the point where Tönnies feared that Michels' enterprise 'will do more harm than good to sociology in its current stage of development [Stadio]'. Not only was Tönnies offended by the low honorarium offered by Veit & Co. for 'heavy intellectual labour', requiring at least twice the sum, he queried a number of names and keywords in the prospectus, including Chamberlain (presumably Houston Stewart) and Otto Weininger, author of Sex and Character. Tönnies also queried the inclusion of Michels' friends Gina and Paola Lombroso, daughters of the late criminologist (and even queried the inclusion of Cesare Lombroso himself). Other names blue-pencilled by Tonnies included Emile Boutroux, author of Psychology of Mysticism (1902) and Science and Religion In Contemporary Philosophy (1908) and the geographer Roland Bonaparte.[107]

Clearly alarmed at the tone and content of Tönnies' letter, Michels responded promptly, undertaking to try to intervene with Veit & Co. on the honorarium issue. He tried to explain away the list of names and keywords as a provisional list that had been sent out against his intentions. On a more substantive issue, he sought to defend some of the choices:

> As far as the names that you find grotesque are concerned, I know just what a hornets' nest I have sat in with this method. On the specific points, I would like to mention that the inclusion of Boutroux and Weininger was recommended to me from a very authoritative quarter. On the other hand, I will gladly sacrifice Bonaparte and a couple of Lombrosos for you.

In general, Michels argued against Tönnies' pessimistic assessment of his venture, stating that with enough goodwill from all concerned, it might still do more good than harm, and he asked Tönnies if he would write on the keyword 'public opinion'.[108] Michels subsequently wrote back to Tönnies stating that Veit could

---

[105] Lenz to Michels, 3 March 1914.
[106] Michels to Tönnies, 28 September 1913, ARM/FLE (photocopy, original in Schleswig-Holsteinische Landesbibliothek, Kiel).
[107] F. Tönnies to Michels, 5 January 1914, ARM/FLE.
[108] Michels to Tönnies, 7 January 1914, ARM/FLE (photocopy, original in Schleswig-Holsteinische Landesbibliothek, Kiel).

ETHNICITY AND RACE   253

meet his demand for a higher honorarium but only on the condition of strict con-
fidentiality, obviously to ensure that other contributors did not find out about
it.[109] There is something incongruous about the former labour movement activist
Michels striking confidential individual pay agreements. On 3 March 1914,
Tönnies responded, agreeing to contribute to the handbook, but continuing to
express his concerns about the social-biological sections of the work. These concerns were an echo of the conflict between Tönnies and adherents of racial-
biologistic approaches to social science which had been fought out in the German
Congress of Sociologists in 1910 and 1912.

Like many other projects of transnational cooperation, Michels' encyclopaedia
of the social sciences foundered on the outbreak of war. On 2 August 1914,
Friedrich Lenz wrote to Michels that he was enlisting in the army and would
therefore not be able to meet his deadlines.[110]

The following month, in late September 1914, Michels also received a letter
from Emile Durkheim. Durkheim had agreed back in January 1914 to contribute
some articles, although he wished to farm some of them out to his students, who
were, he assured Michels, 'fort distingués'.[111] Now, however, Durkheim had to
withdraw: 'there is one fact that can't be helped: the Encyclopaedia will appear in
Germany'. Durkheim felt that in the conditions of August–September 1914, he
could not accept any kind of solidarity with a people whose crimes were shocking
the world: 'One does not accept any contract with a bandit'.[112] Ironically, Michels
had already given up his German citizenship by this time, and was taking up a
chair in Basel in neutral Switzerland.

It is impossible to know whether Michels' *Encyclopedia* would ever have seen
the light of day if war had not broken out in 1914. It may ultimately have been too
eclectic and too uneven in quality to have come to fruition. However, this
neglected episode in Michels' career sheds some light on the extent to which he
was receptive to racial ideology, especially as he moved away from his earlier
involvement in socialism. In accounting for his later embrace of fascism, this is a
factor that should be considered along with his disillusionments with socialism
and democracy and his elitism.

---

[109] Michels to Tönnies 24 January 1914, ARM/FLE (photocopy, original in Schleswig-Holsteinische
Landesbibliothek, Kiel).
[110] Lenz to Michels and publishers Veit & Co., Leipzig (RMs Verlag), 2 August 1914, ARM/FLE.
[111] E. Durkheim to Michels, 19 January1914, ARM/FLE.
[112] Durkheim to RM, 26 September 1914, ARM/FLE.

9

Michels and the Modern

Robert Michels did not engage in a systematic, theoretical way with processes of modernization or the phenomenon of modernity, in the way that Weber did with his concepts of rationalization and the disenchantment of the world.[1] However, underlying Michels' writings is a strong sense that he is taking part in dynamic changes associated with modernity. What strikes a reader of Michels is, firstly, the frequency with which he uses the word 'modern' and its derivatives, and secondly, the overwhelmingly positive valuation with which he invests the term. The terms 'modernity', 'modernism', and 'the modern' have become so diffuse and slippery through overuse that it is necessary to reconstruct as precisely as possible how thinkers understood the terms at the time. Through a close analysis of Michels' attitudes to 'the modern' it is also possible to get a greater understanding of how his thought responded to the social and cultural context of the period.

In the 1890s and early 1900s, the word 'modern' was initially applied most consistently to new directions in literature, and subsequently other forms of art. In many of his early articles Michels took on the role of interpreter between contemporary German and Italian culture, and showed himself to be a champion of the 'modern' in this sphere. He contributed to the (short-lived) Turin-based journal *La Commedia*, which characterized itself as a journal committed to the reform of the 'modern theatre', which was to have 'the task to give expression in artistic form to our present-day life, which is subject to so many problems and questions'. This was to involve a moral and artistic renovation of the theatre, eschewing commercialism, and with an implicit emphasis on national artistic production, rather than foreign works.[2] *La Commedia* was a 'Kampforgan' (an instrument in the struggle), committed to a 'strongly modern and social programme'.[3] In his articles for *La Commedia*, Michels is a firm advocate of modernism in theatre and literature, adopting the stance of the *fin-de-siècle* avant-garde in castigating the intellectually lazy and philistine bourgeoisie and their shallow utilitarian approach to culture.[4]

---

[1] On this, see the discussion between Dieter Henrich, Claus Offe, and Wolfgang Schluchter, 'Max Weber und das Projekt der Moderne', in Christian Gneuss and Jürgen Kocka, eds., *Max Weber. Ein Symposion*, Munich, 1988, pp.155–83.

[2] See Robert Michels, 'Theaterreformen in Italien', *Neue Deutsche Rundschau*, Jg.13, no.6, June 1902, p.667.

[3] Michels, 'Theaterreformen in Italien', p.668.

[4] Roberto [Robert] Michels, 'La "Pochade" in Germania', *La Commedia*, I, no.7, 24 March 1901, pp.2–3, which discusses the popularity of French farce and its imitators on the German theatre; and the more polemical 'Il dramma moderno tedesco', *La Commedia*, I, no.9, 7 April 1901, pp.1–2.

Robert Michels, Socialism, and Modernity. Andrew G. Bonnell, Oxford University Press. © Andrew G. Bonnell 2023.
DOI: 10.1093/oso/9780192871848.003.0010

MICHELS AND THE MODERN   255

Michels contrasted the excellence of modern German drama, citing writers such as Hermann Sudermann, Max Halbe, Frank Wedekind, and (the Viennese) Arthur Schnitzler, with the indifference and hostility of German burghers to modern drama, with the result that some of these authors' works were more often performed outside Germany than on German stages. Michels pilloried the hypocrisy of German burghers, who rejected the gritty realism of plays by Gerhart Hauptmann and Sudermann by invoking their allegiance to the high aesthetic ideal of German classicism ('Cosi parlano quei signori'—'that's how these gentlemen express themselves'), while most of these people were actually enamoured of French farces, of whose vulgarities they were far more tolerant than they were of the realistic moments in serious drama. For Michels, 'questi signori', the average burghers, lacked any aesthetic or artistic sense altogether, merely feeling a need for entertainment. They did not see the theatre as an 'Erziehungsanstalt' (educational institute), in Schiller's sense, but as 'a simple pastime for their petty brains and for their empty hearts'. Modern drama in Germany also had to contend with politically motivated hostility, in the broad sense of the concept 'political'. The social criticism that was conveyed in works by Sudermann, Otto Erich Hartleben, and Arthur Schnitzler, with the latter's exposure of sexual exploitation and moral double standards, aroused condemnation and censorship in imperial Germany, where the Kaiser decreed that the purpose of the theatre was to imbue all classes of the population with an awareness of the greatness and glory of the ruling dynasty. 'Unfortunately', Michels wrote, 'the government protects the enemies of the modern drama and their sentiments', but the resilience of modern German drama in the face of such opposition was a marvellous proof of its vitality.[5] Michels' affirmative attitude to cultural modernism was also shared by his wife Gisela Michels-Lindner, as seen in her article on the 1892 Arts and Crafts Exhibition in Turin for the *Hessische Landeszeitung*, which uses the word 'modern' emphatically and positively.[6] As Timm Genett has pointed out, Michels was dismissive of the cultural pessimism then widely prevalent on the German right, mockingly referring to 'Culturangsthasen'—'frightened rabbits in the cultural sphere'.[7]

Writing about the Italian sculptor Leonardo Bistolfi for the German cultural journal the *Südwestdeutsche Rundschau*, Michels praised Bistolfi as a 'thoroughly

[5] Michels, 'Il dramma moderno tedesco'.

[6] Gisela Michels-Lindner, 'Die erste internationale Ausstellung für modernes Kunstgewerbe in Turin', *Hessische Landeszeitung*, no.258, 2 November 1902, erroneously attributed to Robert Michels in Ravasi's bibliography.

[7] Dr Robert Michels, 'Das Weib und der Intellectualismus', *Dokumente der Frauen*, VII, 4, 15 May 1902, p.109 (here with specific reference to the effects of women's cultural development on the birth rate. Michels argued that a quantitative decline in the birth rate with a higher level of cultural development was compensated for by qualitative improvement, in a kind of Darwinian adaptation effect). Also cited in Timm Genett, *Der Fremde im Kriege. Zur politischen Theorie und Biographie von Robert Michels 1876–1936*, Berlin, 2008, p.40.

256   ROBERT MICHELS, SOCIALISM, AND MODERNITY

modern artist. Anyone seeking the strictly delimited forms of antiquity in his work will be disappointed.' Regrettably, Bistolfi had applauded Kaiser Wilhelm II's recent speech on art, but Michels excused this on the grounds that 'as a foreigner, he was naturally unaware of its implications for German conditions'.[8]

Michels also used the term 'modern' to refer to economic modernization processes, referring to 'the amazing discoveries of the most modern times with their machines and their motors, with the replacement of small-scale industry by large-scale'.[9] Writing on the 'Southern Question' in Italy, the persistence of economic underdevelopment in the region, Michels largely endorsed the arguments of Francesco Ciccotti (economist and 'agrarian socialist') on the need for more intensive cultivation and the consolidation of small-landing holdings (with cooperatives enabling smaller farmers to stand up to larger landowners). 'First of all, the country must be modernized', Michels wrote.[10] Economic modernization would open the way for the further unfolding of class conflict, which would lead to socialism. For Michels, socialism was in the vanguard of modernity. The socialist party could pride itself on 'representing a completely new conception of the dynamic of the universe'. He wrote: 'In all serious questions of modern life, it marches at the head of progress like a proud standard-bearer of reason and morality'.[11] In 1903, Michels wrote in the *Mitteldeutsche Sonntags-Zeitung* that the progressive success of the socialist idea throughout the world would lead to 'the disappearance of continental wars, and in the history books of our grandchildren they will be spoken of as akin to the completely incomprehensible deeds of a horde of cannibals'.[12]

Michels also regarded women's emancipation (discussed in Chapter 5) as quintessentially a sign of progress and the march of the modern. He addressed the readers of the progressive liberal feminist periodical *Die Frauenbewegung* as 'an educated readership with a modern outlook', and stressed the need 'to tear women out of their centuries-old sleep and make them receptive to modern ideas' by giving them the right to vote. Once endowed with the vote, women would be able to participate fully in the 'struggle of modern *Weltanschauungen*'.[13] Women's

---

[8] Robert Michels, 'Leonardo Bistolfi', *Südwestdeutsche Rundschau. Halbmonatsschrift für deutsche Art und Kunst*, Jg.2, no.9, 1 May 1902, pp.334–9, here p.337. In 1909, however, Michels praised Edmondo de Amicis for his distinctly 'un-modern' virtues as a writer. Robert Michels, 'Edmondo de Amicis', *Sozialistische Monatshefte*, Jg.13, H.6, June 1909, p.361.

[9] R. [Robert] Michels, 'Attorno ad una questione sociale in Germania', *La Riforma Sociale. Rassegna di scienze sociali e politiche*, Anno 8, vol.11, ii, 1901, pp.775–94, quotation p.3 of offprint [p.777].

[10] Dr Robert Michels, Review of Francesco Ciccotti, *Socialismo e cooperativismo agricolo nell'Italia meridionale*, in *Documente des Socialismus*, Vol.2, 13, 1902, p.11.

[11] Michels, Review of Francesco Ciccotti, *Socialismo e cooperativismo agricolo nell'Italia meridionale*, p.750.

[12] Dr Robert Michels, 'Der Internationalismus der Sozialdemokratie', *Mitteldeutsche Sonntags-Zeitung*, no.9, 1 March 1903.

[13] Dr Robert Michels, 'Frauenstimmrecht—schon heute eine Notwendigkeit', *Die Frauenbewegung*, Jg.8, no.23, 1 December 1902, pp.177, 178.

political emancipation and the achievement of a progressive modern society clearly went hand in hand, the adjective 'modern' being repeated by Michels to lend the normative force of historical progress to the ethical case for women's suffrage.

In his review of Oda Olberg-Lerda's *Das Weib und der Intellectualismus*, Michels identified with Olberg-Lerda's rejections of popular authors' criticisms of 'the modern woman'.[14] He accepted the proposition that the general 'advancement of cultural development' necessitated an advancement in the situation of women. At the same time, he detected a 'great aversion' on Olberg-Lerda's part (without her actually saying so) 'against the ideas of Nietzsche' concerning the improvement of humanity through breeding out 'all that is sick or weak'. Instead, Olberg-Lerda sought to improve the condition of humanity by the amelioration of social conditions.[15]

Writing on educational reforms for women in Italy since the 1870s (admission to university study, improvement of training and status for women high school teachers), Michels praised these as 'just and modern' actions of the Italian state.[16] Women's economic advancement was a sign of how modern a state was, although Michels noted that Germany was relatively backward in terms of how much women had been able to enter male-dominated occupations, despite being 'a nation that is in many other respects so modern and advanced'.[17] Michels also wrote about the situation of women workers in Italy, praising the Kul-iscioff-Turati bill on the protection of women workers, while noting that some supporters of the bill, like the socialist doctor and gynaecologist Tullio Rossi-Doria, saw the bill as restoring the woman to her household, which evinced an 'unmodern sentimental streak', in Michels' opinion.[18] Timm Genett has stated that Michels' views on women's emancipation, and more specifically on sexual liberation 'are based on a linear view of history, which interprets the progress of civilization as the accumulation of gains in freedom.'[19]

The issue of the ways in which Germany was to be considered backward despite its modernity in the economic sphere recurs in Michels' writings in the early 1900s. As Genett has suggested, Michels viewed the German Empire through the

---

[14] Michels, 'Das Weib und der Intellectualismus', p.112.

[15] Michels, 'Das Weib und der Intellectualismus', p.110. It is not clear how well-acquainted Michels was with Nietzsche, whom he elsewhere described as 'the most modern and fashionable philosopher' in Germany, citing him on men's superiority over women, but referring to him as 'Arthur Nietzsche', in Michels, 'Attorno ad una questione sociale in Germania', p.13 of offprint.

[16] Dr Robert Michels, 'Die Frauenbewegung in Italien', *Die Gleichheit*, Jg.12, no.19, 10 September 1902, p.150.

[17] Robert Michels, 'La Questione della Zitella e della donna professionista', *Unione Femminile*, 2, 19–20 October 1902, pp.144–6, here p.145.

[18] 'Der Kampf um die Arbeiterinnenschutzgesetzgebung in Italien', *Die Frau*, Jg.9, H.9, June 1902, pp.513–18, 612–18, here p.613.

[19] Genett, *Der Fremde im Kriege*, p.49, with references here to Michels' *Grenzen der Geschlechtsmoral*. Genett (p.50) describes Michels as 'an author of pre-reflective modernity'.

258   ROBERT MICHELS, SOCIALISM, AND MODERNITY

prism of assumptions about modernization, and to some extent anticipated the later critical social-historical interpretation of the German *Sonderweg* (special path of development).[20] As noted in Chapter 7, Michels attributed the flawed modernization of the German political system to the political failure of German bourgeoisie: 'The German bourgeoisie has been unable to conquer for itself the position which is due to it under modern industrialization.'[21] The result was the continued dominance of the Prussian aristocracy, which retained privileges that 'modern civilization, despite all its capitalist forms, has abolished everywhere else'.[22] This anachronistic dominance of Germany by the pre-modern agrarian and military elite, with the monarchy at its apex, helped to explain the German Empire's aggressive and irrational colonial and imperial policies, militarism, weakness of pacifism, and the servility of all parties except Social Democracy.[23] Writing in the wake of the Morocco Crisis of 1905, Michels wrote: 'The economically capitalist Germany still stands politically under the rule of a class that economically already belongs to the past: the aristocracy'. The Reichstag was only a weak parliamentary check on the monarchy, as a result of the 'slackness of the bourgeois parties', which failed to stand up for the limited freedoms they had under the constitution.[24] The lack of bourgeois democracy in Germany forced the party of the workers to carry out a democratic role.[25] The German parliamentary system, flawed as it was, represented a grudging concession to modernity by the Prussian-German elite, it was 'that smidgeon of parliamentarism that modern times have granted to the German people'.[26]

Also following the Morocco crisis, Michels wrote in the *Revue Internationale de Sociologie* that Germany had been 'completely unable to divest itself of its medieval past'. Despite Germany being an '*industrial country par excellence*' (emphasis in original), it had not yet experienced the 'historical fact of the coming of the Third Estate'. Consequently, the Morocco crisis had exposed the 'impotence of the modern and democratic, working-class and pacifist forces in Germany'.[27] The government was dominated by conservative aristocrats who did

---

[20] Genett, *Der Fremde im Kriege*, p.83. The *locus classicus* of the so-called Bielefeld School version of the *Sonderweg* thesis is Hans-Ulrich Wehler, *Das deutsche Kaiserreich 1871–1918*, Göttingen, 1980.

[21] Dott. Roberto [Robert] Michels, 'Psicologia e statistica delle elezioni generali politiche in Germania (Giugno 1903)', *La Riforma Sociale*, Fasc.7, Anno X, vol.XIII, seconda serie, 15 July 1903, pp.541–67, quotation p.12 of offprint.

[22] Robert Michels, 'Les dangers du parti socialiste allemande', *Le Mouvement Socialiste*, no.144, 1 December 1904, p.194.

[23] Roberto [Robert] Michels, 'Divagazioni sullo imperialismo germanico e la questione del Marocco', *La Riforma Sociale*, Anno XIII, vol.XVI (2nd series), 1, 1906.

[24] Dr [Robert] Michels, 'Die Kriegsgefahr und die deutsche Arbeiterbewegung', *Die Einigkeit. Organ der Freien Vereinigung deutscher Gewerkschaften*, no.21, 26 May 1906.

[25] Dr [Robert] Michels, 'Die Kriegsgefahr und die deutsche Arbeiterbewegung', *Die Einigkeit. Organ der Freien Vereinigung deutscher Gewerkschaften*, no.22, 2 June 1906.

[26] Michels, 'Psicologia e statistica delle elezioni generali politiche in Germania', p.11 of offprint.

[27] R. [Robert] Michels, *L'Allemagne, le socialisme et les syndicats*, Paris, 1906 (offprint of article for the *Revue Internationale de Sociologie*), p.3.

MICHELS AND THE MODERN   259

little work, but who filled all the ministries.[28] The German bourgeoisie had largely renounced their influence on political life, pursuing economic interests and making a common cause with the aristocracy against the proletariat.[29]

For Michels, this judgement of the German Empire was confirmed by the outcome of the 1907 'Hottentot elections'. The conservative and nationalist success in these elections was, he said, the product of the way in which the 'conservative and semi-barbaric forces' of the country had managed to manipulate the electoral contest, from the weight of official and landowner influence in rural districts to the worsening malapportionment of electoral boundaries that had been largely unreformed since 1871.[30]

Michels' critique of the German Empire found perhaps its most trenchant expression in an article he wrote for an Italian journal in 1908 following the scandal around the publication of the Kaiser's interview with the British *Daily Telegraph*. (Michels might well have risked prosecution for *lèse-majesté* had it been published in Germany.) In a pithy anticipation of the *Sonderweg* thesis, Michels wrote: 'The antinomy of contemporary Germany consists precisely in the fact that its most advanced economic and civil existence has failed to find an adequate corresponding political form'. By comparison with Italy, Michels regarded Germany as representing the distant future in economic terms, but the distant past in political terms. Germany was (after the much smaller) Belgium, the most advanced nation in Europe economically and industrially but 'on the constitutional plane has remained almost a medieval entity'. A pseudo-parliamentary façade covered an almost absolutist monarchical 'dynasty propped-up by an array of petty nobles of the sword and of landed estates'.[31]

In contemporary Germany, Michels argued, the bourgeoisie had failed to convert its dominance in the sphere of political economy to a broader social power, which was exercised by a stratum belonging economically to the past (the Junker landowners).[32] In this respect, Michels suggested, contemporary Germany was a refutation of one of the main theses of Marxism.[33] Wilhelm II personified anachronism as 'the prototype of a dynast from Oriental antiquity, in the middle of a full industrial landscape'. He cited Wilhelm's claims to a Divine mandate and his penchant for inscribing Latin mottoes such as 'sic volo, sic jubeo' and 'lex suprema regis voluntas' in the guest books of German cities, his insistence on referring to the army as 'His' soldiers, and to the judiciary as 'His' judges, and his

[28] Michels, *L'Allemagne, le socialisme et les syndicats*, p.5
[29] Michels, *L'Allemagne, le socialisme et les syndicats*, p.8.
[30] Roberto [Robert] Michels, 'La vittoria dei conservatori nelle elezioni germaniche del 1907. Appunti storici e statistici', *La Riforma Sociale*, Anno XIV, vol.XVII, second series, 15 February 1907, pp.133–51, here p.21 of the offprint.
[31] Roberto [Robert] Michels, 'Guglielmo II e il popolo tedesco', *Rivista Popolare di Politica, Lettere e Scienze Sociali*, Anno XIV, n.24, 31 December 1908, p.659.
[32] Michels, 'Guglielmo II e il popolo tedesco', pp.659–60.
[33] Michels, 'Guglielmo II e il popolo tedesco', p.660.

260 ROBERT MICHELS, SOCIALISM, AND MODERNITY

dicta on the true role of art (which included the depiction of the deeds of 'His Family'). He referred to Wilhelm's dilettantish habit of claiming autocratic authority in the most varied spheres of government and public life. 'He is a demi-god like Lorenzo dei Medici but a Lorenzo run to bad taste, or none'. Commenting on Wilhelm's infatuation with uniforms and military ceremony, Michels relates that he recently saw the Kaiser on horseback in Wiesbaden, dressed in the shining regalia of a general of cuirassiers. In a line reminiscent of Thomas Mann's novel *Royal Highness*, Michels related that instead of feeling 'rebelliousness against such bellicose and autocratic presumption', he felt pity when he saw the 'general attitude of weariness, the dull eye and puffy face' of the ruler. The Kaiser was a product of his country: 'Germany is not a land of marble like Italy, or a land of granite like England or France, but a land of plaster [*stucco*].' Germany's Reich was just 40 years old, so its rulers had not had time to accustom themselves to their new strength—hence the showiness of Wilhelm's rule, like a bourgeois *parvenu*.

Michels posed the question of how a country so advanced in commerce, industry, and science could tolerate submission to such a ruler and his absolutist pretensions. In part, the answer lay in the German national character, he said (Michels' views on German national character have already been discussed in Chapter 7). Wilhelm also pleased the bourgeoisie with his efforts on behalf of German imperial expansion and his fierce hatred of socialism and democracy.[34] The German bourgeoisie, 'instead of acting independently, has put itself under the protection of the God-State', and applauded Wilhelm's 'illiterate and rabiate anti-socialism'. Michels judged: 'The German bourgeoisie's love for Wilhelm is a token of that class's moral hypocrisy in the face of the social question.'[35]

Paradoxically, Germans expressed admiration for Wilhelm's *un*-German personal characteristics, such as his lively temperament (the product of admixtures in the bloodline of the royal house). The German bourgeoisie was also impressed by his apparently modern personal interests: his chats with an inventor of aircraft, his willingness to decorate a Jewish industrialist ('unheard of in feudal Germany'), or to even try to resolve a problem of modern theology: at all these 'the hearts of the most radical Germans leap with inmost satisfaction'. 'The snobbery of modernity [*snobbismo della modernità*] which among true *parvenus* is one of the most inward passions of their soul, paints the emperor for them in the light of a heroic Bengal flame.' Even if Wilhelm promised to mend his ways (after the *Daily Telegraph* affair) and no longer communicate state secrets to British journalists, Michels predicted that Germans would remain in an embarrassing predicament:

> Germany will continue to have a parliament without parliamentary rule, will continue to receive irresponsible ministries by grace of the sovereign, will

---

[34] Michels, 'Guglielmo II e il popolo tedesco', p.661.
[35] Michels, 'Guglielmo II e il popolo tedesco', p.662.

MICHELS AND THE MODERN   261

continue to be governed, body and soul, by a bizarre autocrat and will continue to present to history this rare phenomenon of being simultaneously hated and mocked by foreign peoples.[36]

Despite Italy's relative economic backwardness, especially in the south, Michels saw Italy as less captive to its medieval past than was Germany, with the enduring dominance of its antiquated and economically obsolete feudal caste in the political sphere.[37] Especially in Prussia, according to Michels: 'Feudalism brings the Middle Ages back to life', as shown by the dominance of the nobility over the bourgeoisie in the army, diplomacy, and government.[38] Their unlimited respect for the aristocracy, Michels argued, was a sign of most Germans' excessive attachment to external and superficial things, despite German claims to superior *Innerlichkeit*.

He said, 'The German nobility... still exercises a social dominion as if in the time of the *ancien régime*', despite the fact that many noble families had never played a very distinguished role in their country's history.[39] A 'frenzy' for aristocratic titles, or 'titolomania' prevailed in Germany, he said.[40] In Michels' view, the German bourgeoisie was 'feudalized' in its subservience to aristocratic norms.[41] The Junker-dominated German state had successfully co-opted the bourgeoisie, which submitted to the 'hegemony of a class that economically already belonged to the past, which corresponded to a long-superseded pre-bourgeois economic epoch, namely the Junker class'. The German government was able to tame the bourgeoisie through such means as titles, which affected not only 'civil servants but even the free professions, the doctors and lawyers, and even, indeed, the masters of commerce and industry', as well as through the institution of the reserve army officer, 'which equates to a militarization of the entire bourgeoisie'.[42]

One aspect of Michels' affirmative attitude towards modernity that has aroused relatively little comment (especially when one thinks of the attention paid to questions such as Max Weber's relationship to Protestantism) is his assertively secular outlook. There are plenty of instances in which this outlook found expression, to an extent which his non-socialist contemporaries found unconventional by the standards of the time—his refusal to have his children baptized, for example.[43]

---

[36] Michels, 'Guglielmo II e il popolo tedesco', p.662.

[37] Roberto [Robert] Michels, *Il proletariato e la borghesia nel movimento socialista italiano*, Turin, 1908, p.13.

[38] Michels, *Il proletariato e la borghesia nel movimento socialista italiano*, p.318.

[39] Michels, *Il proletariato e la borghesia nel movimento socialista italiano*, p.301.

[40] Michels, *Il proletariato e la borghesia nel movimento socialista italiano*, pp.300, 302; see also pp.303–8.

[41] Robert Michels, 'Die oligarchischen Tendenzen der Gesellschaft. Ein Beitrag zum Problem der Demokratie', *Archiv für Sozialwissenschaft und Sozialpolitik*, Vol.27 (new series), 1908, p.81. Michels cited Sombart's history of the German economy in the nineteenth century in support of this claim.

[42] Michels, 'Die oligarchischen Tendenzen der Gesellschaft. Ein Beitrag zum Problem der Demokratie', pp.86–7.

[43] Michels' refusal, despite, it was said, his 'Aryan descent', to have his children baptized was one of the issues, along with his socialist views, that were seen as obstacles to him being admitted to a

262 ROBERT MICHELS, SOCIALISM, AND MODERNITY

In his polemics against the National Social Party in 1903, a party which included a number of protestant clergymen, Michels strongly expressed the view that it was inappropriate for a 'modern party' to allow its policies in the secular field to be dictated by a particular religious standpoint. Michels expounded the principle of a plurality of *Weltanschauungen* in the public, political domain: 'materialist, ethical, purely atheist, Jewish'. He characterized his own position as not being an adherent of any particular religion, 'totally hostile towards any kind of mysticism', but 'by no means opposed to a pure belief in God'.[44]

Michels' writings frequently reveal an aversion to clerical influence in society. Writing about rural Italian women workers for a feminist journal in 1902, Michels wrote of the awakening of the women of the rural proletariat of northern and central Italy from the 'quiet of the churchyard':

> Socialism brought new ideals into their dull, barren lives. In place of the confessional, there appeared the feeling of togetherness. Superficial church morality gave way to the purely human morality of mutual aid. No longer was it a matter of wanting happiness after death, but as much as possible in this earthly life.[45]

In Italy, Michels saw 'clerical education and the influence of the confessional' as hindrances to the political and social advancement of women. However, he was pleased to report that these influences 'were giving way more and more to the modern work of enlightenment [*der modernen Aufklärungsarbeit*]'.[46] In a description of a job advertisement for a socialist newspaper editor in a small town in Italy, which Michels published in *Ethische Kultur* in early 1903, he expressed sympathy for the difficulties such a worker would have 'in a small town, in which the priest-rule will surround the enemy journalist with an impenetrable barrier of hatred from the first day on'.[47] In the same journal, Michels wrote in a warmly approving fashion of the mercilessly anti-clerical Italian journal *L'Asino* ('the donkey').[48]

Michels pulled even fewer punches in describing the influence of the Catholic church in Italy when he wrote for Social Democratic newspapers. In an article on the struggle for a divorce law in Italy, published in the Left Marxist *Leipziger Volkszeitung*, Michels branded the papacy an 'enemy in the unified Italian state's

---

Habilitation at a German university. Max Weber, *On Universities*, ed. and trans. Edward Shils, Chicago, IL, 1974, pp.17–18.

[44] 'Aus der Wahlbewegung. Erklärung', *Hessische Landeszeitung*, no.117, 20 May 1903.

[45] Dr Robert Michels, 'Ein italienisches Landarbeiterinnen-Programm', *Dokumente der Frauen*, VII, 6, 15 June 1902, pp.160, 161.

[46] Dr Robert Michels, 'Die italienische Frau in den camere di lavoro', *Die Frau*, Jg.11, Heft 6, March 1904, p.371.

[47] Dr Robert Michels, 'Wie die sozialdemokratischen Hetzer vom Arbeitergroschen leben', *Ethische Kultur*, Jg.XI, Nr.9, 28 February 1903, S.71.

[48] R. [Robert] Michels, Review of *,* [anonymous], 'Der "Esel" als Erzieher', in *Ethische Kultur*, Jg.XI, Nr.33, 15 August 1903, S.264.

own house'. The influence of the papacy also made itself felt across many parts of Europe and America: 'wherever the remnants of the Middle Ages coalesce to form "Catholic congresses"'. The 'power of darkness', represented by the Vatican, resentful of its loss of secular power over its Italian landed possessions in the *Risorgimento*, was taking revenge on the Italian state by resisting liberal reforms in areas like divorce.[49]

In Michels' opinion, the policy of the Social Democratic Party, which declared religion to be a 'private matter' did not go far enough when it came to combatting the regressive influence of the churches in society. At the Social Democratic Party's women's conference at the 1904 Bremen party congress, Michels argued that one of the reasons why men had not given more support to the women's movement was the persistence of 'religious prejudice' among women. Consequently,

> The main emphasis must be placed on replacing the church influence with the socialist element. The sentence: religion is a private matter is no longer appropriate in the programme, because it is misunderstood, as if it says: religion is irrelevant (in original: *Wurst*); whoever is a religious believer, can stay that way. Men have freedom of thought, but women's views are passed on to their children. I would like to see just once a statistical survey of party members adopt the following questions: is your wife in the church? Have you had your children baptized? Is your daughter confirmed? I think a large number of very respected party members would have trouble passing these questions. (Merriment)[50]

Michels' wife, Gisela Michels-Lindner, was not among those women who were susceptible to clerical influence. Her attitude to the church seems to have been no less staunchly anti-clerical than her husband's. In a leading article for the *Mitteldeutsche Sonntags-Zeitung* in 1904, Gisela Michels-Lindner roundly attacked priests and pastors who misused their position to attack socialism, acting as 'advocates of capitalism'. The actions of such representatives of the church, Michels-Lindner concluded, did more to discredit and destroy religion than the socialist movement could.[51]

---

[49] Dr Robert Michels, 'Die Ehescheidung in Italien', *Leipziger Volkszeitung*, Jg.10, no.33, 10 February 1903. See also Robert Michels, Review of Guido Podrecca, *Il divorzio*, in *Ethische Kultur*, Jg.XI, Nr.19, 9 May 1903, p.151.

[50] *Protokoll über die Verhandlungen des Parteitages der Sozialdemokratischen Partei Deutschlands. Abgehalten zu Bremen vom 18. bis 24. September 1904*, Berlin, 1904, pp.343–4. On the question of Social Democracy's relation to organized religion, see Sebastian Prüfer, *Sozialismus statt Religion. Die deutsche Sozialdemokratie vor der religiösen Frage 1863–1890*, Göttingen, 2002; Lucian Hölscher, *Weltgericht oder Revolution. Protestantische und sozialistische Zukunftsvorstellungen im deutschen Kaiserreich*, Stuttgart, 1989.

[51] Gisela Michels-Lindner, 'Christliche Toleranz', *Mitteldeutsche Sonntags-Zeitung*, Jg.11, 9, 28 February 1904.

264 ROBERT MICHELS, SOCIALISM, AND MODERNITY

Michels' incipient estrangement from the German Social Democratic Party after 1904 was partly connected with his views on the party and religion. Michels criticized the party's refusal to engage in anti-religious agitation: the programmatic statement that religion was a private matter was electorally expedient, but it meant abstaining from campaigning against religious superstition in the masses, and allowed people with the most backward views into the party.[52] He quoted Guglielmo Ferrero's admiration expressed in 1897 for 'lo spirito religioso' of German socialism, a spirit which Michels saw as having been displaced by a concern for electoral success.[53] Socialism, in Michels' view, had to replace religion, not accommodate itself to it. Again, in early 1905, Michels argued that a clean break with the church, that 'devourer of consciences', was needed to shake the party out of its lethargy, and make it a revolutionary force, as well as bring out more clearly the party's 'modern scientific essence'.[54]

Michels' expressed desire for a kind of socialism that would not only be impervious to religion, but which would replace it, shows that he had a very different conception of politics from the one famously articulated by Max Weber in his essay on politics as a profession.[55] Michels, of course, expressed his dissatisfaction with the tendency of political parties to become increasingly professionally administered organizations, which Weber also diagnosed, in his major work of 1910/11. It is at least possible that this dissatisfaction was all the greater because he had originally sought a kind of fulfilment in political activity, especially in a party that was ostensibly committed to a strenuous struggle against the powers that be, that might provide a substitute for a religious promise of the transcendental. It is also possible to see in Michels' emphatic secularism and anti-clericalism, along with his affirmative attitude to modern culture and to ideas of sexual liberation, a generational revolt common to many German middle-class youth of the period around 1900, a generational revolt that found expression in the youth movement, many bourgeois life-reform movements, and in the cultural sphere, for example in early expressionist literature. In his rejection of his father's conformist Wilhelmine values, Michels no doubt believed that he had modernity, progress, and reason on his side. However, once Michels left the constricting, repressive sphere of the German Empire with its anachronistic ruling elite, his rebellion could lead him in quite different directions.

---

[52] Michels, 'Les dangers du parti socialiste allemande', p.203.

[53] Michels, 'Les dangers du parti socialiste allemande', p.202.

[54] Robert Michels, 'Le congrès des socialistes de Prusse à Berlin', *Le Mouvement Socialiste*, No.149, 15 February 1905, pp.239–51, here p.246.

[55] Max Weber, *Political Writings*, ed. Peter Lassman and Ronald Speirs, Cambridge, 1994, pp.309–69.

10

Conclusions

Both the common argument that Michels was a disillusioned believer in pure democracy and the view that Michels' extremist tendencies catapulted him from revolutionary syndicalist positions to fascism stand in need of correction in the light of a close analysis of Michels' evolution and the diverse intellectual influences to which he responded. At the same time, this book has sought to avoid reducing explanations of Michels' intellectual positions to mere biographical contingency, although there were certainly strong situational influences on many of his writings, not least his shifts between different national contexts. Like many middle-class youths in Germany at the dawn of the twentieth century, Michels expressed a strong kind of generational revolt against the values of his father's generation, who had aligned themselves with the nationalistic, militaristic, and bourgeois-conformist values of the Bismarckian German upper and middle classes. Michels' family background—part-French, Catholic, and of liberal Rhineland—gave him resources on which he could draw to distance himself from the stifling aspects of Wilhelmine German society. His anti-militarism seems to have been sincere, and was no doubt rooted in his personal experience of military service in the Kaiser's army. One finds no references to positive experiences of military service in any of his writings. His part-French background and upbringing, and a talent for languages saw him strive for a career as a scholar that would take him across national borders in Europe, and at a formative stage in his life he developed a deep and abiding attachment to Italy.

During his time as a socialist intellectual, Michels experienced a tension between his academic ambitions and his political engagement. Contrary to what some writers have assumed, Michels did not consciously turn his back on an academic career to pursue the life of a socialist activist. He seems to have been under the serious misapprehension that if he focused on writing about Italian (and perhaps French) socialism, his socialist sympathies would not be counted against him. Until the First World War broke out, Michels continued to hope for a chair at a German university. His career highlights the exclusion of socialists from public sector employment, especially universities, in imperial Germany, in marked contrast to the situation in Italy.

Michels' reception of Marxism does not appear to have been very profound—he identified with Marx as an exemplar of the educated young man of the bourgeoisie who threw in his lot with the struggles of the working class for social justice, but does not seem to have delved deeply into Marx's theoretical work.

Robert Michels, Socialism, and Modernity. Andrew G. Bonnell, Oxford University Press. © Andrew G. Bonnell 2023.
DOI: 10.1093/oso/9780192871848.003.0011

266 ROBERT MICHELS, SOCIALISM, AND MODERNITY

Immersed in the environment of Marburg, a university town that was home to neo-Kantian ideas in the early 1900s, Michels did not attempt a systematic synthesis of Kantian ethics and Marxian historical materialism. Rather, he developed a strong sense of his own ethical superiority as someone who was fighting for a cause for reasons other than material advancement (unlike working-class adherents of socialism). Like Georges Sorel, Michels appears to have been attracted to the concept of the class struggle not so much by the need to improve the material conditions of the working class, but because he saw the struggle as an opportunity for exercising moral virtue in an ennobling struggle.[1] Far from idealizing the working class, who were after all seeking their own collective self-interest in the labour movement, Michels idealized the class struggle. His largely Platonic and vicarious sympathies for French and Italian syndicalism were not grounded in a theoretical belief in the primacy of the economic over the political struggle, but were based on an approval of the radical sentiments of syndicalist advocates of class struggle, which appealed to Michels' essentially agonistic conception of politics. Indeed, this book has argued that the assumption that Michels ever *was* a syndicalist is questionable.

Michels identified with the radical left of the German Social Democratic Party during the revisionist controversy, and he hoped to be able to revolutionize the sleepy countryside around Marburg with an agitational campaign. He seems to have been temperamentally averse to the prosaic business of gradually building up party and trade union organizations, and found the militance of French and Italian radical syndicalists much more congenial. He was also disappointed by the German Social Democratic leadership's cautious approach to anti-militarist agitation. There is a progressive souring in Michels' views on 'the masses'—while he initially saw the working masses as being in need of guidance from enlightened intellectuals like himself, he became increasingly pessimistic about the prospects of such popular-paedagogical work as time went on.

Michels' consciousness of his own ethical superiority dovetailed easily with his evolving reception of elite theory. His scholarly career drew him into the ambit of Werner Sombart and Max Weber, who helped him develop his critical insights into the mundane and increasingly bureaucratized Social Democratic Party. Contact with Italian elite theorists and Italian social anthropologists, who articulated a belief in natural, biological hierarchies between different groups of people, also had a profound influence on Michels. While racial-biological thought was increasingly aligned with the German right, there was a strong vein of such thought among Italian centre-left and even radical left intellectuals, such as Cesare Lombroso and Lombroso's follower Enrico Ferri, both associates of Michels. The influence of racial-biological thought and ethnic categories on

---

[1] For this interpretation of Sorel's engagement with syndicalism, see F.F. Ridley, *Revolutionary Syndicalism in France*, Cambridge, 1970, especially pp.239–55.

CONCLUSIONS 267

Michels has been overlooked or discounted by many, indeed most, scholars, but a closer analysis shows that it is pervasive, and this helps to explain how he could adopt hierarchical and elitist views by 1910/11. An awareness of Michels' reception of race theory also complements recent scholarship on the long-underestimated relevance of racism to the origins of Italian fascism.

Michels' identification with his adopted Italian home led him to feel a patriotism, nationalism, and understanding for imperialist ambitions that he would have been allergic to in the German context. It is also worth emphasizing that the deep socio-cultural cleavages and the exclusion of socialists from participation in the state in imperial Germany made crossing the political trenches from left to right in the Kaiser's empire more fraught and rare than it became in Italy and France, where trajectories from left-syndicalism to the ultra-right during the rise of fascism were less infrequent than in Germany. Michels' own journey from left to right cannot be fully understood without understanding the changed national context in which it took place. In Germany before the First World War, the socio-cultural milieux that had formed during the Bismarckian period remained intact and largely self-contained, and non-socialist parties collaborated to exclude Social Democrats from political power and participation in public life.[2] The fluidity with which Italian intellectuals could move between university chairs and the socialist party was absent in Germany, and even though united Germany began in 1871 with a wider franchise than most European countries, including Italy at that time, Italy saw a series of electoral reforms before 1914, while the German Reich remained resistant to structural political reform. One factor in Michels' youthful revolt against the political culture of Wilhelmine Germany was his reaction against what he saw as the persistence of anachronistic, feudal-reactionary structures and mores in an otherwise modernizing society, making him an early exponent of a critical view of a German *Sonderweg*—a flawed path of modernization.

There is a generational dimension to Michels' emphatic identification with modern culture, and his rejection of what he saw as the anachronistic elements of Wilhelmine Germany, from the monarchy to its sexual mores. The examination of Michels' involvement with feminism and the sex reform movement highlights the deep divisions between the different political and ideological strands of German feminism before 1914. Michels was unusual, and possibly unique, in seeking to bridge these divisions. Michels' conciliatory attitude to the different strands of socialist and bourgeois feminism—liberal-progressive, conservative-nationalist, and radical on sexual issues—stood in stark contrast to his advocacy of intransigent class struggle when writing for socialist publications, suggesting a

---

[2] For a compelling recent account of the way in which non-socialist parties colluded to combat Social Democracy in imperial Germany, see James Retallack, *Red Saxony: Election Battles and the Spectre of Democracy in Germany, 1860–1918*, Oxford, 2017.

gendered conception of political struggles that analysts of Michels have tended to overlook. In many ways, Michels was in the avant-garde in advocating freedom and autonomy for men and women in matters of sexual life, but his underlying gendered assumptions, and lack of interest in (or even hostility to) the contemporary debate on homosexuality, relativize the degree to which he can be seen as an exemplary pioneer of sexual emancipation.

One dimension of Michels' thought that has not been commented on much by other scholars, partly because it is no longer unusual, was his militantly secular outlook. Michels did not, however, wrestle with the philosophical implications of modernity in the way that, for example, Max Weber did. Weber would not have sought moral absolutes or transcendental experiences in politics. Michels sought satisfactions in political struggle that went far beyond Weber's famous dictum about the politician's need for a slow boring through thick boards. And yet, even in his most politically engaged phase, Michels never abandoned the hope of a professorship at a German university. Some of the contradictions in his thought came from his attempts to straddle ideological and political divides. Without wishing to engage in reductionism, one can add that some of the contradictions in his biography came from the conflicts arising between his search for personal and ethical fulfilment in radical political action and his desire for the dignity of a professorial chair.

Michels' *magnum opus*, *Political Parties*, will probably long continue to be cited by scholars, of varying political-ideological views, for its central sociological observations on the risk that politics as a profession entails, when parties fall prey to the career ambitions of party functionaries, and the instruments of political organization become ends in themselves. But a closer reading of Michels shows how much he was a man of his time, reflecting the psychological, social, and even racial-biological assumptions of a *fin-de-siècle* intellectual who was ill at ease with the 'age of the masses', and someone who ultimately proved susceptible to a cult of action and charismatic leadership.

Bibliography

Archival Sources

International Institute for Social History, Amsterdam
File Robert Michels, Dtl. Div. X/16:
Eduard Bernstein
Luigi Fabbri
Augustin Hamon
Karl Kautsky
Max Nettlau
Gottfried Salomon
Hans Stein
Nachlass August Bebel
Nachlass Eduard Bernstein
Collection Iring Fetscher
Archief Kautsky, K D XVII, 531–43
Collection Gottfried Salomon
Collection Hans Stein
Nachlass Georg v. Vollmar
Sozialistische Monatshefte Archives, 129: Meller, Ch.—Milhaud, Edgard

Bundesarchiv Berlin / Stiftung Archiv Parteien und
Massenorganisationen der DDR
NY4005/90, Clara Zetkin

Geheimes Staatsarchiv Preussischer Kulturbesitz, Berlin-Dahlem
VI. HA, Nl. Schmoller
Nr.158. Fall Michels
VI. HA, Nl. Sombart
Nr.10b. Korrespondenz
Nr.17. Handwörterbuch der Soziologie
Nr.20 Archiv für Sozialwissenschaft und Sozialpolitik

Landesarchiv Berlin
A. Pr. Br. Rep. 030
Nr.8808. Acta des Königlichen Polizei-Präsidiums zu Berlin, betreffend
die Internationale Antimilitaristische Bewegung 1904–1906
Nr.10835. Acta des Königlichen Polizei-Präsidiums zu Berlin, betreffend die politischen
Zustände in Italien
No.16386: Akten der Abteilung VII-4 des Königlichen Polizei-Präsidiums zu Berlin,
betreffend den Schriftsteller, Professor Dr. Robert Michels 1903–1917

270 BIBLIOGRAPHY

Staatsbibliothek Berlin

Handschriftenabteilung
Dep.42 Walter de Gruyter, no.40.2. Eingegangene Briefe 1913 (L-Q).
Kurt Breysig-Nachlass

Hessisches Staatsarchiv Marburg

Bestand 165 Kassel—Preussisches Regierungs-Präsidium,
Nr.706: Special-Akten betr. Die Sozialdemokratie, Bd.4
Nr.1241: Generalakten betr. Die Social-Demokratie
Nr.6420: Betr. Entlassung aus dem Untertanen-Verband, Bd.89
Bestand 180 Kgl. Landratsamt (LA) Marburg:
Nr.752: Volksversammlungen 1902/03
Nr.753: Versammlungen 1904–1906
Nr.2318: Allgemeine Politik Wahlen u. Demonstrationen

Martin-Luther-Universität Halle-Wittenberg, Universitätsarchiv, Halle

Decanat Haym. Promotionen vom 1. Juli 1900 bis Januar 1901, no.8: Robert Michels.

Schleswig-Holsteinische Landesbibliothek, Kiel

Nachlass Ferdinand Tönnies
Briefe (Cb. 54–56: 521.08–18, R. Michels)
Kleinere Werkmanuskripte (Cb. 34: 109)
Akten der Deutschen Gesellschaft für Soziologie (Cb. 54: 61: 1)
Notizkalender 1913–1914 (Cb.54:11:11)

Fondazione Luigi Einaudi, Turin

Archivio Roberto Michels (ARM)
Note: Michels' correspondence is arranged by correspondent and chronologically within each correspondent's file. Name of Michels's correspondent and date of letter are therefore sufficient to locate material.
Inventory of ARM in Stefania Martinotti Dorigo and Paola Giordana, eds., 'L'archivio Roberto Michels. Inventario', in *Annali della Fondazione Luigi Einaudi*, Vol.29, 1995, pp.585–663.
Correspondence: Konrad Adenauer, Alfred Adler, Georg Adler, Viktor Adler, Agitations-Komitee Niederrhein S.P., Friedrich Althoff, Charles Andler, Johan Frederik Ankersmit, Eduard Anseele, Arbeiter-Zeitung, Dortmund, Anita Augspurg, Ottilie Baader, Angelica Balabanoff, Maurice Barrès, Theodor Barth, Gertrud Bäumer, August Bebel, Hermann Beck, Ernest Belfort-Bax, Eduard Bernstein, Regina Bernstein, Edouard Berth, Leonida Bissolati, R. [Rudolf?] Blank, Joseph Bloch, Hans Block, Ivanoe Bonomi, Adolf Braun, Heinrich Braun, Martin Buber, Edward Carpenter, Ernst Cassirer, Minna Cauer, Consum-Verein für Marburg u. Umgegend, Enrico Corradini, Benedetto Croce, Heinrich Cunow, Eduard David, Gertrud David, Hans Delbrück, Heinrich Dietz, Dokumente des Sozialismus, Gustav Droysen, Hermann Duncker, Emile Durkheim, Kurt Eisner, Henry Havelock Ellis, Enrico Ferri, Eugen Fischer, Die Frau, Frauen-Zukunft, Raphael Friedeberg, Eduard Fuchs, Henriette Fürth, Hellmut von Gerlach, Paul Göhre, Hermann Gorter, Jean Grave, Victor Griffuelhes, Ladislaus Gumplowicz, Ludwig Gumplowicz, Konrad Haenisch, Hamburger Echo, Augustin Hamon, Wolfgang Heine, George D. Herron, Hessische Landeszeitung, Camille Huysmans, Gustav Jaeckh,

BIBLIOGRAPHY 271

Edgar Jaffé, Jenaer Volksblatt, Hans Kampffmeyer, Paul Kampffmeyer, Karl Kautsky, Luise Kautsky, Wilhelm Keil, Ellen Key, Siegfried Kracauer, Anna Kuliscioff, Arturo Labriola, Paul Lafargue, Hubert Lagardelle, Karl Lamprecht, Gustav Landauer, Helene Lange, Gustave le Bon, Georg Ledebour, Carl Legien. *Leipziger Volkszeitung*, Paul Lensch, Friedrich Lenz, Enrico Leone, Giovanni Lerda, Oda Lerda-Olberg, Friedrich Lessner, Gabriele von Lieber, Karl Liebknecht, Cesare Lombroso, Else Lüders, Rosa Luxemburg, Magazin für Litteratur, Märkische Volksstimme, Max Maurenbrecher, Gustav Mayer, Franz Mehring, Friedrich Meinecke, Gisela Michels(-Lindner), Mitteldeutsche Sonntags-Ztg, Gaetano Mosca, Friedrich Naumann, Max Nettlau, Hermann Oncken, Anton Pannekoek, Vilfredo Pareto, Wilhelm Pfannkuch, Alfred Ploetz, Adelheid Popp, Henriette Roland-Holst, Alice Salomon, Gottfried Salomon, Carl Schmitt, Gustav Schmoller, Adele Schreiber, Georg Simmel, Paul Singer, Werner Sombart, Othmar Spann, Arthur Stadthagen, Hans Stein, Helene Stöcker, Heinrich Ströbel, Ferdinand Tönnies, Filippo Turati, Emile Vandervelde, Volksstimme, Frankfurt a. M., Georg von Vollmar, Vorwärts, Max Weber, Ludwig Woltmann, Emanuel Wurm, Clara Zetkin

Documenti personali

Printed Primary Sources

Existing Michels bibliographies list most of his publications:

'Opere di Roberto Michels', reprinted from Studi in memoria di Roberto Michels, *Annali della facoltà di giurisprudenza della R. Università di Perugia*, Vol.XLIX, Padua, 1937.

Viviana Ravasi, 'Bibliografia degli scritti di Roberto Michels nel periodo 1900–1910', in Roberto Michels, *Potere e oligarchie. Organizzazione del partito ed ideologia socialista (1900–1910)* (ed. Ettore A. Albertoni), Milan, 1989, pp.73–108.

Books by Michels

Zur Vorgeschichte von Ludwigs XIV.Einfall in Holland (diss.), Halle a.S., 1900.

Il proletariato e la borghesia nel movimento socialista italiano, Turin, 1908 (reprint New York, 1975).

Storia del marxismo in Italia, Rome, 1909.

Zur Soziologie des Parteiwesens in der modernen Demokratie, Leipzig, 1911.

Die Grenzen der Geschlechtsmoral. Prolegomena, Gedanken und Untersuchungen, Munich and Leipzig, 1911.

L'imperialismo italiano, Rome, Milan, and Naples, 1914.

Storia critica del movimento socialista italiano fino al 1911, Florence, 1921 (reprint: Rome, 1979).

Die Verelendungstheorie, Leipzig, 1928 (reprint: Hildesheim and New York, 1970).

Der Patriotismus. Prolegomena zu seiner soziologischen Analyse, Munich and Leipzig, 1929.

Italien von heute, Zurich and Leipzig, 1930.

Anthologies of Michels' Writings

A. James Gregor, ed., *Roberto Michels e l'ideologia del fascismo*, Rome, 1979.

272 BIBLIOGRAPHY

Robert Michels, *Masse, Führer, Intellektuelle. Politisch-soziologische Aufsätze 1906–1933* (ed. Joachim Milles), Frankfurt/New York, 1987.

Roberto Michels, *Potere e oligarchie. Organizzazione del partito ed ideologia socialista (1900–1910)* (ed. Ettore A. Albertoni), Milan, 1989.

Robert Michels, *Critique du socialisme. Contribution aux débats au début du XXe siècle* (ed. Pierre Cours-Salies and Jean-Marie Vincent), Paris, 1992.

Robert Michels, *Soziale Bewegungen zwischen Dynamik und Erstarrung. Essays zur Arbeiter-, Frauen- und nationalen Bewegung* (ed. Timm Genett), Berlin, 2008.

Published Michels Correspondence

Busino, Giovanni, 'Lettres de G. Sorel à L. Einaudi, E. Rods et R. Michels', in *Cahiers Georges Sorel*, no. 1, 1983, pp.71–95.

Genett, Timm, 'Lettere di Ladislaus Gumplowicz a Roberto Michels (1902–1907)', *Annali della Fondazione Luigi Einaudi*, 31, 1997, pp.420–73.

Gianinazzi, Willy, 'La démocratie difficile à l'ère des masses. Lettres d'Hubert Lagardelle à Robert Michels (1903–1936)', *Mil Neuf Cent*, no.17, 1999, pp.103–48.

Malandrino, Corrado, 'Lettere di Anton Pannekoek a Roberto Michels (1905)', *Annali della Fondazione Luigi Einaudi*, 19, 1985, pp.467–92.

Malandrino, Corrado, 'Lettere di Roberto Michels e di Augustin Hamon (1902–1917)', *Annali della Fondazione Luigi Einaudi*, 22, 1989, pp.487–562.

Tommissen, Piet, *In Sachen Carl Schmitt*, Vienna and Leipzig, 1997, pp.83–112 (letters pp.85–96).

Trocini, Federico, 'Sombart e Michels. Due itinerari paralleli?', *Annali della Fondazione Luigi Einaudi*, 48, 2014, pp.291–364.

Trocini, Federico, ed., *Robert Michels e la prima guerra mondiale. Lettere e documenti (1913–1921), Florence*, 2019.

Volpe, Giorgio, ed., *Il carteggio fra Roberto Michels e i sindacalisti rivoluzionari*, Naples, 2018.

Select Secondary Literature

Annali di sociologia / Soziologisches Jahrbuch, Vol.2, 1, 1986 (= Proceedings of Colloquium on Robert Michels on 50th Anniversary of His Death, Held at Trento, 1986).

Beetham, David, 'From Socialism to Fascism: The Relation between Theory and Practice in the Work of Robert Michels', *Political Studies*, 25, 1977, pp.3–24; 161–81.

Beetham, David, 'Michels and His Critics', *Archives Européennes de Sociologie*, 22, 1981, pp.81–99.

Bennett, R.J., 'The Élite Theory as Fascist Ideology—A Reply to Beetham's Critique of Robert Michels', *Political Studies*, 26, 1978, pp.474–88.

Bluhm, Harald and Krause, Skadi, eds., *Robert Michels' Soziologie des Parteiwesens. Oligarchien und Eliten—die Kehrseiten moderner Demokratie*, Wiesbaden, 2012.

Bonnell, Andrew, 'Robert Michels, Max Weber, and the Sexual Question', *The European Legacy*, Vol.3, 6, 1998, pp.97–105.

Bosc, Olivier, 'Eugénisme et socialisme en Italie autour de 1900. Robert Michels et l'"éducation sentimentale" des masses', *Mil Neuf Cent*, 18, 2000, pp.81–108.

Bottomore, T.B., *Elites and Society*, London, 1964.

Busoni, Giovanni, 'Lettres de G. Sorel á L. Einaudi, E. Rods et R. Michels', *Cahiers Georges Sorel*, I, 1983, pp.71–95.

BIBLIOGRAPHY 273

Cavallari, Giovanna, *Classe dirigente e minoranze rivoluzionarie*, Camerino, 1983.

Di Nucci, Loreto, 'Roberto Michels "ambasciatore" fascista', *Storia Contemporanea*, Vol. XXIII, 1, February 1992, pp.91–103.

Drake, Richard, *Apostles and Agitators: Italy's Marxist Revolutionary Tradition*, Cambridge, MA, and London, 2003.

Eisenberg, Christiane, 'Basisdemokratie und Funktionärherrschaft. Zur Kritik von Robert Michels' Organisationsanalyse der deutschen Arbeiterbewegung', *Mitteilungsblatt des Instituts zur Erforschung der europäischen Arbeiterbewegung*, 9, 1989, pp.8–30.

Faucci, Riccardo, ed., *Roberto Michels. Economia, sociologia, politica*, Turin, 1989.

Ferraris, Pino, 'Roberto Michels politico (1901–1907)', *Quaderni dell'Istituto di Studi Economici e Sociali* (Università di Camerino), I, 1982, pp.51–162.

Ferraris, Pino, 'Ancora sul Michels politico attraverso le lettere di K. Kautsky', *Quaderni dell'Istituto di Studi Economici e Sociali* (Università di Camerino), 4, 1985, pp.45–63.

Ferraris, Pino, *Saggi su Roberto Michels*, Camerino, 1993.

Furiozzi, Gian Biagio, *Il sindacalismo rivoluzionario italiano*, Milan, 1977.

Furiozzi, G.B., ed., *Roberto Michels tra politica e sociologia*, Florence, 1984.

Genett, Timm, ' "Ein Land aus Stuck". Robert Michels und die soziomoralische Disposition der Deutschen im Wilhelminismus', in Herfried Münkler, ed., *Bürgerreligion und Bürgertugend. Debatte über die vorpolitischen Grundlagen politischer Ordnung*, Baden-Baden, 1996.

Genett, Timm, 'Vom Zivilisierungsagenten zur Gefolgschaft. Die Masse im politischen Denken Robert Michels', in Ansgar Klein et al., eds., *Masse—Macht—Emotionen. Zu einer politischen Soziologie der Emotionen*, Opladen, 1999.

Genett, Timm, *Der Fremde im Kriege. Zur politischen Theorie und Biographie von Robert Michels 1876–1936*, Berlin, 2008.

Gianinazzi, Willy, 'Il divenire sociale et pagine libere', *Cahiers Georges Sorel*, 5, 1987, pp.119–30.

Gilcher-Holtey, Ingrid, 'Intellektuelle in der sozialistischen Arbeiterbewegung. Karl Kautsky, Heinrich Braun und Robert Michels', in Jürgen Rojahn, ed., *Marxismus und Demokratie. Karl Kautskys Bedeutung in der sozialistischen Arbeiterbewegung*, Frankfurt/M., New York, 1991.

Gregor, A. James, *Phoenix: Fascism in Our Time*, New Brunswick and London, 2004 (chs.3 and 4 on Michels).

Hetscher, Joachim, *Robert Michels. Die Herausforderung der modernen Politischen Soziologie im Kontext der Herausforderung und Defizit der Arbeiterbewegung*, Bonn, 1993.

Kaube, Jürgen, *Max Weber. Ein Leben zwischen den Epochen*, Berlin, 2014.

Keller, Katharina, *Modell SPD? Italienische Sozialisten und deutsche Sozialdemokratie bis zum Ersten Weltkrieg*, Bonn, 1994.

Kelly, Duncan, 'From Moralism to Modernism: Robert Michels on the History, Theory and Sociology of Patriotism', *History of European Ideas*, 29, 2003, pp.339–63.

Lenger, Friedrich, *Werner Sombart. 1863–1941*, Munich, 1994.

Linz, Juan, Robert Michels, *Political Sociology, and the Future of Democracy* (ed. H.E. Chehabi), New Brunswick NJ and London, 2006.

Marucco, Dora, *Arturo Labriola e il sindacalismo rivoluzionario in Italia*, Turin, 1970.

Messeri, Andrea, 'Roberto Michels. Crisi della democrazia parlamentare e fascismo', in Luciano Cavalli, ed., *Il fascismo nell'analisi sociologica*, Bologna, 1975, pp.21–34.

Mitzman, Arthur, *Sociology and Estrangement: Three Sociologists in Imperial Germany*, New York, 1973.

Mommsen, Wolfgang J., 'Max Weber and Robert Michels: An Asymmetrical Partnership', *Archives Européennes de Sociologie*, 22, 1981, pp.100–16.

274 BIBLIOGRAPHY

Mommsen, Wolfgang J., 'Robert Michels and Max Weber: Moral Conviction versus the Politics of Responsibility', in W.J. Mommsen and J. Osterhammel, eds., *Max Weber and His Contemporaries*, London, 1989 (also published in W.J. Mommsen, *The Political and Social Theory of Max Weber*, Cambridge and Oxford, 1989).

Nye, Robert A., *The Anti-Democratic Sources of Elite Theory: Pareto, Mosca, Michels*, London and Beverly Hills, 1977.

Pfetsch, Frank, *Die Entwicklung zum faschistischen Führerstaat in der politischen Philosophie von Robert Michels* (diss., Karlsruhe), 1964.

Pfetsch, Frank, 'Robert Michels als Élitetheoretiker', *Politische Vierteljahrsschrift*, 7, 2, 1966, pp.208–27.

Portinaro, Pier Paolo, 'Robert Michels alla prova della guerra mondiale', *Contemporanea*, Vol.23, 2, April–June 2020, pp.319–33.

Pouthier, Jean-Luc, 'Georges Sorel et Robert Michels', in Jacques Juilliard and Shlomo Sand, eds., *Georges Sorel et son temps*, Paris, 1985, pp.287–94.

Pouthier, Jean-Luc, 'Robert Michels et les syndicalistes révolutionnaires français', *Cahiers Georges Sorel*, 4, 1986, pp.39–60.

Radkau, Joachim, *Max Weber. Die Leidenschaft des Denkens*, Munich and Vienna, 2005.

Repp, Kevin, *Reformers, Critics and the Paths of German Modernity*, Cambridge, MA, 2000.

Roberts, David D., 'How Not to Think about Fascism and Ideology, Intellectual Antecedents, and Historical Meaning', *Journal of Contemporary History*, 35, 2000, pp.185–211.

Röhrich, Wilfried, *Robert Michels. Vom sozialistisch-syndikalistischen zum faschistischen Credo*, Berlin, 1972.

Roth, Guenther, *The Social Democrats in Imperial Germany: A Study in Working-Class Isolation and National Integration*, Totowa, NJ, 1963.

Scaff, Lawrence A., 'Max Weber and Robert Michels', *American Journal of Sociology*, 86, 1981, pp.1269–86.

Spriano, Paolo, *Storia di Torino operaia e socialista*, Turin, 1972.

Sternhell, Zeev, with Sznajder, M., and Asheri, M., *The Birth of Fascist Ideology* (trans. D.Maisel), Princeton, NJ, 1994.

Trocini, Federico, *Tra internazionalismo e nazionalismo. Robert Michels e i dilemma del socialism di fronte alla guerra e all'imperialismo* (= Quaderni della Fondazione Luigi Salvatorelli Marsciano 7), Rome, 2007.

Trocini, Federico, 'Sombart e Michels. Due itinerari paralleli?', *Annali della Fondazione Luigi Einaudi*, 48, 2014, pp.269–91.

Tuccari, Francesco, *I dilemmi della democrazia moderna. Max Weber è Roberto Michels*, Rome-Bari, 1993.

Volpe, Giorgio, 'Riforma o rivoluzione sociale? Il problema della collocazione politica di R. Michels all'interno del movimento socialista', *Rivista di Storia dell'Università di Torino*, Vol.I, 1 2012, pp.43–85.

Volpe, Giorgio, *La disillusione socialista. Storia del sindacalismo rivoluzionario in Italia*, Rome, 2015.

Winkler, Heinrich August, 'Robert Michels', in Hans-Ulrich Wehler, ed., *Deutsche Historiker*, IV, Göttingen, 1972.

Index

For the benefit of digital users, indexed terms that span two pages (e.g., 52–53) may, on occasion, appear on only one of those pages.

Acher, Mathias 240
Adler, Georg 125–6
Albert (Alexandre Martin) 129–30
Alldeutscher Verband – see Pan-German League
Ammon, Otto 248–9
'Anthropogeographie' 15–16, 229
anti-semitism 135n.26, 233–4, 240–3
Arbeiter-Zeitung (Dortmund) 60
Arbeiter-Zeitung (Essen) 76–7, 216
Archiv für Rassen- und Gesellschafts-Biologie 251
Archiv für Sozialwissenschaft und Sozialpolitik 4–6, 22–3, 47–8, 64–7, 69, 74–5, 81–4, 111–12, 114–16, 119–22, 124, 128, 137–40, 142, 177, 190–1, 201, 203, 219, 226–7, 242, 245, 247
Arons, Leo 19
Asino, L (periodical) 262
Auer, Ignaz 38, 242–3
Augspurg, Anita 7
Avanguardia Socialista 28–9, 35–6, 49, 51–3, 55, 101–7, 110, 132–3, 224
Avanti! 51–2, 85, 92–3, 99–102, 119, 130, 169, 190, 246–7

Baader, Ottilie 7
Bader, Paul 33–6
Bakunin, Mikhail 93–4, 111–12, 115–16, 121–3, 125–6, 190–1, 245
Balabanoff, Angelica 162–3
Barrès, Maurice 186–7
Basel University 22, 192, 253
Basler Nachrichten 204–5
Bäumer, Gertrud 7, 23, 152–3, 157–8, 161, 169–70
Bax, Ernest Belfort 158–9, 173–4
 The Legal Subjection of Men 173–4
Bebel, August 2, 10, 15–16, 38–9, 41–2, 50, 55, 61–3, 75–6, 78–81, 87, 92–3, 112–13, 117–18, 130–1, 147–8, 158–9, 164, 166, 173–4, 177, 183–4, 195, 200–2, 215–16
 Woman and Socialism (Die Frau im Sozialismus) 147–8, 150–2, 158–9, 166, 177
Beetham, David 9–10

Bergson, Henri 123
Berlin University 19
Bernhard, Georg 41–2
Bernstein, Eduard 6, 20, 28–31, 39–40, 44–5, 49, 71–2, 86–7, 95–9, 101–2, 106, 125–6, 129–30, 136–7, 183–4, 195, 199–200, 240
 Documente des Sozialismus 6, 20, 30, 95–9, 129, 136–7
 Voraussetzungen des Sozialismus, Die 31
Bertesi, Alfredo 37–8
Berth, Edouard 6, 78–9, 113–14, 117, 123, 126–7, 135–40, 142–3, 187–8, 191
Bethmann Hollweg, Theobald von 79–80
Biermann, W. Eduard 69
Bismarck, Otto von 15–16, 186, 209–10
Bissolati, Leonida 91–2, 97, 112–13
Bistolfi, Leonardo 255–6
Blair, Tony 3
Blanc, Louis 93–4, 129–30
Blank, Rudolf 66–7
Blaschko, Alfred 169–70
Bloch, Iwan 169–70
Bloch, Joseph 19, 27
Bonaparte, Roland 252
Bonomi, Ivanoe 92, 94–5, 105–6, 125–6
Borgius, Walther 169–70
Boschetti, Elisa 153
Boutroux, Emile 252
Bracke, Alexandre-Marie 130–1
Brandes, Georg 6, 79–80
Braun, Lily 156–7, 162–3, 169–70
Bré, Ruth 7, 169–70
Bryce, James 4, 65–6, 118–19
 The American Commonwealth 4, 64–5
Buek, Otto 31
Bülow, Bernhard von 50–1, 76, 160
Bund deutscher Frauenvereine (BDF) 148–9, 160, 163, 169–70, 172–3
Bund für Mutterschutz 7, 147, 163, 167–71, 175, 177–9, 182, 184–5

Caprivi, Leo von 15–16
Carl-Friedrich-Gymnasium, Eisenach 15–16

276 INDEX

Cauer, Minna 7, 153–5, 161, 169–70
Chamberlain, Houston Stewart 252
Chiesa, Pietro 37–8
Ciacchi, Eugenio 30, 95–6
Ciccotti, Ettore 210–11
Ciccotti, Francesco 105–6, 256
Clemenceau, Georges 186–7
Cohen, Hermann 31
Cohen, Max 42
Colajonni, Napoleone
 Latini e Anglo-Sassoni 183–4
Cologne 15–17, 237
Commedia, La (Turin) 17–18, 163–4, 254–5
Communist Manifesto, The 28–9, 187–8
Condorcet, Nicolas de 8–9
Confédération Générale du Travail (CGT) 70–2,
 74, 80–1, 136–8, 141–2
Conrad, Johannes 15–17, 229
Corradini, Enrico 226–7
Correspondezblatt der Generalkommission der
 Gewerkschaften Deutschlands 57–8,
 72–3, 108–9, 137–8
Cosentini, Francesco 122
Costa, Andrea 91–4
Crimmitschau textile workers'
 strike, 1904 106
Crispi, Francesco 90
Croce, Benedetto 30, 95–8, 125–6

Daily Telegraph 259–60
D'Annunzio, Gabriele 209–10
Darwin, Charles 97–8, 147–8, 246–9
Darwinism 15–16, 122–3, 229, 233–4
David, Eduard 43, 48, 55, 75–6, 242–3
De Amicis, Edmondo 27, 188–9, 191
Déroulède, Paul 210–11
 Chants d'un soldat 210–11
Deutsche Soziale Partei 34–5
Dickinson, Edward Ross 178–9
Diehl, Karl 69, 128
Dinale, Ottavio 30
Disraeli, Benjamin 186
Dissmann, Robert 76
Divenire Sociale, Il (periodical) 55, 63–4, 70,
 107–13, 120–1, 135
Dohm, Hedwig 169–70
Dokumente der Frauen (periodical) 149–50
 (see also *Frauen-Rundschau*)
Dreyfus case 186–7
Driesch, Hans 233–4
Droysen, Gustav 15–17
Dubreuilh, Louis 130–1
Dumas, Alexandre (*fils*) 201
Durkheim, Emile 253

Ebert, Friedrich 2, 10
Ehrenfels, Christian von 181
Einaudi, Luigi 246
Einigkeit, Die 72–5, 137–8, 199–200
Eisenach 15–16
Eisner, Kurt 31, 61–2, 87–8, 111–12, 130–1
elite theory 2n.2, 4, 7, 9, 21–2, 83–5, 142–3,
 203–4, 232, 266–7
Ellis, Havelock 7
Engels, Friedrich 28–9, 97–8, 187–8, 191
Erkelenz, Anton 169–70
Ethische Kultur (periodical) 19–20, 29–30, 41–3,
 46, 94–6, 99–100, 129–30, 136, 164–5,
 168–9, 212–15, 221–2, 237–8, 243–5, 262
eugenics 147–8, 150–2, 228, 233–4, 248–9,
 251–2, 257

Fabbri, Luigi 111–12
Fascio Operaio (newspaper) 189
feminism 7, 11, 50–1, 95, 100, 147–52,
 256–7, 267–8
 German feminist movement 148–54,
 156–7, 159–60
 Italian feminist movement 150–3, 159
 Italian proletarian feminist movement 150–3,
 156–8, 262
Fénélon, François de Salignac de la Mothe- 129
Ferraris, Carlo F. 121–2
Ferraris, Pino 7–8, 10, 107, 142, 228
Ferrero, Guglielmo 53–5, 240, 264
 Europa giovane, L' 240
Ferri, Enrico 30, 43–4, 81–2, 92–5, 97, 105–6,
 113–14, 122–3, 125–6, 130, 158–9,
 188–9, 195, 228, 231–2, 246–9, 266–7
 metodo rivoluzionario, Il 97, 125–6,
 158–9, 246–7
Fickert, Auguste 161
Fischer, Eugen 251
Florian, Eugenio 122
Foerster, Friedrich Wilhelm 20, 42
Fraas, Eberhard 229
Franchi, Bruno 122
Frankfurter Zeitung 153, 168–9
Französisches Gymnasium, Berlin 15–16, 129
Frau, Die (periodical) 100, 147, 152–4, 157–8,
 169–70, 184–5, 238–9
Frauen-Rundschau (periodical) 156–7, 167–8,
 170–1 (see also *Dokumente der Frauen*)
Frauen-Zukunft (periodical) 178–9
Frauenbewegung, Die (periodical) 153–6, 165,
 184–5, 197, 256–7
freie Wort, Das (periodical) 18n.14, 19, 93–5,
 195–7, 207
Freud, Sigmund 177, 181

INDEX   277

Friedeberg, Raphael 53–5, 61–2, 133–4
Friedrich, Carl J. 8–9
Fritsch, Theodor 233–4
Fürth, Henriette 7

Galton, Francis 251–2
Garibaldi, Giuseppe 98–9, 207, 209–10
Gebuer, Anna 161
Gehren, Wilhelmine von 161
general strike in Italy, 1904 107
Genett, Timm 7–8, 20–1, 23, 147, 181–5, 206–7, 228, 254–5, 257
Gerber, Adele 161
Gerlach, Hellmuth von 26–7, 33–6, 38–9
German Civil Code (Bürgerliches Gesetzbuch) 148–9, 158–9, 164
German Congress of Sociologists
    1910 (Frankfurt) 250, 252–3
    1912 (Berlin) 225–6, 250, 252–3
Giolitti, Giovanni 104–5
Gleichheit, Die 7, 32, 50–1, 95, 147, 150–4, 158–9, 165–6, 173, 184–5, 188–9, 221, 238–9
Gobineau, Arthur de 233–4, 237, 251–2
Goethe, Johann Wolfgang 164–5, 215
    Italienische Reise 89–90
Gori, Pietro 111–12
Grido del Popolo, Il 99–100, 202, 221
Griffuelhes, Victor 6, 70–2, 135–40
Gross, Otto 177
Guerre Sociale, La 76–8, 80–1, 111–12, 140–2, 216
Guesde, Jules 134–7
Gumplowicz, Ladislaus 208–9, 215, 233–4
    Nationalismus und Internationalismus im 19. Jahrhundert 208–9
Gumplowicz, Ludwig 233–4, 249–50
    Der Rassenkampf 249–50

Haeckel, Ernst 229, 248–9
Halbe, Max 254–5
Halle University 15–17, 148–9, 229
Hamon, Augustin 136
    Socialisme et anarchisme 136
Hamburger Echo 105–6
Handbuch der Frauenbewegung (edited by Bäumer and Lange) 153, 159
Harden, Maximilian 41–2
Harnack, Adolf von 172–3
Hartleben, Otto Erich 254–5
Härtling, Georg 35–7, 61–2
Hauptmann, Gerhart 254–5
Haym, Rudolf 17
Hegel, G.W.F. 245

Heidelberg 65–6
Heine, Heinrich 219, 240
Heine, Wolfgang 34–5, 38–42, 45–6
Hervé, Gustave 76–7, 80–1, 111–12, 128, 139–42, 215–16, 222, 225–6
    Das Vaterland der Reichen (Leur patrie) 142, 215–16
Herzen, Alexander 219–20, 245
Hessische Landbote, Der 45
Hesssiche Landeszeitung 254–5
Hetscher, Joachim 9
Hirschfeld, Magnus 164, 181, 183–4
    Cultur und Ehe 164
historiography 15–18
Hobsbawm, Eric J. 186
Hofmannsthal, Hugo von 6, 79–80
homosexuality 183–4, 267–8
Hubbard, Gustave-Adolphe 131–2
Hué, Otto 56–7
Humanité, L' 134, 139–40
Humanité Nouvelle, L' 44–5, 136
Husserl, Edmund 15–16

I Accuse. By a German (Richard Grelling) 22–3
Ibsen, Henrik 147
Illustriertes Frauen-Jahrbuch (edited by Hermann Hillger) 161
intellectuals 58, 67–8, 74, 90–2, 117, 120–1, 123, 142–3, 147, 163, 186–96, 204–5, 243, 267
International Socialist Congress, Amsterdam, 1904 47–8, 117–18, 133
    Stuttgart, 1907 79–81, 119, 139, 141–2, 216–17, 243
internationalism 206–7, 209–12, 215–16, 220, 225–7, 242–5
Italia irredenta 209–11, 217–19, 234–5
Italian Nationalist Association 226–7
Italian Socialist Party 11, 30, 37–8, 80, 86–7, 89–127, 130, 152–3, 199, 231, 262
    1902 party congress (Imola) 6, 27, 32, 90–4, 153, 188
    1904 party congress (Bologna) 103–6, 111–12, 189
    1905 party congress (Brescia) 111–13
    1906 party congress (Rome) 113–15, 199
    intellectuals in 91–6, 125–6, 188–91, 195–6, 199, 246–7, 267
    social composition 37–8, 91, 93–6, 113–18, 190, 199
    women in 95, 152–3

Jaeckh, Gustav 32
Jaffé, Edgar 4, 64–6
Jaffé, Else 177

278 INDEX

Jahrbuch für Gesetzgebung, Verwaltung und Volkswirtschaft in deutschen Reiche (Schmollers Jahrbuch) 124
Jaurès, Jean 45–6, 49, 52–3, 106, 130–5, 139–40
Jews 49, 67, 183–4, 193–4, 239–43, 245, 260–2
Jüdische Rundschau 239

Kanitz, Count 49
Kant, Imanuel 31, 58–9, 78–9
Kautsky, Karl 6, 19–20, 26–9, 43–4, 47–8, 51–2, 55–6, 75–6, 83, 95, 102–3, 105–6, 111–12, 115–16, 130–3, 187–8, 251
   political break with Michels 83
Kelly, Duncan 225–6
Kirchhoff, Alfred 15–16, 229
Korrespondezblatt – see *Corresponendezblatt*
Krafft-Ebing, Richard von 181
Kritschewsky, Boris 139
Kropotkin, Peter 191
Krupp, Friedrich (Fritz) Alfred 40, 101
Krupp essay prize, 1900 250
Kuliscioff, Anna 6, 92, 95–7, 121–2, 127, 150–3, 162–3, 257

Labriola, Antonio 28–9, 125–6
Labriola, Arturo 6, 20, 81–2, 89–90, 92, 95–8, 100–8, 110, 113–15, 117–18, 122–6, 133–4, 139, 191–3, 199
   Ministero e Socialismo 96–7
   Riforme e rivoluzione sociale 192–3
Lafargue, Paul 130–1
Lafont, Ernest 112–13
Lagardelle, Hubert 6, 20, 81–2, 85, 123, 133–7, 139–40, 142–3, 187–8, 191
Lamprecht, Karl 15–16
Lang, Marie 149
Lange, Helene 152–3, 157–8, 161, 169–70
Lanz von Liebenfels, Jörg 233–4
Lassalle, Ferdinand 93–4, 187–8, 191, 202–3, 240
latinité 212–13, 237, 244–5
Lazzari, Costantino 113–14, 199
Le Bon, Gustave 7, 142–3, 194, 204
   The Crowd 194, 204
leaders 193–4, 200–5
Lega Socialista Milanese 150–2
Legien, Carl 74–5
Leipzig University 15–16
Leipziger Volkszeitung 32, 55–6, 70–1, 104, 224, 231, 262–3
Lenger, Friedrich 80
Lenz, Friedrich (Fritz) 251–3
Leone, Enrico 95–6, 105–8, 111–15, 120–1, 123, 135, 199, 248–9

Lerda, Giovanni 98
   Il socialismo e la sua tattica 98
'*lex Arons*' 18–19, 74, 191–2, 224–5
Liebknecht, Karl 51–3, 55–6, 79–80, 141
Liebknecht, Wilhelm 2, 10
Lindner, Theodor 16–17, 195, 210–11
   Geschichtsphilosophie 195
Lipset, Seymour Martin 2, 25
Liszt, Franz von 195
Lombroso, Cesare 7, 20, 83–5, 89–90, 97, 119–20, 122, 125–6, 149, 158–9, 164–5, 181, 228–35, 238–40, 246–9, 252, 266–7
   momento attuale, Il 231
Lombroso, Gina 7, 162–3, 231–2, 252
Lombroso, Paola 161–3, 252
Loncao, Enrico 113–14, 199
Longobardi, Ernesto Cesare 95–6
Loopuit, Joseph 58–9
Loria, Achille 20, 76, 89–90, 97–8, 119–20, 229, 231
Lotta di Classe (newspaper) 114–15
Louis XIV 16–17, 129, 203–4
Low, Sidney 65–6
Lüders, Else 7
Luther, Martin 201
Luxemburg, Rosa 32, 43, 48, 102–3, 134, 162–3, 203
   Mass Strike, Party, and Trade Union 203

Magazin für Litteratur 167–8, 213–14
Majno-Bronzinin, Ersilia 153
Malon, Benoît 191, 245
Mann Thomas
   Königliche Hoheit 259–60
Marburg 18–19, 25–7, 31–7, 45, 64, 66–8, 76, 89–90, 111–12, 116, 192–3, 213–14, 265–6
Marx, Karl 27–30, 55, 61–2, 66–7, 70, 93–4, 97–8, 111–13, 115–16, 121–3, 126–7, 130–1, 187–8, 191, 202, 215–16, 225–6, 235–6, 240–2, 245–9, 265–6
   Kapital, Das 28–9, 58–9, 76–7
Marx-Aveling, Eleanor 162–3
mass strike debate 61–3, 74–6, 110
masses 23, 83–5, 117, 186–7, 193–205, 225–6, 266, 268
Mazzini, Giuseppe 207, 245
Medici, Lorenzo dei 259–60
Mehring, Franz 41–2
Messina 23–4
Michels, Italia (daughter) 18n.12
Michels, Julius (father) 15–16, 264–5
Michels, Manon (daughter) 181–2
Michels, Mario (son) 26–7
Michels, Peter (grandfather) 15–16

INDEX 279

Michels, Robert
agitational trip to Rhineland and
Ruhr, 1905 48
agonistic conception of politics 107–9, 117,
120–1, 123–4, 126–7, 142, 160–1, 184–5,
265–6, 268
ambition for academic career 18–22, 25, 27,
32, 36–7, 76, 191–2, 265, 268
anti-militarism 20, 33–4, 51–3, 56, 61–3,
70–1, 75–7, 80–3, 112–13, 119, 140–2,
164–5, 199, 207, 211, 215–16, 221–2,
226–7, 261, 265–6
biography 15–24
doctoral dissertation 16–17
ethical conception of socialism 20, 25, 28–31,
39–40, 43–5, 53–5, 58–9, 66–7, 69, 78–9,
82–3, 88, 94–6, 98–101, 107–10, 117,
121, 124–7, 129, 142, 190–1, 193, 195–6,
198, 202, 256, 264–6
ethnic and racial categories, use of 46–7,
53–5, 61, 82–3, 100, 116–19, 123, 132–3,
142–3, 150–3, 170–2, 199–200, 204,
215–20, 228–53, 260, 266–7
family background 15–17, 89–90, 129, 188,
207, 217–19, 237, 245–6, 265
and fascism 7–9, 23–4, 142–3, 204–6, 253
and feminism 147–85
and French socialist movement 128–43
gendered language, use of 184
German citizenship, renunciation
of 20–2, 253
German Social Democratic Party
joins 27
involvement in 25–83, 198, 202–3
disillusionment with 51, 53–6, 63–4,
69–72, 75–83, 107, 126–7, 140–2, 163,
191–2, 198–9, 203, 215–16, 264
Grenzen der Geschlechtsmoral, Die 7, 147,
169–70, 180–3
Handwörterbuch der Soziologie / Encyclopédie
der Sociologie (unpublished) 251–3
intellectual in labour movement, identity
as 25, 37, 67–8, 74, 89–90, 104–5,
115–18, 189–93, 265–6
Italian Fascist Party, joins 23–4, 204–5
Italian imperialism, defends 226–7
Italian Socialist Party, joins 89–90, 93–4
Italophilia 22–3, 89–92, 188, 206–9, 212–13,
219–22, 226–7, 238–9, 246, 267
Marxist theory, reception of 26–9, 31, 87,
121–2, 195, 198, 236, 265–6
military service 15–16, 41–2, 142, 221, 265
nationalism, view of 20–1, 76–7, 206–7,
209–13, 219

parliamentarism, critique of 21–2, 52–6,
59–63, 70, 76–80, 82, 84–5, 101, 104–5,
107–9, 111–14, 117–18, 131, 135–6,
140–1, 160–1, 198–9, 216–17, 225–6
Political Parties 1–4, 7–8, 22, 25, 65–6, 68, 74,
87, 147, 177–8, 191–4, 204, 233–4, 243,
264, 268
proletariato e la borghesia nel movimento
socialista italiano, Il 20–1, 67–8, 115–19,
183–4, 190–1, 245
Reichstag election candidate 33–5, 242–3
republicanism 39–40, 44–5, 53–5, 61–2, 101,
104, 107–8, 131, 160–1, 211, 224
scholarship on 7–11, 24
secular outlook 261–4, 268
and sexual question 147–8, 150–2, 158–9,
163–85, 267–8
Social Democrat, identifies as 19–20, 32,
86–7, 150–2
Storia del marxismo in Italia 121–4
and syndicalism 9–10, 36, 55–6, 63–4, 78–9,
84–5, 107–9, 111–15, 119–21, 126–8,
133–5, 138–40, 142, 199–200, 265–6
Zur Soziologie des Parteiwesens in der
modernen Demokratie – see
Political Parties
Michels-Lindner, Gisela 7, 16–18, 23–4, 26–7,
32–3, 38–9, 48, 89–90, 114–15, 147,
150–2, 165, 176, 181–2, 229, 254–5, 263
Milan 89–90, 98–9, 139, 189
Millerand, Alexandre 45–6, 49, 102–3, 106,
131–3, 141
Mills, C. Wright 2
Mitteldeutsche Sonntags-Zeitung (Giessen) 27–9,
32–4, 39–40, 46, 51–2, 91–2, 256, 263
Mitzman, Arthur 4, 8–11, 25, 67–8, 119–20,
177, 244–5
Möbius, Julius 149
Über den physiologischen Schwachsinn des
Weibes 149
Mocchi, Walter 103, 107–8, 133–4
modernity 5, 8–9, 11, 43–4, 147, 163–4,
254–64, 268
Mommsen, Theodor 18
Monod, Gabriel 235–6
Monticelli, Carlo 100
Morgari, Oddino 113–14
Morgen, Der (periodical) 6, 79–80, 177
Morocco Crisis, 1905 56, 61–3, 70–3, 82–3,
137–8, 199, 215–19, 257–9
Mosca, Gaetano 2n.2, 4, 7, 21–2, 83–5, 119–22,
126–7, 203, 232
Elementi di scienza politica 4
Mosso, Angelo 84–5

280 INDEX

Mouvement Socialiste, Le 6, 20, 51, 53–7, 62–3, 71–3, 75–6, 78–9, 108–9, 111–12, 128, 133–43, 187–8, 191, 198–9, 216–17, 220, 224–5, 243–4
Mozzoni, Anna Maria 95, 150–2
Müller, Hermann 2
Müller von Königswinter, Wolfgang 207
Munich University 15–16
Mussolini, Benito 8, 23–4, 128, 184, 204–6
  Michels' admiration for 23–4, 204–5
Muther, Richard 6
Mutterschutz (periodical) 169–74

Nasi, Nunzio 212–13
National Liberal Party 34–5
National Social Party 26–7, 33–5, 196–7, 212, 233–4, 261–2
nationalism 206–15, 219, 225–7, 237, 244–5
Naumann, Friedrich 169–70, 196–7, 212, 233–4
negative integration 74
neo-Kantianism 31, 232–3, 265–6
neo-Malthusianism 178–80
Neue Generation, Die (see also *Mutterschutz*) 169–70, 173–6, 178–9
Neue Zeit, Die 6, 19–20, 26, 28–9, 46–8, 55–6, 95, 102–3, 134, 166–7, 173–4, 183–4, 187–8, 210–11
Neues Frauenleben (periodical) 153, 161
Niceforo, Alfredo 122, 175–6, 232, 246–9
  Anthropology of the Poorer Classes 247–9
Nietzsche, Friedrich 123, 177, 182–3, 195, 204–5, 251–2, 257
Nieuwe Tijd, De (periodical) 58–9, 162–3
Nieuwenhuis, Domela 216–17
Nordau, Max 239
  Degeneration 239
Noske, Gustav 10, 79–80
Nuova Antologia, La (periodical) 188–9
Nuova Terra, La (periodical) 100

Olberg (or Olberg-Lerda), Oda 149, 257
  Das Weib und der Intellektualismus 149, 257
Oligarchy, "iron law" of 1–2, 4, 7–8, 22, 83–8, 119–20, 126–7, 191–2, 196–7, 201, 203–4
Olivo, Alberto 230
Onetti, Luigi 80–1
Ontwaking (periodical) 75–6
Ostrogorski, Moise 4
  La démocratie et l'organisation des partis politiques 4

Pan-German League 208–9, 212, 226–7, 235, 237
Pappenheim, Karl Rabe von 34

Pappritz, Anna 161
Pareto, Vilfredo 2n.2, 4, 7, 21–2, 83–5, 126–7, 203, 232
  Systèmes socialistes 4
Paris 45–6, 72–3, 78–9, 130–3, 136–8, 171–2, 176–7, 199–200, 224–5
Partito Operaio 98–9, 117–18, 150–2, 189
Partito Socialista Italiano – *see* Italian Socialist Party
patriotism 206–21, 224–5, 241, 243–4
Pensiero, Il (periodical) 108–9, 111–12
Penzig, Rudolf 43
Perugia University 23–4
Pfetsch, Frank 8–9, 194
Pierstorff, Julius 65–6
Pisacane, Carlo 125–6
Ploetz, Alfred 250–2
Politisch-Anthropologische Revue 164–5, 173–4, 196–7, 209–10, 232–9, 249, 251
Proudhon, Pierre-Joseph 123
Prussian Political Police 27, 45, 140–2

racial hygiene 233–4, 250–2
racism 204, 228–9, 232–4, 236–7, 250–1, 266–7
Radkau, Joachim 177
Ranke, Leopold von 16–18
Rappoport, Charles 130–1
Reichstag elections, 1903 32–5, 37–8, 44–7, 49, 101–2, 222, 224, 241
  1907 76–7, 140–1, 216, 221, 259
Reichstag vice-president question 39–42, 44–5
revisionism 30–1, 39–46, 49, 53–5, 58–9, 61–2, 97–8, 102–3, 105–6, 111–12, 123, 130–3, 160–1, 189–90, 198, 200, 232–3, 266
Revue Internationale de Sociologie 258–9
Ribeiro, Pinto 221–2
Richter, Eugen 49
Riehl, Alois 15–16
Riforma Sociale, La (periodical) 37–8, 47–8, 76–7, 83–4, 101–2, 126, 140–1, 147–8, 164, 241
Rigola, Rinaldo 37–8
Rimini 116
Rivista Italiana di Sociologia 126–7
Rivista Popolare 237–8
Röhrich, Wilfried 9
Roland-Holst, Henriette 58–9, 162–3
Rome 23–4, 175–6
Ross—Doria, Tullio 257
Roth, Guenther 74
Rousseau, Jean-Jacques 8–9, 85
Ruhr miners' strike, 1905 56–7, 135–6, 198–9, 221
Russian Revolution, 1905 60–2, 110, 224–5

INDEX 281

Sächsische Arbeiter-Zeitung 104
Saint-Simon, Henri de 191
Salomon, Alice 7, 159
Sand, Shlomo 187–8
Schallmayer, Wilhelm 233–4, 250
Scheidemann, Philipp 10
Schiller, Friedrich 254–5
Schippel, Max 50–1
Schirrmacher, Käthe 50–1, 161
Schmidt, Robert 61–2
Schmoller, Gustav 15–16, 70, 124, 251
Schnitzler, Arthur 163–4, 254–5
  Liebelei 163–4
Schopenhauer, Arthur 164–5
Schreiber, Adele 7, 169–70
Schwäbische Tagwacht 32, 90–2
Schwarz, Hermann 46
Section Française de l'Internationale Ouvrière
  (SFIO, French Socialist Party) 130,
  134–5, 137, 139–40
sex reform movement 7, 11, 167–79, 181–2,
  184–5, 257, 267–8 (*see also* Bund für
  Mutterschutz)
Shaw, George Bernard 81–2
Siebeck, Paul 64
Sighele, Scipio 192
Simmel, Georg 251
social anthropology 97, 122–3, 125–6, 142–3,
  194, 229, 232, 246–9, 251, 266–7
Social Democratic Party of Germany 1–2, 4, 6,
  9–11, 19–22, 25–88, 92, 110–12, 118–19,
  130, 132–6, 141, 148–9, 162–3, 183–4,
  191–4, 196–202, 213, 215–17, 222, 224–5,
  228, 236, 241–4, 257–8, 262–3, 266–7
  'class elevation machine' (Michels) 68–9,
    83–4, 87
  Handbook for Social Democratic Voters 215
  Hessian party congress, 1903 40–1
  Marburg *Wahlverein* 36–9, 41–2, 46,
    48, 61–2
  Party congress 1902 (Munich) 35–6,
    38–9, 92–3
  Party congress 1903 (Dresden) 25, 32–3,
    38–42, 44–6, 61–2, 102–4, 130–2,
    199–200
  Party congress 1904 (Bremen) 25, 49–53, 107,
    160–1, 163, 198, 213, 222, 263
  Party congress 1905 (Jena) 25, 60–3, 110–12,
    198–9, 215–16
  Party congress 1906 (Mannheim) 65–6, 74–6,
    140, 200
  Party congress 1907 (Essen) 80–1, 141–2
  Prussian party congress 1904 55–6
  social composition 37–8, 64–9, 242–3

women's organization 50–1, 150–2, 156–7,
  160–1, 163, 173, 263
Socialismo (periodical) 237–8
*Socialist. Official Organ of the Socialist Labour
  Party, The* 59
Society for Ethical Culture 217–19
Sombart, Werner 4–9, 64–6, 69–70, 79–80,
  115–16, 120–1, 139–40, 169–70, 177,
  194, 201–2, 204, 245–6, 266–7
  Sozialismus und soziale Bewegung 70
  Michels' friendship with 5–6, 79–80,
    177n.149, 245–6
Sonderweg in German history 222, 257–61, 267
Sorbonne, Paris 15–16
Sorel, Georges 6, 9, 71–2, 123, 135–7, 139–40,
  142–3, 187–8, 192–3, 251, 265–6
South-West Africa 50, 76, 214–15
Sozialdemokratische Partei
  Deutschlands – *see* Social Democratic
  Party of Germany
Sozialistische Monatshefte 19, 27, 44–5, 49,
  55, 71–2, 80–1, 86–7, 102–3,
  106, 199–200
Spencer, Herbert 246–9
Spinoza, Baruch 240
Spriano, Paolo 230
Staatswissenschaften 15–16
Sternhell, Zeev 128, 142–3
Stöcker, Helene 7, 167–71
Stölting, Eberhard 228
Strada, La (newspaper) 40, 101
Strauss, Richard 6, 79–80
Strindberg, August 164–5
Stritt, Marie 169–70, 172–3
Ströbel, Heinrich 61
Südekum, Alfred 79–80, 133–4
Sudermann, Hermann 163–4, 254–5
  Ehre, Die 163–4
  Heimat 163–4
Südwestdeutsche Rundschau 255–6
Suttner, Bertha von 161, 181–2
Sybel, Heinrich von 18
syndicalism, French 20, 51, 57–8, 61, 71–2,
  78–9, 108–9, 123, 128, 133–40, 142–3,
  187–8, 265–6
syndicalism, Italian 20, 57–8, 61, 89–90, 96–7,
  101, 107–9, 113–15, 119–21, 123–4, 135,
  142–3, 199, 265–6
Szabó, Ervin 237–8

Talmon, Jacob 8–9
Thesing, Ernst 35–7, 213–14
Tönnies, Ferdinand 8–9, 250, 252–3
totalitarianism theory 8–9

282 INDEX

trade unions 55–9, 61–4, 70–6, 78–9, 108–9, 112–13, 119–20, 126–7, 135–9, 142, 190, 216
   congress of Free Trade Unions, 1905 (Cologne) 57–8, 108–9, 135
Treitschke, Heinrich von 18
Treves, Claudio 92, 102–3, 105–6
Trocini, Federico 7–8
Turati, Filippo 49, 89–92, 94–8, 100–8, 121–3, 127, 130, 150–3, 257
Turin 17–18, 23–4, 76, 79–80, 83–4, 89–90, 99–100, 114–15, 119–20, 126, 141–2, 175–6, 219–22, 229–31, 254–5
Turin University 20–2, 83–4, 87, 119–20, 126, 139, 174, 192

Una donna (novel by Sybille Aleremo, pseud.) 174–5
Unione Femminile 153
universities 18–20, 22, 46, 65–6, 81–2, 156–7, 183–4, 257, 265

Vaillant, Edouard 130–1, 141
Veit & Co. (Leipzig) 251–3
Vezzani, Carlo 94–5
Viazzi, Pio 164–5, 173–4, 235
   La lotta di sesso 164–5, 173–4, 235
Vidal, François 129
Vita Internazionale, La (periodical) 212
Vita Moderna, La (periodical) 188–9
Volksstimme (Frankfurt/M.) 61, 70–1
Volksstimme (Magdeburg) 45–6, 131
Vollmar, Georg von 19, 39–40, 52–3
Vorländer, Karl 31
Vorwärts 32, 34–6, 38–42, 72–3, 86–7, 90, 92, 111–12, 130–1, 137–8

Webb, Beatrice 162–3
Weber, Alfred 177
Weber, Marianne 65–6, 169–70, 172–3, 177, 181–2
   Ehefrau und Mutter in der Rechtsentwicklung 172–3
   Max Weber. Ein Lebensbild 177
Weber, Max 4–9, 11–12, 20–3, 64–6, 70, 74–5, 87, 139–40, 147, 169–70, 172–3, 176–8, 181–2, 192, 194, 204–5, 225–6, 245, 250–1, 254, 261–2, 264, 266–8
   Michels' friendship with 5–6, 172–3, 176–8, 181–2
Wedekind, Frank 163–4, 254–5
Wehler, Hans-Ulrich 222
Weininger, Otto 252
Wilbrandt, Lisbeth 165–6
Wilbrandt, Richard 159, 165–6
Wilhelm II, Kaiser 20–1, 39–40, 50–1, 56–7, 101, 160, 195, 199, 241–4, 254–6, 259–61
Wilser, Ludwig 233–4
Winkler, Heinrich August 206
Woltmann, Ludwig 164–5, 196–7, 209, 232–7, 251–2
Wolzogen, Ernst von 147–8

Zasulitch, Vera 162–3
Zeitschrift für Politik 176
Zetkin, Clara 7, 32, 50–1, 95, 147, 150–3, 156–7, 160–3, 165–6, 173–4, 184–5, 188–9, 221
Zietz, Luise 50–1, 160, 163
Zukunft, Die (periodical) 41–2